PENTAGON PRESS

COMMITTED TO SERVE THE ARMED FORCES

INDIA'S LOOK EAST TO ACT EAST POLICY

Tracking the Opportunities and Challenges in the Indo-Pacific

INDIA'S LOOK EAST TO ACT EAST POLICY

Tracking the Opportunities and Challenges in the Indo-Pacific

Edited by
ManMohini Kaul
Anushree Chakraborty

PENTAGON PRESS

India's Look East to Act East Policy: Tracking the Opportunities and Challenges in the Indo-Pacific
ManMohini Kaul and Anushree Chakraborty (Editors)

ISBN 978-81-8274-847-7

First Published in 2016

Published by
PENTAGON PRESS
206, Peacock Lane, Shahpur Jat,
New Delhi-110049
Phones: 011-64706243, 26491568
Telefax: 011-26490600
email: rajan@pentagonpress.in
website: www.pentagonpress.in

Branch
Flat No.213, Athena-2,
Clover Acropolis,
Viman Nagar,
Pune-411014
Email: pentagonpresspune@gmail.com

Printed at Avantika Printers Private Limited.

Contents

PART II
Key Regional Developments in the Indo-Pacific

PART III
Maritime Security: Challenges and Cooperation

About the Contributors

Aileen S.P. Baviera is Professor of China Studies and Asian International Relations at the Asian Center, University of the Philippines. She is an internationally known scholar specializing on international politics and security in East Asia. She is a former Wilson Center Scholar and is the current editor-in-chief of the *Asian Politics & Policy*, a quarterly academic journal.

Amba Pande is with the Centre for Indo-Pacific Studies, School of International Studies, Jawaharlal Nehru University, New Delhi. She has been involved in research on issues related to Diaspora, Migration, and South Pacific region and has published various articles in national and international journals.

Amit Singh is Assistant Professor at Atma Ram Sanatan Dharma College, University of Delhi, India. He received his Ph.D. degree from the Centre for South, Central, Southeast Asian and South West Pacific Studies, School of International Studies, JNU, New Delhi. He has published articles widely and has been associated as reviewer in reputed journals.

Anushree Chakraborty is currently Assistant Professor at Vidyasagar College for Women, University of Calcutta, Kolkata. She was awarded her Ph.D. at the Centre for South, Central, Southeast Asian and South West Pacific Studies, School of International Studies, Jawaharlal Nehru University, New Delhi. She was also the ICSSR Post-Doctoral Fellow from 2013 to 2014. Dr. Chakraborty has published extensively in leading national and international journals.

Ashok Rai is presently pursuing his Ph.D. at the Center for Indo-Pacific Studies, School of International Studies, Jawaharlal Nehru University, New Delhi. He has served the Indian Navy, with a career spanning 29 years, and has held various appointments at sea and ashore.

Debashis Chakraborty is Assistant Professor of Economics at the Indian Institute of Foreign Trade (IIFT), a deemed university under Ministry of Commerce, Government of India. He is presently Associate Editor of *Foreign Trade Review*, Sage.

Ganganath Jha is Professor at the Centre for Indo-Pacific Studies, School of International Studies, Jawaharlal Nehru University, New Delhi. Prof Jha has several publications in leading national and international journals.

Jasvinder Sidhu is the Ministerial Advisor to the Premier of Victoria, Australia on Multiculturalism. He is also Associate Lecturer at the RMIT University, Melbourne.

Leela K. Ponappa was the former Deputy National Security Advisor and Secretary, National Security Council Secretariat (from May 2007 till October 2009). She was Ambassador to Thailand and Permanent Representative of India to UNESCAP (2002-2004).

ManMohini Kaul is Professor at the Center for Indo-Pacific Studies, School of International Studies, Jawaharlal Nehru University, New Delhi. Prof. Kaul has written extensively on regionalism, foreign policy and security issues in Southeast Asia and South Pacific. Her latest publication is a co-edited book titled *India and New Zealand in a Rising Asia: Issues and Perspectives.*

Mohor Chakarborty is Assistant Professor at the South Calcutta Girls' College, under University of Calcutta, Kolkata. Dr. Chakarborty has a Ph.D. from Jadavpur University, Kolkata. She has published extensively for leading national and international journals.

Nabeel A. Mancheri is a Research Fellow at the Institute of Social Science, University of Tokyo. Prior to joining Tokyo University, he was Assistant Professor at India's National Institute of Advanced Studies, Bangalore. He has worked as a consultant to OECD Paris, ICRIER New Delhi and CUTS International and has been involved in research related to trade issues.

Omprakash Dahiya is Assistant Professor at Amity University, Noida. He has an M. Phil. and a Ph.D. in International Relations from the Centre for Indo-Pacific Studies, School of International Studies, Jawaharlal Nehru University, New Delhi. Dr. Dahiya has worked as an Associate Fellow at the National Maritime Foundation, New Delhi.

Premesha Saha is a doctoral candidate at the Centre for Indo-Pacific Studies, School of International Studies, Jawaharlal Nehru University, New Delhi.

Richard A Herr is Professor at University of Tasmania since 1973. He is currently the academic coordinator for the Law Faculty's ANZACATT "Parliamentary Law, Practice and Procedure" course, serving the eleven Parliaments of Australasia. He is also the Adjunct Professor of Governance and Ethics at the Fiji National University where he drafted the first Candidates' Manual for Fiji to assist Candidates in the September 2014 elections. He was awarded the Medal of the Order of Australia (OAM) in 2007 as part of the Queen's Birthday Honours List "for service to higher education". He is also the recipient of the 2013 Blamey Medal for his security assessment of Melanesia and an AusAID Peacebuilder Award in 2002 for work in Solomon Islands.

Shishir Upadhaya is a doctoral candidate at the Australian National Centre for Ocean Resources and Security, Wollongong, New South Wales, Australia. Earlier, he was the Regional Head (Aerospace, Defence and Maritime) at HIS Global Pvt. Ltd. He served the Indian Navy prior to joining the HIS Global.

Shubhamitra Das is Assistant Professor at the Centre for Indo-Pacific Studies, School of International Studies, Jawaharlal Nehru University, New Delhi. Dr. Das has published on South Pacific and her interests and writings range from environmental issues in the South Pacific to Australia's foreign policy.

Sushma Negi is a doctoral candidate at the Centre for Indo-Pacific Studies, School of International Studies, Jawaharlal Nehru University, New Delhi.

Vibhanshu Shekhar is an adjunct faculty at the ASEAN Studies Center, School of International Service, American University, Washington DC. Dr. Shekhar has a Ph.D. on Southeast Asian Studies from Jawaharlal Nehru University (JNU), New Delhi and has conducted post-doctoral research at the Australian National University, Canberra.

List of Abbreviations

ACMECS	Ayeyawady-Chao Phraya-Mekong Economic Cooperation
ADB	Asian Development Bank
ADMM	ASEAN Defense Ministerial Meeting
AIELTF	ASEAN-India Economic Linkages Task Force
AIIB	Asian Infrastructure and Investment Bank
APEC	Asia Pacific Economic Cooperation
APT	ASEAN Plus Three
ARF	ASEAN Regional Forum
ARMM	Autonomous Region in Muslim Mindanao
ASEAN	Association of South East Asian Nations
BAP	Bali Action Plan
BDF	Bali Democracy Forum
BIMST-EC	Bay of Bengal Initiative for Multi-Sectoral Technical and Economic Cooperation
CADP	Comprehensive Asia Development Plan
CECA	Comprehensive Economic Cooperation Agreement
CEPEA	Comprehensive Economic Partnership in East Asia
CPA	Commonwealth Parliamentary Association
CS	Continental Shelf
CUES	Code for Unplanned Encounters at Sea
DCA	Defence Cooperation Agreements
DFAT	Department of Foreign Affairs and Trade
DOC	Declaration of Conduct of Parties in the South China Sea
EAEC	East Asia Economic Cooperation
EAMF	Expanded ASEAN Maritime Forum

EAS	East Asia Summit
EEZ	Exclusive Economic Zones
ENDC	Eighteen Nation Disarmament Committee
ERIA	Economic Research Institute of ASEAN and East Asia
FLP	Fiji Labour Party
FICCI	Federation of Indian Chambers of Commerce and Industry
FTA	Free Trade Area
GCC	Great Council of Chiefs
GMS	Greater Mekong Sub-region Programme
IBSA	India Brazil South Africa
IIT	Intra-Industry Trade
IMAC	Information Management and Analysis Centre
IONS	Indian Ocean Naval Symposium
IOR	Indian Ocean Region
IORA	Indian Ocean Region Association
IPN	International Production Networks
IR	International Relations
LDC	Least Development Country
LEP	Look East Policy
LASEDECO	Land Settlement and Development Corporation
MGC	Mekong Ganga Cooperation
MILF	Moro Islamic Liberation Front
MNLF	Moro National Liberation Front
MOG	Multinational Observation Group
MPAC	The Master Plan on ASEAN Connectivity
MSG	Melanesian Spearhead Group
NAASP	New Asian-African Strategic Partnership
NAM	Non-Alignment Movement
NARRA	National Authority for Reforestation and Rehabilitation Administration
NCBBF	National Council for Building a Better Fiji
NCGUB	National Coalition Government of the Union of Burma
NDA	National Democratic Alliance
NDF	National Democratic Force

NFP	National Federation Party
NLD	National League for democracy
NLTB	Native Land Trust Board
NPT	Non-Proliferation Treaty
NUP	National Unity Party
ONGC	Oil and Natural Gas Corporation
PAD	People's Alliance for Democracy
PIF	Pacific Islands Forum
PMC	Post Ministerial Conference
PNG	Papua New Guinea
PR	Proportional Representation
PR	Permanent Residency
RCEP	Regional Comprehensive Economic Partnership
REDD	Reducing Emissions from Deforestation and Degradation
ReCAAP	Regional Cooperation Agreement on Combating Piracy and Armed Robbery against Ships in Asia
RFMF	Republic of Fiji Military Forces
SAARC	South Asian Association for Regional Cooperation
SCS	South China Sea
SEATO	Southeast Asia Treaty Organisation
SIGINT	Signals Intelligence Facility
SLOC	Sea Lanes of Communications
SLORC	State Law and Order Restoration Council
TPP	Trans Pacific Partnership
TRT	Thai Rak Thai Party
TVET	Technical and Vocational Training
UNCLOS	UN Convention on the Law of the Sea
UNFCCC	United Nations Framework Convention on Climate Change
UPA	United Progressive Alliance
USDP	Union Solidarity and Development Party
VKC	Virtual Knowledge Centre
WPNS	Western Pacific Naval Symposium

Acknowledgements

This book was conceived during endless academic discussions over cups of tea in the JNU campus. Belonging as we did to the division of Southeast Asian and South Pacific Studies at the School of International Studies, JNU, it was natural for us to observe the transformation of the region into a constructive strategic and economic hub. This inspired us to bring out a volume which would focus on the themes and issues concerning the region and delineate them from the perspective of India's foreign policy.

The use of the normative term "Indo-Pacific" became significant for us, once the programme of Southeast Asian and Southwest Pacific Studies was given an independent status as the Center for Indo-Pacific Studies. This development further encouraged us to publish an edited book that would explore not just Southeast Asia but also extend the scope to the Indo-Pacific region which meant including the South Pacific region and assessing the role of Look East, and now Act East Policy in shaping partnerships with this emergent, strategically important region. We decided to track internal and external developments and challenges in the Indo-Pacific region, which involved broad strategic and domestic elements especially those that echo our own domestic and neighbourhood problems. We believe this volume is a step forward, however small it may be, towards a better understanding of the region and of India's strategic options in Southeast Asia and the South Pacific.

This volume would not have been possible without the effort of the entire team and supporters. Though it is not possible to mention them all here, there are a few to whom we owe such debt of gratitude that their names must be mentioned. We are indebted to Ruth Rhea Khan, Assistant Professor, Krishnanagar College for her deep interest, constant encouragement and valuable inputs. We must also record our deep gratitude to Arun Kumar

Oraon, M. Phil student at the Centre for Indo-Pacific Studies, for his support and valuable assistance.

We are indebted to all our contributors for having shown consideration in being prompt in their response.

EDITORS

Introduction

The Indo-Pacific region, combining the Indian and the Pacific Ocean, is an evolving geostrategic arc. The social construction of the 'Indo-Pacific' has added new actors with corresponding identities seeking responsibilities, building partnerships and simultaneously promoting defence links for prevention of possible conflicts resulting from traditional and nontraditional security threats. India has emerged a major actor expected to play a critical role in shaping the contours of the 21st century Indo-Pacific. The importance of the concept of 'Indo-Pacific' for India's geo-strategic setting has been recognized by Indian policy makers and analysts, especially from a geostrategic and geo-economic prism. India is physically placed sitting atop the strategic route linking the region "spreading from Bab-al-Mandab and the Straits of Hormuz through the Malacca and the South China Sea to Australia and the Western Pacific.

Earlier, India was seen as an external power invited by the Asia Pacific region for deeper engagement. Today in the new millennium, India is advantageously positioned – politically, economically and strategically on the Indo-Pacific map as a major stakeholder. Geographically, the 'Indo-Pacific' region covers almost half of earth's surface from the East Indian Ocean-South China Sea-Western Pacific Ocean continuum. The regions such as South Asia, Southeast and East Asia in addition to the South Pacific, fall into this arc. The terminology encompasses massive landmass, along with long coastlines and vast water surface. With immense opportunities, there are numerous challenges as well and tracking these is important for a critical understanding of this complex region.

Since the earliest times, the region (Southeast Asia in particular) was influenced by the two Asian power centers — India and China. The two Asian civilizations impacted their indigenous culture and political set up.

Despite inheriting all the drawbacks of post-colonial societies, Southeast Asian countries have achieved a level of stability and prosperity, which is exemplary. The significant rise of Southeast Asia as an economic hub has led India to support ASEAN's centrality in the multilateral fora like ASEAN Regional Forum (ARF), Asia-Europe Meet, East Asia Summit (EAS) and ADMM PLUS. Today, with the presence and interest of multiple stakeholders, a global shift is taking place towards the Indo-Pacific with its geo-strategic and economic environment becoming extremely complex and challenging. Thus the wide ranging issues which include domestic and external elements have developed into critical subjects of scrutiny. Geographically distant countries like Australia and the South Pacific Island states are part of India's Look East policy; with Act East Policy the gaps in India's foreign policy towards both the regions is being addressed by the government of Prime Minister Modi.

One of the aims of this study is to examine the factors contributing to India's desire to play an active role in Southeast Asia and South Pacific, with a view to making a rational assessment of the political, strategic and economic forces that have shaped this policy and are now shaping the Act East Policy. To put India's relationship in the trajectory of further growth, an introspection of India's relationship with the region is imperative, with a view to consolidate the gains so far and to remove the road blocks that are holding back further progress.

As the concept of "Indo-Pacific" is gaining traction in Indian strategic thinking, the book recognises the need for experts to explain and analyse the major contemporary developments in this region. The detailed deliberations addressed by the contributors give fresh insights on the ensuing academic debates on the challenges that confront or may confront the region. India as an emerging global power needs to understand the extent of these problems, both old and new, so as to facilitate the construction of an Indo-Pacific order in the future that would contribute to peace, stability and wellbeing of the countries that comprise this region. For meaningful contribution, India needs to work proactively and open channels of consultation and dialogue with the concerned countries for building a robust mechanism that absorbs risks posed by competition, as well as generate synergy to propel the region into becoming a strategic powerhouse. Most chapters in the volume are written from an Indian perspective, except for the ones on the South China Sea (SCS) dispute, Fiji's recent constitutional changes, and the third on Indian migration to Australia. The chapters in the volume provide useful policy directions which would help in cementing relations between India and Southeast Asia and with the now not-so-distant neighborhood of the South Pacific.

Chapter Summaries

The book is organised into four parts. They are as follows: Dynamics of India's Engagement with the Indo–Pacific; Key Regional Developments in the Indo-Pacific; Maritime Security: Challenges and Cooperation; and Conflicts and Conflict Resolution.

In the first section, the book begins with an overview of India's engagement with the entire gamut of Indo-Pacific in order to provide a background for understanding India's Look East Policy. The chapters trace the historical links and the recent foreign policy priority of the Government of India. This section also deals with bilateral relations of India with two countries belonging to two different spectrums — Myanmar and Australia. Myanmar is India's neighbouring country, holding significant strategic interest for India, while Australia has emerged a potential partner of India in the evolving Indo-Pacific architecture. Bilateral relations of India with the other major countries of the Indo-Pacific region are to be covered in the upcoming volume.

The two sections, Internal Dynamics: Regional Implications (PART II) and Conflicts and Conflict Resolution (PART IV) deal with the issues that at first glance may not seem to be directly related to India's interest in the region, but from the editors' point of view they have special significance. First, awareness of problems concerning neighbouring countries leads to better handling of relations both at the bilateral and at the multilateral level. Two, some of these issues reflect our own domestic and neighbourhood problem. The rest of the sections have chapters that are dealing with India's strategic and security relations and its trade and economic interests in the Indo-Pacific region.

The first chapter by Prof ManMohini Kaul is a detailed overview of the Look East Policy and now Act East Policy. Besides exploring the development of India–ASEAN relations, the chapter analyses the present contours of India's policy towards ASEAN and the South Pacific in the new regional strategic landscape. The author suggests the focal points to be considered under the Act East Policy and evaluates the prospects under the Modi Government for a more meaningful cooperation within the complex geopolitical and strategic environment of the Indo-Pacific.

Leela Ponappa's paper in the following chapter assesses the relationship between India and Southeast Asia and examines the dynamics of the former's engagement with the latter, and the Look East Policy, which in her words "was both a restoration of historical links and the crafting of contemporary relationship incorporating political, economic and security interests, extensive cultural linkages apart." Some of the key factors that have direct and current relevance for India have been delineated in the paper. She also highlights the conceptual argument around the geographical contours and the subsequent continuum between the Pacific and the Indian Ocean. Also, emphasis is laid on the crucial projects that must receive priority under the current Act East Policy, thus leading to opportunities ahead. Leela Ponappa recommends that India needs to start thinking of itself as a Pacific Ocean country in order to explore the opportunities in eastern Asia.

Anushree Chakraborty analyses the latest introduction to the security architecture in Southeast Asia and East Asia, that is, the East Asia Summit. The author examines the role played by EAS in managing the broader strategic balance. She highlights India's participation in shaping agendas and confronting with the challenges of this work-in-progress forum.

Debashis Chakraborty provides an in-depth analysis on the intra-bloc trade experience of ASEAN and examines the comparative account of their participation in production networks across major sectors. The author observes India's participation in the ASEAN production network and notes that recent Indian initiatives, such as the 'Make in India' campaign, trade route promotion with ASEAN countries through infrastructural augmentation, implementation of Indo-ASEAN FTA tariff reform commitments, removal of non-tariff barriers, introduction of trade facilitation measures etc. will contribute significantly in integrating India with the region.

The subsequent chapter by Nabeel A. Mancheri explores the political and economic aspects of India-China and Southeast Asia relations. The author questions the relationship between these actors, based on their dependence on trade and economic interests. He points out that trade and market are important strategic tools, and explains that those nations which are bigger buyers and sellers have a potential leverage that is utilised for political gains and national power projections. In this case, China's strategic interest in the region is highlighted. The author notes that trade dependence on China would shape the strategic choice of the Southeast Asian countries. Explaining further he states that "from the trade data it can be inferred that in case of any conflict between India and China, most of the countries in the region are going to take a neutral stand as it would be too risky for them to align with any side that could cost them billions worth of trade".

Shubhamitra Das's chapter explores the different perspectives shared by India and Australia on the term 'Indo-Pacific'. She examines how the geopolitical construct merges from their perspective and turn into a lucrative relation, with a rippling effect for the countries in the zone. She goes on to explain the geopolitical big picture in the Indo-Pacific and looks at the convergences and divergences in the Indo-Australian relation.

Omprakash Dahiya's chapter is the last essay in the first section on Dynamics of India's Engagement with the Indo–Pacific. He explores the emerging strategic partnership between India and Myanmar in the subtext of the Indo-Pacific region and analyses some of the issues like the China factor, and economic and strategic issues which have far reaching impact on the bilateral relationship. India's land connectivity with mainland Southeast Asia is through Myanmar, with which India shares a 1,643 km long land border through India's North-East, and maritime connectivity through the Bay of Bengal. Describing in detail the geo-strategic importance of Myanmar for India, he analyses the contours of this relationship which in his opinion should be India's top foreign policy priority.

The second section on the Key Regional Developments in the Indo-Pacific studies some of the relevant domestic themes in Fiji, Australia, Myanmar and Indonesia. The chapter by Ganganath Jha is on democratic transition in Myanmar. After decades of military rule, a transition towards democracy has begun to happen in the country. President Thein Sein has introduced several reforms in the political and economic sectors. Prof. Jha analyses the dynamics of the ongoing internal change and the lopsided aspects of Myanmar's political reforms in this chapter. He makes a pertinent point that the Chief of Staff of the Defence Forces in Myanmar is a powerful person and is above civilian control as he has the power to nominate 25 percent of all members of the Parliament and of State and regional assemblies. He concludes by noting that despite aberrations, the current political scenario does reflect hope and confidence in Myanmar emerging as a fully democratic country.

Vibhanshu Shekhar examines the evolving foreign policy principles of Indonesia, the largest country in Southeast Asian region. He questions a rising Indonesia's global diplomacy as it grapples with what its appropriate response should be, what position and status befits the country and how Indonesia should contribute to the new debates of the 21st century. He identifies the answer in the idea of principled pragmatism and multilateral activism which has contributed to Indonesia's emerging desire for greater role in shaping the evolving global order.

With the transition to democracy in Fiji, India's relations with it are being pursued with greater vigour, reflected in Prime Minister Modi's visit to Fiji in November 2014. The articles on Fiji review the new constitution and the politics of race which has been the central determinant of the political discourse in Fiji.

Richard Herr has given a detailed analysis of the political reforms in post-coup Fiji. He reviews coup leader Bainimarama's cure for the perceived malignancy of communalism, with a special emphasis on the changes to the Westminster model of Parliament in Fiji. Arguably, his cure has created a more liberal, non-racial order for Fiji, albeit with a strong corporatist party. There is a noticeable undertone of personal ambition in Prime Minister Bainimarama's leadership. With regard to India-Fiji bilateral relations, Herr writes that India has played an important role in insuring international acceptance of the Fiji election results by co-chairing the Multinational Observation Group (MOG).

Continuing with Fiji's disjointed political reform process, the subsequent chapter by Amba Pande assesses the impact of constitutional developments at different times in Fiji's political history and observes that these have been completely entangled with the racial politics and the political aspirations of the feudal elements in the Fijian society, with grave consequences for ethnic Indians. On the recent changes introduced by Prime Minister Binimarama, she is of the view that although a post-coup Fiji appears to be moving in the right direction, it has a long way to go in giving a fair representation to ethnic Indians in civil service, judiciary, police, army and educational institutions as these have so far remained heavily tilted towards ethnic Fijians.

The last chapter of the section deals with the recent migration of Indians to Australia, within the context of Australian multiculturalism. From an Indian perspective the harassment of Indian students was a major irritant in India-Australia relations. However, Australia by deft diplomacy expressed its sincerity in pursuing multiculturalism and was able to prevent this issue from adversely impacting the overall bilateral ties. Jasvinder Sidhu's article is relevant in the context of India's Act East Policy, in which building connectivity with Indian Diaspora is one of the major tenets. He examines critically Australian multiculturalism in the context of recent Indian migration to Australia. His perspective on India-Australia linkage is based on the necessity of empowering the Indian Diaspora. However, for this to be achieved the Indian Diaspora must address their internal issues that are linked with settlement and migration and once they become empowered and confident they can make a significant impact on the India-Australia relationship.

The third section on Maritime Security: Challenges and Cooperation has four chapters. As an Indian Ocean nation, India with its expanding trade and dependence on energy exports, supports freedom of navigation and is pursuing close ties with those nations which have vital interests in maritime security. Its Navy's growing capability and the capacity to respond immediately to threats in its neighbouring seas, and the ability to provide immediate disaster relief have helped India to foster closer links with the countries to its east and beyond to Australia. India is also seeking stronger ties with littoral states like Indonesia and Malaysia. The following articles including those on the South China Sea are crucial to India's security discourse.

In the first essay in this section, Aileen S.P. Baviera analyses in great depth the complex maritime security environment in the South China Sea. According to her there are at least four interconnected layers of challenges, having different sets of stakeholders and interests. She describes the various mechanisms, institutions and cooperation initiatives that have come to the fore in order to manage and find a solution to the complex security challenges in East Asia and Southeast Asia. She observes that South China Sea is China's critical area for maritime power projection in its drive to become a global maritime power. It has also become central to the question of power shift and the future of East Asian regional security order. Baviera recognises India's growing interest and engagement in security affairs of South China Sea, resulting from China's endeavours in gaining a foothold in India's neighbourhood. This leads to India seeking a greater and deeper engagement with East Asia and highlighting India's need for hedging the options involving China's own strategic backyard in East Asia. She argues that to counterbalance China in East Asia, India is being encouraged by Japan, US and to some extent Australia, and this is evident from the new concept of "Indo-Pacific" security region.

The subsequent chapter by Amit Singh also deals with the South China Sea dispute, but from the Indian perspective. The chapter analyses the strategic and economic significance of the South China Sea vis-à-vis India, especially for its energy security. It highlights the overlapping and conflicting claims in the SCS and explores possibilities for New Delhi to improve its bilateral and multilateral relations with Southeast Asian countries in order to safeguard the interests of nations on freedom of navigation in the SCS and maritime security in the region.

Shishir Upadhayaya highlights the key maritime security challenges before India and defines the broad strategy that could be adopted to foster maritime security cooperation in the IOR. His chapter concludes with specific recommendations for forging close maritime security cooperation with Southeast Asian littorals, led by the Indian Navy. This chapter is a significant contribution since it addresses India's maritime diplomacy in the region, an important foreign policy tool in the Look East Policy.

Since the previous chapter focused on maritime multilateralism, the subsequent chapter by Ashok Rai takes up the subject of bilateral cooperation in the maritime domain. The author narrows down on one particular country in Southeast Asia, that is, Malaysia. The chapter examines the prevailing maritime security dynamics of the Asia-Pacific Region, the existing India-Malaysia maritime engagements and recommends areas where India and Malaysia could cooperate to further enhance their maritime security.

The last section of the volume on Conflicts and Conflict Resolution includes case studies of three conflicts, namely, Southern Philippines, Scarborough Shoal, and the Preah Vihear Temple. Each of these conflicts is different from the other, with each teaching the same important lesson, that 'intransigence of the disputant parties aggravates the conflicts and its resolution.' Since India is now engaged in a big way with countries to its east, it is pertinent to understand the ongoing issues in the neighborhood and also draw valuable lessons.

The first chapter of the section is on Southern Philippines written by Mohor Chakraborty, who analyses the trends of the separatist movement led by the Moros and the manner in which it has been dealt with by the Government of Philippines. The chapter concludes with the present status of this conflict under President Benigno Aquino III, thereby flagging this case study as the culmination of a long and arduous process of conflict resolution, which could well be a panacea for countries both within the region and beyond for those who are forging peace with secessionist groups.

Premesha Saha writes on the maritime dispute between China and the

Philippines. She examines in details the overall importance of the Scarborough Shoal, the origin of the dispute and its present status between the Philippines and China. While enumerating the course of the dispute, the impact that it might have on the "politico-strategic" landscape of Asia is examined.

Sushma Negi deals with the Preah Vihear temple dispute between Thailand and Cambodia. The author examines how the domestic factors contributed to the inflaming of the dispute, in order to uphold the interest of a section of the political group. The chapter provides an interesting insight into how a foreign policy issue has been exploited by the political leaders of respective countries for their personal advantage.

PART I

Dynamics of India's Engagement with the Indo–Pacific

1

From Look East to Act East:
Evolution of India's Foreign Policy towards Southeast Asia and South Pacific

Manmohini Kaul

In the changing geo-political, geo-economic and geo-strategic landscape of the Indo-Pacific region, India, as a major Indian Ocean nation and as an emerging global power, has an important role in ensuring the security and stability of the Indian Ocean Region (IOR) and of the contiguous regions of Southeast Asia and South Pacific. Although India's Look East Policy has helped bridge the gaps in its foreign policy towards Southeast Asia and South Pacific, there is still an immediate need to define the exact nature of future commitment towards the extended neighbourhood. To some extent this realisation has already dawned upon the NDA government of Prime Minister Narendra Modi, causing it to reshape India's Look East Policy into an Act East Policy. At the ASEAN-India Summit in Myanmar in November 2014, Prime Minister Modi had a clear message about prioritising the engagement with Southeast Asia when he said: "I also assure you that there will be major improvement in our trade policy and environment. We will also move ahead with connectivity projects with ASEAN with speed. I also suggest that we conduct a review of our free trade agreement on goods to improve it further and make it beneficial to all. I also urge that the FTA on Service and Investment be brought into force at the earliest."[1]

In fact, the Act East Policy is not new and its origins lie in the durable initiative of Look East Policy. The difference lies in the active socialising by Prime Minister Modi in undertaking official visits and building personal equations with the leaders of these countries. His official trips to Australia and Fiji, which had not been visited for decades by an Indian Prime Minister, and to Japan and Myanmar underscore two things—the wide ranging nature of the new government's foreign policy and the push for greater economic and strategic engagement with the countries to India's east at the bilateral and multilateral level[2]. More importantly, the Act East Policy is nuanced to selectively reiterate the importance of some countries (like Japan and Vietnam), where the government is focusing particularly in building partnerships.

It is too early to judge how these promises, perhaps made through a skillful articulation of words according to skeptics, will ultimately translate into action. However, Modi's foreign policy has already received accolades in the country and abroad and he is seen to be resolute in enhancing India's reputation as a global power[3]. This is illustrated by an article in a recent edition of Time magazine by President Obama, where he praises the leadership quality of the Indian Prime Minister by stating "Today, he's the leader of the world's largest democracy, and his life story—from poverty to Prime Minister—reflects the dynamism and potential of India's rise".[4]

This paper is divided into three parts. The first part explores the development of India-ASEAN relations and reviews the factors that lead to India's Look East Policy. The second part analyses the present contours of India's policy towards ASEAN and the South Pacific region in the new strategic landscape. The third part looks at the way ahead for the Act East Policy and evaluates the prospects for a more meaningful cooperation within the complex geopolitical and strategic environment of the Indo-Pacific region.[5]

The Early Years

India and Southeast Asia share a vibrant past, reflecting long standing land and maritime connectivity which has led to extensive influence of Indian culture and religion in the region. These relations were affected by India's turbulent history of invasions and the advent of British colonizers, but until then the interface was entirely peaceful and willingly accepted and adapted by Southeast Asia.[6] When India achieved independence in 1947, Prime Minister Jawaharlal Nehru stressed two major pillars of India's Foreign Policy: non-alignment and centrality of India's role in Asia[7]. Despite this, the ensuing years saw some major gaps in India's foreign policy towards Southeast Asia. In hindsight, what then appeared to be lack of interest on India's part now seems to be a preoccupation with upheavals in the immediate neighborhood beginning with the India-China War of 1962 and the subsequent wars with Pakistan. This continues to the present day, with the unresolved border issue with China and the Kashmir issue aggravated by cross border terrorism, destabilising the geostrategic environment of South Asia.

When ASEAN was formed in 1967 not much interest was shown by the Indian political elite in joining it. In the words of Sunanda K. Datta Ray, "the ASEAN that emerged represented everything India claimed to abhor".[8] India seemed to view it as a forum of pro-west countries, with the two core members (Thailand and the Philippines) committed to the US military alliance system both bilaterally and multilaterally through the US led Southeast Asia Treaty Organisation (SEATO); such military alliances were contrary to the principles of India's non-aligned policy. However, India's non-alignment policy was compromised in the eyes of the ASEAN countries when it signed the Indo-Soviet Treaty of Peace, Friendship and Cooperation in 1971.[9]

In the mid-1970s, India did try to expand relations with the growing economies of the ASEAN countries. This included visits by senior Indian ministers to all ASEAN nations in the summer of 1976 to allay their doubts about India's negative perception of the organisation. The visiting ministers assured them that India was not "averse to the formation by others of regional groups for co-operation in economic, cultural and technical fields".[10] As a result, some joint ventures with Indian participation were set up in a few ASEAN countries; but trade and investment between India and Southeast Asia did not grow significantly, especially as many of these joint ventures did not see the light of the day.

The diplomatic initiative shown by India was not a complete washout however, and it did have a positive outcome to the extent that these countries were now inclined to include India as a dialogue partner of ASEAN. However, India's support for Vietnam in Cambodia in 1978 and for the USSR in Afghanistan in 1979 embittered relations with ASEAN and postponed the granting of dialogue status. According to Mahbubhani, "the merit of the case" that "decided India's stand" was "the Soviet Union, Vietnam and India on one side, China, Pakistan and the United States on the other."[11] This was particularly true during Mrs. Gandhi's second term in power in 1980.[12]

When Rajiv Gandhi became Prime Minister in 1984, visible efforts were made to broaden and deepen the relations with Southeast Asia, including visits by him to many of these countries. It was during his administration that the South Asian Association of Regional Cooperation (SAARC) was established in 1985. However, the enthusiasm expressed in the region at the formation of SAARC did not last as Pakistan embarked on extensive militarisation and India followed suit by expanding its defence forces and machinery. Not only did this aggravate the ongoing tension between the two countries, it also sent wrong signals to the ASEAN states, which saw with trepidation what appeared to them as India's projection of its military power and naval strength in the region. Anxieties about India's intentions increased when it sent peacekeeping forces to Sri Lanka in 1987 and intervened militarily in Maldives in 1988, and with the divergent views on the Cambodian issue continuing as before, there were no signs of improvement in the India-ASEAN relationship.

Development of a New Policy

The end of the Cold War and its appendage of 'bloc politics', and the resolution of the Cambodian crisis, scaled down the differences between India and the pro-west ASEAN countries in the early 1990s. Making amends for lost opportunities, India laid the framework for engaging with ASEAN through the Look East Policy of 1991. This coincided with the liberalization of the Indian economy and a generally more open and progressive government. ASEAN's response was immediate and positive—India was included as a sectoral partner in January 1992, upgraded to a full dialogue partner in December 1995, and made a member of the ASEAN-led ARF in 1996. Some ASEAN leaders continued to be less optimistic about India's inclusion as they feared that issues like Kashmir and India-Pakistan tension may divert attention from the main goals of these organisations; it was Singapore's quiet diplomacy that helped India to secure a foothold in ASEAN and ARF.[13]

Since the initiation of the Look East Policy, apart for a minor setback over India's nuclear tests in 1998, the relationship between India and ASEAN has forged ahead with a new attentiveness for greater economic engagement and convergence of views on the emerging security architecture. India has been proactive in initiating several multilateral fora to take this relationship further such as India-ASEAN Business Summits, ASEAN-India Economic Linkages Task Force (AIELTF), and the 2003 Comprehensive Economic Cooperation Agreement (CECA). India's growing role and influence in

ASEAN is particularly reflected in improved economic links: ASEAN was India's fourth largest trading partner in 2015 and trade between them stood at over US $76 billion (2013) with an "average growth of 22 per cent per annum over the past decade."[14] The India-ASEAN Trade in Goods Agreement was signed in 2009[15] and it stated that a Free Trade Agreement (FTA) in services and investments will come into force on July 15, 2015, thereby providing greater opportunities for investors and professionals.[16] However, the pace of these developments has been slow primarily due to India's cautious policies and domestic compulsions. For example, it took six years of negotiations before the FTA on goods could be signed and another two years for the FTA on services and investments to be finalised. India also continues to lag behind considerably in comparison to China in terms of trade and investment with the ASEAN. It is expected that things will improve once the FTA in services and investment comes into force, with bilateral trade expected to grow up to "$100 billion by 2015 and double that volume by 2022."[17]

India's elevation to a Summit Partner during the Phnom Penh Summit of November 2002 was an acknowledgment by ASEAN of India's emergence as a key player in the Asia-Pacific region. To further promote economic and political integration, the partnership was institutionalised through the India-ASEAN multilateral dialogue at the highest level and establishment of a framework for intra-regional cooperation at the Vientiane Summit in 2004 through the agreement on "ASEAN-India Partnership for Peace, Progress and Shared Prosperity.[18] All these developments have had positive results culminating in the signing of the India-ASEAN Strategic Partnership in 2012.

India is now regularly interacting with ASEAN through a series of consultative meetings which include summits, ministerial meetings, senior officials meetings, and meetings at experts level, as well as through the ARF, PMC 10+1, EAS and ADMM Plus. These interactions have further widened the scope of the relationship and led to a convergence of views on security. By celebrating events like the 20th anniversary of the dialogue partnership and the 12th anniversary of the summit-level partnership, and hosting the ASEAN-India Commemorative Summit in New Delhi in 2012, a concerted effort has been made on all sides to showcase the strong bond that has evolved. India publically signaled the significance it attaches to this relationship by designating for the first time an ambassador to the ASEAN in April 2014.

China

China continues to be the main concern for India, the United States and many others in the Indo-Pacific region.[19] China's assertiveness and military posturing has irked several countries and India is seen as a counterbalance and therefore a natural partner by the US 'pivot to Asia policy'.[20] Several ASEAN countries would like to see like-minded powers to be proactive in keeping the region stable and check China from turning Southeast Asia into its backyard.[21]

In this respect, India's capability to respond to non-traditional and traditional threats is recognised by the Southeast Asian countries, the US, Japan, Australia and New Zealand. At the end of the day of course, the political will of the Indian government will determine how it chooses to respond to future challenges and position itself in the region. What is apparent now is India's activism in deepening a strategic partnership with the US and its allies like Australia and Japan. The presence of President Obama as chief guest at India's Republic Day Parade on January 26, 2015, the first time ever by an American president, was a forceful public message about the strong ties shared by India and the US. This also underscores the significant difference between the UPA and NDA governments, with the current administration diligently pursuing wider diplomatic relations and constructing multiple partnerships.

As for China, its policies have worked at paradoxical levels. On the one hand it is a country that can deliver economic benefits to those that engage with it bilaterally or multilaterally; on the other hand however, its brazenness in claiming sovereignity rights over the South China Sea has led to serious apprehensions about its future intentions.[22] India is also very concerned about China's claims to Arunachal Pradesh, incursions into the unresolved border areas and its increasing influence in neighbouring countries.[23]

Even though China has emerged as India's top trading partner, the strengthening of economic cooperation has not resolved border issues; bilateral talks continue as before though both countries now reiterate the importance of the dialogue process for managing this major irritant in their relationship. India in particular seems to have learned a lesson from the 1962 war with China—the Henderson Brook Papers suggest that the war could have been avoided had India agreed to a dialogue process at that time.[24] Today, China and India are the two major Asian countries vying to make the most of their influence in the emerging economic architecture that is acquiring institutional shape and form in the region, especially with the ASEAN Economic

Community coming into existence in 2015. India's economic rise, growing influence and its proactive policy pivoting towards the region is appreciated and accepted by most—and it is increasingly seen as a strategic partner that shares their view that no hegemon be allowed to emerge in the region.[25]

Engaging the South Pacific

Phase II of India's Look East Policy began in 2003, with a concerted effort to engage with the South Pacific region which has received added attention since the term "Indo-Pacific" with its geostrategic connotations has gained acceptance although it is still used interchangeably with the Asia-Pacific when describing the region. India's former foreign secretary Shyam Saran explains "...the term "Indo-Pacific" has gained currency in strategic discourse in India. From a geopolitical perspective it represents the inclusion of the Western Pacific within the range of India's security interests, thus stretching beyond the traditional focus on the Indian Ocean theatre... As India's regional and global profile increases, it will inevitably gravitate towards the centre of this expanded geopolitical and geo-economic space. The concept of an Indo-Pacific theatre fits in neatly with this evolving trend.."[26] Historically, the South Pacific island states have not featured in Indian foreign policy discourse and interaction in the region was limited to the major South Pacific powers of Australia and New Zealand.[27] There are three explanations for this—the decolonisation process in the island states started as late as 1962 which restricted their interaction with India; Australia and New Zealand's policy of alignment in the 1940s and 1950s heightened during the Cold War years and polarized them from India; and the island states were tied to the metropolitan powers through their aid dependence which limited the scope for trade and commerce with India.[28]

The growing convergence with Australia and New Zealand helped India's foreign policy take a tangible shape towards the South Pacific island states. At the second India-ASEAN Summit in September 2003, Foreign Minister Yashwant Sinha stated that India's Look East Policy which had focused primarily on ASEAN countries in Phase 1, had expanded in Phase II with the "definition of East extending from Australia to China and East Asia with ASEAN as its core".[29] Thereafter, India's relationship with the island states became more active, which included India becoming a dialogue partner of the Pacific Islands Forum (PIF) in 2002; this was obviously initiated by the two antipodean nations.

Act East Policy, today, showcases India's economic, political and strategic power and simultaneously conveys Modi's interest in building networks with smaller countries that, according to him, had remained in the periphery of India's foreign policy calculus. In his address to the joint session of the Australian Parliament on November 18, 2014, Modi laid the framework for cooperation with Australia when he stated: "Australia will not be at the periphery of our vision, but at the centre of our thought. So, we stand together at a moment of enormous opportunity and great responsibility. I see a great future of partnership between India and Australia and, a shared commitment to realise it".[30]

Australia

Bilateral relations between India and Australia have gone through significant transformation since Foreign Minister Gareth Evan delivered a speech in New Delhi in June 1995 on "The Indian Ocean; An Australian Perspective". The Indian response to Evan's projection of Australia as an Indian Ocean nation was one of indifference with no apparent interest in forging closer ties. During the administration of Prime Minister Keating from 1992-96, Australia tended to alienate India by its response on certain sensitive issues. One such irritant was Australia's decision to sell mirage aircraft to Pakistan. The Indian High Commissioner Sudarshan Bhutani and Foreign Minister Gareth Evan were reported to have clashed at a seminar in Melbourne on the mirage deal and on Australia's indifference towards the racist policies of Fiji towards Indo-Fijians particularly after the 1987 military coups. India was also not happy with the Australian media's projection of the Indian blue water naval capability. The subsequent government of Prime Minister John Howard too did not earn brownie points when it responded most abrasively to India's 1998 nuclear tests, which naturally caused a strain in the bilateral relationship.

Seeing the negative impact of its posturing in bilateral relations, Australia has worked hard on creating strategic policies that would help build closer links with India. Although the 1990s were not an easy period in the bilateral relationship, the academia and the research wing of the Department of Foreign Affairs and Trade (DFAT) contributed valuable work on Australia-India relations. The Indian Ocean Centre for Peace Studies published two papers titled *Prospects for the Future* and *India: The Outlook* while the East Asia Analytical Unit of DFAT published a detailed study on strengthening economic cooperation between India and Australia titled *India's Economy at the Midnight Hour: Australia's India Strategy*. More recently, the *Asian Century White Paper* was launched by the Australian Government in October 2012 which provided a roadmap for enhancing and broadening relations with Asian countries, including India.[31] The Australia India Institute was established in 2010 in the University of Melbourne with its stated goal of "building Australia's understanding of India and deepening and enriching the relationship between the two countries."[32] The premise here is that it is Australia that has laid the roadmap for embarking on a closer bilateral engagement.

Possible explanations for Australia's desire to deepen relations with India include the fact that changes taking place in Asia are shaping the discourse on security and the emerging economic architecture; Australia began to share a common perception on order, stability and cooperation in international relations with countries like India; there are common values of democracy and multiculturalism and the belief in the "new geopolitics" of interdependence and "new regionalism;"[33] and finally, a belief in the recent discourse on the neighbourhood connect. This aspect was emphasised when the then Australian Foreign Minister Stephen Smith in September 2008 pointed out: "It is under-appreciated that Perth and Chennai are closer to each other than Sydney is to Seoul, to Shanghai, or to Tokyo."[34] In addition, India's growing strategic partnership with the United States has also had a positive fall out on India-Australia relations. By means of economic opportunities and strategic interests in India, Australia has pragmatically and effectively implemented its policy of engagement towards India and views it as a natural partner in fighting "asymmetrical wars" and maintaining maritime security. The relationship was further energised when Prime Minister Howard visited India in 2000 and also with the first India-Australia Strategic Dialogue held in 2001. In recent times, joint naval exercises are being conducted on a regular basis and the MOU on Defence Cooperation has been a major accomplishment in promoting defence relations.

India and Australia are also focusing on closer economic ties, and with the Act East Policy firmly in place, it is expected that a FTA will be signed by the end of 2015. Australia has recently signed similar FTAs with China, Japan and Korea.[35] India's trade with Australia has increased tremendously with two-way trade in goods and services almost doubling between 2003-04 and 2013-14 (from $6.8 billion to $14.8 billion).[36] If India's market is of growing attraction to Australia then natural resources from Australia are equally important for India. The change in Australia's uranium export policy to India under the Australia-India Civil Nuclear Cooperation Agreement has removed a major irritant in bilateral relations. Danielle Rajendram of the Lowy Institute observes "Aside from the economic benefits of nuclear commerce between the two states, the conclusion of the deal has removed a major source of mistrust from the relationship, signalling that Australia considers India a responsible nuclear power".[37] The Indian Diaspora is another "important point of contact" for the growth of bilateral relations and Prime Minister Modi attaches great importance in connecting with the Indian Diaspora and encouraging them to participate in his 'Make in India' initiative. According to 2011 census data, "there were 295,373 India-born people living in Australia, an increase of 148,000 people when compared to the 2006 census".[38] This 'new Indian Diaspora,' continues to maintain their links with their homeland and has helped Australia's growing proximity with India.

India's foreign policy response towards Australia is now based on cooperation and constructive engagement, and in the current enthusiastic atmosphere Indian policy makers have responded positively to Australia seeking greater links. The emerging partnership is vital for the long term interests of both countries, as is the growing convergence on issues concerning comprehensive security. The much anticipated bilateral Strategic Partnership Agreement was signed in November 2009. In November 2014, during Prime Minister Modi's trip to Australia a new Framework for Security Cooperation was concluded. According to the Joint Statement, the new framework is "to guide closer bilateral collaboration across the security spectrum." The Framework demonstrates the unshakeable resolve of the two countries in combating and defeating terrorism, including the threat posed by foreign fighters joining extremist groups".[39] There are however some Australian analysts who hold the view that there are "limits of strategic convergence", especially in the Indian Ocean.[40]

New Zealand

India and New Zealand relations are now being viewed from a shared belief in democracy and multiculturalism and shared views on maritime security and non-traditional security threats. They are also part of a growing regional architecture and members of various regional and international fora. Both are keen to strengthen this partnership as has been apparent from various reciprocal high level visits in recent years. No longer is New Zealand seen as geographically apart and culturally different, and major links are being shaped in particular through the growing Indian community (approx. 100,000 residents and about 11,349 fee-paying students[41]). The number of Indian tourists visiting the antipodean country has also increased dramatically with a recent count being 29,000 in 2012.[42] A combination of growing economic interaction and the Act East Policy have led to expectations that the implementation of a FTA with New Zealand would not be delayed further. Negotiations on the FTA have been underway since 2010 and in October 2011, New Zealand Prime Minister launched the NZ Inc India Strategy explaining the benefits that will accrue once the FTA is in place.[43] In fact, the lack of an FTA has in no way impeded trade between the two countries, and India has emerged as the 15th largest bilateral trading partner of New Zealand with trade in goods over NZ $1.1 billion in June 2013."[44] The two countries are committed to support efforts to safeguard freedom of commerce and navigation; both have expressed concern about the maritime environment in the Asia-Pacific region and are keen to safeguard SLOCs from inimical powers. Fundamental changes in their security relations took place in 2001 when bilateral defense links were forged and Indian Naval warships visited Wellington the same year and Auckland in 2006.[45] Besides joint naval exercises, there are regular bilateral high level visits of senior officials from the Army, Air Force, and Navy and New Zealand appointed a defense adviser to India in June 2011.[46] The ushering of Act East Policy and New Zealand's agenda of "implementing an interagency strategy that is working towards India being a core trade, economic and political partner for New Zealand by 2015,"[47] are helpful in moving forward the relationship.

Fiji

Of all the South Pacific island states, India has had close relations with Fiji even before the latter became an independent country in 1970. This connect is mainly due to the large Indian Diaspora who in Fiji, brought by the British in 1879 as indentured labourers to work on sugar plantations. Under colonial rule, distinct local administrations were evolved for the Indo-Fijians and the Fijians, and this "divide and rule" policy of the British laid the foundation for separation between the two communities. Once indenture labour was abolished in 1920, the majority of Indians chose to stay on in Fiji even though it meant living under insecure conditions. The political system worked out by the British was discriminatory and institutionalised supremacy of indigenous rights and as a result there has been a continuous struggle for power-sharing between the two communities.[48] Fiji has a total population of about 800,000 of which Indians constitute 41 percent, though their number has been declining due to migration to other countries especially since the coups of 1987.

Despite a few ups and downs, bilateral ties between India and Fiji have been fairly close since 2001. It has deepened further after Commodore Bainimarama's coup of 2006[49] as Indian policy makers held that his military government was not racist, unlike the regimes that followed the coups of 1987 and 2000. Fiji's return to democracy under his leadership in 2014 has enhanced bilateral relations even more. Under the new constitution which was ratified in 2013, there are reasons to believe that democratic Fiji will hopefully emerge as a truly multicultural state. Some of the major changes introduced in the new constitution that will definitely impact the future political narrative of the country include: firstly, declaration of Fiji as a secular country which is a courageous and incredible departure from the previous dynamics of politics dominated by racial divide; secondly, the political system now being based on a common electoral role which follows the principle of "one man, one vote" instead of the discriminatory communal electoral system in place since Fiji's independence; thirdly, all the citizens of Fiji under the new constitution to be known as Fijians—earlier this nomenclature only referred to indigenous Fijians; and lastly, parliamentary seats not to be reserved on the basis of ethnicity, a practice which even the much heralded 1997 constitution could not do away with. All of this leads to the expectation that in the future race would no longer be the central determinant of political discourse in Fiji.[50]

There has been a marked change in Fiji's foreign policy during the eight years of military rule. The focal point is the shift from "West to Asia" through the active pursuit of a "Look North policy."[51] On its part, India must build on this policy and engage more actively with Fiji through its Act East policy. This is even more important now as Fiji is emerging as a leader of the Melanesian Spearhead Group (MSG) which has important island countries like PNG, Solomon Islands, and Vanuatu as its members. Prime Minister Modi's official visit to Fiji in November 2014 was timely as he expressed faith in the recently held elections and the country's return to democracy after eight years of military rule. He received a resounding reception in Fiji which reinforced India's positive image in the South Pacific and could lead to India playing a more visible role in the region, thereby also balancing China's growing influence. In his address to the Fiji Parliament, Prime Minister Modi stated:

> "For India, Fiji will always have a special place. The tide of history brought many from India to your shores. It has forged our ties of culture and kinship. But, our relationship today stands on a much broader platform of our shared values and our common interests as developing countries. And now, together we are partners in making history."[52] In recent years, the island states have experienced an alarming rise in sea levels due to climate change and global warming, and this is another area where they are aware of India's capability to assist in the sustainable development of the region. During the Fiji visit Prime Minister Modi also addressed the Summit of Pacific Island nations, a first such meeting between an Indian Prime Minister and the islanders, and he offered help and commitment on the issues of development and climate change in the Pacific islands.[53]

The Way Forward: Focal Areas

The Act East Policy, with its mantra of three Cs representing Commerce, Culture and Connectivity, is laudable, but there is a need to focus on important ground realities to ensure it remains relevant. Going forward, there are certain focal areas the Indian government will have to keep in mind as it continues to broaden and deepen these relationships.

Firstly, India's northeast region is an important determinant in the Act East Policy and it is imperative that infrastructure projects linking it with Myanmar are fast-tracked and successfully completed. Although India has actively initiated a number of connectivity projects (such as Kalandan multi-modal transit transport facility, upgrading Sittwe port, upgrading and extending the India-Myanmar friendship road), in reality implementation has been poor or nonexistent. A recent report in the *Economist* says: "...the state badly needs a better road to Myanmar. Driving the 100km from Imphal to Moreh takes five hours as the highway ascends from the rice paddies of the Imphal valley. The road is much as it was in 1942, when it was hastily built by the British."[54]

Secondly, if links with the fastest growing CLMV countries are to be realized then it is essential to develop infrastructure.[55] Indian companies are keen on fast implementation of infrastructural links through road, rail and sea for better "trade and business ties" with the ASEAN region. Indian policy has to assert its geographical proximity with Myanmar in particular, as without a comprehensive approach and with the growing number of stakeholders vying for influence in Myanmar, India would lose out in the economic sector.[56]

Thirdly, India must focus on the Bay of Bengal Initiative for Multi-Sectoral Technical and Economic Co-operation (BIMSTEC). This sub-regional initiative of India with Bangladesh, Bhutan, India, Myanmar, Nepal, Sri Lanka and Thailand as members was expected to build links between South Asia and Southeast Asia, and have a potential of US $43-59 billion trade.[57] The proposed Asian rail link envisaged for BIMSTEC nations would enhance connectivity by linking India with the five Southeast Asian countries. India has been keen to emphasise that BIMSTEC is the connecting link between SAARC and ASEAN, though in practice the infrequency of Summit Meetings hardly justifies such claims. The other sub-regional grouping, Mekong Ganga Cooperation (MGC) was formed in 2000, consisting of Myanmar, Thailand, Cambodia, Vietnam and India. Though closer economic cooperation with Mekong countries is the main rationale behind this group, India also expects to strengthen its connectivity and influence with ASEAN through MGC. It is still in the initial stage of development, and has not made significant progress.

Fourthly, from the point of view of security, India is committed to support efforts to safeguard freedom of navigation through the seas. Any obstruction to free passage of ships would have major consequences for its maritime interests. With expanding trade and dependence on energy exports, freedom of navigation is crucial and requires an integrated approach for combating traditional and non-traditional threats. The recent visit by Prime Minister Modi to some Indian Ocean littoral states is an optimistic step towards projecting India's interest in IOR. India must strengthen its strategic partnership with its most important maritime neighbour, Indonesia, and efforts must be made to move the partnership to a higher level ensuring Indonesia's cooperation in the Indian Ocean.

Lastly, to put the relationship with the South Pacific nations in a trajectory of further growth, it is imperative to review India's relationship with the island states and identify renewed opportunities for co-operation. A meaningful exercise can be undertaken by focusing on specific sectors, like education, health, trade and commerce, forests, fishery, environment, culture, tourism, and infrastructure. Small gestures go a long way in moulding opinions in the region, and in fact they are wary of big ventures as, according to them, "many of the existing projects are not viable to small economies".[58]

Conclusion

The creative shaping of the Act East policy would not have been possible without the continuous process of Look East policy which has been in force for more than two decades. Its emphasis on economic integration and strategic cooperation has, to a large extent, given credibility to India's commitment to further these causes in the Asia-Pacific region. The Act East policy affirms India's pledge to play a pivotal role in building consensus and in focusing on economic and development issues in the region. Future trends in the region could also be affected by certain activities—a pessimistic appraisal sees India facing security challenges in the Indian Ocean and in Myanmar, leading to confrontation between India and China.[59] On the other hand, an optimistic point of view does not see democratic India provoking a situation with China or any other country, and continuing to be viewed by ASEAN and the South Pacific countries as a trustworthy partner.

The future contours of India's Foreign policy and its ability to cope with the emerging challenges are difficult to predict. It's obvious that the Indo-Pacific region is witnessing complications, with tensions on the rise and strategic manipulations due to the involvement of external powers. As challenges get more complex, new ways of building and maintaining strategic partnerships have to be explored in consonance with these trends. Foreign policy will now need to be more sensitive to non-military threats because the complex patterns of interdependence and security are increasingly being interpreted as human security. In the words of the pioneering economist, Mahbub ul Haq, "And the imperatives of this human security have become universal, indivisible, and truly global today. The choice before us is simple, though stark. We can either learn to live together, or we can all die together."[60]

Author's Note

Some of the focal areas mentioned in this paper had been highlighted at the CII, 3rd ASEAN/ANZ Regional Committee Meeting, September 3, 2013. This meeting was attended by the author as a member of the Committee.

This paper builds on the work of the author in the previous articles "ASEAN-India Relations During the Cold War" in Fredric Grare and Amitabh Mattoo (eds), *India and ASEAN; The Politics of India's Look East Policy,* New Delhi: Manohar Publishers,2001 pp.41-66. and "Indian Perspectives on Security Dimensions of India and Southeast Asia", in V.R. Raghavan and Karl Fischer (eds), *Security Dimensions of India and Southeast Asia,* Tata McGraw-Hill, New Delhi 2005, pp.3-21. "India's Look East Policy: Posture and Reality" in Y. Yagama Reddy (ed), *Emerging: India in Asia-Pacific* New Century

Publications, New Delhi, 2007, pp.240-259. "Regional Groupings: An Overview of BIMSTEC and MGS" in *South Asian Survey* 13/2 July-December 2006, pp.313-322.

END NOTES

1. Remarks by the Prime Minister at the 12th India-ASEAN Summit, Nay Pyi Twa, Myanmar, 12 November 2014 http://www.narendramodi.in/remarks-by-the-pm-at-the-12th-indiaaseansummit-nay-pyi-taw-myanmar/ (Accessed March 22, 2015)
2. Through existing cooperative forums like ASEAN, ASEAN Regional Forum (ARF), the Post Ministerial Conference (PMC) 10+1, the East Asia Summit (EAS), ASEAN Defence Ministerial Meeting Plus (ADMM PLUS), G20, Indian Ocean Rim Association (IORA) and the Pacific Islands Forum (PIF).
3. See C. Raja Mohan From Looking East to Acting East http://mea.gov.in/in-focusarticle.htm?24714/From+Looking+East+to+Acting+East (Accessed on March 26, 2015.)
4. http://www.hindustantimes.com/india-news/obama-writes-article-on-pm-modi-in-timemagazine-calls-him-india-s-reformer-in-chief/article1-1337899.aspx (Accessed on March 17, 2015)
5. See ManMohini Kaul, "ASEAN—India Relations During the Cold War" in Fredric Grare and Amitabh Mattoo (ed) *India and ASEAN; The politics of India's Look East Policy*, Manohar Publishers, New Delhi, 2001, pp.41-66 and "Indian Perspectives on Security Dimensions of India and Southeast Asia", in V.R. Raghavan and Karl Fischer (ed) *Security Dimensions of India and Southeast Asia*, Tata McGraw-Hill, New Delhi 2005, pp.3-21. Concept note of two-day International Seminar on India's Look East Policy: Gleanings from the Past to the Present, 18-19 December 201, University of Burdwan.
6. Ibid.
7. Sarvepalli Gopal, *Jawaharlal Nehru, A Biography* Vol.1: 1947-1956 Oxford University Press, Delhi,1979, p.345
8. Sunanda K. Datta, Ray, *Looking East to Look West: Lee Kuan Yew's Mission India*, Penguin Books, New Delhi, 2009, p.84.
9. Mohammed Ayoob, *India and Southeast Asia: Indian Perceptions and Policies* Routledge, London, 1990, p.18
10. *Amrita Bazar Patrika*, Calcutta, August 20, 1976.
11. Quoted in Sunanda K. Datta –Ray, n.7, p.219
12. Kripa Sridharan, "The ASEAN Region in India's 'Look East Policy'" in K. Raja Reddy (ed) *India and ASEAN: Foreign Policy Dimensions for the 21st Century*, New Century Publications, New Delhi, 2005 pp. 118-120.
13. Sunanda K. Datta, Ray n.7, p. 289.
14. Keynote Address by External Affairs Minister Smt. Sushma Swaraj at the Inaugural Session of Delhi Dialogue VII in New Delhi, 11-March-2015, http://pib.nic.in/newsite/PrintRelease.aspx?relid=116864 (Accessed on March 22, 2015)
15. Keck, Zachary, India, ASEAN Celebrate 20th Anniversary With Two FTAs, December 21, 2012, http://thediplomat.com/2012/12/india-asean-celebrate-20th-anniversary-with-twoftas/(Accessed May1, 2014).
16. http://articles.economictimes.indiatimes.com/2015-01-15/news/58108785_1_malaysianminister-services-and-investments-rcep (Accessed March 26, 2015)
17. Manish Chand Act East: India's ASEAN Journey http://mea.gov.in/in-focusarticle.htm?24216/Act+East+Indias+ASEAN+Jouroney (Accessed March 27, 2015)

18. C.S. Kuppuswamy, India's Look-East Policy: More aggressive, Better Dividends: http://chantikaturi.blogspot.in/2008/01/indias-look-east-policy-more-aggressive.html (Accessed May 2, 2014)
19. Mohan Malik, China's Strategy of Containing India: Tensions brew between burgeoning world powers, http://www.utne.com/community/chinasstrategyofcontainingindia.aspx#ixzz310adFgsi (Accessed May 3, 2014)
20. Barack Obama's speech to Parliament, *Herald Sun,* November 17, 2011.
21. Mark Beeson, "Southeast Asia and the Major Powers: The United States, Japan and China", in Mark Beeson (ed) *Contemporary Southeast Asia: Regional Dynamics, National Differences,* Palgrave Macmillan, Hampshire, 2004, p.209, see also Denny Roy," Southeast Asia and China: Balancing or Bandwagoning", *Contemporary Southeast Asia*, vol. 27, no.2, 2005, pp. 305-22
22. Thomas J. Christensen., "The Advantage of an assertive China: Responding to Beijing's Abrasive Diplomacy", *Foreign Affairs,* vol. 90, no. 2, 2011, p. 55.
23. Mohan Malik, n. 19, http://www.utne.com/community/chinasstrategyofcontaining india.aspx#ixzz310adFgsi (Accessed May 3, 2014)
24. B.R. Deepak, Henderson Brooks Report on 1962 War: 'Secrecy' an Ostrich Act, Paper No. 5669, 21 March 2014, [Online: web] http://www.southasiaanalysis.org/node/1483 (Accessed May 3 2014.)
25. C. Raja Mohan, "India and the Balance of Power", *Foreign Affairs*,: http://www.cfr.org/india/india-balance-power/p10948 (Accessed May 7, 2014)
26. Shyam Saran, "Mapping the Indo-Pacific: India and the strategic inter-linkage between Indian and Pacific Oceans", The Indian Express, October29, 2011.
27. ManMohini Kaul, "Imagining the South Pacific: An Indian Construction of the Region, in N.N. Vohra (ed) India and Australasia, History, Culture and Society, Shipra Publications, New Delhi, 2004, p. 132
28. Ibid.
29. C. Raja Mohan, "Is India an East Asian Power? Explaining New Delhi's Security Politics in the Western Pacific, ISAS Working Paper No. 81, 11 August 2009, p. 6.
30. 'Prime Minister Narendra Modi's Address to the Joint Session of the Australian Parliamenthttp'://www.narendramodi.in/prime-minister-narendra-modis-address-to-thejoint-session-of-the-australian-parliament/ (Accessed April 4, 2015)
31. http://australianpolitics.com/downloads/foreign/12-10-28_aust-in-the-asian-century-whitepaper.pdf (Accessed on April 24, 2015)
32. http://www.aii.unimelb.edu.au/about us (Accessed on April 24, 2015)
33. Paul Bowles, "ASEAN, AFTA and the 'New Regionalism'," *Pacific Affairs,* Vol. 70, No. 2 (Summer, 1997), pp. 219-233.
34. http://www.mea.gov.in/Portal/ForeignRelation/Australia_July_2014.pdf Accessed on April
35. Ibid
36. Australia-India Comprehensive Economic Cooperation Agreement, http://www.dfat.gov.au/trade/agreements/aifta/Pages/australia-india-comprehensive-economic-cooperationagreement.aspx. (Accessed April 4,2015)
37. Danielle Rajendram India's new Asia-Pacific strategy: Modi acts East, http://www.lowyinstitute.org/publications/indias-new-asia-pacific-strategy-modi-acts-east. (Accessed April 4, 2015)
38. http://indianexpress.com/article/world/indians-abroad/indians-make-up-over-1-per-cent-ofaustralias-population/ (Accessed on April 17, 2015)

39. http://pib.nic.in/newsite/PrintRelease.aspx?relid=111502
40. David Brewster, "Australia and India: the Indian Ocean and the limits of strategic convergence" in *Australian Journal of International Affairs*, 64;5,549-565, DOI: 10, 108/ 10357718, 2010, 513369 http// dx.doi.org/ 101080/10357718.2010.513369. (Accessed on October 2013)
41. Jacqueline Leckie,*The story of a New Zealand South Asian Community Indian Settlers,* Dunedin: Otago University Press, 2007.
42. New Zealand-India Free Trade Agreement (FTA) http://mfat.govt.nz/Trade-and-Economic-Relations/2-Trade-Relationships-and-Agreements/India/index.php. (Accessed on April 4, 2015)
43. Ibid.
44. http://mfat.govt.nz/Trade-and-Economic-Relations/2-Trade-Relationships-and-Agreements/India/index.php.
45. New Zealand Ministry of Defence: *Defence White Paper 2010,* http://www.defence.govt.nz/reports-publications/defence-white-paper-2010/chapter3-nz-strategic-outlook-to-203. (Accessed on March 4, 2015)
46. See for details ManMohini Kaul, "India in New Zealand's Asia Policy", in ManMohini Kaul and Vibhanshu Shekhar (ed), *India and New Zealand in a Rising Asia: Issues and Perspectives*, Pentagon Press, New Delhi, 2012.
47. http://mfat.govt.nz/Trade-and-Economic-Relations/2-Trade-Relationships-and- Agreements/India/index.php. (Accessed on April 4, 2015)
48. ManMohini Kaul, *Pearls in the Ocean: Security Perspectives in the Southwest Pacific*, UBSPD, New Delhi, 1993, pp.27-50
49. For an alternative view see Brij V. Lal, "Editorial: Fiji's Coup Conundrum", in *The Round Table: The Commonwealth Journal of International Affairs*, 101: 6, 489-497, DOI: 10,1080/ 00358533.2012.749097 HTTP:// DX.DOI.ORG/10.1080/00358533.2012.749097 (Accessed on October 25, 2013)
50. ManMohini Kaul, Multicultural Becomings, http://www.lilainteractions.in/fiji/
51. Ibid
52. http://www.narendramodi.in/primeministers-address-to-fiji-parliament/ (Accessed on April 25, 2015)
53. Prime Minister Narendra Modi reaches out to Pacific nations; announces $1 million fund, visa on arrival http://pacificidf.org/pm-narendra-modi-reaches-out-to-pacific-nationsannounces-1-million-fund-visa-on-arrival/ (Accessed on April 2, 2015.)
54. India's north-east ;Missing link http://www.economist.com/news/asia/21632649-promisescloser-ties-over-border-myanmar-are-long-way-reality-missing-link (Accessed on April 2, 2015)
55. CII, 3rd ASEAN/ANZ Regional Committee Meeting, September 3, 2013. This meeting was attended by the author as a member of the Committee.
56. Ibid.
57. http://www.mofa.gov.np/en/bimstec-170.html (Accessed May 7, 2014)
58. Author's interview during the trip to some of the Island States as a team leader of experts/ officials which visited the South Pacific between May 14-June 5, 2004, to conduct a 'needs and capacity' study on technical and developmental cooperation.
59. See Robert D. Kaplan, *Monsoon: The Indian Ocean and the Future of American Power,* Random House, New York, 2010 , pp.213-239.
60. http://mhhdc.org/index.php (Accessed on March 22, 2015)

2

India and East Asia: Opportunities Ahead

Leela K Ponappa[1]

The subject of India's opportunities in East and Southeast Asia is of direct and current relevance to India's foreign policy, encompassing its political, economic, strategic and cultural interests. In looking at East Asia, within which term I include Southeast Asia as well, we are necessarily addressing the restoration of India's natural and historical linkages, which are evident throughout the region. What this calls for is a reorientation of India's own mindset regarding where its neighbourhood lies, the nature of its contemporary strategic interests and the extent of outreach that is sustainable.

While continuing to handle bilateral relations with its neighbours as a foreign policy priority, India has perhaps understood the need to expand its neighbourhood engagement with regions beyond what is termed 'South Asia'. We speak today of a Look East policy. Harking back to the kinds of external linkages that India had sustained long before the colonial interregnum, let us recall that from the time of Ashoka to the Mughals, areas that are today considered parts of Central Asia were natural domains of operation for their commerce, military and strategic campaigns, and that there was a two-way flow of people and ideas; likewise, the Cholas and other major peninsular and coastal rulers had a natural tendency to head east, across the Bay of Bengal and the Straits of Malacca, primarily in pursuit of trade. The influence of such outreach is encapsulated in the very term "Indo-China", and evident in the easy melding of economic interaction, culture, religion, language, architecture, food, textiles and aesthetics in general, in a seamless manner that is taken for granted. Throughout history, India and China have always had an awareness of each other even though the realities of geography and transport technology prevented the degree of interaction that is possible today. India's historical linkages with eastern Asia did not come about because of any conscious policy to look east. It is the naturalness of the engagement that offers India fresh opportunities now, to develop contemporary relationships based on new realities.

During the colonial interregnum, the British mindset governed the direction of India's regional linkages. Britain's perceptions from within India were land-based and the focus of the Indian Army was primarily the north-west, as part of the Great Game. However, to sustain its imperial reach, Britain reserved for itself the dominance of the Indian Ocean through the Royal Navy. Post-Independence, India's terms of reference were largely determined by the consequences of Partition and the country's pre-occupations with the economic legacy of the colonial past. India had relations with East and Southeast Asia, but the degree of engagement did not match the attention paid to relations with the west.

At the risk of over simplification, one could say that today, over six decades after Independence, India is seeking to create new realities through fresh economic direction, new political developments, internally and externally and wider strategic concepts. These measures are all part of a process of India's maturing as a nation state, with a comfort level in handling its own growing power in the social, economic, military and political fields and a consciousness of the need to use this power with responsibility.

Looking East beyond SAARC

After a slow start in accepting regionalism as a foreign policy instrument in the 1980s, essentially through SAARC, India's thinking grew progressively, primarily towards eastern Asia. By the early 1990s and after the end of the Cold War, Prime Minister P.V. Narasimha Rao's Look East policy led to full engagement with ASEAN as a dialogue partner, membership of ARF in 1995, a Summit relationship in 2002 and membership of new fora such as the ASEAN Defence Ministers Meeting plus Eight (ADMM+8) and the Expanded ASEAN Maritime Forum (EAMF) more recently. In 2005, India was present at the first East Asia Summit, thanks to friends in ASEAN. The Look East policy was both a restoration of historical links and the crafting of contemporary relationships incorporating political, economic and security interests, extensive cultural linkages apart.

India's rethinking about its neighbourhood also saw its involvement in the establishment of other regional fora. In 1997, BIMSTEC was formed, incorporating select members from SAARC (Bangladesh, India, Sri Lanka) and ASEAN (Myanmar, Thailand) around the Bay of Bengal. India thus found an alternative forum for itself together with two other SAARC members, joined later by Bhutan and Nepal. The year also saw the establishment of the IOR-ARC, now the IORA. In 2000, Mekong-Ganga Cooperation began, in furtherance of the Look East policy, particularly with the CMLV component of ASEAN (Cambodia, Myanmar, Laos and Vietnam).

In 2002, Asian Cooperation and Development was initiated under a Thai initiative, with cross-regional participation by select members of ASEAN+3, the GCC and SAARC working towards an Asian community. (ACD did considerable preliminary work on conceptualising an Asian bond market, much of it by India, although the follow up took place through the ASEAN+3).Further, in 2005, India joined the East Asia Summit as a founder member and the SCO as an Observer. In 2008, the Indian Ocean Naval Symposium (IONS) was convened, as an Indian initiative. In 2010, the ADMM+8 was formed. Thereafter in 2012, the Expanded East Asia Maritime Forum (EAMF) was formed.

Separately, India started FTA and CECA/CEPA negotiations with several countries and regions. A pioneering FTA process with Sri Lanka in 1998 was followed by Thailand in 2003, ASEAN (2003), BIMSTEC (2004), Singapore (2005), Korea (2009), Malaysia (2011) and Japan (2011). An early but long-dormant PTA, the Bangkok Agreement (1975) was revived and rechristened the Asia Pacific Trade Agreement in 2005, with China as a new member in addition to Bangladesh, India, Laos, South Korea and Sri Lanka. How the APEC, RCEP and TPP processes will evolve remains a question; they seem to be works in progress and it is to be seen whether they will become more inclusive and cohesive.

In another domain, India's security dialogue with several countries in a wider neighbourhood led to fruitful cooperation in some key areas. The significance of this progression since 1985 clearly established that the determination of India's neighbourhood based on organisational constructs and appellations had conceptual limitations, to the same extent that, for example, the earlier Japanese idea of Asia as ending in Burma was unrealistic.

Maritime Dimension

The maritime dimension is self-evident throughout this discussion. Today, beside the earmarked regions of Asia, whether South, East, West or Central, the Asia-Pacific is a generally accepted concept, amid a growing debate about the newer concept of the Indo-Pacific. The idea stands endorsed by some like Australia and Indonesia; it has been both contested and acknowledged by Chinese Track II participants; in India, the issue is still being debated.

The Pacific Ocean has been a key element in the westward movement of the United States from the 19th century onwards. It has necessarily remained a major factor as the US engaged diversely with Asia after World War II—through alliance, partnership, confrontation and war—with Japan, Korea, Russia, Vietnam, Thailand, ASEAN as a whole, Mongolia, now Myanmar, and of course with China. The role of the US and its overarching naval presence in the Pacific and Indian Oceans is a factor that affects all the littorals, India included.

Are these separate theatres, as some have argued? There is a natural geographical continuum between the Pacific and Indian Oceans, in use for centuries, with no man-made linkages to each other like either the Suez or Panama canals. Unlike the Atlantic and the Pacific, the Indian Ocean has no major northern passage of exit, hemmed in as it is by Asia's land mass, barring a few choke points towards the east and west. India is a sea-locked country, strategically located atop the northern Indian Ocean, with no dispensations for land transit unlike the international norms that require neighbours to provide a land-locked country with access to the sea. However, being sea-locked for a country of India's size with a coastline of over 7,000 kms provides opportunities and this too is part of the historical neighbourhood that India is increasingly aware of, given its locational advantage astride the SLOCs connecting the Gulf, the Red Sea and the Mediterranean with the South China Sea and the Pacific Ocean. ASEAN is typically considered to have a greater orientation towards the Pacific, perhaps because of the overwhelming presence of China. However, five of the 10 ASEAN countries are also Indian Ocean littorals (Myanmar, Thailand, Malaysia, Indonesia and Singapore) and three of these are India's neighbours. The historical pattern of India's engagement by sea—economic, social and cultural—has ranged from eastern Africa to the northern Indian Ocean including the Red Sea and the Gulf and extensively towards the Straits of Malacca and beyond. Today, a major part of India's foreign trade with ASEAN, China, Japan, Korea, the US and the rest of the Americas passes through the Malacca Straits to the South China Sea and the Pacific Ocean. India energy interests encompass not just the Gulf and the rest of the Indian Ocean but also the South China Sea.

Maritime security and the safety of the SLOCs thus become important factors through bilateral and regional cooperation, for purposes of trade, energy supplies and security against piracy and disasters, natural and man-made. While the UNCLOS establishes rules of the road in a manner that does not exist on land, strategic rivalry is inevitable but need not necessarily become confrontational. It would behove major countries to give substance to the statement that there is enough space for all, by not letting rivalry degenerate to a threat. Codes of conduct are essential for the management and the peaceful settlement of the several territorial disputes in the East and South China Seas.

Key Factors

Amidst this progression of India's thinking about its regional identities, some key factors warrant attention:

- The first would obviously be China. Let us step back a bit, and set aside our bilateral perceptions, to recognise the realities involved. China is a Civilisational State. It has also functioned as a political entity since the 2nd century BC, when it was first unified under a single ruler. We see it today as a fast growing, assertive, economic and military power. Despite the appearance of a cohesive strategy, there are indications of divergent positions within China on how to handle such power. Two[recent] articles [in 2011] provide pointers: one in Qiushi,[2] the authoritative journal of the Chinese Communist Party's Central Committee titled "How China Deals with the U.S. Strategy to Contain China", makes the case that China has never gained peace by giving in, but only through war. The author also advocates the use of trade as a weapon. Contrast this with the Foreign Affairs article by Wang Jisi, Dean of the School of International Studies at Peking University in Beijing on 'China's Search for a Grand Strategy',[3] which advocates collaboration as the approach of choice. Thus, China appears to be internationally collaborative when dealing with North Korea's nuclear capabilities or with international financial issues; it is combative on issues like the South China Sea, or nuclear proliferation to Pakistan. There are clearly contradictions, possibly deliberate and simultaneous, which India—like other countries—will need to identify and craft responses to. There are also several question marks about the internal situation in China amidst reports of workers' protests and ethnic alienation, even if there is no apparent threat to the predominance of the Chinese Communist Party. India will have to device methods to deal with all the complexities involved given the range of its own relations with China, involving local, bilateral, regional and international dimensions.

- Maritime issues as cited above constitute the second major factor. India's preoccupations with land boundary issues with China and Pakistan foreclosed adequate attention to the maritime aspects of India's neighbourhood dealings for many decades. If a neighbour is defined as a country with which India shares a border, it is worth noting that of India's 11 neighbours, we have only land boundaries with four [Afghanistan, Bhutan, China, Nepal], both land and sea boundaries with three [Bangladesh, Myanmar, Pakistan] and only maritime boundaries with four [Indonesia, Maldives, Sri Lanka, Thailand]. Without underestimating the importance of secure land boundaries, particularly with neighbours that have been troublesome, I would like to emphasise that the maritime dimension of India's security requires equal attention, as the Mumbai attacks on 26/11 so forcefully showed. Even earlier, piracy in the Straits of Malacca posed a serious threat to trade until regional collaboration tackled it with some success. India's commanding position in the Indian Ocean gives it a unique opportunity to bring together the forces of stability in ensuring the safety of the Sea Lines of Communication.
- Economic and military cooperation thus become key factors in India's engagement with East and Southeast Asia. Our historical linkages with this region were established through trade and culture and an important element in the Look East policy is the move towards FTAs, bilaterally as with Thailand, Singapore, Malaysia and South Korea or multilaterally, as with ASEAN as a whole. China is today India's largest trading partner. India has also come a long way from fighting shy of establishing defence partnerships with

confidence. Our armed forces, primarily the Navy, have active linkages with all countries in the region, have exercised bilaterally or multilaterally with most of them including China and collaborated closely in various ways. Further economic and military engagement can lead to growth and stability if India engages with transparency and confidence. It should be noted that India has been a security provider of choice to smaller countries in this region.

- Connectivity also becomes critical. There has been rapid growth in China's links from north to south, with the building of the Kunming-Singapore highway and railway, and east to west via the northern branch of the Trans Asian Railway, by which it would be possible to ship a container by rail from Shanghai to Brussels. India organised an exciting car rally with ASEAN in 2004, with teams from each of the 10 ASEAN countries and India moving from Guwahati in India through Myanmar, northern Thailand, Laos, Vietnam, Cambodia, central and southern Thailand, Malaysia, Singapore to Indonesia. The rally demonstrated the ground linkages but much more remains to be done to give these linkages substance.

Three major projects warrant India's attention:

- Around the time that the great canal projects at Suez and in Panama were thought of, a canal across the Kra Isthmus was also contemplated, to link the Bay of Bengal to the Gulf of Thailand. In current circumstances it is not likely that a Kra Canal will ever become a reality, for a variety of reasons; however, a land bridge across the Kra Isthmus is a very real possibility, with roads and pipelines that could bypass the Malacca Straits, reduce transit time and costs and connect the Bay of Bengal not just to the Gulf of Thailand but onward, to the South China Sea. Access to Kra from India would lie through the 10 degree channel, i.e. right through the Andaman Islands. India should clearly partner Thailand and Malaysia in initiating such a project and invest in it.
- The Myanmarese port of Dawei [previously Tavoy] on the Andaman Sea lies about 120 km west of the Thai town of Kanchanaburi [known for the bridge on the river Kwai]. A feasibility study for a road connecting Dawei to Kanchanaburi indicates trade benefits through multi-modal movement: by sea across the Bay of Bengal just north of the Andamans to Dawei, thence by road via

Kanchanaburi and on to Bangkok, with further movement by sea to the South China Sea and the Pacific.

- The proposed Trilateral Highway connecting India, Myanmar and Thailand would in effect provide road connectivity from India's westernmost point, Port Okha in Gujarat to Danang in Vietnam, on the South China Sea, given existing eastward connectivity from Thailand through Laos. The alignment has been identified and the project is technically feasible; there appear to be some hitches involving the funding arrangements in Myanmar. These should be resolved quickly.

So-called soft power also presents India with several opportunities in creating common stakes with East and Southeast Asia. The sharing of India's experience is an exercise that we should not underestimate. There is room for two-way traffic, with India learning, for example, from the excellence of tourist facilities and packaging in eastern Asia, while contributing with the teaching of English. Apart from some of our well-established technical training programmes under the ITEC scheme and military training, a large number of areas ranging from India's political evolution through the practice of democracy to the application of science and technology to development through our space programme's inputs into water management, telemedicine etc could contribute to intensified engagement. Nuclear safety is an obvious area for cooperation. Finally, security cooperation is waiting to be strengthened, perhaps within a new, overarching concept of Asian security architecture.

Conclusion

Politically, India has the advantage of its rise not being seen as threatening or exploitative.It has the ability to set itself an agenda without hyphenation between either the US or China. While strengthening links with newer partners like Japan, Australia and the US, India will need to maintain a fine balance in its relations with China, expanding engagement where beneficial while clearly conveying and safeguarding its security concerns. While acknowledging the reality of strategic rivalries and participating in responsible dialogue, India should ensure that it has the capabilities to counter any threat enhancement and unilateral alteration of the *status quo*.

Given both the multiplicity and the linkages of diverse regional organisations, Asia's governments will at some stage have to enter into a pan-

Asian dialogue on security issues. Till then, India should participate in the regional discourse towards security architecture which is multipolar, transparent, rule-based inclusive and non-hegemonic.

Economically, trade and investment hold the key. Even as India pursues the revival of its manufacturing capabilities, it should maximise its trade and economic ties throughout its neighbourhood. The feasibility of greater connectivity by land, sea or multimodal means is a key factor in strengthening linkages and developing a sense of community and neighbourhood. Enhanced connectivity and infrastructural linkages between the diverse regions which constitute India's neighbourhood would provide additional channels for trade and contact between civil societies.

At the heart of the matter of exploring the opportunities in eastern Asia is India's own mindset and notions of what constitutes its geographic space. Mongolia employs the concept of the 'third neighbour' to help identify priority countries beyond the two—China and Russia—which surround it. India needs to start thinking of itself as a Pacific Ocean country and initiating or strengthening the measures that would make this possible. The promise of such linkages stands squarely in front of us and it remains for us to use our national assets, be they the holy places of Buddhism, our investment capabilities or the reach of the Indian Navy, to make them new realities.

END NOTES

1. This contribution is largely based on a presentation at the Centre of Advanced Studies, Pune in March 2011. In order to provide the reader with a view that reflects the position at that time in the context of the Look East policy, it has deliberately not been updated in 2015 to encompass the Act East policy since the assessments and conclusions continue to hold good.
2. http://chinascope.org/main/content/view/3291/92/, (accessed on December 10, 2010).
3. Foreign Affairs, March/April 2011 issue.

3

India's Role in the East Asia Summit

Anushree Chakraborty

Southeast Asia is one of the fastest growing regions in the world. The region, comprising small and medium ranged powers, has elevated its visibility and diplomatic assertiveness in the last two decades. The region's successful integration effort, in addition to its economic boom and prosperity drive, has distinguished it from the other regional initiatives around the world. Nonetheless, what marks the region from the rest is the enormous normative weight it carries in the 21st century international polity. Southeast Asia as a region has put forward an alternative discourse of managing security, the one distinct from the Western rationale. Security is understood differently in the Southeast Asian region and it has effectively organised itself as a body with their indigenous outlook on security through the ASEAN Way. Today, ASEAN's security structure and norms have moved towards comprehensive security, distinct from the collective security promoted by the West.

One of the greatest achievements of the Southeast Asian region in the preceding century was that it managed to reduce security competitions and conflicts among hostile post-colonial nations, while maintaining order and stability, similar to its counterpart in Europe. In the post-Cold War period, despite an impressive record of stability and economic growth, security challenges became a major preoccupation in the region. With the changing strategic environment and re-arrangement of powers, from uni-polar moment to multi-polar world, Southeast Asian region adjusted itself in the new world order to remain relevant and reinvented itself as an epicenter of managing great power relations. This ambitious role called for institutions and norms that will keep the major powers hooked to the region.

ASEAN's first dedicated security related institution was the ASEAN Regional Forum (ARF).Since it is backed by substantial amount of literature debating about its relevance, I will restrict myself to the latest introduction to the security architecture in Southeast Asia and East Asia, that is, the East Asia Summit (EAS). Although EAS is not considered an exclusive security forum, nevertheless, it provides impetus to manage the broader strategic balance. This chapter therefore will analyze the EAS and its functioning as it completes a decade. Since this forum is relatively new, it is too early to assess its achievements. Nevertheless, the chapter will highlight the core work of the institution and evaluate India's role in it.

Genesis of EAS: Exclusive Club for Exclusive Purpose

The idea of EAS originated from the report published by the East Asian Vision Group within the ASEAN Plus Three (APT) circle in 2001. The report titled "Towards an East Asian Community: Region of Peace, Prosperity and Progress," spoke about establishing the EAS for enhancing functional cooperation between members with the aim of building the East Asia Community. In the past, there have been academic debates questioning the utility of multiple institutions within the ASEAN circle, thereby resulting in duplication, which finally produces an 'alphabet soup'.

Nevertheless, the effectiveness of APT as a platform for cooperation provided the incentive to elevate it to another institutional format in the name of EAS. This helped in expanding the mandate of the APT and linking it to ASEAN Summit meetings, meanwhile ensuring the centrality of ASEAN in the wider circle. Moreover, East Asian region *per se* is yet to realize regionalism. The regional lackluster in East Asia fails to address the security dilemma among their members. This leads to uncertainty and consequently, builds up a threat perception for the neighbouring Southeast Asian region. Therefore, it makes sense for ASEAN to involve East Asian countries into greater East Asia Community building efforts. ASEAN accordingly is continuing with the dialogue between themselves and the East Asian countries. Since an ASEAN member's economic prosperity and security is intimately linked with East Asia, ASEAN countries are keen to expand their relationship with more benefits of functional cooperation through EAS. Therefore, the most important norm for EAS is that it is based on the premise of centrality of the ASEAN.

In addition, the creation of EAS cannot be appreciated without deliberating upon the strategic paradox facing the region and the history of international politics, especially of 19th century Europe, which is looming large upon the psyche of regional leaders and intellectuals.[1] Yusuf Wanandi, one of the leading minds in Indonesia noted that the EAS is going to be the 'Concert of Powers' for East Asia.[2] Drawing from Hugh White's[3] idea, Wanandi comments that the EAS should be utilised "in order to create peace, stability and development in East Asia, especially to create an environment where China and the US can cooperate better and alleviate the antagonism or tendencies to confront each other."[4]

It is important to note that ARF was created for specific security goals, that is, for the non-traditional security issues, which cannot be addressed by one single country in the region. This therefore raised the need for an all-encompassing security architecture that will cover geographically much wider space and involve as many members as possible. As a result, ARF has twenty seven member countries across different continents, institutionalising security dialogue among them. With the large number of participants and wide coverage of geographical space, the agenda and the pace with which the Forum proceeds is insignificant.[5] ASEAN Defense Ministers Meeting (ADMM), the latest addition to ASEAN security architecture, focuses on traditional security. Because of the prior discomfort, the ASEAN leaders kept traditional security at the back burner. However, at 27 years of existence, ASEAN has reached maturity and is daring to move beyond its comfort zone; formation of the ADMM and the establishment of ASEAN Intergovernmental Commission of Human Rights being the case in point. With the inception of the ADMM, ASEAN has built a forum for the Ministry of Defense of each participant country to be part of the regional community building process and contribute towards greater security and confidence in the region.

One of the stated objectives of the EAS is 'promoting peace, stability and economic prosperity in East Asia'. The EAS also states the need for promoting strategic dialogue and cooperation on political and security issues for peaceful coexistence. These statements explain the raison d'état of EAS. In addition to community building, what distinguishes EAS from previously established ASEAN initiated institutions is that EAS seeks to balance the great power politics in the region. The primary purpose of EAS is managing the strategic rivalry that is underpinning the 21st century Asian corridors. This is indeed an ambitious task compared to the earlier objectives of ASEAN institutions. Another stated objective of EAS is to bring the region at par with global standards of universally recognised values. This suggests that despite lapses of democratic consolidations in some parts of ASEAN, there are aspirations within the region to meet the globally required democratic standards. This is reflected in the initial membership given to countries outside the ASEAN Plus Three. India, Australia and New Zealand have set the example for the region to emulate. The ASEAN Charter established thereafter also highlights the forward looking path in which the ASEAN leaders hope to tread.

ASEAN has made possible an inclusive regionalisation process within the entire Asia Pacific region. There are several countries which have established regular interaction with ASEAN by sending ambassadors. Realising their seriousness, ASEAN members sought to capitalise their interest in the region by forming another regional club in the name of EAS. However, ASEAN members were careful to make it a limited club, thereby restricting its membership to five big countries in addition to ASEAN Plus Three. Its genesis lies in developing increasingly interlinked and interdependent societies among the members, fostering strategic dialogue and promoting cooperation in political, economic and security issues.[6] This will help the ASEAN members to bring their issues at the forefront, extend cooperation beyond their immediate circle and seek support from some of the important countries in the neighbourhood. The result will be enhanced confidence and trust building among the EAS countries.

The year 2015 marks the 10th year of EAS' establishment. Over these years, EAS members have focused attention on areas such as promoting development, financial stability, energy security, economic integration and growth, eradicating poverty and narrowing the development gap in East Asia. This has been done through technology transfer and infrastructure development, capacity building, good governance and humanitarian assistance, as well as by promoting financial links, trade and investment expansion and liberalisation, environmental protection, prevention of infectious diseases and natural disaster mitigation.[7] At the 8th EAS Finance Minister's Meeting held on 2nd July 2013 in Brunei, EAS identified six priority areas, namely environment and energy, education, finance, global health issues and pandemic diseases, natural disaster mitigation and ASEAN Connectivity.[8] These issues were brought into focus in order to avoid some of the controversial subjects among the participants, while also addressing the immediate challenges facing the region. However, despite the absence of official acknowledgement in the EAS proceedings, it is seen as the platform which will accommodate rising powers such as India and China, recognise the geopolitical interests of the US, and define a role for the middle powers in pursuit of peace and security.[9]

The East Asia Summit's journey since its first meeting in Kuala Lumpur in 2005, reveals the issues that have been deliberated upon in the last ten years. At the first summit, the members adopted the EAS Declaration on Avian Influenza Prevention, Control and Response. At that time, there were concerns over some continuing cases of avian influenza in the region.As a result, EAS decided to coordinate efforts and increase cooperation in addressing this challenge, including ensuring the availability of medicine and health personnel. At the second EAS in 2007 at Cebu, underlined areas of cooperation were energy security, renewable and alternative energy sources, energy efficiency and conservation, and finally climate change. EAS members also agreed to develop deeper, more diversified and better-integrated financial markets, and to strengthen regional mechanisms to prevent and manage financial crises. In addition, natural disaster mitigation received attention and Track Two study on a Comprehensive Economic Partnership in East Asia (CEPEA) was conducted.

At the third EAS in Singapore in November 2007, there was a separate section on Energy, Environment, Climate Change and Sustainable Development. Given that most of the members of EAS are developing countries, it is interesting that they showed commitment to these issues. There was a mention of Myanmar in the summit and the comments made were positive since it encouraged the concerned country to face the international response and move towards political reforms. Another step forward was the establishment of the Economic Research Institute of ASEAN and East Asia (ERIA) which was to be accommodated temporarily at the ASEAN Secretariat. At the fourth meeting, in Cha-am Hua Hin, Thailand in October 2009, issues related to trade finance, environment and climate change were discussed. However, most significant was the Cha-am Hua Hin Statement on EAS Disaster Management, trafficking issue and the support for Intra-ASEAN connectivity. Notably, for the first time, the EAS members officially acknowledged that the Summit has rapidly developed as a strategic forum and an important component of the evolving regional architecture.

Subsequently, at the 8th EAS Finance Minister Meeting on 2nd July 2013 at Brunei, six priority areas for EAS were identified. Further, there was an implementation of the Declaration of the 7th EAS on Regional Responses to Malaria Control and talk on the revival of Nalanda University in India. However, in the recent EAS meeting, issues of non-traditional security, maritime security and disaster management were brought in, which is already part of the agenda in other forum such as ARF and ADMM. EAS needs to be careful to avoid repetition of efforts.

External Partners

The East Asia Summit was formed with the aim of constructing East Asian regionalisation. In this geographical contour, China, Japan and South Korea cannot be treated as external partners. Who, then, should be considered the external partners of East Asia Summit? The answer lies in the rest of the five countries, barring ASEAN members and the above three East Asia countries. These include Australia, New Zealand, India and more recently, United States and Russia.

It is important to examine the motivation behind the participation of external powers in the region. The United States joined EAS in 2011. When the EAS was formed in 2005, there was an agreement to evolve the ASEAN+3 framework and make it into the EAS platform. The consensus was reached to bring in countries like Australia, New Zealand and India, in addition to the ASEAN+3 members. However, some of the EAS members such as China were not keen to expand the platform beyond the ASEAN+3 set up by including countries like the US and India. On the other hand, the US dreaded its role getting constraint in the Asian multilateral affairs. Several US opinion stated that with the growing ASEAN confidence in its regionalism and China's rising influence, the centrality of the United States is under challenge .[10] In fact, there was a strong sense in Washington DC that the East Asia Summit, to which the United States had not been invited in the formative period, could lead to a new regional forum led by China, that would exclude the United States and increasingly displace APEC, and other more inclusive fora, as the leading multilateral group of Asia.[11]

Indeed, the US joined the EAS as part of a broader strategy to pivot American foreign policy away from the Middle East toward the dynamic Asia-Pacific region. The United States wants to help build the regional architecture through which future challenges will be addressed. The US does not want the EAS to be mere symbolism and a talk shop with the limitations found in other ASEAN-driven institutions. As a result, it accepted EAS to be ASEAN driven and ASEAN-centred, nevertheless, putting across more broad based issues into the ASEAN driven agendas. Two most notable US contributions in the EAS agenda so far includes, nonproliferation and maritime security, which was deliberated during the 9th EAS in 2014 at Nay Pyi Taw. However, the US does seek greater say for the non-ASEAN members in the agenda-setting.[12] It is keen to use the EAS podium to express its views on concern interests and retain its strategic leverage *vis-à-vis*China among the major powers in Asia.

The inclusion of Russia's membership in the EAS along with the US is noteworthy. Russia's membership was sought to expand the range and scale of opportunities for the ASEAN members in the EAS.[13] It was understood that presence of Russia will fill the table for major power interactions, which in turn will address global security and strategic challenges such as Korean Nuclear crisis, situation in Middle East, etc. However, Kremlin's lack of high level representation in the EAS since its joining is notable.[14] Russia's lack of involvement can be understood from the point of view of lack of strategic interest and sway in the Asia Pacific region. Moscow has no post-imperial influence in the region that it must fight for.[15] Moreover, the current security challenges in the Asia Pacific region are not in tune with the Russian interest. Therefore, there is vast difference in the approach of the two former super powers towards the region and its institutions.

Australia being the founding member of EAS, considers the regional group to have an important role in building closer regional integration and cooperation at a time of particular dynamism in East Asia.[16] Australia has both economic and security interest in the East Asian region. On the commercial side, EAS countries received more than 77 per cent of Australia's total exports and two-way trade with EAS countries was worth $440 billion in 2013-2014.[17] On the strategic and security point, Australia's security is linked to the East Asian security. In addition, Australia plays an important anchor for the larger US's pivot to the strategic Asian game plan. Therefore, Australia has serious stakes in the political, security and functional cooperation in the region. Australia identifies and welcomes the six priority agendas that have received focus in the ten years of EAS proceedings. New Zealand, on the other hand, is not as indispensable as its big neighbourAustralia is for the ASEAN countries. Nonetheless, since economic integration is an important step for the EAS vision, New Zealand is a country that cannot be left aside. Therefore, in view of the benefits to be accrued through closer financial and economic integration, New Zealand became the founding member of the EAS in 2005.

Among the sixteen founding members of EAS in 2005, India is an important member to be invited despite resistance from some members in the initial negotiation phase. India has both economic and strategic interest in participating in the EAS. Economically, India is among the top ten trading partners of ASEAN. Although its trade is presently 2.7 per cent of ASEAN's share of total trade figure, nevertheless, the share is increasing.

Strategically, India considers the Southeast and East Asian region as its extended neighbourhood with substantial strategic stake. New Delhi seeks a role in the emerging Asian security architecture given its size of economy, population and other normative weight it carries in global politics. Moreover, the 18 EAS member countries represent collectively 55 per cent of the world's population and account for around 56 per cent of global GDP. Therefore, it is significant for India to link itself with the ASEAN-driven institutional network to carve for itself a prominent role in creating stability and prosperity in the region.

India's Contribution in the EAS

There are six priority areas of regional cooperation within the framework of the EAS – energy and environment, finance, education, natural disaster management, pandemics and connectivity. India endorses regional collaboration in all six priority areas.[18] In the area of human resource development, India has taken lead in three projects on harmonisation of national qualification frameworks to assure their interoperability and facilitate student and people mobility in the region, the EAS regional leadership development program and facilitating technical and vocational training (TVET) for teacher-student mobility.[19]

Moreover, India seeks to continue its role as a security provider in the region. As a result, India has shown enormous interest in capacity building particularly in the field of disaster management and maritime security. In ARF, India held several workshops and training programmes for the regional countries. In the EAS as well, India seeks to continue with this role. For example, New Delhi held a "EAS-India Workshop 2012: Building Regional

Framework for Earthquake Risk Management" on 8-9 November 2012.It subsequently, extended the proposal to establish a network of 24×7 Points of Contacts among the National Disaster Response Agencies of the EAS participating countries and a Virtual Knowledge Centre (VKC) to share knowledge and best practices related to natural disaster risk assessment, mitigation and response. Such initiative enhances India's credibility as a security provider and anchors it for a greater role in the Asian strategic architecture.[20]

In the recent years in the EAS deliberation, India has made its presence felt with its initiative of Nalanda University project at Rajgir, Bihar. The EAS appreciates India's commitment to revive the ancient centre of learning.[21] At the Chairman's Statement of 9thEAS in Nay Pyi Taw, Myanmar on 13 November 2014, it was noted that India is working to set up the University as a non-state, non-profit and self-governing international institute of excellence.[22]

Connectivity is another area which is considered as strategic priority for India. The Master Plan on ASEAN Connectivity (MPAC) adopted in 2010, aims at physical, institutional and people-to-people connectivity in order to create a single market and production base required for building an ASEAN Community by 2015. But the connectivity of ASEAN cannot be complete if the region is unable to connect itself with its neighboring East Asian and South Asian countries. MPAC talks about fifteen priority areas wherein ASEAN can integrate through connectivity. It is believed that if ASEAN could accomplish 50 per cent implementation of the Master Plan by 2015, then it will already be well positioned for an unprecedented era of regional economic expansion and progress.[23] India does not want to stay behind and seeks to reap the benefits of connectivity. As a result, the Master Plan talks about including India by "upgrading the extension of ASEAN Highway Network to China and India, particularly sections from Ha Noi via northern LaoPDR through Myanmar to the border with India, by 2015."[24]

India is an important pillar of the ongoing negotiations within the Regional Comprehensive Economic Partnership (RCEP), another initiative on regional trade arrangement by the sixteen EAS members. The RCEP negotiations aim at achieving substantial improvement over the ASEAN+1 FTAs by the end of 2015. Since the negotiations began in the middle of 2013, the RCEP members have made little progress towards defining the contours of the eventual agreement. The modalities are yet unclear, with the major proponents struggling to find an approach that will be acceptable to all the 16 members.[25]

Notably, India had agreed to eliminate tariffs on nearly 79 per cent of its tariff lines when the FTA is fully implemented. India is being asked to top up this commitment by undertaking a further dose of tariff liberalisation. On the other hand, most of its partners in the region have also been rather conservative in opening their market to India. Six of the ten ASEAN members had made tariff elimination commitments comparable to that of India's.[26]

It must be understood that India has been rather open to imports from the ASEAN region. In the RCEP negotiations, India has a lot to gain provided it pushes for negotiations in goods and services on parallel tracks. In addition, areas of investment and intellectual property rights must be taken care.[27]

At the academic and research level, important collaborations are taking place. Research and Information System for developing countries (RIS), a think tank under Ministry of External Affairs, is partner institute of Economic Research Institute for ASEAN and East Asia (ERIA) in India. ERIA was established in 2008 in Jakarta for providing research inputs for policy making.[28] ERIA has completed several key reports on issues pertinent to India, including the Comprehensive Asia Development Plan (CADP) which includes a study on the Mekong-India Economic Corridor. They also came up with a report on ASEAN-India Connectivity: The Comprehensive Asia Development Plan Phase II in December 2011. Recently, Dr. Rajiv Kumar, Senior Research Fellow, Center for Policy Research and former Secretary General of FICCI has been nominated as India's representative in the ERIA Governing Board.[29] Therefore, since India's involvement in the EAS is from the inception stage of ideas and policy formulation, India can contribute effectively at norm building and develop policies that will have mutual beneficiaries.

Evaluation

Although EAS has identified some of the priority areas, nevertheless, there is a lack of well-defined objectives. Initially, the ASEAN members were reluctant to add the traditional issues in the EAS deliberations. Later on, traditional issues were involved, such as maritime security and non-proliferation. Therefore, the members themselves are not united in their vision and focus at the EAS dais.

What is the exact nature of role that the ASEAN members have sought for EAS? As we know, EAS discussed issues such as conundrum in Korean Peninsula and maritime security. These issues are overlapping with the ARF agendas. Therefore, there is no clear separation of issues and agendas among the various institutions, which suggest, lack of clarity and partial division of labour, within the ASEAN-driven institutions.

In addition, ASEAN members have brought together all the major powers in Asia and the Pacific in the EAS forum, namely, China, India, Australia, Japan, the US and Russia. Such congregation of major powers requires the EAS to grow into a podium that will sustain their regional interests and accommodate their geostrategic agendas. If the EAS continues with its deliberations on modest issues of nontraditional threats and capacity building programs for the small and medium ranged ASEAN powers, it will fail to endure the major powers' engagement in the EAS for long term.

However, India should continue to participate with the EAS deliberations since it has much to gain. Already, there are studies coming up on Mekong-India Economic Corridor. Therefore, India's positive approach and active presence and implementations thereafter, might add substantial value to its growth and address some of the serious security concerns it is facing at the domestic as well as regional level.

END NOTES

1. Refer article, Aaron L. Friedberg, "Ripe for Rivalry: Prospect for Peace in a Multipolar Asia", *International Security,* 18 (3) (Winter, 1993-1994), 5-33.
2. Yusuf Wanandi, "Strategic Developments in East Asia: the East Asian Summit", 7, available at http://www.eastwestcenter.org/sites/default/files/filemanager/PECC_20_GM/Wanandi.EAS.pdf.
3. See details in Hugh White, *The China Choice: Why America Should Share Power,* (Collingwood, Australia: Black Inc., 2013).
4. Wanandi, ibid.
5. For detailed analysis, refer Ralf Emmers and See Seng Tan, "Strategic Developments in East Asia: the East Asian Summit", RSIS Working Paper No. 189, 2009.
6. Kuala Lumpur Declaration on the First East Asia Summit, 14 December 2005, available at http://mea.gov.in/bilateral-documents.htm?dtl/7120/Kuala+Lumpur+Declaration+on+the+First+East+Asia+Summit.
7. Asian Development Bank Report, "Regional Cooperation and Integration Strategy", July *India's Role in the East Asia Summit* 2006, available at http://aric.adb.org/aid-for-trade-asia/pdf/final-RCI-strategy-paper.pdf.
8. Chairman's Statement of the 3rd East Asia Summit Foreign Ministers' Meeting at Brunei Darussalam, 3 July 2013, available at http://www.mea.gov.in/in-focus-article.htm?21896/

Chairmans+Statement+of+the+3rd+East+Asia+Summit+Foreign+ Ministers+Meeting+at+ Brunei+Darussalam

9. In an Interview with Ann Marie Murphy, The National Bureau of Asian Research, available at http://www.nbr.org/research/activity.aspx?id=183.
10. Bruce Vaughn, "East Asian Summit: Issues for Congress", (Washington D.C.: CRS Report for Congress, 2005).
11. Ibid.
12. Ann Marie Murphy, ibid.
13. It has been argued that Russia has much to offer East Asia. The development of Siberia would meet Asia's resource crunch. Moscow could be the important source energy in addition to making a valuable contribution in preventing and managing conflicts and natural disasters in the region. For details, see AlicaKizekova, "Russia's role in EAS: Promoting Inter-Regional Cooperation", *PacNet Newsletter* 62, 4, November 2011, available at http://csis.org/files/ publication/pac1162.pdf
14. After formally joining the EAS in 2011, Russian Head of State failed to attend the EAS proceedings for the subsequent years. In 2014, Russia was represented by the Premier Dmitry Medvedev.
15. ArtyomLukin, "Putin Skips the East Asia Summit (again)", East Asia Forum, 21 October 2014, available at http://www.eastasiaforum.org/2013/10/22/putin-skips-the-east-asiasummit-again/.
16. Australian Government, Department of Foreign Affairs and Trade, available at http:// www.dfat.gov.au/international-relations/regional-architecture/eas/pages/east-asia-summiteas.aspx
17. Ibid.
18. "About East Asia Summit", available atURL://http://www.aseanindia.com/about/eas/.
19. Ibid.
20. Ibid.
21. Founded in the 5th Century A.D., Nalanda is known as the ancient seat of learning. 2,000 Teachers and 10,000 Students from all over the Buddhist world lived and studied at Nalanda, the first Residential International University of the World.(see for details Nalanda University website, available at http://www.nalandaopenuniversity.com/about.html#history)
22. ASEAN document, available at http://www.mea.gov.in/bilateral-documents.htm?dtl/24252/ Chairmans+Statement+of+9th+East+Asia+Summit+EAS+in+ Nay+Pyi+Taw+Myanmar+13+ November+2014
23. SanchitaBasu Das, "Foreword", in *Enhancing ASEAN's Connectivity*, (ISEAS: Singapore, 2013), viii.
24. ASEAN document, "Master Plan on ASEAN Connectivity", 39, available at http:// www.asean.org/resources/publications/asean-publications/item/master-plan-on-aseanconnectivity-2.
25. BiswajitDhar, "India's RCEP Challenge", *The Financial Express*, 3 December 2014, available at http://www.financialexpress.com/article/fe-columnist/indias-rcep-challenge/15030/
26. Ibid.
27. Ibid.
28. About EAS, available at http://mea.gov.in/aseanindia/about-eas.htm
29. Ibid.

4

Deepening of International Production Networks in ASEAN Countries:
India's Role in the Integration Process[1]

Debashis Chakraborty

Introduction

It has been noted that both economic (e.g., trade creation, inward FDI flows, regional energy cooperation) and political factors (e.g., intra-regional and extra-regional security) can play important roles in shaping regional trade agreements (RTAs) between two or more countries.[2] The Association of Southeast Asian Nations (ASEAN), which was formed in 1967, provides a classic example where all of the conditions have been fulfilled in sequential manner. While the security concerns were of primary importance in the earlier phase of integration, the economic factors have received prominence in recent period. For instance, on internal security front, one of the major objectives of ASEAN has been to reduce tensions between Indonesia and Malaysia.[3] On the other hand, on external security front, ASEAN originated as response to the perceived threat of communism,[4] in particular, China's promotion of communist ideology in several countries of the region. After the initial period of discord, ASEAN identity evolved through the shared norms of 'ASEAN Way'.[5] The principle has been greatly beneficial for intra-bloc conflict management by preventing disputes from escalating into armed conflicts with far-reaching regional ramifications.[6] As a result of the growing harmony,

ASEAN was able to form a sustainable regional cooperation backed up by treaties and secretariat, which is now being deepened further through trade integration.

Given the regional proximity of the ASEAN countries to Japan and the motivation received by witnessing the export-oriented growth experienced by South Korea, Taiwan and Hong Kong, since eighties these economies increasingly moved towards outward-oriented growth policies. The urge to harness regional comparative advantages through deep trade integrations was subsequently felt and the ASEAN Free Trade Area (AFTA) agreement was signed in 1992. In the following period, ASEAN allowed entry to Vietnam (1995), Laos and Myanmar (1997) and Cambodia (1999), whose labour-cost advantage and natural resource base ensured further integration within the bloc. AFTA has led to significant reduction in trade barriers among ASEAN countries, as 90 percent of product classifications were covered in the trade liberalisation programme, with full support of the member countries.[7] Over the last decade deep production integration, as reflected through enhanced *Intra-Industry Trade* (IIT) flows in manufacturing products including the same in semi-finished products and parts and components, has emerged as one of the major success stories of ASEAN, giving rise to the urge of creating greater cooperation through establishment of ASEAN Economic Community (AEC) by 2015.[8]

Since the initiation of the economic reforms in 1991, 'Look East Policy' has been a defining feature of the India's export oriented programme.[9] The growing relationship between the two sides was further consolidated in 1992 with India becoming the Sectoral Dialogue Partner of ASEAN, covering trade, tourism, investment and science and technology. Negotiations to enter into a Free Trade Agreement (FTA) with the ASEAN countries started from 2004 onwards, but the process was delayed due to political compulsions on both sides.[10] Although Indo-ASEAN FTA finally came into existence from 2010 onwards, the trade growth continues to be modest vis-à-vis the expected level.[11]

In this background, the present chapter intends to analyze the intra-bloc trade experience of ASEAN. In particular, given the deeper integration experience in ASEAN, a comparative account of their participation in production networks across the major sectors has been noted here. Furthermore, India's participation so far in the ASEAN production network is also explored. The analysis is arranged along the following lines. The trade integration experience of the ASEAN countries is briefly discussed first, followed by an account of their production network-related performance, and the same vis-à-vis India. Finally, on the basis of the observations, a few policy conclusions are drawn.

Trade Integration among ASEAN Countries

Southeast Asian countries, given their proximity to Japan, which is a major source of foreign direct investment (FDI) and technical know-how, started moving towards liberalised trade policies since late sixties and early seventies. Singapore moved in this direction first given the resource-constraint of the economy that makes adoption of an 'inward-looking' policy less rewarding, and the policy was replicated by other countries in subsequent period. The phenomenon has been known as the 'flying geese' model in trade literature, where Japanese capital boosted manufacturing sector productivity across Southeast Asian countries.[12] While the first wave of Japanese investment initially went to Hong Kong, South Korea, Taiwan and Singapore, it subsequently reached the original ASEAN-5 countries, e.g., Indonesia, Malaysia, Thailand and the Philippines. In terms of sectoral investment patterns, the perspective was only too visible—the FDI came first to the textile and clothing sector, and subsequently followed by technologically more sophisticated sectors like chemicals, iron and steel, automobile, electronic goods etc., in that order. The process ensured that every time investment came to a technologically superior sector, a sizable skilled workforce was already present in the country due to existing operations of the multinational corporations (MNCs). Moreover, as Japanese and South Korean FDI entered the original ASEAN-5 countries simultaneously, the stage of their manufacturing sector progress remained at a comparable level, paving the path for future intra-ASEAN collaborations in this segment.

After expansion of AFTA and following gradual liberalisation in newer ASEAN members, since late nineties FDI and technology from Japan, Singapore and South Korea targeted Vietnam, Cambodia and Lao PDR.[13] While in the initial period FDI came to Southeast Asian countries because of their cheap labour supply in production of low-tech products, skill formation through learning and regular technology spillover effects and scale advantages have gradually enhanced the percentage of skilled workforce and production efficiency.[14] As a result, the prominence of high-technology products has increased in the export basket of the ASEAN countries.[15]

At present, Singapore, China, Japan and South Korea are among the major investment sources to the ASEAN from the Asian region. The intra-region investment flows in Southeast Asia has facilitated development of international production networks (IPN) in the region, where the countries increasingly specialise in a narrow set of product lines as per their comparative advantage rather than the entire range of the product category. For instance, it has been observed that in automobile products Thailand specialises in engine and electronic parts, Philippines specialises in fuel system and suspension parts, Malaysia specialises in bumper and drive shaft, while Indonesia specialises in engine valves and steering handle[16] making the final assembled automobile products truly regional in nature. The intermediate products are brought to the country with best capabilities for speedy and cost-efficient assembling (for instance, Thailand), and also from where the product can be exported outside AFTA with greater ease. While the AFTA tariff liberalisation has facilitated greater intra-region trade flows in semi-finished and final products by offering zero percent tariff on partner exports that deepened the IPNs[17] the deepened connectivity linkages by land, sea and air routes significantly contribute in enabling seamless movement of the goods across borders.[18]

Figure 1 shows growing importance of ASEAN countries in international commerce, measured in terms of their collective share in world exports in percentage terms. While in 2001, the figure stood at around 6.2 per cent, it has increased to 6.7 per cent in 2013, declining from the earlier peak of 6.8 per cent in 2010.[19] While the recession in EU-US since 2010 has lowered the share of ASEAN in global exports, it has also set the stage for deeper intra-bloc as well as intra-region collaboration. For instance, ASEAN has entered into FTA with China and India in the recent period.[20] It is also part of the ongoing negotiations on the Regional Comprehensive Economic Partnership (RCEP), also known as ASEAN+6, i.e., trade integration involving six RTA partners of ASEAN, namely Australia, China, India, Japan, New Zealand and South Korea.

Table 1 shows the intra-bloc trade destination (by source) for the ASEAN countries in percentage terms. While the exporting countries are noted row-wise, their export destinations are reported column-wise. For obvious reason, no trade is reported along the diagonal. The last column summarises the intra-ASEAN export destination for the individual bloc members. To understand the temporal perspective, data for 2010 and 2013 are compared separately in the upper and lower panels of the table. It is observed that in 2010 barring the exception of Brunei, Cambodia and Vietnam, the intra-bloc export shares

Figure 1: Presence of ASEAN in World Merchandise Exports (%)

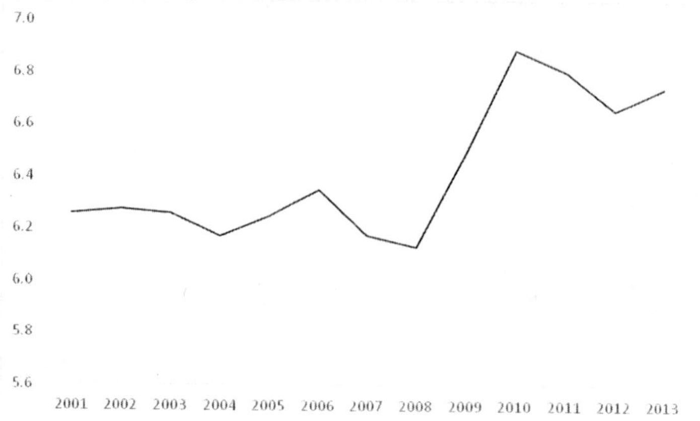

Source: Constructed by the author from WITS and Trade Map data.

of all the countries were higher than 20 percent, signifying vibrant trade integration. The corresponding figure has increased sharply for Brunei in 2013, but a fall has been reported for Philippines. The figures are particularly high for Lao PDR and Singapore, signifying their trade dependence on regional partners. While higher intra-regional export orientation has been noted for Myanmar in 2010, the data for 2013 has not been obtained. The intra-ASEAN trade integration is more pronounced for imports, as reflected from Table 2. It is observed that barring the exception of Thailand and Vietnam, for all the ASEAN countries the share of their intra-region import is higher than 20 percent. The corresponding figures are found to be relatively larger for several smaller economies, namely, Brunei, Lao and Myanmar.

It has often been noted that the pace of trade integration among the bloc members suffer considerably if the member countries are guided more by the protectionist instincts. The protectionist mind-set often persists if the economic and export structures of the bloc members are too similar. The degree of export basket similarity among ASEAN economies can be understood with the help of Table 3, which summarises the estimated bilateral export basket correlation coefficients at HS 2 digit level of aggregation, as computed through the STATA software. Higher values of the obtained pair-wise correlation coefficients indicate greater similarities between export baskets of two countries. This may pose a problem for future trade liberalisation, as the partner economy would then be viewed as a potential competitor rather than a collaborator. It can be noted from the table that a number of country-

Table 1: Trade Integration among the ASEAN Countries: The Recent Scenario (Exports)

	Importing Partners, 2010										
Exporting Countries	*Brunei*	*Cambodia*	*Indonesia*	*Lao*	*Malaysia*	*Myanmar*	*Philippines*	*Singapore*	*Thailand*	*Vietnam*	*ASEAN*
Brunei Darussalam	-	0.0007	7.0716	0.0001	1.5113	0.0004	0.0692	2.7888	0.8636	0.0767	12.3824
Cambodia	0.0005	-	0.0746	0.0158	0.3475	0.0001	0.0473	7.6918	2.6849	1.7199	12.5824
Indonesia	0.0386	0.1380	-	0.0035	5.9338	0.1801	2.0159	8.6978	2.8943	1.2335	21.1355
Lao PDR	0.0020	0.0725	0.0298	-	0.1096	NT	0.0006	0.1366	36.2464	14.1108	50.7083
Malaysia	0.2263	0.0994	2.8316	0.0076	-	0.1859	1.5642	13.3572	5.3466	1.7840	25.4028
Myanmar	0.0052	NT	0.5011	0.0001	2.1356	-	0.2555	3.6236	41.6675	0.7950	48.9836
Philippines	0.0116	0.0165	0.8723	0.0006	2.7118	0.0218	-	14.2122	3.4616	1.1109	22.4193
Singapore	0.2686	0.6266	9.3943	0.0065	11.9276	0.3295	2.0415	-	3.6095	2.1011	30.3052
Thailand	0.0659	1.1992	3.7615	1.0936	5.4102	1.0614	2.5017	4.6129	-	2.9929	22.6993
Vietnam	0.0197	2.1649	1.9843	0.2768	2.8976	0.0686	2.3622	2.9366	1.6375	-	14.3482

(Contd.)

Table 1: Contd.

	2013										
	Brunei	*Cambodia*	*Indonesia*	*Lao*	*Malaysia*	*Myanmar*	*Philippines*	*Singapore*	*Thailand*	*Vietnam*	*ASEAN*
Brunei Darussalam	-	0.0000	4.6982	NT	3.8585	0.0003	0.7271	4.3599	4.1951	5.2632	23.1023
Cambodia#	0.0001	-	0.0942	0.0184	0.6746	0.0013	0.0210	6.5911	2.8411	2.2199	12.4617
Indonesia	0.0401	0.1275	-	0.0042	5.4035	0.1766	1.8177	9.0635	2.8977	1.1569	20.6877
Lao PDR	0.0000	0.0307	0.0428	-	0.0249	-	0.0033	0.0156	37.4549	15.2514	52.8236
Malaysia	0.2399	0.1138	2.9978	0.0061	-	0.2462	1.5752	12.6932	5.1429	1.6825	24.6976
Myanmar@						-					
Philippines	0.0130	0.0203	1.2611	0.0013	2.2876	0.0294	-	8.9041	3.9631	1.4945	17.9744
Singapore	0.3844	0.2215	10.4473	0.0085	12.2070	0.2962	1.6525	-	3.4280	2.4935	31.1389
Thailand	0.0599	1.2697	4.4043	1.2191	5.4185	1.2437	2.0281	5.0039	-	3.0850	23.7322
Vietnam#	0.0147	2.5583	2.0586	0.3777	3.9294	0.1029	1.6340	2.0673	2.4729	-	15.2158

\# As 2013 data is not available, data for 2012 has been considered.

@ Data not available.

NT No Trade.

Source: Computed by author from Trade Map Data, ITC (undated).

Table 2: Trade Integration among the ASEAN Countries: The Recent Scenario (Imports)

	Exporting Partners, 2010										
Importing Countries	*Brunei*	*Cambodia*	*Indonesia*	*Lao*	*Malaysia*	*Myanmar*	*Philippines*	*Singapore*	*Thailand*	*Vietnam*	*ASEAN*
Brunei Darussalam	-	0.0004	2.5443	0.0016	23.6380	0.0039	0.2644	19.0837	5.3786	0.2446	51.1595
Cambodia	0.0108	-	3.5758	0.0306	3.3768	0.0011	0.1502	3.1760	14.0891	9.9396	34.3500
Indonesia	0.4911	0.0035	-		6.3751	0.0235	0.5206	14.9199	5.5068	0.8420	28.6825
Lao PDR	0.0003	0.0271	0.1687	-	0.4625	0.0001	0.0092	0.7040	65.4592	6.1289	72.9600
Malaysia	0.0294	0.0197	5.5601	0.0014	-	0.1393	2.1389	11.3810	6.2372	1.5791	27.0861
Myanmar	NT	NT	4.8817	NT	3.2261	-	0.3372	26.9564	11.3689	0.9122	47.6825
Philippines	0.0050	0.0046	4.2234	0.0000	4.5260	0.0228	-	9.3087	7.0180	3.0001	28.1086
Singapore	0.0421	0.0514	5.4196	0.0009	11.6935	0.0267	2.9589	-	3.3081	0.5182	24.0194
Thailand	0.0540	0.1177	3.1118	0.4109	5.8713	1.5427	1.3023	3.4509	-	0.7658	16.6274
Vietnam	0.0118	0.3261	2.2504	0.3439	4.0234	0.1212	0.8255	4.8341	6.6035	-	19.3399

(Contd.)

Table 2: Contd.

	2013										
	Brunei	*Cambodia*	*Indonesia*	*Lao*	*Malaysia*	*Myanmar*	*Philippines*	*Singapore*	*Thailand*	*Vietnam*	*ASEAN*
Brunei Darussalam	-	0.0003	2.0018	NT	18.4720	0.0096	0.2568	19.4618	4.1951	0.2164	44.6138
Cambodia#	0.0072	-	2.7556	0.0151	3.4138	0.0021	0.1328	3.8751	11.8255	14.3720	36.3992
Indonesia	0.5739	0.0045	-		5.8640	0.0402	0.4804	14.6333	5.8642	1.3430	28.8035
Lao PDR	0.0000	0.0356	0.0944	-	0.3697	NT	0.0129	0.4256	60.6975	7.4510	69.0867
Malaysia	0.0265	0.0355	6.1149	0.0004	-	0.1246	0.8326	12.7926	6.0119	1.8003	27.7393
Myanmar@						-					
Philippines	0.0102	0.0020	3.9939	0.0002	4.3508	0.0322	-	8.0762	5.7170	1.4314	23.6139
Singapore	0.0148	0.0486	5.1506	0.0015	10.9454	0.0480	1.3636	-	2.4875	0.8197	20.8797
Thailand	0.2180	0.1417	3.2200	0.5425	5.2840	1.6086	1.0479	3.2812	-	1.3039	16.6478
Vietnam#	0.5366	0.4768	1.9753	0.3963	2.9988	0.0962	0.8477	5.8806	5.0904	-	18.2987

As 2013 data is not available, data for 2012 has been considered.

@ Data not available.

NT No Trade.

Source: Computed by the author from Trade Map Data, ITC.

pairs display strong export basket similarities, especially involving the more advanced economies of the region (e.g., Indonesia, Malaysia, Philippines, Singapore, Thailand). Nevertheless, thanks to the AFTA operations and deepening of the ASEAN spirit, instead of the intra-bloc competition, a collaborative approach has so far been witnessed.

It can further be noted from the table that India's export basket displays greater degree of similarity with Brunei, Indonesia, Malaysia, Myanmar and Singapore. Degree of similarity with other ASEAN countries is however found to be moderate. The result indicates that India may not be viewed as a competitor across all the ASEAN countries as far as merchandise trade is concerned and this offers a positive expectation for Indian exports in coming days. However concern areas do remain in these five markets.

To understand the production and trade integration within the region as well as with India, the bilateral IIT index for intra-ASEAN and ASEAN-India trade has been summarised in Table 4. The higher values of IIT indicate higher trade flows in intermediate and semi-finished products at disaggregated level, which can be interpreted as greater participation in IPNs. The bilateral country-pair wise aggregate IITs are calculated by the Grubel-Lloyd Corrected (GLC) index by using the following formula:

$$GLC = \frac{\Sigma\ (X_i + M_i) - \Sigma\ |\ X_i - M_i|}{\Sigma\ (X_i + M_i) - |\ \Sigma X_i - \Sigma M_i|} \times 100$$

where, X_i and M_i represent the simultaneous export and import of the i-th product at HS 4-digit level respectively. To understand the temporal perspective, IIT has been calculated for 2011 and 2013 separately, and reported in the upper and lower panels of the table respectively.

The obtained results clearly indicate that intra-ASEAN trade is becoming increasingly integrated as the IIT index is rising for most of the country-pairs over 2011 to 2013. The IITs are particularly high for Indonesia, Malaysia, Philippines, Singapore, Thailand and Vietnam. The result indicates that the firms located within these economies are increasingly trading among themselves in semi-finished products and parts and components, essentially to exploit the labour cost and raw material availability advantages, ease of exporting etc. On the contrary, Brunei, Cambodia, Lao and Myanmar are yet to join in the intra-region IPNs in a substantial manner, which is expected to improve over time.

The table further denotes that India's participation in the ASEAN IPN has so far been limited, as reflected from the IIT figures. A relatively higher value of the IIT indices is noted in case of Indonesia, Malaysia, Philippines, Singapore and Vietnam, signifying growth in simultaneous export and import across product categories. However, trade with other countries are mostly found to be inter-industry specialisation-based and does not involve deepening of production networks.

But what has been the overall production integration scenario in ASEAN countries? Table 5, which draws data from OECD's Trade in Value Added (TIVA), summarises the aggregate and select sectoral participation index for the ASEAN countries. The upper panel shows forward participation index, which indicates the "share of exported goods and services used as imported inputs to produce other countries' exports" (OECD, undated). Since 1995, the index has considerably increased for nearly all the countries, showing their inclination in integrating with other economies. The bottom panel displays the backward participation index, showing "the value of imported inputs in the overall exports of a country" (OECD, undated). This denotes the importance of importing the raw materials and other semi-finished parts and components in promoting exports, which the countries are increasingly reckoning. Rising value of both the indices for ASEAN and India creates further room for bilateral trade promotion not only in the final products but also in the semi-finished and intermediate products.

Finally, Tables 6-8 summarises the decomposition of exports (in percentage terms) within six major sectors in the ASEAN countries and India, on the basis of the data obtained from OECD-TIVA database.[22] The gross exports here have been categorised under four sub-components, namely, direct domestic value added content, indirect domestic value added content, re-imported domestic value-added content and foreign value-added content. The first component clearly indicate the level of development and spread of the domestic sector, and indirectly underline the support received from the policymakers. The second component stresses the production linkages with other sectors of the economy. The third component underlines the process of exporting of raw materials and other semi-finished components and later importing a different level of processed product, which is used in the final export subsequently. The last component shows the presence of foreign value added in final exports, which indicates import of raw material, semi-finished products etc. from the trade partners. To understand the temporal perspective,

Table 3: Export Correlation Coefficients between ASEAN Countries and India for Merchandise Trade[21] (2013)

	India	*Brunei*	*Cambodia*	*Indonesia*	*Lao*	*Malaysia*	*Myanmar*	*Philippines*	*Singapore*	*Thailand*	*Vietnam*
India	1										
Brunei	0.78	1									
Cambodia	0.07	-0.01	1								
Indonesia	0.77	0.90	0.05	1							
Lao	0.44	0.51	0.10	0.54	1						
Malaysia	0.59	0.59	-0.01	0.74	0.33	1					
Myanmar	0.80	0.85	0.08	0.81	0.67	0.51	1				
Philippines	0.20	0.07	0.04	0.27	0.16	0.81	0.11	1			
Singapore	0.51	0.44	-0.01	0.54	0.20	0.93	0.36	0.85	1		
Thailand	0.46	0.21	0.03	0.38	0.11	0.69	0.21	0.67	0.71	1	
Vietnam	0.28	0.16	0.29	0.33	0.13	0.78	0.19	0.89	0.82	0.62	1

Source: Estimated by the author from Trade Map data, ITC

Table 4: Intra-Industry Trade between ASEAN Countries and India for Merchandise Trade

	2011										
	Brunei	*Cambodia*	*Indonesia*	*Lao*	*Malaysia*	*Myanmar*	*Philippines*	*Singapore*	*Thailand*	*Vietnam*	*India*
Brunei	-										
Cambodia	0.00	-									
Indonesia	2.01	12.74	-								
Lao PDR	0.00	7.67	0.00	-							
Malaysia	10.85	7.95	26.78		-						
Myanmar	0.00	6.41	0.18	NA	1.54	-					
Philippines	1.08	16.00	31.32	10.20	56.00	5.65	-				
Singapore	46.18	6.37	30.38	6.44	72.90	11.68	55.26	-			
Thailand	1.12	12.04	30.59	9.82	41.49	0.37	33.26	44.45	-		
Vietnam	1.67	8.35	15.87	2.71	22.25	1.81	16.12	53.29	47.81	-	
India	0.01	2.72	11.32	2.41	31.64	3.26	19.84	52.44	10.38	12.98	-

(Contd.)

Table 4: Contd.

	2013										
	Brunei	*Cambodia*	*Indonesia*	*Lao*	*Malaysia*	*Myanmar*	*Philippines*	*Singapore*	*Thailand*	*Vietnam*	*India*
Brunei	-										
Cambodia	0.00	-									
Indonesia	0.38	8.76	-								
Lao PDR	0.00	2.47#	0.31	-							
Malaysia	13.12	3.88	26.78		-						
Myanmar	0.00	1.20#	0.96	NA	1.61	-					
Philippines	2.03	2.70	42.39	0.00	61.65	3.87	-				
Singapore	19.05	8.00	27.90	16.95	66.94	15.85	45.04	-			
Thailand	1.31	27.22	37.76	13.76	39.49	0.64	29.21	49.69	-		
Vietnam	1.20	14.18#	16.90	4.73#	26.24	1.13	21.88	38.00	37.86	-	
India	0.00	2.64	10.80	0.06	17.21	0.47	21.96	35.73	7.11	11.92	-

#Data for 2012 has been reported.

Source: Computed by the author from Trade Map Data, ITC.

Table 5: Deepening Production Integration of ASEAN and India in International Trade

Country	Forward Integration											
	Overall		*Chemicals*		*Base Metals*		*Machinery & Equipment*		*Electrical Equipment*		*Transport Equipment*	
	1995	*2009*	*1995*	*2009*	*1995*	*2009*	*1995*	*2009*	*1995*	*2009*	*1995*	*2009*
India	14.2	20.3	2.5	1.9	0.6	1.0	0.1	0.3	0.2	0.9	0.1	0.2
Indonesia	18.8	29.3	2.5	4.6	0.5	1.2	0.1	0.3	0.3	0.9	0.1	0.2
Brunei Darussalam	19.3	32.2	0.8	1.7	0.1	0.1	0.0	0.0	0.0	0.0	0.0	0.0
Cambodia	17.7	6.3	0.1	0.1	0.1	0.2	0.0	0.1	0.1	0.1	0.1	0.0
Malaysia	15.2	27.7	1.4	2.7	0.5	0.7	0.4	0.8	3.2	7.4	0.1	0.2
Philippines	16.6	28.3	1.1	0.6	1.3	0.3	0.1	0.1	2.2	14.3	0.0	0.3
Singapore	13.8	20.7	1.8	3.6	0.4	0.4	0.1	0.4	3.5	5.4	0.1	0.2
Thailand	12.0	18.3	1.4	2.9	0.5	0.9	0.1	0.2	3.4	5.3	0.3	0.3
Viet Nam	12.6	14.7	0.2	0.5	0.1	0.2	0.1	0.0	0.1	0.2	0.1	0.1

(Contd.)

Table 5: Contd.

Country	Backward Integration											
	Overall		*Chemicals*		*Base Metals*		*Machinery & Equipment*		*Electrical Equipment*		*Transport Equipment*	
	1995	*2009*	*1995*	*2009*	*1995*	*2009*	*1995*	*2009*	*1995*	*2009*	*1995*	*2009*
India	9.6	21.9	3.0	2.6	0.4	1.1	0.3	0.5	0.2	2.1	0.2	0.9
Indonesia	14.7	14.4	3.0	2.7	0.7	0.8	0.6	1.7	1.2	2.1	0.3	0.5
Brunei Darussalam	18.4	11.6	2.3	0.1	0.4	0.0	0.0	0.0	0.1	0.1	0.0	0.0
Cambodia	26.0	34.1	0.5	1.0	0.5	0.8	0.4	0.6	1.0	1.7	0.2	0.4
Malaysia	40.3	37.9	7.1	5.8	1.2	1.2	5.6	5.7	13.8	13.0	0.4	0.4
Philippines	30.9	38.4	1.7	0.3	2.1	0.2	0.4	0.4	8.5	32.4	0.2	0.8
Singapore	46.7	49.9	8.0	14.4	0.7	0.9	0.5	2.9	27.7	12.9	0.3	1.5
Thailand	29.8	34.5	3.2	3.7	1.1	1.6	0.5	0.8	15.2	17.2	0.8	1.5
Viet Nam	24.4	36.5	0.3	0.9	0.2	0.7	0.4	0.7	0.8	1.7	0.1	0.4

Source: Constructed by author from the OECD TIVA database.

the value addition is compared for 2005 and 2009 separately. As evident from the discussion, gradual rise in the last two components indicate how closely a particular country is getting linked with the IPNs.

The upper panel of Table 6 shows the value addition scenario for the textile and clothing sector. The figures reveal that foreign value added has increased over 2005-09 for Brunei, Indonesia and Vietnam. Despite decline in foreign value added in 2009 vis-à-vis the 2005 figure, the figure has remained considerably high for the other countries, particularly in Cambodia and Singapore. Re-imported domestic value-added content has been lesser than one percent for all countries in both the reported years. The scenario in chemical sector has been summarised in the bottom panel of the same table. Increase in foreign value added over 2005-09 has been observed in case of Brunei and Vietnam. A sharp decline has been however noted for the corresponding figure of Indonesia. Re-imported domestic value-added content however remains non-important for all countries in both the years. In both the cases, participation of foreign players in India's export pattern has risen only marginally.

The upper panel of Table 7 depicts the value addition scenario for base metals and metal products. It is observed that foreign value added has increased over 2005-09 for Brunei and Vietnam, while a reverse scenario is noted for other countries. Nevertheless the decline is not very high and the importance of foreign participation in production network is very much obvious. Interestingly, re-imported domestic value-added content has increased for Philippines, Singapore and Thailand, implying deepening of networks. The bottom panel shows the scenario for machinery and equipment sector, where foreign value added content has increased in Singapore and Vietnam. On the other hand, re-imported domestic value-added content has increased for Philippines, Thailand and Vietnam. As in the earlier case, India witnessed only a marginal rise in participation of foreign value-added in exports.

The upper and lower panel of Table 8 shows the value addition scenario in electrical and transport equipment sectors respectively. It is observed from the table that the share of foreign value added in export is quite high in all the ASEAN countries, as there exist tremendous possibilities of network deepening in these two sectors. In particular the figure has increased in Vietnam for both sectors, which underlines the fact that that the existing production networks are taking increasing note of the changed business climate, deepened connectivity and prevalent labour cost advantage of the

Table 6: Decomposition of Participation in Select ASEAN Countries – Textile & Clothing and Chemical Products

(*% of Gross Exports*)

Countries	*2005*				*2009*			
	Direct domestic industry value added content of gross exports	*Indirect domestic content of gross exports (originating from domestic intermediates)*	*Re-imported domestic value added content of gross exports*	*Foreign value added content of gross exports*	*Direct domestic industry value added content of gross exports*	*Indirect domestic content of gross exports (originating from domestic intermediates)*	*Re-imported domestic value added content of gross exports*	*Foreign value added content of gross exports*
				Textile & Clothing				
India	29.49	54.59	0.07	15.85	27.66	54.32	0.09	17.93
Brunei Darussalam	34.37	30.89	0.00	34.70	39.67	23.52	0.02	36.79
Cambodia	22.29	14.51	0.00	63.20	22.82	14.89	0.00	62.29
Indonesia	36.80	40.71	0.19	22.29	38.43	37.04	0.19	24.35
Malaysia	37.71	19.09	0.30	42.90	37.39	24.44	0.26	37.91
Philippines	41.06	19.46	0.02	39.47	40.50	30.06	0.02	29.41
Singapore	28.25	16.16	0.37	55.24	32.16	13.21	0.32	54.32
Thailand	36.96	32.99	0.07	29.99	36.37	37.92	0.08	25.63
Viet Nam	19.55	19.15	0.09	61.20	19.49	17.74	0.14	62.62

(*Contd.*)

Table 6: Contd.

Countries	*2005*				*2009*			
	Direct domestic industry value added content of gross exports	*Indirect domestic content of gross exports (originating from domestic intermediates)*	*Re-imported domestic value added content of gross exports*	*Foreign value added content of gross exports*	*Direct domestic industry value added content of gross exports*	*Indirect domestic content of gross exports (originating from domestic intermediates)*	*Re-imported domestic value added content of gross exports*	*Foreign value added content of gross exports*
				Chemical Products				
India	26.58	47.06	0.10	26.27	24.87	47.70	0.10	27.33
Brunei Darussalam	43.48	39.13	0.00	21.74	37.84	34.05	0.00	28.11
Cambodia	33.86	14.00	0.00	52.26	34.56	14.07	0.00	51.37
Indonesia	45.83	29.19	0.09	24.90	45.42	39.62	0.07	14.89
Malaysia	23.98	35.95	0.32	39.75	23.41	42.48	0.24	33.86
Philippines	30.71	23.02	0.02	46.24	31.22	33.05	0.02	35.71
Singapore	27.05	13.82	0.17	58.96	25.44	18.73	0.16	55.66
Thailand	35.68	24.52	0.06	39.73	36.64	30.30	0.06	33.00
Viet Nam	32.38	17.12	0.16	50.34	32.29	15.76	0.12	51.83

Source: Constructed by the author from OECD-TIVA database.

Table 7: Decomposition of Participation in Select ASEAN Countries – Base Metals & Metal Products and Machinery & Equipment

(% of Gross Exports)

Countries	*2005*				*2009*			
	Direct domestic industry value added content of gross exports	*Indirect domestic content of gross exports (originating from domestic intermediates)*	*Re-imported domestic value added content of gross exports*	*Foreign value added content of gross exports*	*Direct domestic industry value added content of gross exports*	*Indirect domestic content of gross exports (originating from domestic intermediates)*	*Re-imported domestic value added content of gross exports*	*Foreign value added content of gross exports*
				Base Metals & Metal Products				
India	26.39	52.53	0.07	21.01	24.33	53.40	0.07	22.20
Brunei Darussalam	33.33	33.33	0.00	33.33	30.77	15.38	0.00	53.85
Cambodia	21.94	11.33	0.00	66.73	22.65	12.02	0.00	65.33
Indonesia	27.61	49.34	0.14	22.91	31.88	51.71	0.12	16.29
Malaysia	40.87	7.76	0.29	51.09	38.89	11.77	0.27	49.07
Philippines	30.65	22.22	0.02	47.11	31.42	29.99	0.04	38.55
Singapore	31.71	14.88	0.23	53.19	32.20	16.73	0.24	50.84
Thailand	42.11	15.21	0.06	42.62	42.20	20.45	0.08	37.27
Viet Nam	20.73	16.75	0.12	62.40	20.67	15.47	0.12	63.73

(*Contd.*)

Table 7: Contd.

Countries	Machinery & Equipment							
	2005				2009			
	Direct domestic industry value added content of gross exports	Indirect domestic content of gross exports (originating from domestic intermediates)	Re-imported domestic value added content of gross exports	Foreign value added content of gross exports	Direct domestic industry value added content of gross exports	Indirect domestic content of gross exports (originating from domestic intermediates)	Re-imported domestic value added content of gross exports	Foreign value added content of gross exports
India	31.34	47.37	0.07	21.21	29.00	47.97	0.09	22.94
Brunei Darussalam	-	-	-	-	-	-	-	-
Cambodia	32.59	9.11	0.00	58.30	33.39	9.87	0.00	56.74
Indonesia	25.60	23.16	0.26	50.97	32.92	28.12	0.25	38.71
Malaysia	38.26	4.10	0.96	56.68	37.06	6.53	0.76	55.66
Philippines	30.50	25.72	0.03	43.75	30.35	34.37	0.05	35.24
Singapore	30.15	14.57	0.26	55.01	30.42	12.88	0.25	56.46
Thailand	34.66	19.10	0.10	46.13	33.35	22.46	0.15	44.04
Viet Nam	31.14	14.05	0.07	54.76	31.09	13.33	0.08	55.50

Source: Constructed by the author from OECD-TIVA database.

Table 8: Decomposition of Participation in Select ASEAN Countries – Electrical Equipment and Transport Equipment

(% of Gross Exports)

Countries	*2005*				*2009*			
	Direct domestic industry value added content of gross exports	*Indirect domestic content of gross exports (originating from domestic intermediates)*	*Re-imported domestic value added content of gross exports*	*Foreign value added content of gross exports*	*Direct domestic industry value added content of gross exports*	*Indirect domestic content of gross exports (originating from domestic intermediates)*	*Re-imported domestic value added content of gross exports*	*Foreign value added content of gross exports*
				Electrical Equipment				
India	32.99	47.67	0.08	19.26	30.87	46.87	0.10	22.15
Brunei Darussalam	38.46	23.08	0.00	38.46	36.00	22.00	0.00	42.00
Cambodia	25.53	9.40	0.00	65.07	26.25	9.91	0.00	63.91
Indonesia	35.68	32.81	0.19	31.31	38.43	33.89	0.18	27.51
Malaysia	35.38	4.77	1.01	58.84	35.83	7.26	0.77	56.14
Philippines	30.06	10.62	0.29	59.04	30.90	18.32	0.34	50.44
Singapore	25.10	10.25	0.71	63.94	26.45	11.54	0.77	61.24
Thailand	30.68	10.40	0.27	58.64	31.26	13.50	0.36	54.88
Viet Nam	23.48	13.73	0.08	62.71	23.40	12.93	0.10	63.56

(Contd.)

Table 8: Contd.

Countries	*2005*				*2009*			
	Direct domestic industry value added content of gross exports	*Indirect domestic content of gross exports (originating from domestic intermediates)*	*Re-imported domestic value added content of gross exports*	*Foreign value added content of gross exports*	*Direct domestic industry value added content of gross exports*	*Indirect domestic content of gross exports (originating from domestic intermediates)*	*Re-imported domestic value added content of gross exports*	*Foreign value added content of gross exports*
				Transport Equipment				
India	29.85	49.61	0.08	20.46	27.14	49.11	0.10	23.64
Brunei Darussalam	50.00	50.00	0.00	50.00	40.91	22.73	0.00	36.36
Cambodia	30.93	12.37	0.00	56.70	31.77	12.76	0.00	55.47
Indonesia	41.27	26.73	0.20	31.80	42.08	40.67	0.12	17.13
Malaysia	33.62	15.25	0.30	50.83	31.49	20.88	0.27	47.36
Philippines	24.80	32.66	0.05	42.49	24.51	40.98	0.06	34.44
Singapore	34.18	23.79	0.23	41.80	36.87	18.54	0.18	44.41
Thailand	35.82	15.70	0.15	48.34	34.91	20.05	0.18	44.86
Viet Nam	26.75	16.78	0.12	56.35	26.65	15.92	0.11	57.32

Source: Constructed by the author from OECD-TIVA database.

country. Interestingly, the rise in foreign value participation in Indian export for these two sectors have been sharper vis-à-vis the other four sectors.

Conclusion

The classical trade theories, e.g., Comparative Advantage Theory proposed by David Ricardo and the Factor Abundance Theorem proposed by Heckscher-Ohlin predicted complete specialisation while explaining the trade pattern across countries. However since eighties, the Scale Economy models proposed by Paul Krugman and other economists, have been applied to explain the trade flows in the presence of imperfect competition framework in a more successful manner. In the settings of ASEAN countries, gains from trade can be explained with the deepening of the production networks and country specialisation in narrower product lines.

With concerted sequential reform measures, the ASEAN countries have considerably improved the intra-bloc trade scenario. The FDI reforms have paved the stage for foreign MNCs to come with technical know-how and their presence have facilitated the process of technology spillover, thereby adding to the efficiencies of the domestic entrepreneurs as well in long run. Coexistence of a vibrant manufacturing sector in almost all of the ASEAN countries, especially in the developed ones, therefore has fulfilled the precondition of the successful trade integration. The process has further been facilitated though the development of regional connectivity and tariff reforms resulted by AFTA, both of which lead to seamless flow of merchandise products. In particular, the specialisation in narrower product categories in line with comparative advantage has deepened the production networks.

Although India hopes to benefit significantly by successfully integrating with ASEAN economies, especially in the manufacturing sector, its aspirations are yet to be fulfilled. As the calculated IIT coefficients indicate, there is ample scope to improve Indian participation in ASEAN IPNs. However, the growing trend in both ASEAN and India to source raw materials, parts and components from abroad for their exports is a heartening trend and it is expected that both the sides will subsequently find a collaborative strategy worth their while in long run.

As all the ASEAN countries are increasingly deepening the intra-region production networks and no exceptional regional concentration of the bloc benefits from the AFTA trade liberalisation has been witnessed, the dissatisfaction quotient among members is minimal. More importantly, as within the IPN no firms in a country needs to close down, but simply need to readjust within the sector in lines with the national/sectoral comparative advantage, the negative repercussions on the labour market are also minimised. This is an integral reason behind the observed 'ASEAN success' as the members optimistically fulfil their commitments with utmost enthusiasm in light of their past positive experiences. The resulting sustainable trade-investment integration has augmented the ASEAN economies to stay competitive in the global market. This has enabled them to expand the export basket and enhances the attractiveness of the bloc as a whole. The eagerness in the recent RCEP initiative, which is moving towards much wider trade integration by keeping ASEAN as the hub, underlines its charm to the partners in no uncertain terms. The trend of events therefore indicate that the ASEAN drive to maturity, aided further by the deepening of the production networks, will continue in full steam in the coming decades with no apparent signs of slowing down. Furthermore, there exist considerable scopes for ASEAN countries to enhance both their forward and backward integration in trade with India for several industrial categories in long run, which will be mutually beneficial. The recent Indian initiatives, e.g., 'Make in India' campaign, trade route promotion with ASEAN countries through infrastructural augmentation, implementation of Indo-ASEAN FTA tariff reform commitments, removal of non-tariff barriers, introduction of trade facilitation measures etc. will contribute significantly in this regard.

END NOTES

1. The views expressed by the author is personal and do not represent the same of his organisation.
2. World Bank, "Trade Blocs Policy Research Report", (World Bank and Oxford University Press, New York, 2000).
3. Ibid.
4. Ibid.
5. Mely C. Anthony, "Regionalisation of Peace in Asia: Experiences and Prospects of ASEAN, ARF and UN Partnership", *IDSS Working Paper* 42, (The Institute of Defense and Strategic Studies, Singapore, 2003).
6. Kripa Sridharan, "Regional Organisations and Conflict Management: Comparing ASEAN and SAARC, Crisis States", *CSRC Working Papers Series 2*, Crisis States Research Centre, (London School of Economics, London, 2008).
7. Hector Calvo-Pardo, Caroline Freund and Emanuel Ornelas, "The ASEAN Free Trade Agreement: Impact on Trade Flows and External Trade Barriers", World Bank Policy Research Paper No. 4960, (World Bank, Washington DC, 2009).
8. Junianto James Losari and Joseph Wira Koesnaidi, "Indonesia and the Establishment of the

ASEAN Economic Community in 2015: Are We There Yet?", *OREI Policy Brief 10*, (Asian Development Bank, Manila, 2014).

9. Isabelle Saint-Mezard, 'The Look East Policy: An Economic Perspective', in Frederic Grare and Amitabh Mattoo (Eds.).*Beyond the Rhetoric: The Economics of India's Look East Policy*.(Centre de Sciences Humanines and Manohar, NewDelhi, 2003).
10. Debashis Chakraborty and Dipankar Sengupta, "Integration Experience and Trade Performance of the Indo-ASEAN FTA: A Review of Issues", in P. Gugler and J. Chaisse (Eds.).*Competitiveness of the ASEAN Countries: Corporate and Regulatory Drivers*, (Cheltenham: Edward Elgar, 2010), pp. 207-237.
11. Debashis Chakraborty, "The Upcoming Indo-ASEAN CECA: Of Great Expectations and Areas of Concern", *China Report*, 50(3), (2014), 259-276.
12. Roger Hayter and David W. Edgington, "Flying Geese in Asia: The Impacts of Japanese MNCs as a source of industrial learning", *Tijdschrift voor Economische en Sociale Geografie*, 95(1), (2004), 3–26.
13. Jayant Menon and Sharad Bhandari, "The Mekong Region Foreign Direct Investment", (Asian Development Bank, Manila, 2006).
14. Tu Yonghong and Tan Xiao, "Technology spillovers of FDI in ASEAN sourcing from local and abroad", *China Finance Review International*, 2(1), (2012), 78-94.
15. United Nations Economic and Social Commission for Asia and the Pacific (2014), "Asia-Pacific Trade and Investment Report 2014: Recent Trends and Developments", UNESCAP, New York.
16. World Trade Organisation, "Trade patterns and global value chains in East Asia: From trade in goods to trade in tasks", in collaboration with (Institute of Developing Economies (IDE) and Japan External Trade Organisation (*JETRO), Geneva*, 2011).
17. UNESCAP "Fighting Irrelevance: The Role of Regional Trade Agreements in International Production Networks in Asia", Asia-Pacific Research and Training Network on Trade Study, (UNESCAP, New York, 2011).
18. Asian Development Bank, "Aid for Trade in the Asia and the Pacific: An Update", (Report to the Second Global Review on Aid for Trade, Manila, 2009).
19. World Trade Organisation "Aid For Trade Country Factsheets 2013", *Geneva*, 2014.
20. Debashis Chakraborty and Animesh Kumar, "ASEAN and China: New Dimensions in Economic Engagement", *China Report*, 48(3): 327-349, (2012).
21. Shujiro Urata, "Constructing and Multilateralising the Regional Comprehensive Economic Partnership: An Asian Perspective", ADBI Working Paper No. 449, (Asian Development Bank Institute, Tokyo, 2013).
22. Organisation for Economic Cooperation and Development, "Trade in Value Added (TIVA) database", http://stats.oecd.org/Index.aspx?DataSetCode=TIVA_OECD_WTO (last accessed on September 5, 2014).

5

Why Trade Matters in India-ASEAN and China Relations

Nabeel A Mancheri

Trade has traditionally molded the ways nations established their interactions. On the one hand, it brought regions together—in terms of commerce, culture and politics—on the other hand, it created rivalries in the quest for resources. Civilisations flourished and perished, metropolises created and dissolved-trade forming the nucleus of all these processes. Trade and power were then integrally linked, whereby the location of power was determined by the control over trade.[1]

The countries in wider East Asia are highly integrated in the post-globalisation world. From an economic perspective, this is reflected in the rapid increase in international trade and investment flows. China is the largest economy in the region followed by Japan, India and South Korea. Trade constitutes almost 50 per cent of the GDP of all countries in the region. This has led to greater economic interdependence among East Asian countries.

As these countries grow fast and trade relations among them grow bigger, this may lead to a stiuation where they use trade strength as a political tool or may invoke trade interdependence as a deterrence against a rival country. The threat will be dependent on the import volume or export volume of a particular country. If the country is a large importer, it might possess power as a buyer. Power will increase with the size of the market in the importing country or with the size of exports from an exporting country.[2] Such power can sometimes be coercive if a large buyer suddenly uses the refusal of purchases as a threat for political concession from a target country.[3] So becoming large trading nations, countries invariably possess strategic strengths that it can leverage upon others.

The present study tries to analyse how the import and export dependence among East Asian countries work as a potential leverage that is utilsed for political gains and national power projections. China's strategic interests in the region are especially highlighted. China's assertiveness in East Asia shows the confidence of being foremost in the region. China's political interests in the region are especially overlapped with China's economic interests and vice-versa. East Asia is stuck in a number of territorial disputes among the member countries and there is a possibility of miscalculations and military conflicts in the future. The East China Sea disputes among China, Japan and Korea or the South China Sea disputes among China and ASEAN members or the long and unsettled border problems between India and China are the major concerns to the peace and stability in East Asia.

According to P.M. Goodman, economics and diplomacy is two sides of a same coin. One side represents diplomacy promoting exports, investment, and other economic activity that contributes to a country's prosperity; and the other side represents as an economic tool—from sanctions to trade negotiations—to shape the behaviour of other countries in support of a nation's security and other foreign policy goals.[4] Passive side of this proposition is that the economics or greater trade can deter the potential conflicts among countries.

There is also a collision between economics and security that pose a strategic challenge in Asia today. According to A.E. Feigenbaum, "the same countries that are trading, investing and growing together are beset by security tensions and dysfunctional diplomatic relationships". Beijing's long-term strategic intentions inspire deep anxieties among other nations in the region despite China has become the top trade partner for many of Asia's major economies.[5]

The trade data shows China as the top importer as well as exporter in the region followed by Japan and South Korea. China also had a robust trade surplus of 177.3 billion euros in 2011. Singapore and South Korea are the two other countries in the region having the trade volume over 500 billion and also have positive trade balance. Japan is the second largest exporter and

Table 1: Total Trade of China, India and ASEAN Countries (2011)

Ranks	*Country*	*Export*	*Import*	*Trade*
1	China	1,340,162	1,162,848	2,503,010
2	Japan	555,251	597,976	1,153,227
3	South Korea	386,141	366,356	752,497
4	India	217,946	328,874	546,820
5	Singapore	284,272	247,297	531,570
6	Thailand	159,721	158,991	318,712
7	Malaysia	157,969	128,646	286,615
8	Indonesia	141,444	124,491	265,935
9	Vietnam	65,058	68,948	134,006
10	Pakistan	18,123	36,310	54,434
11	Philippines	33,053	40,250	53,304
12	Bangladesh	14,133	25,451	39,583
13	Sri Lanka	7,179	14,642	21,820
14	Nepal	572	3,601	4,173

Source: Euro Stat, 2012. (http://ec.europa.eu/trade/creating-opportunities/bilateral-relations/statistics)/

importer and had a positive trade balance until recently, helping it to finance various projects in developing world. However, since last few years, the import has outperformed export in Japan with 42.7 billion trade deficit in 2011 and continued this trend till the first quarter of 2014. India is the fourth largest trader from the region with huge trade deficit of 110 billion euros in 2011, making additional burden to India's current account deficit which is close to six percent of Indian GDP.

China has taken over the world as the largest economy and trader, but unlike the mercantilist past, the world is much more interdependent now. In case of China, even the rivals are partners in its growth through trade and investment. This is apparently true of China's neighbors as they are highly integrated with China, reflected in the rapid increase in trade, production networks and investment flows.[6] The intra-regional production networks involving India, China and others are analyzed more elaborately in the previous chapter of this book. China's status can be interpreted as that of a regional power, its military and economic capabilities far outstrip other nations from the region.

The above table represents India's and China's trade with countries in South, East and Southeast Asia. The table reveals that China is the top trading

Table 2: India's and China's Trade with South Asian and Southeast Asian Countries

India's Trade with South Asian and South East Asian Countries				*China's Trade with South Asian and South East Asian Countries*			
Rank	*Country*	*Million Euro*	*Share of India's total trade (%)*	*Rank*	*Country*	*Million Euro*	*Share of China's total trade (%)*
1	China	56,129.7	9.8	1	Japan	257,750.6	9.8
2	Singapore	18,395.7	3.2	2	S. Korea	184,504.6	7
3	Indonesia	15,710.6	2.7	3	Malaysia	67,827.4	2.6
4	S. Korea	12,963.4	2.3	4	India	55,774.9	2.1
5	Japan	12,717.4	2.2	5	Thailand	48,834.5	1.9
6	Malaysia	9,833.9	1.7	6	Singapore	47,565.2	1.8
7	Thailand	6,254.8	1.1	7	Indonesia	45,695.9	1.7
8	Sri Lanka	4,168.3	0.7	8	Vietnam	30,320.4	1.2
9	Vietnam	3,728.2	0.6	9	Philippines	24,326.5	0.9
10	Bangladesh	3,279.2	0.6	10	Pakistan	7966.3	0.3
11	Nepal	2,407.4	0.4	11	Bangladesh	6,228.2	0.2
12	Pakistan	1,531.9	0.3	12	Myanmar	4,904.9	0.2
13	Philippines	1,097.5	0.2	13	Sri Lanka	3,861	0.15
14	Myanmar	1,300.6	0.2	14	Nepal	989.4	0.03
	Total	149,518.60	27.3		Total	786,549.8	31.42

Source: Directorate General for Trade Statistics, 2012.

partner of India. China contributes almost 1/10th of India's total trade. However, India has a huge trade deficit with China, which indicates that China's imports to India are much greater than India's exports to China. Hence, China is a better import market rather than an export market for India. Other countries in lead as trade partners for India are Singapore, Indonesia, South Korea, Japan and Malaysia from East and Sri Lanka and Bangladesh from South Asia. East Asia dominates India's trade basket compare to South Asia making the region economically important as in the case of security. This high trade dependence makes the whole argument in this book more relevant and an active pitch for India's Act East Policy. Though in terms of population and market South Asia and Southeast Asia is at comparable level, India's trade with EAC community is much higher than India's trade with South Asian countries. The notion of geographic and cultural proximity determines a country's trade is incomprehensible in case of India's trade with South Asia. It is rather political relations and relative size of the economies matter much more and this explain the political economy of India's trade with South Asia and East Asia.

Table 3: India's and China's Export to South, East Asian and Southeast Asian Countries (2011)

India's Export to South Asian and South East Asian Countries				*China's Export to South Asian and South East Asian Countries*			
Rank	*Country*	*Export in Million Euro*	*Share of India's total exports (%)*	*Rank*	*Country*	*Export in Million Euro*	*Share of China's Total exports (%)*
1	China	14,417.4	6.3	1	Japan	111,103.6	7.9
2	Singapore	12,180.2	5.3	2	South Korea	62,551.6	4.4
3	Indonesia	5,174.9	2.3	3	India	38,084.5	2.7
4	Japan	4,272.1	1.9	4	Singapore	26.625.5	1.9
5	S. Korea	3,639.3	1.6	5	Indonesia	22.068.7	1.6
6	Sri Lanka	3,626.0	1.6	6	Vietnam	21,941.5	1.6
7	Malaysia	2,954.8	1.3	7	Malaysia	21,046.6	1.5
8	Bangladesh	2,839.9	1.2	8	Thailand	19,386.0	1.4
9	Vietnam	2,566.9	1.1	9	Philippines	10,754.3	0.8
10	Thailand	2,432.3	1.1	10	Pakistan	6,365.0	0.5
11	Nepal	2,026.8	0.9	11	Bangladesh	5,890.5	0.4
12	Pakistan	1,264.4	0.6	12	Myanmar	3,639.6	0.3
13	Philippines	760.5	0.3	13	Sri Lanka	2,255.1	0.2
14	Myanmar	351.9	0.10	14	Nepal	979.9	0.07
	Total	58,507.40	25.6		Total	303,998.20	23.67

Source: Directorate General for Trade Statistics, 2012.

India also retains a negative balance of trade with almost all East and Southeast Asian countries barring Singapore, Vietnam and Philippines though the trade with the Philippines is negligible. Trade deficit with Asian region makes almost half of India's total trade deficits. The trade imbalance with China is a major concern to India and this constitutes about a quarter of India's total trade deficit. The huge trade imbalance is a concern in maintaining good political relation whether it is India-China trade or China's huge trade surplus with many countries. This is also true in case of how South Asian countries perceive India's economic size and their unfavorable trade with India. Unlike the trade with East Asia, India has a considerable trade balance with South Asian countries.

China's trade relations particularly with East Asian countries are manifold higher compared to India. The above table reveals that Japan in lead as the biggest trade partner of China from the region, though both countries have been at logger heads over various issues, historically and politically. South

Korea is the second largest trade partner with a total trade of 184 billion euros, contributing seven percent of China's total trade. India ranks fourth after Malaysia amongst the other Asian trade partners of China. China's all weather friend and ally, Pakistan occupies the 10th position with total trade of about seven billion euros, while India's trade with Pakistan is just 1.5 billion. Comparing the situation of China with India, it is evident that China's trade with these countries is much higher. This is another crucial factor that will determine how events pan out in the region. China's dependence on the region for its trade is about 31.4 per cent of its global trade, while India's dependence on the region is about 27.3 percent of its global trade, slightly lower than that of China.

Even though China is a huge import market for India, it still ranks as number one export market for India from the region, exporting 14.41 million worth of commodities. India's engagements with other countries in terms of exports is considerably low and this will play an important factor in shaping relations with other countries if there is an India-China conflict in the region. To balance India's trade with the East Asian region, India will have to increase its exports particularly to big economies of East Asia along with increasing the trade volume with small countries like Myanmar and Philippines. In the South Asian region, India's export is fairly better in comparison with China, but the trend is rapidly shifting towards China in recent years. Still, the countries like Vietnam, Sri Lanka, Bangladesh and Nepal are a considerable market for Indian exports. The above table also reveals that India's imports and exports to countries like Philippines, Pakistan and Myanmar is almost similar and India is a good export as well as import market for these countries in terms of their global trade.

Japan, Korea, India and all East Asian tigers including Vietnam are huge export market for Chinese goods. India is the third largest export market for Chinese commodities from the region after Japan and South Korea. The combined market share of these three countries for Chinese commodity exports is about 15 percent of China's total exports. China's exports of 304 billion worth of commodities to the region in 2011 constituted about 23.6 percent of its global exports while India's dependence on the region is about 25.6 percent of its global exports. As China's export with small economies of South and South East Asia is comparably lower now, the country has initiated various plans including financial assistance and infrastructure investments to improve its exports to smaller countries such as Nepal, Sri Lanka and Myanmar.

Table 4: India's and China's Imports from South Asian and South East Asian Countries (2011)

India's Imports from South Asian and South East Asian Countries				*China's Imports from South Asian and South East Asian Countries*			
Rank	*Country*	*Export in Million Euro*	*Share of India's total imports (%)*	*Rank*	*Country*	*Export in Million Euro*	*Share of China's total imports (%)*
1	China	41,712.4	12.1	1	Japan	146,647.1	12.0
2	Indonesia	10,535.7	3.1	2	South Korea	121,952.9	10
3	S. Korea	9,324.1	2.7	3	Malaysia	46,780.8	3.8
4	Japan	4,445.3	2.4	4	Thailand	29,448.5	2.4
5	Malaysia	6,879.1	2.0	5	Indonesia	23,627.2	1.9
6	Singapore	6,215.5	1.8	6	Singapore	20,939.7	1.7
7	Thailand	3,822.6	1.1	7	India	17,660.4	1.4
8	Vietnam	1,161.3	0.3	8	Philippines	13,572.2	1.1
9	Myanmar	948.7	0.3	9	Vietnam	8,378.8	0.7
10	Sri Lanka	542.3	0.2	10	Pakistan	1,601.3	0.1
11	Bangladesh	439.3	0.1	11	Bangladesh	337.7	0.02
12	Nepal	380.6	0.1	12	Myanmar	1,265.5	0.10
13	Philippines	337.1	0.1	13	Sri Lanka	1605.9	0.13
14	Pakistan	267.5	0.081	14	Nepal	9.5	—
	Total	87,011.50	26.18		Total	433,827.50	35.23

Source: Directorate General for Trade Statistics, 2012.

In case of Indian imports, China has a lion's share of contributing more than 12 per cent to India's total imports. India's import from China is almost equal to the combined share of India's imports from all other countries in the region. India also depends quite largely on Indonesia, South Korea, Malaysia and Japan for its imports. An over-reliance of India on all other countries for imports also suggests that India is not in a great position in the region as the market in India is heavily dependent on other countries. However India's huge domestic market provides an alternate option to ASEAN countries to depend upon in case of a conflict with China.

For China, Japan ranks as the number one import partner from the region. China's imports from South Korea, Malaysia are also considerably high. China's import market suggests that China is overly dependent on two or three countries for imports. With regard to other countries, China engages only in minimum imports in proportion to its world imports. China's import from India stands at seventh position even below the smaller countries of the region such as Thailand, Singapore and Malaysia and China is a good export market for majority of countries in East and South East Asia in terms of their total trade.

From the overall trade statistics, it is evident that Japan and South Korea lead as the best import as well as export market for China with a trade deficit of euro 35.5 billion and 59.4 billion respectively. India ranks third on the list with a 20 billion trade surplus in favour of China. Japan, South Korea, Malaysia and Thailand are important to China with regard to import whereas India, Singapore, Bangladesh, Pakistan are important to China with regard to exports. In terms of numbers, China's engagement with countries in the region is far greater than that of India and hence puts China in a far more commanding position than India. China may try to consolidate its trade position with these smaller countries in the region to attain its political and strategic goal.

Table 5: Trade Dependence of South, East and South East Asian Countries on China and India (Million Euro)

Countries	*Total trade with China*	*Total trade with India*	*Share of exports to China (C-4)*	*Share of exports to India (C-5)*	*Share of imports from China (C-6)*	*Share of imports from India (C-7)*
Japan	257,750.6	12,717.4	26.41	0.80	18.57	0.71
South Korea	184,504.6	12,963.4	31.58	2.41	17.07	0.99
Malaysia	67827.4	9,833.9	29.61	4.35	16.36	2.29
Thailand	48,834.5	6,254.8	18.43	2.39	12.19	1.52
Indonesia	45,695.9	15,710.6	16.70	7.44	17.72	4.15
Singapore	47,565.2	18,395.7	7.36	2.18	10.76	4.92
Philippines	24,326.5	1,097.5	41.06	1.01	26.71	1.88
Vietnam	30,320.4	3,728.2	12.87	1.78	31.82	3.72
Pakistan	7966.3	1,531.9	8.83	1.47	17.52	3.48
Bangladesh	6,228.2	3,279.2	2.38	3.10	23.14	11.15
Myanmar	4,904.9	1,300.6	21.88	16.40	37.29	3.60
Sri Lanka	3,861.	4,168.3	1.12	7.55	15.40	24.76
Nepal	989.4	2,407.4	1.66	66.53	27.21	56.28

C-4 and C-5 = Xij/Xiw × 100 (Country i's export to country j divided by country i's total exports to the world multiplied by 100)

C-6 and C-7= Mij/Miw × 100 (Country i's import from country j divided by country i's total imports from the world multiplied by 100)

Source: Directorate General for Trade Statistics (2012; http://ec.europa.eu/trade/creating-opportunities/bilateral-relations/statistics/

Unlike the previous case of India's and China's trade, here I examine the trade dependence of South and Southeast Asian countries on India and China in terms of their global trade. This is the most important matrix which gives us an idea of the dependence of these countries for their exports and imports on China and India. The data reveals that any escalation of conflict in the region will be more damaging to these countries in relative trade terms than to China and India as their trade dependence is skewed towards China and to a lesser extent towards India. China has become the number one trade partner, export and import partner for many of these countries replacing either U.S. or Japan in recent years. The PRC's emergence as a major trading power and an investment partner is not a zero sum proposition from the perspective of the region. The PRC's imports of components from countries in ASEAN and other developing East Asian countries have grown rapidly, in line with the equally rapid expansion of manufacturing exports from the PRC to extra regional markets, mostly North America and Europe.

From the trade data we can infer that in case of any conflicts between India and China, most of the countries in the region are going to take a neutral stand as it would be too risky for them to align with any side that could cost them billions worth of trade. Escalation of any conflict between China-Japan or China-South Korea over territorial disputes is remote as China has become the leading trade partner for these countries and about 26 percent of Japan's total exports and 31 percent of Korea's exports are destined to China. These two biggest economies of the region also depend on China for about 18 percent and 17 percent of their imports. It is also bewildering that many countries in the Southeast Asian region largely depend on China, close to a quarter of their total trade, either originate or destined towards China, even though political relations have been going southward. For example, Philippines a staunch U.S. ally in the region with an unresolved territorial dispute with China depends on China for astonishing 41 percent of its total exports and 27 percent of imports.

The trade matrix is a clear indication of bilateral ties between countries. From the table, it is evident that the major economies in the region like Japan, South Korea, Malaysia and a few others, the bilateral trade with China is more intensive than bilateral ties with India. These countries are better export and import markets for China rather than for India. As a result, these countries would choose to side with China or at least will take a neutral stand on any issues concerning India and China. The pure economics suggest that China's role in the region is one of complete dominance. In developing strong bilateral ties with almost all the powerful countries in the region, China has stamped its authority and will now look ahead to try to consolidate its position.

The overall picture emerging from the trade matrix of East Asia helps us to draw the conclusion that China's engagement in terms of trade in the region makes it a potent force and China has become the driving force in the region. India on the other hand, engages in much weaker numbers and China itself has a huge role to play in India's trade. All these factors taken into account make India seem rather vulnerable in the region and not in a position to dictate terms. This means that India is effectively left to fend for itself in a region where China's domination is very strikingly evident by mere numbers.

This over dependence has led to a precarious catch-22 situation for China's trade partners in Asia, who have contested claims in the region. The region is stuck in a number of territorial disputes and there is possibility of miscalculations and military conflicts in the future. China has unleashed a new wave of aggressive posture in the region started with the rare earth embargo to Japan in 2010 after a territorial incident in East China Sea and then the incidence such as de facto seizure of the Scarborough Shoal from the Philippines in 2012, declaration of an Air Defense Identification in 2013 over an area of the East China Sea, siege of the Second Thomas Shoal in the Spratlys in early 2014, construction of an airstrip on the Johnson South Reef, and the naval skirmishes with Vietnam over Chinese deployment of Haiyang Shiyou 981 floating oil rig off the central coast of Vietnam.

Trade as a Potential Leverage

Trade restrictions are one way to flex muscles. The control can be powerful when the trade is strategic items or critical resources. China used this tool as an informal embargo on rare-earth exports to Japan during the 2010 Senkaku crisis. In this case, China used its dominant position in rare earth industry to settle the political crisis.[7] The confrontation between China and Japan in September 2010 over the detention of the crew members of a Chinese fishing vessel by Japanese coastguard resulted in a number of retaliatory measures by China. The most controversial among them was the halting of shipment of rare earths and related material to Japan. This was a rare case of using rare earth materials as a strategic tool. The REE embargo episode had sent clear indication to the leaders around the world that a more powerful China might use its economic strength as a weapon.

The concentration of trade with a single partner is argued to represent vulnerability. This will determine how events pan out in the region with a growing economic clout of China. Will any of them bet on these huge trade volumes over the tiny islets in East or South China Sea? As the developed countries in the Western hemisphere are in economic doldrums with declining demands in their imports, importance of emerging countries like India, China and ASEAN will increase many folds, making the conflict escalation too costly affair to afford.

Will this huge trade dependence between China and others in the region prevent conflicts from escalation? Some scholars argue so. For example, *Richard Katz* argued that the conflict between China and Japan over the Senkaku did not escalate to a war because of 'mutual assured production,' or China needs to buy Japan's products as much as Japan needs to sell them. Japan's total trade with China has tripled since 2000 rising by 30 per cent year-on-year to more than $300 billion. Both China and Japan share a mutual trade relation as 60-70 per cent of goods imported by China from Japan comprises of machinery used to make China's own exports.[8]

Trade dependence also means that if one country overly depends on another either for exports or imports, it may give the rival a wedge in strategic matters. For example, Philippines a staunch US ally in the region with an unresolved territorial dispute depends upon China for 41 per cent of its total exports and 27 per cent of imports. Whereas Philippine's export to the US was about 10 per cent of its total exports and imports was just about 6.4 per cent of its total imports. This over dependence of Philippines on China has proved to be a disaster.

In recent years, Chinese vessels have been involved in aggressive behavior near the borders of Philippines in the South China Sea. Moreover, China resorted to economic measures like temporarily restricting the import of agricultural products to punish the Philippines over Scarborough Shoal incidents.[9] Also, Chinese mainland tourist agencies stopped sending groups to the Philippines, which as the third largest source of tourists was a great blow to Manila.

Another case point is Malaysia's deliberate silence over a 2013 Chinese naval expedition in an area just 80 kms away from Malaysia in South China Sea.[10] China is Malaysia's largest trade partner and its export to China accounts 30 percent of its total exports along with huge bilateral investments and tourism. This huge dependence on China has compelled Malaysia to compromise its position on the South China Sea disputes. If the trend continues, other nations too will fall in line like Malaysia.

The implications of this economic over dependence on China, an aspiring global power will be multi-faceted. Continued occurrence of Chinese assertiveness in the region such as declaration of ADIZ, naval maneuvering in East and South China Sea or the continued infiltrations in Indian border areas may become routine affairs. China may again use its trade power as a bargaining chip by selectively restricting exports or banning imports. China's engagement in terms of trade in the region makes it a potent force where its domination is very strikingly evident by mere numbers. This would allow China to dictate terms in the region as Beijing expands and enforces Chinese sovereignty claims in the region, rewarding those who fall in line and punishing those who do not.

No country from the region will be in a position to take a particular side if a bilateral confrontation occurs between China and an individual country from the region as the economic benefit for doing so will be higher than taking a side. Therefore, most of the countries would take a neutral stand. Some smaller countries like Cambodia or Laos may even align with China. China remains an important economic player even in smaller countries like Bangladesh and Vietnam. As a result, these countries might choose to remain evenhanded as taking sides would be detrimental to their business. In effect, the trade relations of China neutralise all the soft power capabilities that India or Japan possesses in the region.

END NOTES

1. N Mancheri and R Nair, "China and Its Neighbors: Trade Leverage, Interdependence and Conflict", *ICS Wednesday Seminar*, (Institute of China Studies, New Delhi, 2014), available at http://www.icsin.org/ICS/WednesdaySeminarReport/87.pdf.
2. It Chen, "Balance of payments and power: assessing China's global and regional interdependence relationship" *International Relations of the Asia-Pacific*, (Oxford University Press, 2014), doi:10.1093/irap/lcu00.
3. D.M. Lampton, D.M, The Three faces of Chinese Power: Might, Money, and Minds, (University of California Press, Berkeley, 2008).
4. M.P. Goodman, "Economics as a Strategy", *Global Economics Monthly*, volume 3, issue 1 January, 2014.
5. A.E. Feigenbaum, "Ten Trends That Will Shape Asia in 2014", *Carnegie Endowment*, December 30, 2013.
6. T. Marukawa, Ito and Zhang, China's Outward Foreign Direct Investment Data *ISS Contemporary Chinese Research Series*, No.15, Tokyo University, 2014, available at http:/ /web.iss.u-tokyo.ac.jp/kyoten/research/ISS_China_series_No.15.pdf

7. N. Mancheri, "Does the WTO ruling against China on rare earths really matter?, *East Asia Forum* (October 30, 2014), available at http://www.eastasiaforum.org/2014/10/30/does-the-wto-rulingagainst-china-on-rare-earths-really-matter/
8. R. Katz, "Mutual Assured Production", *Foreign Affairs*, 92-4 July/August, 18-24, 2013.
9. Mastro Oriana, "The Problems with the Liberal Peace in Asia," *Survival*, 56 (6), April / May, 2014, 129-158.
10. S. Lockman, "Why Malaysia isn't afraid of China (for now)", *The Strategist*, The Australian Strategic Policy Institute, 24 April, 2013, available at http://www.aspistrategist.org.au/why-malaysia-isnt-afraid-of-china-for-now/

6

India's Relation with Australia within the Indo-Pacific Dynamics

Shubhamitra Das

The 21st Century gives primacy to concrete issues like energy security and maritime security, which was camouflaged earlier under ideology, civilisation and religion. The emerging nomenclature, 'Indo-Pacific' gained tremendous scholarship since the Indian and the Pacific Ocean, which are the world's busiest trading routes got submerged with both traditional and non-traditional security threats like piracy, trafficking and terrorism. Power projection, balance of power and territorial disputes joined hands with increased interconnectivity through trade, multilateralism and regionalism. The operatic intermixing of ideas and perception is the nature of the concept of Indo-Pacific, while the orchestration is done during the US declaration of 'pivot' or rebalancing Asia. It would be interesting to see how the security architecture emerges and likewise how the strategic partnership unfolds. India and Australia standing at the nodal points of the two oceans will have an exhaustive role to play, which was never fathomed by either of the countries' policy framework. This chapter will be an attempt to understand the different perspectives shared by India and Australia on the term Indo-Pacific and how the geopolitical construct merges their perspective into a lucrative relation and its rippling effect for the countries in the zone.

India and Australia were less visible in a responsible role in the Asia-Pacific nomenclature. While 'Asia-Pacific' emphasised the western need to Asian oil[1], 'Indo-Pacific' gave the impetus to the Asian (China, India, Southeast Asia and East Asian) demand and security of oil for sustained economic growth, energy resource which has from antiquity been the reason for power play and wars. US preference to Indo-Asia-Pacific with the centrality to Asia explains "Indo-Pacific' strategically that does not include China but engulfs China from the two oceans where China has increased its presence. But it would be too early to predict that all countries of the Indo-Pacific instead of strategically engaging with each other on multi-directional issues will bandwagon with US in its efforts to contain China. Australia in its Defence White Paper 2012 mentioned that 'China will not be a threat as much as an opportunity'[2] for Australia to perceive its Asian regional cooperation; especially with the Southeast Asian Nations. Australia in its Defence White Paper 2013 has mentioned the Indo-Pacific region as the zone of strategic importance. The 'two-Ocean navy' concept that was floating in Australia ever since 1980s, and issues of 'trade routes, energy flows, diplomatic bonds and strategic connections' became the center stage for Australia's new nomenclature[3]. For the first time Australia linked itself as an inclusive member of the region and not being in the 'periphery' due to its different identity from the Asians. As Rory Medcalf aptly puts, 'At last, here is a definition of Asia that automatically includes Australia'[4].

The Indo-Pacific region is seen to be dynamic and ambiguous. The rising defence budgets, unresolved territorial disputes, growing nuke proliferation threats and mounting nationalistic sentiments are causes enough to derail the regional security,[5] and rising Asian powers and great power rivalry led to the construction of a geopolitical premise engulfing all the issues of concern under one banner. Increased military activity in the region has been credited to the post-9/11 'War on Terror' but gradually gained momentum with the rising China and mostly due to its capability for air and sea denial leading to anxiety among the states having regular and active economic transactions.

Australia's Indo-Pacific—Concept and Strategy

Conceptually, Indo-Pacific has long been available in the marine biology and other sciences. Culturally too, we are familiar with the notion of Indo-Pacific due to the travel of Buddhism from India, to China to Southeast Asian countries. Geopolitical significance to 'Indo-Pacific' is due to the changed and aggravated strategic, economic and diplomatic challenges/engagement for an ever increasing demand for energy resources leading to the vital concern of freedom of navigation, movement of air-sea spaces and control of the region from transborder issues of piracy, trafficking and terrorism. This has been the reason to either 'power projection capabilities due to the fear of conflict or the need for an expansive foreign policy'[6] in the new world of globalisation, interconnectivity and juridical compulsions.

'Geography is given the central focus in foreign policy or statecraft due to its permanence' with the design of land and seas, distribution of resources and people, their social institutions and behavioral patterns[7] a geopolitical construct emerges. What the Indo-Pacific means geopolitically is to consider Spykman's 'Rimland' theory; i.e. those countries that are touching the mainland of Asia and are also touching the sea, i.e. the littoral countries, that connects sea and land for unhindered naval operations[8].

On the other hand, reterritorialising the region with the nomenclature of Indo-Pacific has been a grand strategy of Australia that could accommodate the US 'Pivot' to the 'Indo-Asia-Pacific'. Australia, the only ally closer to the region was relied on while US declared its efforts to rebalance the region[9]. The other reason to contain a growing power which is beyond/opposed to the western concept of political, diplomatic or economic growth the '*Beijing consensus*' to the '*Washington consensus*' which is very less worked upon and considered as a decadent thesis, since the western understanding of democracy, economic growth and social justice being on tandem for human development is not to be refuted. On the other hand, the US' earlier emphasis on East Asian countries like Japan and South Korea became strategically inadequate since China is a continental power whiles US is basically a maritime power[10]. This made the US to focus more on the region's continental powers like India and with its older partners like Vietnam and Philippines. With the presumed decline of the US hegemony and its simultaneous declaration to '*pivot*' or rebalancing Asia gave a clear ambiance to power projections and military alliance or partnerships that is best defined by Raja Mohan that 'cooperative security, great power concert and a balance of power system[11], may form the broad contours of the geopolitical map of Indo-Pacific.

India's Indo-Pacific

Within this grand strategy of Indo-Pacific how comfortable and/or ready is India? Will India join the concert of democracies or will India maintain its strategic autonomy and consider having a strategic partnership with these countries? Can Australia and India's relation help in garnishing India's Look-East policy? Is India really interested in containing China to secure its interests or to support US efforts to rebalance the region? India had readily accepted the nomenclature not because 'its strategic perspective could be influenced by a geo-political construct'[12] but because it exactly portrays its strategy in the region. The timing of the concept and India's increased presence within the international system and its security policies and the presumed role India aspires to play certify its acceptance of the term readily. India's 'naval capability, strategic positioning and robust presence'[13] in the Indian Ocean further confirmed its role within the Indo-Pacific paradigm. India is not as much as a security provider but a serious regional player in the Indian Ocean, after its tremendous leap from perceived isolation to becoming a global economic and strategic partner, player and competitor. India was also grappling for the need of a nomenclature which was put in a platter by Australia that exactly fits India's view of its strategic role in the near future. The terminology also helped to build a strategic and institutional landscape to thwart Chinese hegemony[14] to maintain a code of conduct of the sea lanes of communication and for freedom of navigation and movement on the sea-air spaces and to prevent the region from being dominated militarily and economically. The changed perception of the region by India brought the latent 'look east' policy to the forefront with closer economic, trade, defence and security cooperation with the Southeast and East Asian countries.[15] As a matter of fact, in 1990 the 'Look-East policy' was basically 'designed to curtail the major threat coming from China on Southeast Asian region'.[16] In the recent years, India has signed security agreements with Singapore, Indonesia, Malaysia, Vietnam and Cambodia.[17] India urgently requires a paradigm shift in its overall social, political and diplomatic structures; especially 'a sound defence industrial base and its Ministry of Defence needs to have institutional depth and political vision'[18] and not be entwined in between the bureaucratic hassles leading to delay and non-implementation of policies.

India's growing demand for energy resources became apparent for sustained economic growth, removal of hunger and poverty, regional stability and security and also for gaining a dominant role in the Indian Ocean. India became alert with its failed efforts in building pipeline on the India-Bangladesh-Myanmar or in the India-Pakistan-Iran. Incidentally, India is in between four choke points, namely Suez Canal, Bab-el-Mandeb, Strait of Hormuz and the Malacca Straits. Hence, the issue is no more just the demand and struggle for oil but also to secure the resources on the pirate ridden region from east coast of Africa to the Southeast Asian region. India could find its strategic reach by extending towards Central Asia and the whole of African Coast and towards Southeast Asia, East Asia and the South Pacific. India being both a 'continental and a maritime power' but weaker among the Asian powers namely, China and Japan requires to gear itself for a bigger role in the region.

India's 'neo-Curzonian foreign policy' emphasises the 'centrality of India' with a multidirectional approach in its engagement from major powers of East Africa to Pacific Asia'.[19] This stretches from the Gulf of Eden to Malacca Strait, also considered by Robert Kaplan as the 'center stage of 21st Century'.[20] The accessibility is to revive commercial cooperation, to build physical, political and institutional links and enhance energy security with new suppliers and gaining assets and to increase defence cooperation with the countries of the region.[21] Neo-Curzonian mapping of India's Indo-Pacific would be limiting since India's expanded scope will be on the east coast of Africa which touches the Indian Ocean till the Pacific that reaches the US from the eastern side via Australia, New Zealand and South Pacific Island countries. K.M. Panikkar, said that 'Indian Ocean has to be truly Indian and India needs to build a 'steel ring' in the region around Yemen, Mauritius and Sri Lanka and Singapore.[22] But before India could even visualise a 'steel ring', China has built its enigmatic 'string of pearls'. What India needs at the moment is to increase its naval capabilities that could 'operate at distant regions from the Indian coast along with force deployments, port visits, exercise and operations'[23] on the one hand and bring the dormant 'Look East' Policy activated with 'multiple engagements with Asian powers, enhance its relation with the regional institutions, build defence and security cooperation with key actors of the region and improve its international image and its geopolitical standing in Asia'.[24] India could be credited to be one of the first countries to sign ASEAN's Treaty of Amity and Cooperation, being outside the region.[25]

India started bilateral and multilateral economic cooperation with the Southeast, East Asia and South Pacific countries along with strengthening South Asian Association for Regional Cooperation (SAARC) and Bay of Bengal Initiative for Multi Sectoral Technical and Economic Cooperation (BIMSTEC).[26] India will have to think of possibilities of associations and groupings that could sustain its efforts on the Indian Ocean and also gain it a permanent seat in the UN Security Council. Australia, India and Indonesia has tremendous potential in coming together for better regional cooperation in Indian Ocean Rim Association (IORA) and Indian Ocean Naval Symposium (IONS).[27] IONS, if successful, have tremendous potential to become the counterweight against Shanghai Cooperation and the presumed Silk Route of China. India's location on the Indian Ocean is considered as its destiny since the Ocean is linked with India in varied historical, cultural, civilisational, economic and political ways that the Ocean bears its name.[28] India could truly become a security provider as US and Australia presumed it to be in the near future. Likewise, India's active participation is seen in the Pacific Island Forum (PIF), and the top Asian multilateral institutions like ASEAN Regional Forum, East Asian Summit, ASEAN Defence Minister Meeting with the East Asian Summit members (ADMM+) and Asia-Pacific Economic Cooperation.

The bilateral relation with the Southeast Asian countries like Singapore, Vietnam, and Indonesia is gaining ground followed by Malaysia, Cambodia and Philippines. India's relation with the US is more of a strategic partnership from the Indian side. Indo-US relation has a positive future due to shared political values and convergent geopolitical interests. India is a lot concerned about Pakistan which continues to get US weapons to be used in a 'conventional conflict with India'.[29] Hence, Indo-US relation is not without its glitches and India needs to move with caution. The nuclear agreement is more than mere nuclear technicality but is a 'new configuration of global balancing[30] in the face of emergent nuclear threats. The US has long been expecting India to play a strategic role over the region; especially the Indian Ocean and expand its naval capabilities by coordinating with the US near the Persian gulf, Southeast Asia and towards Taiwan straits.[31] India's strategic autonomy would depend on its prioritisation and premise on its expansion of its naval capabilities, which is one of the examples is its initiative in forming IONS and reviving the IORA. Nevertheless, the Look East Policy stretches as far as South Pacific islands. India has always been an ardent advocate for decolonisation and human rights and can play a major role on 'global governance and political modernisation' with the countries in the region, collaborating with Australia and New Zealand to transform the so-called 'arc of instability'.

India and Australia's Merging Interests with the Indo-Pacific

The sheer enormity of Indian and Australian coast or their maritime jurisdiction and the multivariate traditional and non-traditional security issues in the region would have brought the two countries together sooner or later. Post 9/11 has made the world aware of the scale of destruction capable through terrorism, further merging the domestic and international security concerns within a singular fold; the national security.[32] Moreover, the geopolitical emphasis of the term Indo-Pacific has implied the natural partnership between India and Australia. Australian Defence White Paper 2009 made an initial attempt to cooperate with India and adds "as India extends its reach and influence into areas of shared strategic interests, we need to strengthen our defence cooperation and understand India's strategic thinking'.[33] A little further back in 2007 when Prime Minister Kevin Rudd aspired for a Asia-Pacific community which involved East Asia and Southeast Asia, including India, China, Indonesia and US by 2020, though it did not materialise, a little credit goes to Rudd's effort too for the evolution of the geopolitical concept of the Indo-Pacific. Being at the focal points on Indo-Pacific map will India and Australia take the role of security guards or 'super-policeman'[34] is a case in point. Australia expects India to act as a democratic counterbalance to China and a potential commercial alternative to shed it's over dependence on Chinese trade. And hence by 2002 Australia's trade with India increased by leaps and bounds and is faster than its trade with China.[35] China's so-called 'non-confrontational assertiveness' and its air-sea denial capabilities has made the countries in the region wary and various ways of hedging China is done by almost all the countries in the region.

If India and Australia's relation could garnish India's Look-East policy, then that could be best answered with Australia's Defence White Paper 2013 which gave central focus to Southeast Asia in its 'Look West' Policy. While India too framed its reach on the Indian and the Pacific Oceans, its Look East Policy shows similar grounds to cooperate. The 'military variant involves Andaman and Nicobar Tri-Command Services'[36] for balancing the region. India's expansion on the Indian Ocean is given a positive nod by Singapore, Indonesia, Vietnam, Malaysia, Philippines and Australia. India developed security cooperation through joint naval patrolling, bilateral exercises, biannual naval get-together like 'Milan'[37] with Southeast Asian states and Australia. The annual Malabar Indo-US naval exercises started as early as 2000 has also been quite a success. It remains to be seen if India's bilateral relation with Indonesia which is one of the main features of India's expanses in the 'Look East' policy gains momentum with India's role in bringing both Australia-Indonesia in one platform in the Indian Ocean.

India and Australia has signed many agreements in the post 9/11 like 2003 Memorandum of Understanding on Cooperation in combating international terrorism, 2006 Memorandum of Understanding on defence cooperation and track II bilateral security dialogue every 18 months was decided,[38] while in 2007 defence information-sharing arrangement, and in 2008 agreements on intelligence dialogue, extradition and terrorism[39] were cleared. Related to security aspects both have signed many agreements related to cooperation on intelligence, law enforcement, border security, terrorist financing and money laundering.[40] Apart from these, India and Australia can come together on issues of 'disaster management and environmental protection; specifically of oil spills and ameliorate and prevent transnational security threats like piracy, trafficking and terrorism'.[41] India and Australia have been sharing many military exercises like US-Indian Malabar exercises, Australia's Kakadu and Pitch Black exercises. As early as 2007, Australia, Japan and Singapore were invited to take part in the Indo-US Military exercise, i.e. the Malabar exercise[42] which almost seemed to nurture the idea of a quadrilateral relation between India, US, Japan and Australia as a concrete mechanism to contain China.

The future of India-Australia relation depends upon how well they shed their past misunderstanding. The similarities such as British legacy, membership in Commonwealth, English language and cricket could not bring the two countries together all through the Cold War days. The contrast was very well put by Christopher Waters in terms of "alignment versus non-alignment, military alliance versus peaceful co-existence, military strength versus non-military confidence building measures, and western nations versus Asian nations'.[43] The Nehru-Menzies era in 1952 was one of the starting points of conflict, when Menzies was invited to join the Eighteen Nation Disarmament Committee (ENDC) which was in 1961 set up by UN General Assembly as an autonomous body on disarmament issues and also of joining Non Alignment Movement (NAM), Menzies rejected both and joined SEATO, a military alliance to prevent Communist advances in Southeast Asia.[44] In July 1959, when for a moment Australia agreed to sell uranium to India with a clause that India allows free inspection of its nuclear facilities,[45] it was similarly rejected by India. Other issues that brought each other apart were the Suez crisis in 1956, Australia's support to South Africa's Apartheid regime, but what made India angry and indifferent to Australia was the way it handled the nuclear issue, selling Uranium to France, Taiwan, China and Pakistan and refusing to sell to India for not signing NPT and the hardly forgotten incident i.e. Australia's severity of reaction towards Pokhran II nuke test[46] in 1998. The history of nuclear deal and its ultimate signing has a long story of lost opportunities, inconsistencies within Australia's policy. The geostrategic interests of both the countries harmonised with the changed international perspectives on economic and security issues.

Conclusion

The Indo-Pacific region is one of the largest entities of growing economies and political perplexity. The economic growth, regional conflicts like India-Pakistan, India-China, China-Japan, China-Taiwan, the multilateral arrangements like ASEAN, EAS, APEC, BIMSTEC, IORA, IONS and the new bilateral relations of India-US, India-Australia, India-Vietnam, Singapore, Indonesia and the potential other strategic engagements on the South China Sea completes the big picture of Indo-Pacific.

It needs to be seen how well Australia and India manages their relationship without any baggage and maintain a matured and responsible role for constructive cooperation and engagement to balance rising powers peacefully. In addition, for India, with its domestic and border disputes, it will be interesting to see its readiness to play the coveted role of 'security provider'.

END NOTES

1. See Simon Dalby, "Imperialism, Domination, Culture: The Continued Relevance of Critical Geopolitics", *Geopolitics*, 13 (3), (2008), 413-436.
2. Rahul Mishra, "Australia's Defence White Paper 2013: Seeking a Fine Balance", *Strategic Analysis*, 37 (6), (2013), 688-693.
3. Rory Medcalf, "In Defence of the Indo-Pacific: Australia's New Strategic Map", *Australian Journal of International Affairs*, 68 (4), (2014), 470-483.
4. Ibid.
5. Zue Feng, "An Emerging Trend In East Asia: Military Budget Increases and their Impact", *Asian Perspective*, 33 (4), (2009), 17-45.
6. Patrick Porter, "The Maps are too Small: Geography, Strategy and National Interest" https://www.gov.uk/government/uploads/system/uploads/attachment_data/file/207210/Geography__Strategy_and_the_National_Interest.pdf
7. Harvey Starr, "On Geopolitics: Places and Space", *International Studies Quarterly*, (2013), 57, 433-439.
8. Phil Kelly, "A Critique of Critical Geopolitics", *Geopolitics*, 11 (2006), 24-53, and also see Raghavendra Mishra, "India and Indo-Pacific: Involvement rather than Entanglement", *Indian Foreign Affairs Journal*, 9 (2), (April-June 2014), 112-118.
9. Laura Neack, "Pathways to Power: A Comparative Study of Foreign Policy Ambitions of

Turkey, Brazil, Canada, Australia", *Seton Hall Journal of Diplomacy and International Relations*, (Summer/Fall, 2013), 53-73.

10. See Evan Braden Montgomery, "Competitive Strategies Against Continental Powers: The Geopolitics of Sino-Indian-American Relations", *Journal of Strategic Studies*, 36 (1), (2013), 76-100.
11. C. Raja Mohan, "Samudra Manthan: Sino-Indian Rivalry in the Indo-Pacific", (Carnegie Endowment for International Peace, Washington, 2012), 211.
12. A. Vinod Kumar, "Indo-Pacific: India will be a fringe player", *Indian Foreign Affairs Journal*, 9 (2), (April-June 2014) 136-141.
13. Barthelemy Courmont and Geragthy Colin, "India and Australia: Emerging Partnership in the Indian Ocean", *Korean Journal of Defence Analysis*, 25 (2), (2013), 281-299.
14. Raja Menon, "The India Myth" *The National Interest*, (Nov-Dec 2014), 46-57.
15. Sumit Ganguli and S. Manjeet Pardesi, "Explaining 60 years of India's Foreign Policy", *India Review*, 8 (1), (Jan-Mar 2009), 4-19.
16. Balaji Chandramohan, "India Looks Outward", *New Zealand International Review*, 38 (3), (May-June 2013), 17-20.
17. C. Raja Mohan, "An Uncertain trumpet? India's role in Southeast Asian Security", *India Review*, 12 (3), (2013), 134-150.
18. Ibid.
19. W Jeffery Legro, "The Politics of the New Global Architecture: The US and India" *Strategic Analysis*, 36 (4), (July-August 2012), 640-644.
20. Ibid., n. 16.
21. C. Raja Mohan, "The Return of the Raj" (2010), available at http://asialink. unimelb.edu.au/__data/assets/pdf_file/0007/467962/The_Return_of_the_ Raj.pdf
22. David Brewster, "Australia and India: The Indian Ocean and the Limits of Strategic Convergence", *Australian Journal of International Affairs*, 64 (5),(Nov 2010), 549-565.
23. Barthelemy Courmont and Geragthy, "India and Australia: An Emerging Partnership in the Indian Ocean" *The Korean Journal of Defence Analysis*, 25 (2), (June 2013), 281-299.
24. Ibid, n.17.
25. Walter C. Ladwig, "India and the Balance of Power in the Asia-Pacific", *JFQ*, 57, (2nd Quarter, 2010), available at http://users.ox.ac.uk/~mert1769/JFQ.pdf.
26. Ibid, n. 16.
27. Ibid, n. 2.
28. Ibid, n. 10.
29. C. Uday Bhaskar and Geoffery Kemp, "Maritime Security Challenges in the Indian Ocean Region" A Workshop Report, Center for the National Interests, The Maritime Foundation, Feb 23-24, 2011, India International Center, New Delhi.
30. Harsh Pant, "The Indo-US Nuclear Deal: Beginning of a Beautiful Relation", *Cambridge Review of International Affairs*, 20 (3), (2007), 457-472.
31. Ibid., n. 22.
32. Andrew O'Neil, "Conceptualizing Future Threats to Australia's Security" *Australian Journal of Political Science*, 46:1, (2011), 19-34.
33. Ibid, n. 22.
34. Ibid, n. 23.
35. Peter Mayer and Purnendra Jain, "Beyond Cricket: Australia-India Evolving Relations" *Australian Journal of Political Science*, 45 (1), (March 2010), 133-148.
36. Balaji Chandramohan, "Australia's White Paper 2013: A View from India" *Strategic Analysis*

Paper (June 2013), available at http://www.futuredirections.org.au/publications/indian-ocean/1085-australia-s-defence-white-paper-a-view-from-india.html

37. David Brewster, "India's Defence Strategy and the India-ASEAN Relationship" *India Review*, 12(3) (2013), 151-164.
38. Ibid, n. 35.
39. Ibid.
40. Ibid.
41. Jenelle Bonnor and Varun Sahini, "India-Australia Reengagement: Common security Concerns, Converging Strategic Horizon, Complementary Force Structures", *Australian Strategic Policy Institute, Strategic Insight*, (October 2004), 1-8.
42. Ibid, n. 35.
43. Christopher Waters, "After Decolonisation: Australia and the Emergence of the Non-Aligned Movement in Asia, 1954-55", *Diplomacy & Statecraft*, 12 (2), (June 2001), 153-174.
44. Edmond Roy, "Australian Uranium and India: Ideology verses Pragmatism", *South Asia: Journal of South Asian Studies*, 34 (1), (April 2011), 113-140.
45. Ibid.
46. Marika Vicziyani, "Australia-India Security Dialogue: Academic Leadership in the Diplomatic Vaccume", *South Asia: Journal of South Asian Studies*, 23, (Special Issue, 2000), 159-178.

7

India's Strategic Partnership with Myanmar in the Indo-Pacific Region

Omprakash Dahiya

Myanmar[1] is of extreme strategic and economic importance for India. The two nations share a 1,600 km land border and a long maritime boundary in the strategically important Bay of Bengal and Andaman Sea. They are bound by religious, cultural and ethnic linkages in addition to the fact that four of India's politically-sensitive Northeastern states share international borders with Myanmar. India has been pursuing friendly relations with its eastern neighbour since the early 1990s with the goal of countering China's influence in the region as well as exploiting the tremendous energy resources of Myanmar. Critics have however, argued that India's Myanmar policy is flawed and have called for a re-evaluation.

Since the formulation of its Look East Policy in the early 1990s, India has realised the significance of Myanmar in strengthening its economic links with Southeast Asia. The official visit paid by J.N. Dixit, the then foreign secretary to Yangon in March 1993 was a turning point in Indo-Myanmar relations when India decided to change its policy and cautiously engage the junta.[2] Myanmar is India's gateway to the ASEAN as it is the only member of the regional formation which shares a land and maritime boundary with India.[3] With India becoming a summit level partner of ASEAN and a member of the East Asia Summit, good bilateral relations with Myanmar will benefit

India's national interests. Besides, Myanmar and India are members of sub regional groupings such as the Bay of Bengal Initiative for Multi-Sectoral Technical and Economic Cooperation (BIMST-EC) and the Mekong Ganga Cooperation (MGC). It is also part of the Ayeyawady-Chao Phraya-Mekong Economic Cooperation Strategy (ACMECS) and the Greater Mekong Sub-region Programme (GMS).

Geographically, Myanmar is located at the middle of the Indo-Pacific region. It could be considered the transitional area (spot) of South Asian Association for Regional Cooperation (SAARC); Association of South East Asian Nations (ASEAN) and East Asia Economic Cooperation (EAEC). Myanmar is the second largest nation amongst the Indian neighbours, the largest on its eastern flank that can provide the eastern littoral areas an access up to the Bay of Bengal Sea. This chapter provides insight to the emerging strategic partnership between India and Myanmar in the Indo-Pacific region and analyse some of the issues concerning the bilateral relationship.

Historical Background

India and Burma has a historical connection that goes back to the fifth century and since then they have enjoyed mutual contact in the realm of trade, commerce, religion, law, political philosophy and culture. Hinduism and Buddhism came to Burma from India by the seventh century. Both countries came under British colonial rule, and the Burmese leaders had deep association with the Indian leaders during the struggle for national independence.

The series of conflicts known as the Anglo-Burmese Wars from early to late 19th century resulted in the British Raj seizing different territories of the Kingdom of Burma and eventually annexing the whole nation as part of British India.[4] The years that followed saw the integration of Burma and its economy with the undivided India and its economy; and the burden of defending Burma naturally fell on the British Rule. The separation of Burma from the British Rule in 1937 did not in any way reduced the responsibilities of the British India in defending what was its large eastern flank. With British India establishing comfortable relations with Siam that borders Burma, there was little concern in Calcutta (and later Delhi) of a threat to the Raj from the East. The weakening of the Chinese empire limited any potential threats from the north. The Second World War, however, shattered the quiescence on the eastern front.

The fall of Singapore and the rapid advances of Japanese armed forces almost to the doorstep of India in the Second World War underlined the huge strategic significance of Burma. Located between India and China, and between the subcontinent and the East, Burma became critical to the new theatre that was widely described as CBI (China-Burma-India).[5] The Southeast Asia Command was set up by the Allies to push the Japanese out of Myanmar; and undivided India contributed nearly 750,000 troops. Burma also provided the backdoor to China that let the Allies supply the Chongqing government in the fight against Japanese occupation. The American General Joseph Stilwell built the famous Ledo Road from India to Yunnan through northern Burma.[6]

Writing during the Second World War and looking ahead to the security of the region after the decolonisation of the Subcontinent which was then on the cards, the Indian historian and diplomat K.M. Panikkar highlighted the indivisibility of Indian and Burmese security, "the defence of Burma is in fact the defence of India, and it is India's primary concern no less than Burma's to see that its frontiers remain inviolate. In fact, no responsibility can be considered too heavy for India when it comes to the question of defending Burma".[7] Panikkar was convinced that Burma was not in a position to defend itself and the country's domination by another power would be disastrous for India. Panikkar also understood that post-colonial nationalism would make substantial defence cooperation between Delhi and Rangoon difficult. Yet, he was confident that the logic of a defence union will suit Delhi and Rangoon. What emerged, however, was a more complex story of India-Burma defence cooperation after the Second World War.

India-Burma Friendship Treaty

The decolonisation of India and Burma in the late-1940s set the stage for redefining the framework of their bilateral relations, including defence ties. The Indian national movement strongly supported the aspirations of Burmese people for separation from the British India and independence from Britain. The Indian National Congress, in its very first session in 1885, opposed the annexation of Upper Burma, and its leaders including Mahatma Gandhi strongly backed the Burmese nationalist demand for separation from the British India.[8] The strong bonds of friendship between Jawaharlal Nehru and Burma's first premier U Nu provided the basis for managing the transition to nationalist rule. While Burma sought to reclaim its national economy from foreigners, the large Indian population present in the country was badly affected. Nehru did not let the issue derail the bilateral ties. India and Burma also shared the commitment to empower the newly liberated states, articulate their independent viewpoints on world affairs and create an area of peace in Asia amidst the then-unfolding Cold War.

Panikkar had argued that a "long-term alliance between India and Burma" would be advantageous for both countries. He considered and rejected two potential arguments against a strategic union between the two countries. He argued that the massive difference in the sizes of the two populations and the emerging Burmese nationalism could raise questions about India's dominance over Burma and might undermine the potential defence partnership between the two. He argued that the resources and location of Burma would make it so important for India that it could not afford to sour the relationship and that it was in India's interest to make a success of voluntary security association between the two.[9] On his part, Nehru seemed fully conscious of Burma's geopolitical significance and the need for great patience and understanding in building a long-term partnership with Burma.

The severe internal security threats faced by Burma in the immediate aftermath of independence provided the context for substantive Indian military assistance to Rangoon. Immediately after independence, Rangoon confronted major insurrections by the Burmese Communist Party, ethnic Karen and other militias in 1949. Rangoon was under direct threat from the rebel forces. Nu sought military assistance from India and other Commonwealth nations as well as the United States. Nehru helped convene a meeting of the Commonwealth representatives in Delhi in late-February 1949. While being empathetic to Nu's request, the meeting suggested that Burma reconcile its differences with the Karens and offered the good offices of the Commonwealth for talks on reconciliation. Rejecting the proposition as an unwanted interference in Burmese affairs, Nu reached out again to Nehru. Facilitating eventual Commonwealth assistance, and working with Pakistan and Ceylon to strengthen the hand of Rangoon, India also provided direct bilateral military and financial assistance to Burma that was acknowledged with much grace by Nu once the situation was brought under control.[10] The Indian assistance prevented the fall of Rangoon to rebels and included the supply of six Dakota transport aircraft to Burma.[11] Speaking in the Indian Parliament in March 1950, Nehru declared that India's support to Burma was not about interfering in the internal affairs of its neighbour. "It is not our purpose and is not right for us to interfere in any way with other countries, but whenever possible, we give such help as we can to our friends, without any element of interference".[12]

Beyond immediate crisis management, Nehru and Nu sought to put the bilateral relationship on a firmer footing. Nu apparently wanted an explicit agreement for military cooperation but Nehru sought to keep the defence ties informal and flexible. The idea of defence and security cooperation, however, is hinted at in the peace and friendship treaty that Nehru and Nu signed in July 1951. Article IV of the treaty says: "The two States agree that their representatives shall meet from time to time and as often as occasion requires to exchange views on matters of common interest and to consider ways and means for mutual cooperation in such matters."[13] Article II of the treaty outlines a broader sentiment declaring that "there shall be everlasting peace and unalterable friendship between the two states who shall ever strive to strengthen and develop further [the] cordial relations [already] existing between the peoples of the two countries".

Seen from the perspective of Delhi, the treaty would seem akin to the kind of security treaties that Nehru had signed with Bhutan, Nepal and Sikkim during 1949-50. The language of Article II in the treaty with Burma is entirely similar to the one found in the other three treaties. More fundamentally, it could be argued that much as Britain had developed a treaty system to secure the subcontinent from external threats, Nehru too had to structure a similar system. At the same time Nehru understood that Myanmar was very much unlike those three Himalayan kingdoms and had to be approached very differently. Unlike those Himalayan kingdoms towards which Nehru adopted the British protectorate framework, the Burmese Republic became India's partner in articulating Asia's voice on the international stage. Therefore, the security clauses were subtle and the Indo-Burmese defence cooperation was part of a larger effort to create an area of peace in Asia. It is important to note that the India-Burma friendship treaty was signed at around the same time as both countries concluded similar agreements with Indonesia. The three countries became the most vocal proponents of Asian identity in the early-1950s.[14] While, all three were members of non-alignment and opposition to the emerging military blocs in the East and the West, they also understood the importance of greater military cooperation among themselves. However, with the passage of time and the growing focus in Delhi and Rangoon on questions arising from the impact of the Cold War on Asia, the salience of the special security ties at the bilateral level steadily diminished.[15]

India's foreign policy approaches towards Myanmar from the 1960s to the early 1990s represent a classic case in which India's strategic interests were given a go-by in pursuit of moralistic policies. India during this time maintained that no effective relationship could be maintained with Myanmar because of Army rule and lack of democratic institutions. India's postures towards her Eastern neighbour Myanmar contrasted sharply with those towards Pakistan, her Western neighbour.

This approach towards Myanmar was not the least due to the presence in India of a sizeable number of Burmese displaced political families and others with connections at the higher echelons of power. The lowest point came after the 1988 people's uprising when India was the first neighbouring country to criticise the Burmese military Junta. The Indian Embassy in Rangoon actively supported the pro-democracy student activists and many entered India for shelter after the military coup in 1988. Under such pressures, after 1988 when the SLORC (State Law and Order Restoration Council) took over Myanmar, the All India Radio carried anti-Myanmar broadcasts, souring relations between the two countries still further. The anti-Myanmar broadcasts went along for a long time until the Foreign Ministry realised the damage that was being inflicted on Indo-Myanmar relations. Foreign policies are structured to further a nation's national interests and strategic goals and not the personal pre-delictions of a few political leaders. India's national interests demanded that Myanmar should remain a friendly state on the Eastern flank, that it should not come in the Chinese strategic embrace, and that at a time when Myanmar was battling for its national security and survival, it should not be subjected to meaningless propaganda on democratic norms. From 1988 to 1990, India followed a policy committed to open support of the forces of democracy and "complete disengagement" with the ruling military junta in Burma.

Instead of having a "constructive engagement" as other East Asian countries did, India's policy only resulted in China making a strategic headway from about 1988 to 1992. India's policies were all the more regrettable in that Myanmar even under Army rule and Chinese pressures did not allow anti-Indian activity from its soil. North East insurgents in their gun-running used Myanmar territory in the last leg after landing on the coast of Chittagong Hill Tracts. This also could have been curtailed earlier on in case a political and strategic dialogue existed between the two countries.

Fortunately, when former PM Narasimha Rao initiated 'Look East' policy, the long years of not nourishing the India-Myanmar links came into focus. PM Narashimha Rao reversed India's policies towards Myanmar and put initiatives into place to rebuild a viable relationship.

The China Factor

India's current defence diplomacy towards Myanmar and their broader political engagement are widely viewed through the prism of its rivalry with China. India's Defence Minister Antony's visit to Nay Pyi Taw has been projected in the media as part of this rivalry.[16] Yet when they became independent in the late-1940s, it was India that loomed large over Myanmar. But Indian strategists were conscious of the historic links between China and Myanmar and the re-emergence of China as a power of consequence after the Second World War. Panikkar also foresaw that the rise of China would complicate India's strategic calculus in Myanmar and Southeast Asia. China's "mere existence as a great military power on the borders of Burma", Panikkar argued, "and the increasing importance she will attach to the Burma Road and access to Rangoon, and the dynamics of Chinese population problems in relation to Burma and Malaya will create grave complications in India's foreign policy".[17] The triumph of the Communist Party of China in the civil war and its establishment of a People's Republic in Beijing became an important factor in the evolution of political relations between India and Burma.

The emergence of China as a communist state generated deep anxieties all across Asia; Delhi and Rangoon were no exceptions. With communist insurgencies raging in both India and Burma, there was incentive for Delhi and Rangoon to consult each other. The initial logic of bilateral defence cooperation was driven by the same consideration. At the same time, Nehru and Nu had to come to terms with the fact that they should actively seek a working relationship with communist China, a neighbour for both India and Burma. The two also concurred on the proposition that they had no interest in supporting Western efforts to isolate China. Nehru had agreed to Burma's request to be the first to recognise the People's Republic of China and India soon followed.[18] A series of developments relating to China since then have had an effect on political and security cooperation between India and Burma.

One issue was the fallout of the Chinese civil war in Burma. Rangoon was deeply concerned at the presence of Kuomintang troops the stragglers from the civil war who drifted into Burma on its territory. Rangoon objected to the transgression of its frontier by the PLA in pursuit of its defeated rivals.

When Rangoon went to the United Nations in 1953 for international support, India strongly backed the resolution, demanding disarmament, internment and evacuation of foreign troops. Speaking in the debate, India's Permanent Representative Krishna Menon said, "What hurts Burma hurts us equally. We have no military alliance but Burma is closely linked to us and it is naturally of great concern to us that she should suffer".[19] As Rangoon and Delhi pushed the Western powers to get the Formosa (now Taiwan) government to evacuate the Chinese nationalists who were in Burma, China had every reason to be pleased.

The improvement in Sino-Burmese relations during the mid-1950s was tested in 1956 amidst reports of the PLA's incursions into Burma in pursuit of the nationalist troops. Nu sought Indian assistance, and Nehru asked the Chinese Premier Zhou Enlai to discuss the problems on the frontier with Nu; Zhou accepted the advice.[20] By the turn of the 1960s though, India's ties with China were headed south and Sino-Burmese ties on the upswing. As tensions on the border with India rose, China signed a boundary settlement with Burma in 1960 that generated much unhappiness in Delhi. Rangoon sought to placate Nehru, but what irritated him was the suggestion that India should emulate Burma in resolving the boundary dispute with China. Of special concern to Nehru was the map attached to the agreement that conformed to Chinese territorial claims against India at the tri-junction with Burma.[21] Burma's neutrality during the Sino-Indian border clashes of 1962 also shocked the political classes in Delhi that had gone out of the way to support Burma in the preceding years.

During this period, China offered its first aid package to Burma and began to purchase rice at higher than market prices. Burma also discussed the possibilities of facilitating the transit of goods produced in Yunnan. The idea would not make much progress in the 1950s, but it acquired great traction by the turn of the 21st Century. The Sino-Burmese warmth, however, was disturbed once again during the years of the Cultural Revolution that rocked China for nearly a decade from the mid-1960s. Meanwhile, India and Burma signed an agreement in 1967 to delimit and demarcate their 1643 km land boundary. The China factor came to the fore again in the late-1980s, when Burma's military rulers drew close to Beijing in the aftermath of their crackdown on the pro-democracy movement and the resulting international condemnation. India's strong support to the pro-democracy movement increased the political distance between Delhi and Rangoon. But as Burma found itself isolated and China's influence began to grow rapidly, Delhi reviewed its policy and moved towards 'constructive engagement' with the military regime. Security cooperation was at the heart of India's new engagement with Burma since the early-1990s.

Economic Cooperation

Economic interest has pushed India to establish a good relationship with the Burmese junta, and it plays a very major role in the present India-Myanmar relationship. From the viewpoint of Indian industry and business, Myanmar is a bridge between India and Southeast Asian markets, and a gateway to Southeast Asia. While Indian economic relations with other ASEAN countries such as Thailand and Singapore are relatively good, Indian business sees Myanmar as a potential not only for bilateral economic cooperation but also for regional cooperation due to its geographical proximity with India. As Myanmar is part of both BIMSTEC (Bangladesh, India, Myanmar, Sri Lanka and Thailand Economic Cooperation) and ASEAN, Burma is crucial for some regional projects like the Trans-Asian highway and railway projects. (Myanmar is being linked to the rest of Southeast Asia under the trans-Asian highway project from Iran to China.) And India is keen to import gas from Myanmar. India's Oil and Natural Gas Corporation (ONGC) Videsh Ltd., is reportedly negotiating with South Korea's Daewoo International Corp. to buy a 30 per cent stake in Daewoo's offshore exploration block in the Arakan offshore in north-western Myanmar. Myanmar authorities have also suggested the possibility of opening a third border point at Paletwa township in Rakhine State in Myanmar and South Mizoram in India. To boost border trade, the Government of India has agreed to equip better communication facilities in Moreh and also to sanction necessary funds to the government of Manipur State for organising seminar-cum-awareness programmes/workshops on border trade. Moreover, the Central government was considering a 100-crores budget proposal of the Manipur government to set up an "Export Promotion Industrial Park" in Manipur State.

Myanmar possesses resources that are required desperately by India e.g. natural gas, minerals, and pulses. Myanmar has 2.54 trillion cubic metres of natural gas reserves and largest copper mines in Asia. India public and private sectors can invest in Myanmar's underdevelopment secondary and tertiary sectors like educational, telecom and healthcare systems. That can enable binding relationship that can change the economic character of North-eastern

India. It would be in India's interests to focus on areas west of Irrawaddy River and south to strengthen bilateral relations through trade and investment links. Reforms presently underway in Myanmar have opened up enormous economic opportunities for several countries. It is now up to New Delhi to prioritise the implementation of identified projects, so that the goal of economically integrating its Northeast with Myanmar does not simply remain a nightmare. While China is far ahead of India in engaging Myanmar through military and economic cooperation, India has still got the option of enhancing its economic cooperation with Myanmar. Moreover, Myanmar's venture for regional economic cooperation and military procurement beyond China should be used by India for taking the dual advantage of securing energy resources and strengthening geostrategic cooperation in countering Chinese influence. This will depend on how India counters the emerging military threat and maintains a balance in engaging China both on the western and eastern flanks.

Strategic Cooperation

Strategic analysts have identified many drivers of India's intensive outreach to Burma in the last two decades.[22] These include the competition with China for influence, access to natural resources, connectivity to India's Northeast, and building a land bridge to Southeast Asia. These factors are indeed important, but none of them more consequential for India than the imperatives of border management. While the China factor certainly shapes the overall strategic environment in which India will have to pursue its relations with Myanmar, Delhi's approach in many sectors has an autonomous logic of its own. Having inherited a complex frontier with restive minorities that were not fully integrated with their respective new nation-states, both India and Myanmar confronted quite early on the problems of securing their borders and recognised the importance of bilateral cooperation.

After India outlined a policy of constructive engagement with the military in Myanmar in the early-1990s, cooperation between the security forces on both sides of the border has steadily deepened. To be sure, there were many initial glitches. When the two armies were conducting an important joint operation—code-named Operation Golden Bird—in 1995, the President of India announced that Aung San Suu Kyi, Myanmar's pro-democracy leader, was chosen for the 1993 Jawaharlal Nehru Award for International Understanding. The Burmese army suspended the operations. India then moved to a more consistent position of engagement with the Burmese armed forces.[23] While India stepped up its efforts to improve connectivity with Myanmar, develop road links through Myanmar to Thailand and beyond, and encouraged its companies to take up projects in Myanmar, security cooperation remained the most sustained feature of the bilateral relationship.

The joint and coordinated campaigns against the insurgents on both sides of the border since the mid-1990s have been rooted in the shared political understanding and confidence that neither side would give shelter to elements hostile to the other. On the other borders of India, with Pakistan and Bangladesh, Delhi's strategy had focused on fencing, in the absence of requisite cooperation from its neighbours. In the case of Myanmar, Delhi would focus on prevailing through cooperation with Nay Pyi Taw's security forces.[24] The general assessment is that the security cooperation between India and Myanmar has been a major success. "The drastic reduction in insurgency-related violence in Manipur and Nagaland—states sharing borders with Myanmar—has allowed New Delhi and Nay Pyi Taw to explore policy options to seal the gains".[25] These include stronger institutional exchanges between local governments and military units across the border, arms supply and capacity building. The initial focus on security cooperation on the land frontier has steadily been complemented by maritime cooperation.

The institutional exchanges have intensified over the last decade to include all the major stakeholders on both sides—including the paramilitary forces, the armies, and the defence and interior ministries. Frequent high-level exchanges at the national level have been complemented by local liaison among the officials at the border. During Prime Minister Manmohan Singh's visit to Myanmar in 2012, the two sides chose to expand their security cooperation to a more comprehensive partnership for development cooperation in the border regions. Manmohan Singh and Thein Sein signed a Memorandum of Understanding on India-Myanmar Border Area Development that would help promote prosperity along their shared frontiers. In the joint statement issued at the end of Manmohan Singh's visit, the two sides identified "the need for special focus on the development and prosperity of the people in bordering areas", agreed on cooperation "to bring about overall socio-economic development in the border areas by undertakingboth infrastructure development and micro-economic projects, including upgradation of roads and construction of schools, health centres, bridges, agriculture and related training activities".[26] The framework detailed in the MoU on border area development is a new approach, and it remains to be seen how the two sides will implement this.

The first-ever visit to Myanmar by an Indian defence minister was Shri A.K. Antony who travelled to Nay Pyi Taw on 21 January 2013. Although no major agreements were signed during his visit, Antony's brief sojourn in Myanmar underlined Delhi's political commitment to deepen security cooperation between the two countries.

While recognising the importance of non-traditional security, India has also slowly expanded its focus on hard core security cooperation. There has been greater frequency of exchanges by senior military officials. The three service chiefs were in Myanmar within a span of 18 months during 2011-13. "These visits and other exchanges", according to a statement in Delhi following Antony's visit to Myanmar, "had provided each side a better understanding of mutual concerns, needs and strengths".[27] Although there were no specific agreements, the two sides reportedly discussed the possibilities of greater Indian support for building up the capacities of Myanmar's armed forces. Media reports quoting defence ministry officials have said Delhi is willing to respond to requests from Myanmar for across-the-board expansion of training opportunities in India.[28] Upgrading of Myanmar's military equipment has been another item on the bilateral agenda. During a visit to Myanmar in 2006, the chief of Indian Air Force reportedly offered to modernise the avionics in Myanmar's fighter inventory. India also had plans to establish a naval aviation training centre in Myanmar.[29]

Of special importance to India has been the expansion of naval engagement with Myanmar. While the initial and enduring Indian focus has been on cooperation between the armies and security forces along their long border, the maritime significance of Myanmar was not lost on the Indian defence decision-makers. Reports of a Chinese base in the Coco Islands owned by Myanmar in the Bay of Bengal generated much public awareness of maritime issues in the Bay of Bengal.[30] Myanmar was quick to dispel India's concerns. It offered Delhi access to the Coco Islands and let its officials see for themselves the inaccuracy of those reports. This episode and the Chinese have developed a commercial port at Sittwe on the Arakan coast triggered strong interest in the Indian Navy for sustained engagement with Myanmar. This has covered frequent port calls by India's naval ships, the negotiation of turn-around arrangements for Indian ships while transiting to the Malacca Straits, the inclusion of Myanmar Navy in the biennial 'Milan' exercises in the Andaman Sea, coordinated naval patrols to secure the long maritime frontier between the two countries in the Bay of Bengal, and the Indian Navy's participation in the humanitarian relief operations after Cyclone Nargis devastated Myanmar in 2008.[31] In early 2012, Myanmar was part of a 14-nation joint naval exercise with India in the Bay of Bengal aimed at combating piracy and terrorism. The stability of Malacca Straits remains a key concern for the economies of Indo-Pacific including India and Myanmar. China too remains worried about the US naval presence in the region. It views its trans-Burma Shwe pipeline project as a possible solution to its Malacca dilemma.

Transfer of Indian arms to Myanmar is a more interesting but controversial issue. India's supplies of military hardware "ranged from Islander maritime patrol aircraft, naval gun-boats to 105mm light artillery guns, mortars, grenade launchers and rifles" as well as non-lethal equipment including radars.[32] More recently, India has reportedly offered the sale of military helicopters to Myanmar and has agreed to train Myanmar pilots.[33] The supply of Indian hardware has unsurprisingly invited political controversy. At a time when Myanmar's military regime was isolated and was the target of many international sanctions, the Indian supply of arms was criticised by the international community as well as by Myanmar's political activists. Delhi responded by arguing that much of the equipment it had supplied was non-lethal and defensive in nature. At the end of 2012, India was accused of transferring weapons, bought from Sweden, to Myanmar's armed forces in violation of European sanctions. These weapons have been reportedly used by the Myanmar forces against Kachin rebels in the north of the country.[34] While India promised to investigate the issue, some Indian analysts are cautioning against entering into a substantive arms supply relationship with Myanmar at a time when its armed forces are continuing operations against a number of rebel groups. They suggest, instead, that India "work towards facilitating a rapprochement among the Burmans and other ethnic groups".[35]

At a general level, India's contemporary engagement with its eastern neighbour has been marked by a big gap between potential and performance.[36] In the defence field, in particular, structural constraints in Delhi have limited India's record on the ground. These include the absence of an effective institutional framework for security diplomacy, the inadequate defence industrial base, and the inability of the Indian government and the private sector to undertake and operate critical dual-use infrastructure like ports. As Myanmar seeks to modernise its military, India's emphasis for quite some time to come is likely to be on training and capacity building rather than arms supply.

In terms of objectives, India's main goal will continue to be the stabilisation of its land frontiers with Myanmar. What started in the early-1990s as simple cooperation in the area of counter-insurgency across the frontiers has been transformed into a more comprehensive engagement on 'border management'. This transformation is now being reinforced with the ambitious plan for bringing development into the restive areas. As India's stakes in the maritime space rise, Myanmar's importance in India's naval calculus is likely to steadily rise. As the major powers begin to see the eastern Indian Ocean and the Western Pacific as a single maritime theatre, the Indo-Pacific, the Andaman Sea is gaining strategic salience. Along with the South China Sea, it forms the critical link between the Indian and Pacific Oceans.

As China seeks to protect its vital sea lines of communication through the Malacca Straits amidst fears of American efforts to disrupt them, and develops alternative routes to the Indian Ocean, Myanmar's waters in the Bay of Bengal are likely to become contested zones in the coming years.[37] Myanmar provides the natural outlet to the sea for the provinces in Southwest China as well as a route to import oil and natural gas into China by skirting the Malacca Straits. The emerging Chinese interest in the Bay of Bengal has aroused concerns in India. If China is focused on North-South connectivity through Myanmar, India is looking at developing East-West connectivity through the land and waters of Myanmar. Realists in Delhi have begun to recognise that India's objectives cannot be about preventing deeper cooperation between China and Myanmar but expanding India's own engagement with the eastern neighbour.

It is not a surprise that India's recent security diplomacy with Myanmar has too often been framed in terms of a rivalry with China.[38] While a rising China does shape the regional environment, Indian security cooperation with Myanmar, as we have noted, has its own logic and limitations. While there is an undeniable element of rivalry between India and China, their competition in Myanmar has never been symmetric.[39] As its international isolation comes to an end, Myanmar is diversifying its great power relations, and it no longer has to rely on the goodwill of China and India or seek to play one against the other. The United States' outreach to Myanmar and the prospect of resuming defence contacts between the two set a very different context to the geopolitics of Myanmar.[40] Myanmar's incipient defence contacts with the West, its participation in the construction of an ASEAN defence community, and its expanding engagement with Japan and Russia tend to liberate India's own security diplomacy with Nay Pyi Taw. For, Delhi no longer needs to bear the presumed burden of balancing China in Myanmar.

Conclusion

The emergence of a vibrant and independent Myanmar embedded in a strong regional institution like the ASEAN, therefore, is in India's strategic interest. The reality is that, since partition and independence, India has not been in a position to guarantee this outcome on its own in Myanmar. An outward-looking and self-assured Myanmar will have enough common ground with India to facilitate deeper security cooperation, the foundation for which has already been laid. The real challenge for India lies in improving its own defence capacities to respond to some of Myanmar's security needs and demands and emerge as a reliable partner for Nay Pyi Taw in a few specific areas.

The round of sanctions on Myanmar, lifted or suspended, provides enough opportunity for economic activity to surge. The country has already displayed the courage not to sink any deeper into a Chinese orbit. Considering the fact that President Thein Sein must had to battle the hardliners, the road ahead requires constant vigil as well as rewarding incentives. India's support to Myanmar in lifting of sanctions can become a major opportunity for establishing a lasting political, economic and social relationship. India can help Myanmar in political reforms and a sustainable constitutional order. That would be helpful not for Myanmar but also for the Northeast regional stability. Besides, a democratic, independent minded Myanmar is more likely to lean towards India than China.

Long years of non-alignment did not in any way serve India's national security interests and needs. Collective security groupings are not the order of day though the future does portend that the regional economic groupings would ultimately don security colours too, if nothing else in terms of conflict resolution or conflict management. Strategic partnerships do provide intermediate solutions, especially when they are bi-lateral in nature and incorporate economic co-operation and assistance in a major way.

In India's quest for strategic partnerships, Myanmar acquires top priority being a vital geo-strategic entity on her Eastern flank and sharing a long border with China. Myanmar's providing the major Eastern littoral to the Bay of

Bengal imparts added strategic significance to India's naval strategies. Myanmar has not permitted China to turn it into a strategic de-stablising entity for India, like Pakistan. India should therefore make a determined effort to forge a strategic partnership with Myanmar.

END NOTES

1. Both terms, *Myanmar and Burma*, are used in this paper.
2. Hlaing, Kyaw Yin and Talor Robert H, Myanmar: beyond politics to societal imperatives, Institute of Southeast Asian Studies, 2005, p. 40.
3. "Exchange of Visits", Embassy of India in Myanmar, Ministry of External Affairs, Government of India, available at http://www.indiaembassy.net.mm/index.php?option=com_content&view=article&id=52&Itemid=63&lang=en.
4. Htin Aung, *The Stricken Peacock: Anglo-Burmese Relations, 1752-1948*, (Lieden: M. Nijhoff, 1965).
5. C. RajaMohan, "India's Security Cooperation with Myanmar: Prospect and Retrospect", *ISAS Working Paper No. 166*, 21 February 2013.
6. Ashley Jackson, *The British Empire and the Second World War* (London: Hambledon Continuum, 2006), pp. 351-404; Leslie Anders, *The Ledo Road: General Joseph W. Stilwell's Highway to China* (Oklahoma; University of Nebraska Press, 1965)
7. K.M. Panikkar, *The Future of South East Asia* (London: George Allen & Unwin, 1943), p. 45.
8. Bimla Prasad, *The Origins of Indian Foreign Policy* (Calcutta: Bookland, 1960), pp. 36-38.
9. Panikkar, op. cit., pp. 45-50
10. Richard Butwell, *U Nu of Burma* (Stanford, CA: Stanford University Press, 1963), p. 186.
11. Soe Myint, *Burma File: A Question of Democracy* (Singapore: Marshall Cavendish), p.89.
12. Jawaharlal Nehru, *India's Foreign Policy: Selected Speeches*, September 1946-April 1961 (New Delhi: Publications Division, 1974), pp. 292-293.
13. Available at http://www.commonlii.org/in/other/treaties/INTSer/1951/12.html
14. The India-Burma agreement was signed on 7 July 1951; India-Indonesia accord on 3 March 1951; and Indonesia and Burma signed their agreement on 31 March 1951.
15. Uma Shankar Singh, *Burma and India, 1948-1962* (New Delhi: Oxford and IBH, 1979), p 63.
16. Vivek Raghuvanshi, "India, Myanmar seek closer ties with an eye on China", *Defense News*, 22 January 2013; see also Press Trust of India, "Myanmar's ties with India, Japan and Western countries concern China", *The Times of India*, 6 January 2013.
17. Panikkar, op. cit., pp.35-36.
18. K.M. Panikkar, *In Two Chinas: Memoirs of a Diplomat* (London: George Allen & Unwin, 1955), p. 66.
19. Uma Shankar Singh, op. cit, pp. 63-65.
20. Butwell, op. cit., p. 187.
21. Uma Shankar Singh, op. cit., pp. 74-79.
22. Rajiv Bhatia, "India must strengthen bilateral ties with Myanmar", *Economic Times*, March 23, 2012
23. Soe Myint, op. cit., p. 99.
24. Bibhu Prasad Routray, "Myanmar and India's Northeast: Border Cooperation, Better

Connectivity and Economic Integration", *IPCS Article no. 3788* (New Delhi: Institute of Peace and Conflict Studies, January 10, 2013.)

25. Ibid.
26. Joint Statement on the occasion of the visit of Prime Minister of India Dr Manmohan Singh to Myanmar; available at http://pib.nic.in/newsite/erelease.aspx?r elid=84517
27. "India and Myanmar should work together to address common concerns: Antony", Press Information Bureau, Government of India, New Delhi, 22 January 2013.
28. Rajat Pandit, "Now, Antony headed for Myanmar to bolster defence ties", *The Times of India*, 5 January 2013.
29. Vijay Sakhuja, "India and Myanmar: Choices for Military Cooperation", *ICWA Issue Brief* (New Delhi: Indian Council of World Affairs, January 2013).
30. Andrew Selth, "Burma, China and the Myth of Military Bases", *Asian Security*, 3 (3), (2007), pp. 279-307.
31. Sakhuja, op. cit.
32. Pandit, op. cit.
33. Vivek Raghuvanshi, "Amid warming ties, India may give Helos to Myanmar", *Defense News*, 26 November 2012.
34. David Stout, "Indian officials accused of providing Burma with embargoed weapons", *Democratic Voice of Burma*, 25 January 2013, available at http://www.dvb.no/news/indian-officials-accused-of-providing-burma-with-embargoed-weapons/25199
35. Gautam Sen, "Cooperation between Indian and Myanmar Armed Forces: Need to Move Away from a Weapons & Equipment Supply-Based Relationship", *IDSA Comment* (New Delhi: Institute for Defence Studies and Analyses, 15 January 2013.)
36. Renaud Egretau, "India's Ambitions in Burma: More Frustration than Success?", *Asian Survey*, 48 (6), (November/December 2008), pp. 936-957.
37. Vijay Sakhuja, "Bay of Bengal Littorals in Chinese Strategic Calculus", *China Brief*, 10 (14), 9 July 2010.
38. J. Mohan Malik, "Sino-Indian Rivalry in Myanmar: Implications for Regional Security", *Contemporary Southeast Asia*, 16 (2), (September 1994), pp. 137-56; Harsh V Pant, "China Shakes up the Maritime Balance in the Indian Ocean", *Strategic Analysis*, 36 (3), (May-June 2012), pp. 364-68.
39. Thant Myint U, *Where China Meets India: Burma and the New Crossroads of Asia* (New York: Farrar, Straus and Giroux, 2012).
40. Gwen Robinson, "US courts military contact with Myanmar", *Financial Times*, 20 September 2012; Sam Holmes, "U.S. Military visits Myanmar, Stepping toward New Role", *Wall Street Journal*, 21 October 2012.

PART II

Key Regional Developments in the Indo-Pacific

8

Myanmar towards Democratic Transition

Ganganath Jha

Myanmar is strategically located between South Asia and Southeast Asia and shares contiguous land frontiers with five countries, namely India, China, Bangladesh, Thailand and Laos. It has a land area of more than 676,000 sq kms and a coastline stretching over 2,200 kilometres. Its frontiers have prominent natural frontiers in the form of mountain ranges in the northwest, north and east and rivers in the west and south-east. There are eight major ethnic group in the country namely; Bamar, Chin, Kachin, Kaya, Mon, Rakhine and Shans. According to 1983 census, Bamar constituted 69 percent of the population followed by Shan 8.5 percent, Karens 6.2 percent and Rakhine 4.5 percent. Buddhist comprises 89.4 percent, of the total population, Christians 4.9 percent and Muslims 3.9 percent. The country is endowed with rich natural resource where the soil is fertile and oil and natural gas are in abundance. It has hydrocarbon reserves of 2.512 trillion cubic meters (TMC) of natural gas and 3.2 billion barrels of crude oil.[1] The hydropower potential is put at 37000 megawatt. Besides it has potentials to produce hydro-power to fulfil the needs of the countries in the neighbourhood. Myanmar is also a part of golden triangle, where opium is produced for the global market. Opium production in Myanmar was estimated to be from 450 to 600 metric tons in 1985, which increased to 1470-2000 metric tons in 1989.[2] The production showed increasing trends in the post 1990 era because it was considered a much needed source of income for the military as well as the insurgent.[3]

Historical Overview

Burma, called Myanmar since 1989, is resourcefully a rich nation. It was richest of all countries in Southeast Asia on the eve of its independence but became poorest under the military rule of General Ne Win. Although Ne Win had participated in the freedom struggle and supported Bogyoke Aung San, he played an ambitious role as commander in chief of the Armed Forces under the leadership of Prime Minister U Nu (1948-1962). General Ne Win did not like federal ideas of civilian leaders and therefore led a coup d'etat in 1962 to disband democratic system. Ne Win clamped authoritarian rule and centralised all power of the government to crush the ethnic demands for autonomy of the Karens, Shans, Kachins, Chins and Royingyas. His policy of snapping ties at the international level, his brand of socialism and crusade for nationalisation were aimed at strengthening the role of military in the politics of the country. He remained in power till 1988 and this period was sufficient to destroy democratic institutions built in Burma in the pre and post independence period. He resigned after August 1988 uprising but this did not usher into the democratic era. General Saw Maung who was more hawkish in temperament, came into power and ruthlessly crushed the aspirations for restoration of democracy.

However, General Saw Maung promised to hold general elections soon to divert public anger. The general elections were indeed held in May 1990 which was free and fair. All the parties supported by the military got crushing defeats. The oppositions led by National League for Democracy (NLD) got a massive mandate. It got 392 out of 485 seats of Parliament (Pyidaungsu Hluttaw) and its allies, Karens, Shans, Rohingyas, Kachins and Chins etc, which got most of the seats in their respective areas, supported Aung San Suu Kyi to from the new government. But the military refused to hand over power and passed order 1/90 to nullify election results.[4]

There were worldwide condemnation of military rulers, but they did not take the cognizance of the condemnation.[5] On the other hand, they become vengeful against NLD supporters who were persecuted, jailed or compelled to seek asylum outside the country. Any opposition to government was violently crushed. The economic situation started deteriorating and Burma had already achieved the status of Least Development Country (LDC) in

1987. The problem of food, clothing and shelter became acute as a result of internal turmoil and also because the western world had imposed trade sanctions.

The national honour of the Burmese had suffered setbacks due to its poverty, lack of democracy and human rights. There were some who projected Myanmar as a rogue state and there were some who questioned the role of China in building military bases in Myanmar. International opinion was so adverse that Myanmar herself had refused to take ASEAN's rotating chair in 2006. It had to do something to take care of the adverse world opinion. Thus, it was necessary to evolve constitutional processes to indicate a roadmap for transition to democracy.

In 2007, Thailand, its neighbour adopted a new constitution which protected the interests of the military and on that basis the elections were held for democratic transition. The military leaders argued that they were not interested in remaining clinged to power permanently. The military had come to power only a year before after ousting Thaksin Shinawatra and thereafter completed the constitutional processes to hold election for the restoration of civilian rule. In Myanmar, the military remained in power for decades and it was not serious for transition to civilian rule. However, the experiences of Thailand inspired them to finalise a constitution in which the prerogatives of the military was to be retained and at the same time give an impression that they too were not interested in remaining clinged to power now.

But there were differences in the system of the two countries. Thailand has a constitutional monarchy and its Royal Privy Council's approval is sufficient to get the constitution passed. On the other hand, Myanmar had a Constituent Assembly to write a constitution in which there was no consensus at the outset.[6] NLD, the main opposition had been marginalised and thus it had walked out of the Constituent Assembly in protest. It had boycotted participation in the constitution making process because their opinions were ignored. The members left in the Constituent Assembly, who did not support boycott, were not opposed to military viewpoint. The people of the country did not have much expectation from the constitution makers. The domestic situation worsened and especially after the silent demonstration of the Buddhist monks against spiralling price rise in 2007. The international community continued to apply pressure on Myanmar for change and so something to suggest that it also belong to the civilised world and cared for its people. Thus, attention was given on constitution making processes and getting approval of the people through a referendum.

The new constitution of Myanmar was finalised and approved under the guidance of the military in 2008 and the government announced that the elections will be held on 7 November 2010. The opposition group, and then led by NLD boycotted participation in that election. Suu Kyi continued to remain in house arrest and the NLD had the legitimate grudge that their opinion was not solicited while adopting a new constitution. NLD had a grievance that the new constitution protects the monopoly of the military in politics of the country. Despite NLD boycott, the elections were held in November 2010 in which 42 parties contested. Union Solidarity and development Party (USDP) of Thein Sein, National Democratic Force (NDF) and pro-establishment National Unity Party (NUP) etc fielded their candidates and USDP got the majority of seats, winning 129 seats of Pyithu Hluttaw (Lower House) out of 224 and 259 seats of Amyotha Hluttaw (Upper House) out of 440 seats. The election results did not suggest any drastic change in the politics of the country as Thein Sein had military background, but his government which came into power in March 2011 started showing dynamism and vision to transform the system.

General Than Shwe resigned in March 2011 and he was replaced by Thein Sein who always attached important to reconciliation and harmony in the society. He began to take initiative to contact the opposition leaders for peace and development. His agenda included release of political prisoners, freedom of the press, right to form unions and finally the democratic transition. He started taking initiatives for peace talks with opposition leaders and make constitution arrangements to resolve ethnic violence. His initiative, actions and statements proved his sincerity and his commitments for reforms became popular. His peace overtures to NLD were reciprocated and Suu Kyi extended support. When the government announced to hold by-election for 45 seats of the two houses of Parliament, NLD agreed to participate.

On 1 April 2012 the by-elections were held in Myanmar in which 17 political parties contested. There were 157 candidates for 45 seats of Parliament and all the major political parties were given equal opportunity to campaign and win. Suu Kyi decided to contest from Kawhmu constituency.[7] The NLD fielded candidates for 44 out of 45 vacant seats of Parliament. There were election observers from the UN, EU and ASEAN and the election was held peacefully. The NLD volunteers while canvassing were always carrying NLD flags, Suu Kyi Logos, and sang nationalist songs. Suu Kyi attracted crowds everywhere that she went for canvassing. She talked about alleviation of poverty and price rise which was possible through cooperation and reconciliation. She wanted to address the issues of trust deficit between civilians and the military.[8] Suu Kyi talked about helping the government in bringing about good governance. She stated that process and institution of the government produce result to meet the need of the society by making the best use of the resources available. It needs to insure a balance in utilisation of resources and creating an environment conducive for sustainable development. She appealed to the voters to vote for NLD and the response was encouraging. Myanmar's state media confirmed on 4 April 2012 that NLD was victorious in 43 constitutions out of 44 that it had contested.

Suu Kyi has been constantly talking about political and judicial reform. Union Parliament (Pyidaungsu Hluttaw) has large number of nominated members. According to 2008 constitution, 25 percent of the seats of union Parliament are reserved for the military. Thus 56 out of 224 seats of Pyithu Hluttaw and 110 out of 440 seats of Amyotha Hluttaw are reserved for the military. The chief of staff of the Defense forces is the powerful person, beyond the control of the civilians. He will nominate 25 percent of all members of Union Parliament, State and Regional Assemblies. Thus, the loyalties of such members are towards the military and their opinion is biased. There are several other critical issues that require to be amended. For instance, fundamental rights are not guaranteed. The President is not answerable to the election commission or any authority. He has absolute rights to appoint Chief Ministers, Chief justices and Attorney General. Again the military representatives in civil services are overwhelming. Active and retired military officers are appointed as officers and executives. However, provision which is a matter of concern is that the Supreme Commander would assume state power on a national emergency if there is danger of disintegration of the Union, national solidarity as well as the loss of national sovereignty. There is no check on the central government being centralised are the stumbling blocks to implement reforms. Again the process of amendment has been made very cumbersome. The constitution can be amended only with the approval of 75 percent of the members of the both Houses of Parliament and one half of the eligible voters.

There has been demand for autonomy or the federal system to bring ethnic minorities in the mainstream but such issues will demand structural reforms.

The NLD has been demanding rules for a genuine federal system by reorganisation of states, whereby the states could be organised on the basis of ethnicity. According to NLD sources, at least eight states should be created on the basis of ethnicity, namely, Bamars, Chins, Kachins, Karens, Kaya Mons, Rohingyas and Shans. They believe that federalism is a pre-requisite for establishing reconciliation, peace and development in Myanmar. This is possible only if the military and civilians have understanding of each other and cooperate hand in hand to achieve their goals of nation building and prosperity.[9]

However the aim of this chapter is to examine recent development in the politics of Myanmar, which needs to be understood in its proper perspective. There are observers who find it against the Chinese interests. There are others who find it pro-western and pro-Indian. To me the developments in Myanmar are neither pro-western nor pro-Indian or anti-Chinese. Whatever has happened since the release of Suu Kyi from her house arrest in 2010, are the steps towards democratisation. The restoration of democracy has been the demands of the people of Myanmar, which were strongly supported by the leaders of the Association of Southeast Asian Nation (ASEAN), whose policy of "Constructive Engagement" with Myanmar had been mooted to detract Myanmar's total dependence on China. The ASEAN leaders at the same time thought that greater interaction with ASEAN will tempt Myanmar for democratisation in tune with the rest of the ASEAN countries. Myanmar was offered the membership of ASEAN in 1997 but nothing was done against the political system to end military rule. Though General Khin Nyunt came out with a roadmap for restoring democracy in Myanmar, but he was ousted from power. General Than Shwe did not like to hear the name of Daw Aung San Suu Kyi. Many leaders in ASEAN felt frustrated that the policy of constructive engagement could not yield the desired results.

The constitution of Myanmar which was announced in 2008 was opposed by the activists of the democracy movement. When general elections were announced in November 2010 for the formation of a popular government, structural changes were not envisaged, but it was to legitimate the position of the ruling establishment. However, when the elections were held, the changes in the political order started, which is momentous. General Than Shwe paved the path for the emergence of ex-General Thein Sein, who has a vision and agenda to transform Myanmar from authoritarian to democratic system. He has displayed overtures to establish rapprochement with Daw Aung

San Suu Kyi and other civilian leaders. He has taken steps for reconciliation with the opposition groups and adopted policies for reconstruction and nation building. Unlike General Than Shwe, he is trying to gain the trust of the general people and end isolation and trust deficit between government and people. President Thein Sein has already taken steps to introduce changes in the domestic and foreign policy of Myanmar which is highly appreciated by the ASEAN and the free world. The changes in the politics of Myanmar suits geostrategic interests of India, which treats Myanmar as a gateway to Asia-Pacific. Any connectivity through land and sea routes to the ASEAN region cannot avoid Myanmar, whose support and access is important for the success of Look East policy, Mekong-Ganga Cooperation, BIMSTEC and ASEAN.

Changes in the Domestic Policy

Now let us examine the changes in domestic policy of Myanmar that has been adopted in the post 2010 era. First of all, Thein Sein became the new president, who had his road map to cooperate with the civilians and resolve the shortage of rice, milk and fruits in the country. He thought that the cooperation of the civilian leaders, especially Suu Kyi is important and in that endeavour, he sought the cooperation of U Aung Kyi, the minister of labour and social welfare. U Aung Kyi was one of those leaders of the government who had some rapport with Suu Kyi, who took up this task very seriously. He succeeded in arranging a meeting between Suu Kyi and Sein on 21 August 2011, which paved the path for reconciliation and cooperation with civilian leaders.

The meeting between Thein Sein and Suu Kyi was held at Naypyitaw with the photography of Bogyoke Aung San in the background. This was different experience from the past as the photographs of military leaders were missing from the venue. The contents of the talks included the matters pertaining to the release of political prisoners, end of ethnic conflict and the political role of Suu Kyi in future.[10] The agenda of the meeting which had been included in the four points agreed by both were the following: (a) To work together for governments stability, (b) To cooperate for country's economic and social development, (c) To shelve disputed views for evolving the democratic system and (d) To continue dialogue.[11]

This meeting was extremely successful as both sides were satisfied with the outcome. Now the photographs of Suu Kyi and Thein Sein together, were displayed and sincere efforts were made on both sides for reconciliation and cooperation. Neither Suu Kyi nor Thein Sein allowed their prejudices to be discussed. Suu Kyi must have had the grievances that she had been persecuted ever since 1989. She had been jailed or kept under house arrest on flimsy grounds and her party NLD had been banned. In fact, when general elections on 27 May 1990 had been held, NLD had got 80 percent of seats and 60 per cent of votes. In ordinary situation, she was to be handed over power of the government. But the military leaders decided otherwise. They pleaded that the elections were simply to form constituent assembly to formulate new constitution. SLORC Declaration no.1/90 spelled out steps towards civilian rule that precluded transfer of power to the NLD.[12] There were reign of terror against all those who talked about Suu Kyi and when she was about to be released before 2010 elections, fresh charges of allowing trespassing were slapped to keep her continued in house arrest till the elections were over.[13] Suu Kyi did not allow all those issues to come in the way of dialogues. On the other hand, Thein Sein also did not display prejudices of the military that Suu Kyi had proximity with ethnic leaders and also that she was a threat to the unity of nation. Thein Sein sought cooperation with Suu Kyi in this meeting and it was warmly reciprocated.

Suu kyi wanted cooperation with the military for national solidarity and communal harmony. After her release from house arrest on 13 November 2010, she had expressed her eagerness to have a dialogue with the military leaders. The continued dialogue was projected as a key to bring about national reconciliation and harmonious social conditions. As the trust deficit prevailed and general public and the military Generals both felt insecure, we have to work hand in hand to feel safe and secure. While addressing the crowds gathered to welcome her release, Suu Kyi had stated, "I am glad to see so many people here and so happy to be free. This is a time to be quiet and a time to talk. People must work in unison. Only then we can achieve our goal."[14] However no initiative for dialogues was visible for nine months following her release, but when the meeting was arranged in August 2011, roadmap for restoration of democracy became clear.

Now the first thing that needed attention was the release of 200 political prisoners who were languishing in the jails. A student leader named Min Ko Naing had been arrested in 1989 and was awarded 65 years of jail sentence for supporting the democracy movement. Another leader, U Gambira of All Burma Monks Alliance, was in jail for supporting anti-military demonstrations. Comedian Zargnar who had mobilised funds for relief work in the aftermath of cyclone Nargis had been convicted as an external agent fomenting trouble in Myanmar.[15] Tint Swe, a powerful leader of NLD and foreign minister in the Nnational Coalition Government of the Union of Burma (NCGUB), formed in exile at a rebel camp on Thai-Myanmar border in 1990 was persecuted to go out of the country and remain in exile. There were several such cases which needed attention so that their viewpoint could be taken for reconciliation and to assure welfare of the masses in Myanmar. Thus the parleys with the government officials started and positive result were witnessed. The Parliament passed a bill entitled "Peaceful Assembly and Procession Bill", allowing citizen to stage peaceful protests. Although there is a provision that advance permission should be taken for demonstrations, yet it is regarded as a major step towards political liberalisation. The farmer's groups in Yangon's Dagon Township and other places have already staged protest demonstrations against forced takeover of their lands for government projects and the regime has agreed to pay compensation.[16]

Most of the political prisoners have been released and the press is allowed to report about politics and crime. In October 2011, a new Labour law has been passed under which Myanmar's workers are entitled to stage protested and set up labour unions which were banned in the past.[17] The President has promulgated a new media law to end censorship aimed at institutionalising the right to speech and expression. The Times of India has editorially commented on 27 August 2012 that Myanmar abolished pre-publication censorship of the media after a span of nearly five decades. The move does away with the earlier practice of submitting news reports and articles for vetting to the country's Press scrutiny and Registration department prior to publication. Read along with efforts to pass a new legislation to upgrade media laws, it marks a significant departure from the previous military regime that used strict censorship to curtail criticism of the junta and its policies. The move to ease media restrictions also bears testimony to the commitment of President Thein Sein and his government to democratic reforms. While commenting about it India's former foreign secretary, Shyam Saran has remarked that "the government has recognised the right to public protests, and made Labour Unions and strikes a legitimate right of workers. Restrictions on access to the internet have been relaxed and there is greater media freedom. The pace with which these changes have been coming has led even liberal elements to express the fear that there may be backlash. It appears that Thein Sein has the support of younger military leaders who wish to see a steady economic and political transformation of their country.[18]

Another landmark initiative is to assuage, the bitter feelings of ethnic minorities.[19] In 1962, Ne Win had staged a military coup d'etat to prevent the legislation aimed at granting autonomy to frontier provinces i.e. Shans, Karens, Kachins, Chins and Rohingyas. He was of the firm view that if the frontier provinces of Myanmar will get autonomy, the union of Burma will disintegrate. His strong views against ethnic minorities in the frontier areas never changed. His successors, General Saw Maung and General Than Shwe also treated ethnic minorities as anti-national and did everything to alienate them from decision making and nation building. It is only after the advent of Thein Sein that dialogues have started for ending their alienation from the national mainstream. The NLD had a meeting with all the ethnic leaders at Kale on 22 October 2010, which called for a federal system based on equity and democracy to be established through a second Panglong Conference.[20] In fact, the first Panglong agreement had been signed on the eve of independence of Myanmar whereby all the top leaders had agreed to concede autonomy to ethnic areas and there was also a provision that if the autonomous areas were not satisfied with a Centre Rule, they were entitled to secede. However, the main architect of the agreement, Aung San, who had signed the Panglong agreement, was assassinated subsequently and the agreement was kept under the carpet by his successor.[21] However, when six decades later, the meeting of ethnic leaders was held at Kale and Kale Declaration was announced, they once again reiterated their support for the provisions of Panglong Agreement. It emphasised that dialogues with ethnic leaders are important and the ways to resolve the problems of the Kachins, Karens, Shans, Chins or Rohingyas can be found with continued dialogues and understanding.[22] In view with the resolve of Kale Declaration, Suu Kyi has appealed in Parliament to amend and enact laws to safeguard the right of ethnic minorities, making in clear that this will mean more than preserving their language and culture.

Suu Kyi has refused the ideas of separatism and violence and argued that the desired objective can be achieved through peaceful and nonviolent means. She had stated that she agreed with the broad objective of Panglong Agreement but she will never support secession of any part of the country. The issue of autonomy can be discussed under the rubric of federal structure and her opinion is supported by majority of ethnic leaders. Kuensai Jai-Yen, a Shan intellectual is quoted as saying that, "Of course the decisive authority is in junta's hands, but we have only Suu Kyi who holds Bogyoke Aung Sang's legacy to bring it from the military to us".[23]

The government has already lifted the ban against NLD and supported the candidature of Suu Kyi to stand in the elections. She has already contested successful for membership of National Assembly on 1 April 2012. The public meeting and canvassing has been allowed and the reports are that wherever Suu Kyi was going for canvassing, large numbers of people were gathering to listen to her.[24] Being charismatic, her wisdom and appeal proves her iconic. She talks about solving the problem of food, clothing and shelter and the people in Myanmar has lot of expectations from her. Being a Nobel laureate, she has been awarded Sakharin and Nehru award for her precious views about democracy, human rights and federalism. She has attracted the attention of the western world and she can use her vision, charisma and wisdom for development of Myanmar. Thein Sein administration is aware of the realities and therefore trying to bring Suu Kyi in the forefront to address socio-economic problem as well as change the overall image of the country from a dependent state on China to self-reliant and vibrant nation.

Changes in the Foreign Policy

President Thein Sein has taken some decisions to bring Myanmar on non-aligned path. From 1998 to 2010, Myanmar was considered a client state of People's Republic of China. It was a reality that China was the most important factor in the security and economic affairs of Myanmar. It was with the support of Myanmar that China became a factor in the politics of Indian Ocean region, Myanmar and China had been historically linked through land routes know as Burma Road, but in the post 1998 era, connectivity for business and trade between the two increased. Several roads have been constructed and the Chinese goods are coming to Myanmar and from there to South Asian countries. The business and trade however was not objectionable for the countries in the region but it was the role of the Chinese in the security matters of Myanmar that aroused apprehensions. China established Signals Intelligence Facility (SIGINT) at Coco Islands located in the Indian Ocean which is merely 30 nautical miles away from the Andaman's. Besides that, China developed Hainggyi in the Indian Ocean as an important port for naval activities. Again Irrawaddy and Bassein River have been developed to cater to the strategic interests of the Chinese. It is understood that the Chinese presence at Coco and Hanggyi can jeopardise security interest of India as well as the ASEAN states. It can paralyze shipping in the Bay of Bengal and create problem in the movement of ships in the Malacca straits. While commenting about the

Chinese installations in the region, Sanjoy Hazarika has stated that the Chinese presence at Coco Island in Myanmar may enable China to monitor activities on the missile testing ranges of Balasore and Chandipur in Orissa.[25] The strategic build-up of the Chinese in Myanmar had security implications on India but its concerns were not addressed by the Myanmarese leaders. Although ASEAN felt concern at the Chinese build up in Myanmar and South China Sea and mooted constructive engagement policy so that Myanmar is enabled to evolve a balanced view of the regional realities, but Than Shwe was opposed to any change as far as deeper strategic ties with China was concerned. However, when Thein Sein came into power transformation from absolute dependence to self-reliance was give importance and review of China policy hitherto pursued became apparent.

In September 2011, Thein Sein took a bold step to cancel the $ 3.6 billion Chinese hydro-electric dam project, even at the cost of hefty cancellation fee of $ 42.5 million.[26] Although there were opposition to the project, known as Myitsone project at the local level, but its cancellation was not expected. China had planned to construct a series of dams on the northern tributaries of the Irrawaddy in the upper reaches of the main river, and preparatory work on the project had started. Ethnic Kachins were opposing the construction of the dam because thousand had been displaced and many more were to be displaced and evicted from the area. Although ethnic Kachins were the admirers of the Chinese in the past but Myitsone dam project offended them and they turned strong critics of the Chinese later. It was due to opposition of the dam that Kachins had boycotted participation in 2010 elections. They were furious that despite their historic support to the Chinese interests in the past, the latter has come with a project that would dilute their existence and identity. Moreover, it was understood that after the completion of the dam, most of the power were to be supplied to the Chinese, but the anger of the displaced Kachins will be left on the government to resolve. Hence, Thein Sein decided to cancel the project, but this decision annoyed the Chinese who were dictating so far the government of the Myanmarese and using their natural resource for their own purposes.

Various opinions and comments have come ever since the cancellation of the deal. The Time weekly newspaper reported that "although this incident will not cause long-term damage to overall relations between China and Myanmar, the relations can no longer stay in their traditional form."[27] Some Chinese enterprises have been secretive about all kinds of events that have happened while investing in Myanmar so as to obtain profits. This has resulted in Chinese policy makers not understanding or even misjudging the actual situation in Myanmar. If serious political changes occur in Myanmar, it is very likely to jeopardise China's investment interests. The losses will not only be the recent hydroelectric station project, but may also include already operational China-Myanmar oil and gas pipelines and even the China-Myanmar highway, high speed railway and other planned projects will not be able to proceed.[28]

Again Taipei Time reported that "what worries China most about the suspension of the Myitsone project is not the economic loss, but the apparent change in Myanmar's political orientation. The Burmese, for their part, want to move out of China orbit. They don't want to be a Chinese province anyone. This trend is as hard to stop as an arrow in flight. As Myanmar escapes from its isolation, China will find itself even more isolated, and that is a prospect that the authorities in Beijing find very worrying".[29] In retrospect we find that the Thein Sein administration has taken a popular decision to cancel Myitsone deal. This has pleased the people in the area and the step is regarded as a landmark for reconciliation with ethnic minorities. This decision has pleased not only the countries in the neighbourhood but the entire world. The United Nations, the United States, the European Union and the ASEAN have welcomed the positive decisions of Myanmar as it has displayed its determination to take reformative measures in the realm of foreign policy also.

In September 2011, Thein Sein took another decision to invite the US Secretary of State, Hillary Clinton, to visit Myanmar which coincided with the release of 200 political prisoners. The invitation was sent as a part of initiative to opening up the country to the world. The US responded warmly to the invitation and thus the interaction with US officials started. There was a high level meeting between state department officials and Myanmar's defence chief on 3 November 2011 which was followed by President Barrack Obama's conversation with Suu Kyi on telephone and subsequent announcement that Hillary Clinton will visit Myanmar soon. Hillary Clinton came to Myanmar on December 1 and 2, 2011. This was a visit by the US Secretary of State in 50 years, which signified the beginning of new era of relations. On this occasion a letter from the US President Barrack Obama was delivered to Suu Kyi, promising eternal support for her role in the politics of the country. At the same time, the US President sent a message to President Thein Sein and offered to begin a new phase in ties. Obama said that "Washington wanted to explore how it can support and advance your efforts to transition to democracy and promote human rights" and Thein Sein reciprocated by saying that there will be reforms in Myanmar.[30]

Hillary Clinton met Suu Kyi on a private dinner and talked about the politics of the country. She indicated plans for lifting of decades old sanctions against Myanmar. In short, Clinton's visit has proved a landmark in inspiring the reformist leaders in Myanmar and it is bound to open new vistas of co-operation with the United States and the Western world. On the other hand, this visit has indicated some new trends in the politics of the region.[31] Nayan Chanda, a renowned expert, has remarked that "Clinton's arrival is marking the beginning of a new Great Game in Myanmar to block, or even roll back, Chinese advances to the South".[32]

Thein Sein is gradually opening up in the economic sphere. Foreign investors including the United States are assured that 100 percent foreign investment in lucrative sectors like energy and mining will be allowed along with repatriation of profits. They will not require seeking tie-ups with local firms. The local banks have been given permission to open dollar accounts and Myanmar Investment commission is to follow four principles while attracting foreign investment. They are to protect the interests of Myanmar's citizens, protecting the dignity of the state, guarding national sovereignty, as well as allowing only environment friendly investments. The pace of reforms has been welcomed in the west. Hillary Clinton, the US Secretary of State praised Thein Sein for moving his country to such a long distance in such a short period of time.[33] In this connection, it is noteworthy to cite the statement of Stephen P. Gruff of Asian Development Bank (ADB), who after his visit to Myanmar said "I was immediately struck by the vibrancy and a palpable sense of change in the air. The country's immense potential is reflected in the ADB's most recent analysis, which shows that Myanmar has the potential to follow Asia's fast growing economic and expand 7 percent to 8 percent if it continues on the path of across-the-board reforms initiated earlier this year".[34]

Japan is satisfied with the ongoing pace of reforms and it has resumed its aids to Myanmar which had been stopped years ago. The ASEAN is also satisfied with the process of reform as Malaysian Prime Minister, Najib Razak said that "Southeast Asian leaders were satisfied with the momentum of reforms in Myanmar" on the eve of ASEAN summit in Bali in 2011.[35] Myanmar thus won ASEAN approval to chair the ASEAN in 2004 as a reward for hints of reforms after decades of military rule. Marty Natalegawa, Foreign Minister of Indonesia said that "All leaders are in agreement that significant changes, significant developments have taken place in Myanmar and those changes have made it more conducive to carry out this responsibility". In retrospect, we find that Myanmar was forced to renounce the ASEAN rotating presidency in 2006 in the face of criticism over its human right record and the ruling junta's failure to shift to democracy.[36] However, there was no resistance to the proposal in 2014 and Myanmar hosted the East Asia Summit subsequently.

Indo-Myanmar Relations

Indo-Myanmar relations have witnessed several problems in the past affecting mindset of the leaders of the two countries. The Britishers colonised Burma and integrated them with British India. Large numbers of Indians were recruited in the military and police forces to be stationed in Burma and the overall impression given was that India had occupied Burma. Again it was the Britishers who encouraged the migration of Indians to go to Burma and induced them to invest in the agriculture sector. South Indian chettiars were given the incentive that if they invest in the expansion of agricultural areas, they will be given land ownership rights. They invested generously in de-forestation and expansion of cultivable lands. They were also given the ownership rights over the land as the incentive for investments. Simultaneously, a mischievous propaganda was also supported by the colonial rulers that Indians have occupied the lands of the Burmese. The British policy of divide and rule in Burma was extremely successful and the differences between Indians and the Burmese became unbridgeable and the unity between ethnic Burmans and others very difficult. The divide in the Burmese society was so sharp on the eve of independence that Bogyoke Aung San, the father of the nation along with six of his cabinet colleagues were assassinated in 1947. The complicity of the British officials in this crime was apparent but U Saw was convicted and punished swiftly.[37] The whispering gossips and propaganda against some Indians close to U Saw was highlighted to implicate Indians also in the assassination which proved costly for Indians then domiciled in that country.

When the Britishers approved 1948 constitution and supported Burma's citizenship laws, the implication was clear that it will rob the Indians of their rights over citizenship, land and industries. On the surface, the Britishers showed that they were supporting the sabotage, the backbone of Burmese economy. They had already closed Burmese shells during the Second World War. Myanmar has been struggling ever since to strengthen its economic infrastructure but the success has been elusive. However, Indian has become active now to strengthen fraternal ties with Myanmar and thus the opportunity has been bestowed to strengthen relations.

India and Myanmar, sharing 1640 Km long border, are slowly and steadily coming closer to each other. Though the relations were cool for decades due to ideological differences but the situation started improving under the paradigm of Look East Policy. However, the experiences were not encouraging in certain areas. Two Indian owned state companies ONGC Videsh and GAIL—along with South Korean Daewoo had made investment in Rakhine offshore area to explore and extract oil and gas and when it was found and negotiations were underway for better pricing and building a pipeline through Bangladesh to India, Myanmar ignored Indian and signed a MoU with China, committing all gas from Block A-I and A-III to China. This was to be wheeled through a 2,380 km pipeline connecting Myanmar's Kyakphyu in the Bay of Bengal to Rili in Yunnan.[38] This was indeed disappointing but Indian government did not lose its patience. India's the then Foreign Minister, Pranab Mukherjee visited Myanmar in January and May 2007 and discussed the issue of energy supplies with General Maung Aye and Brigadier General Thura Myint Maung and the response of Myanmar government was quite assuring about the concerns of the government of India. Myanmar side showed that the losses could be addressed through cooperation with India's presence at Block and A-111 was kept intact and Mous were signed to promote defence and economic relations.[39] India always wanted cooperation of Myanmar to address the threat of insurgency in the Northeast. India had felt great relief when the armies of the two countries had participated in operation Golden Bird in 1995 to flush out Indian insurgents from Myanmar. After General Malik's meeting with his Myanmarese counterpart General Maung Aye in 2000, deeper level of cooperation to address the problem of cross border terrorism and drug trafficking had been agreed. In November 2001, Myanmar Army had arrested about 40 Manipuri insurgents after raiding their camps at Tamu, Namphalong and Khunjao. All those captured belonged to United National Liberation Front, People's Liberation Army and People's Revolutionary Party of Kangleipak. However, such activities were considered a partial success only because there were several such camps in Myanmar which needed to be destroyed. Myanmar agreed to India's proposal to institutionalise cooperation between the armies of the two countries for operations against ULFA and other insurgent outfits. Pranab Mukherjee who visited Myanmar in May 2007, was assured to take a stock in A-III block and at the same time extend security cooperation. Myanmar was pleading that lack of infrastructure in Myanmar was hindering the troops from extending full cooperation to India and the Chief of Myanmarese Army had already stated in New Delhi in December 2006 that 35 millimetre field guns, helicopters, mortars, Submarine detecting sonars, islanders aircraft and spares for MiG fighters will enhance their infrastructure to nab the Indian outfits in Myanmar.

India agreed to the proposal of Myanmar and at the same time transferred two BN-2 defender Islander maritime surveillance aircraft to Myanmar to promote relations between the navies of the two countries. The two nations also agreed for joint exercises and exchange of intelligence to prevent sea piracy and smuggling of narcotics. It also gave deck-based air defence guns and varied surveillance equipments.[40]

When Thein Sein came into power, he extended sincere support to nab the Indian insurgents in Myanmar. On 7 September 2011, Myanmar army attacked the so called head quarters of the Northeast rebels at Saigaing and destroyed several ULFA camps. The ULFA cadres were intermittently attacking Indian security forces and seeking shelter in Myanmar. They have been spreading hatred against Indians and keep themselves busy in kidnapping the people for ransom in the Northeast. They mingle with the people in Myanmar of the basis of their ethnicity and remain engaged in perpetual campaign of violence and hatred. This has disturbed the quest for connectivity between the two countries. The construction of roadways, railways and industrial infrastructure are delayed because of disturbances in the area. The investors are thinking twice before committing their resources in the region. It is also because of disturbances in the northeast that the proposal of Chennai-Dewei transport corridor is attracting the attention of the experts in the region. However, the development of the Northeast and its uninterrupted connectivity with countries in the neighbourhood are essential for economic prosperity of South and Southeast Asia.

While writing about India-Myanmar relations, Rajiv Bhatia, former Indian ambassador to Myanmar has stated "Cooperation in security management, regular intelligence-sharing, defence cooperation, maritime security and long-term energy and connectivity cooperation are the central challenges".[41] All these endeavours can be achieved if we have understanding of each other. When the President of Myanmar, Thein Sein visited New Delhi in October 2011, a joint statement was issued through which all necessary assistance was assured by India in Myanmar's political, economic and social reforms. Both reiterated their shared commitment to strengthening and broadening the multi-faceted relationship based on shared history, civilisation ties and close religious, linguistic and culture affinities and take it to a new level.[42] On the other hand, Myanmar also extended support and said that it would not allow sanctuaries to secessionist elements from Northeast of India.

In fact, the up gradation of economic relationship with Myanmar would give a tremendous boost to the development of northeast region. The planned infrastructure development of road, rail and waterways are important steps in that direction. This includes Kaladan multi-nodal transport project in the Rakhine state and road project to improve access to a border trade crossing in Chin State.[43] Ranjit Gupta has further explained that "India is upgrading the Sittwe port and making 225 kilometer of the Kaladan River from Sittwe to Setpyitpyin navigable. It is to be connected to Mizoram by a 62 km road. Presently Kolkata-Sittwe sea route is 539 kms. These projects are designed to provide connectivity between mainland India and its North-eastern states. But we should think about setting up of multi-purpose special economic zones around Sittwe. It should be considered on a priority basis. The SEZ would provide an avenue for utilisation of the gas from the exploration blocks currently with ONGC Videsh and Essar.[44] Power for downstream industries in the SEZ could be supplied from the two hydropower projects that India is involved in Tamanthi and Shwezaye. RITES are involved in the development of rail transportation. The SEZ would synergise the objectives of these projects and become the symbol of India's presence and commitment to Myanmar's economic development in non-exploitative fashion, in strong contrast to what other major investors are doing.[45]

The Indo-Burmese relations are expanding in other areas also, such as health and farming sectors. India has agreed to modernise the children's hospital in Yangon by supplying the latest modern equipments. Talks are also on building a state of the art general hospital in Sittwe. India has extended its support to work for in cyclone-prone areas. It has handed over 10 modern and disaster-proof rice silos (warehouses) built at a cost of two million dollars to preserve grains during natural calamities. External affairs minister, S M Krishna who visited Myanmar in June 2011, inaugurated the silos. Each silos, having a combined capacity of 5000 tone storage is handy. A team led by agriculture scientist, M S Swaminathan has been authorised to understand the country's needs in the agricultural sector and the possible help that India can extend. India has already to provide a grant of 10 million US dollars for procurement of agricultural tools, besides 100 computers to the central land records as requested by Myanmar. India is also willing to setup agricultural research centre in Yezin, near the capital.[46]

India has agreed to send a team from the Archaeological Survey of India to render its services in restoration of eleventh century Ananda temple in Pagan at Mandalaya. On the economic side, both countries are satisfied at the rapid growth of trade and target for bilateral trade has been fixed at US$ 3 billion by 2015.[47] The Ministry of Commerce figures for import and export in 2010 had estimated that the total trade between the two countries was of US$ 1497. US$ 77 million in which exports amounted to US$ 207.97 million and imports are US$ 1289.80 million. However, the figure mentioned does not show the actual figure because India and Myanmar has had the history of clandestine trade, whose figures are difficult to account. There are immense potentials of natural gas, petroleum, teak, pearls, gems, rubber, timber, sugar and rice in Myanmar and similarly immense areas of cooperation between the two, which can be explored for mutual benefits.

India's Prime Minister, Manmohan Singh paid a visit to Myanmar on 27-29 May 2012 to give new thrusts to relationship with Myanmar. Prime Minister stated before his departure that the focus of his visit would be on strengthening the existing trade and investment links, building agreements for greater connectivity and for development of areas along their shared 1640 km. border." Four of India's north-eastern states straddle this border—Arunachal Pradesh, Nagaland, Manipur and Mizoram. Indian Prime Minister had a proposal for bus service to connect Imphal to Mandalaya, which aimed at promoting both trade and people to people ties, is a component of development in the region that India see as crucial to its internal stability as well as to its Look East Policy. It was subsequently reported that Prime Minister Manmohan Singh and President Thein Sein agreed to the proposal and set a deadline, 2016 for trilateral road connectivity, which will make it possible to drive right up to Thailand from India via Myanmar.[48] India would undertake the repair of 71 bridges on the Tamu-Kalewa Friendship road and will link it with a place know as Yargyi which will effectively link March in India to Mae Sot in Thailand. On the other hand, Myanmar would upgrade the Yargyi-Monywa stretch to highway standard by 2016.[49] Prime Minister portrayed his visit to Myanmar as a voyage and termed it "a historic milestone" in the long story of relationship that was impregnated with enormous potential and promise. Accompanied by 25 Indian CEOs, representing all sectors of Indian industry, Indian Prime Minister displayed vision to strengthen relations.[50]

The signing of 12 agreements after Prime Minister's arrival at Naypitaw included several areas of cooperation. Besides greater connectivity, there was an agreement for setting for Myanmar Institute of Information Technology. A Memorandum of Understanding (MoU) between the two countries was signed for India-Myanmar border area development. Prime Minister announced India's support extending financial assistance of $ million per year for five years for undertaking small developmental projects such as schools, health centres and dispensaries small roads and bridges, agriculture and agro-processing projects and related training programmes in the Naga Self Administered Zone (Saigaing Division and the Chin State). The MoU was also signed for establishment of border hats in Arunachal Pradesh.

India's Exim Bank had earlier reported that Myanmar had 2.54 trillion cubic meters of gas reserves[51] (at par with Malaysia and Indonesia). India which was already involved in the onshore and offshore gas exploration had to compete with international bidders in Myanmar. President Thein Sein assured India's Prime Minister through a joint statement those investments from Indian companies in Myanmar oil Myanmar's oil and gas sector would be appreciated. He expressed his happiness to allocate available blocks with good prospects to Indian companies.[52] Talking about energy cooperation, President Thein Sein expressed appreciation for India undertaking the preparation of detailed project report of the Tamanthi and Shwezaye hydropower project also.

India's foreign secretary Ranjan Mathai was satisfied with the agreements in oil and gas sector. He hinted at the possibility of a gas pipeline running into India from Myanmar. He said that Myanmar's economy has so much potential for development that we feel the scope for cooperation in virtually all fields of industry—agro-based industries, resource-based; industry information technology, communication, hydro-carbon transport. India's main infrastructure venture in Myanmar is the Kaladan project to link Sittwe port to Mizoram road and connect it with an inland water way, which started in 2008. The waterway is expected to be completed by 2013 and the road link by 2014.[53]

The bilateral trades of India with Myanmar are increasing. It was worth US$ 1.2 billion in March 2012 almost two-thirds of that is from Myanmar's exports of moong dal to India. If the infrastructural issue for connectivity are resolved and Myanmar is modernised, it will be a major hub of trade from India to ASEAN and vice versa.[54] The Times of India has rightly observed that a number of reforms since March 2011 spearheaded by President Thein Sein have raised hope of a democratic renaissance. Scores of political prisoners have been released, media restrictions eased, formations of unions allowed and ceasefires implemented with several insurgent ethnic group coming in the wake of encouraging signs, the international community has already pledged support for Myanmar's reform process with US announcing restoration of diplomatic ties and lifting economic sanctions. India is keen to contribute its efforts in the modernisation of Myanmar and the levels of relations are bound to rise.[55]

Conclusion

To conclude it can be stated that Myanmar is undergoing changes and they are aimed at reforms for democratic restoration. In the realm of domestic politics, they have allowed NLD to play their political role. Suu Kyi has participated in the elections in 2012 and has assured support to President Thein Sein for cooperation in nation building. She was disliked by the military in the past and all those who tried to isolate her in the past, are silent at present. This is a cause of worry as their agenda is not known. Thein Sein is enthusiastic to take the cooperation of Suu Kyi, which will help the nation in establishing, ethnic reconciliation and also pave the path for international prestige. In the realm of foreign policy, the aim of Thein Sein government is to diversify relations from total dependence on China to equidistance in relations with its neighbours. It has attached importance to India and other ASEAN countries in solving its socio-economic problems. It has also given importance to cooperation in matters with neighbouring countries and has decided to destroy the bases of ULFA, Nagas and Manipuri insurgents which existed in Myanmar for decades. The country has taken positive steps towards democratisation and the overall trends are in tune with the political realities in ASEAN countries.

Although President Thein Sein is repeatedly saying those reforms in Myanmar are irreversible but there is scepticism. Suu Kyi is very charismatic and a great mobilise of public opinion. Her NLD has recently become victorious in by-elections for 43 seats of Union Parliament out of 44 that it contested. The general election is likely to be held in Myanmar in 2015 and if the objective conditions will prevail as in 2012, NLD is likely to come into power. Thein Sein, as leader of USDP is conversant with this reality. The military elements in Myanmar's politics have not shown their trust in Suu Kyi or NLD so far and they will like to prevent Suu Kyi's emergence as head of the state. However, if they will do anything to contain her influence, it will instigate civil disobedience in the country. The entire world, including China will disapprove such an action.

Suu Kyi is the ardent follower of the policy of non-violence as Mahatma Gandhi. She is keen to lead Myanmar on the path of development and it is in that endeavour that she has extended support to Thein Sein. She is renowned and reputed leader who has made sacrifices for the nation. However, if she will get an opportunity to lead the nation, she will have to consider Manerplaw Agreement signed by National Coalition Government of the Union of Burma (NCGUB) on 31 July 1992. The essence of this agreement was directed against military rule, but its preamble is still relevant. It stated that "Burma is a country where indigenous nationalities have lived together in adjacent territories for the last several millennia. It belongs to all indigenous nationalities. Only when a true federal structure is established based on the desires and aspirations of all the indigenous nationalities will Burma stand united and stable. We will draw up a true federal union constitution in accordance with the desires of indigenous nationalities and all people. We will follow the principle that no nationality shall have special privileges" (Manerplaw Agreement or NCGUB, 31 July 1992).

END NOTES

1. K. Yhome, Myanmar's changing Geo-Strategic value: Key Drivers and Implications India-Burma Relations: Trends and Developments, (1990-2011), Burma Centre, Delhi 2011, 37.
2. *The Nation* "Opium Burning", 5 March 1992.
3. The Nation "Burma's Multi-Million-Dollar Heroine crop is Expected to reach Record Levels this Season", 3 March 1992.
4. John Funston, Ed. Government and politics of Southeast Asia, ISEAS, Singapore, 2001, 226.
5. In May 2010, an American known as John Yettow swam to the lakeside home of Suu Kyi without taking permission from the military. The military regarded this event unlawful. They were angry that even Suu Kyi did not inform the military about the event immediately and therefore they projected Suu Kyi as a culprit that she allowed the event of trespass a secret. Thus the military court slapped 18 months of house arrest to Suu Kyi. The military action was so arbitrary that it invited world-wide condemnation. The UN Secretary General Ban Ki-Moon and the US President Barack Obama condemned it along with other great leaders.

6. Burma Lawyer's council, The Military and its Constitution in Burma, NCGUB office, Bangkok, 1999, pp. 1-67.
7. *The Nation*, Bangkok, 1 April 2012.
8. Prashant Jha, "Myanmar votes today in historic by elections", *The Hindu*, 1 April 2012.
9. See Manerplaw Agreement 31 July 1992, Manerplaw Agreement signed by Dr. Sein Win, U Tin Aung, Saw Bo Mya and Nai Shwe Kyin of NCGUB, NLD, DAB and NDF on 31 July 1992 had resolved to implement the following: 1. The Kachin, Karen, Chin Mon, Burman, Araka, Shan peoples and etc. Will have National state incorporated in a Federal Union of States. 2. The National State will assign certain power to the Federal Union and the remaining powers will be exercised by the National States including legislative, administrative and judicial powers. 3. The federal Union will consist of two house of Parliament: the National Assembly (Upper House) and the People's Assembly (Lower House). 4. In accordance with the principle of civilian supremacy over the military the Federal Union and state armies will be put under the direct supervision of the Elected Governments. 5. The legislative, administrative and judicial branches of the Federal Union Government will be checked and balanced in power, and the judiciary will be independent. 6. The Constitution will be designed to prevent any re-emergency of chauvinism and fascist dictatorship in the future.
10. Xinhua General News Service, Yangon "First Dialogue between new government of Myanmar and Aung San Suu Kyi paves way for future cooperation", 26 July 2011.
11. The Observer, London, "For the first time-Myanmar President U Thein Sein met Aung San Suu Kyi", 22 August 2011.
12. Following the electoral victory of opposition party, NLD in May 1990, the military issued order 1/90 to justify their refusal to recognise the election result. It stated that the duty of the elected representatives is nothing more than drafting a new constitution, and the military that held power under martial law, was not bound by any constitution and would hold power until it ensures that a sufficiently strong constitution is in place.
13. Ganganath Jha, "Politics of military in Myanmar", *Area Studies*, a journal of International Studies and Analysis, Tirupati, January-June 2011, 5 (1), 121-123.
14. The Observer, London, "The Generals Think they have sidelined Her, They are Wrong", 14 November 2010.
15. "Suu Kyi Released from House Arrest", *The statesman*, New Delhi, 13 October 2011.
16. "Democratic Reforms", *The Times of India*, New Delhi, 25 November 2011.
17. "Myanmar of Reforms Spree", *The Times of India*, 25 November 2011.
18. Shyam Saran, "The pivot of Change in Asia", *Indian Express*, New Delhi, 1 December 2011.
19. The six cabinet colleagues of Aung San who were assassinated along with him were Ba Win (commerce and supplies), Thakin Mya (Finance), Abdul Razak (Education), Mahn Ba Khaing (Industry and Labour), Ba Choe (Information), and Sao Sam Htun (Forntier Areas). U Saw, a well know leader was alleged and convicted for this crime. He is believed to have planned and directed the killing with the weapons supplied by the Britishers. The complicity of British officials who were friendly to U Saw, namely Major young, Major Moore Major Daine, captain Vivian, John Steward Bingley etc. Before and after the assassination are considered circumstantial evidences of their complicity. The hasty trial and execution of death sentence to u saw prevented punishment to real culprits. The BBC had reported immediately after the assassination that the British were behind the Killings. Bertil Lintner, Outrage: Burma's Struggle for Democracy, Hong Kong, 1989: BBC Worldwide Monitoring, pp. 1 59.

20. The Nation "Call for second Panglong Conference", 16 November 2010.
21. Shelby Tucker, *Burma: The Curse of Independence*, (Penguin Books, 2001), 153.
22. Supalak Ganjanakhundee, "The World will welcome Myanmar if it Reforms", *The Statesman*, 22 August 2011.
23. Supalak Ganjanakhundee, "Call for Second Panglong Conference", *The National Bangkok*, 16 November 2010.
24. Delphine Shrank, "Testing Burma's Political Dispensation", *Deccan Chronicle*, 31 March 2012.
25. Sanjoy Hazarika, "Wisdom in Wooing Myanmar", *The Statesman*, New Delhi, 5 December 2000.
26. Nayan Chanda, "Winds of Change in Myanmar", *The Times Of India*, 26 November 2011.
27. "Myanmar Round up", *The Time Weekly*, 30 November 2011, available at www.time-weekly.com.
28. Interview with Hong Bo, employee of large Chinese owned enterprise in Yangon, 17 October 2011.
29. Interview of Wilson Chen, US Based Democracy Activist, 17 October 2011.
30. "More Reforms, More Rewards", *The Times of India*, 2 December 2011.
31. Nayan Chanda, "Global Eye More Than a Tactical Strift", *The Times of India*, 21 January 2012.
32. Nayan Chanda, "Winds of Change in Myanmar", *The Times of India*, 26 November 2011.
33. Subir Bhaumilk, "Myanmar's Date with Destiny", *The Times of India*, 8 August 2012.
34. Stephen P. Gruff, "Myanmar: Asia's Next Rising Star", *The Statesman*, 28 August 2012.
35. "ASEAN rewards Myanmar for Reforms", *The Times of India*, 18 November 2011.
36. "Fruits of Democracy", *The Times of India*, 27 August 2012.
37. Ibid, n. 21.
38. Ganganath Jha, "Indo-Myanmar Relation—An overview", *World Focus*, 28 (6), (June 2007), 238.
39. "Indo Myanmar Pact to tackle Terror", *The Times of India*, 22 January 2007.
40. As reported by *Kashmir Time*, 21 March 2011, "India supplied 98 truckloads of arms and ammunitions to Myanmar as part of the agreement reached at the Home Secretary level talks. It also offered unspecified number of T-55 tanks, armored personnel carriers, 105 millimetre light artillery guns, mortars and locally designed advanced light helicopters to Myanmar".
41. Rajiv Bhatia, "Why Myanmar President's Visit to India matters?", 11 October 2011.
42. Text of the Joint Statement between India Myanmar, New Delhi, 14 October 2011.
43. Syed Ali Mujtaba, "India has abandoned Aung San Suu Kyi, Indians have not", *Kashmir Times*, 22 March 2011.
44. "Trilateral contract Reached for Gas exploration in Myanmar", *Xinhua General News Service*, Section world news, 5 April 2012.
45. Ranjit Gupta, "Building Bridges across Irrawaddy to Myanmar", *The Times of India*, 17 October 2011.
46. Pt9 News Agency Report on Myanmar, 22 June 2011.
47. Rajiv Bhatia, "Why Myanmar President's Visit to India matters?" available at htsyndication@hindustantimes.com, 11 October 2011.
48. Nirupama Subramanian, "In scramble for Myanmar, India tries to build on Earlier gains", *The Hindu*, 28 May 2012.
49. Sachin Parashar, "By 2016, Drive Down to Thailand", *The Times of India*, 29 May 2012.

50. Rajiv Bhatia, "Striking the Right Note", *The Times of India*, 31 May 2012.
51. *Xinhua General News* on 5 April 2012 stated that Myanmar has abundance of natural gas resources in the offshore areas. There are three main large offshore oil gas fields and 19 on shore ones. Myanmar has proven recoverable reserve of 18.012 trillion cubic feet (TCF) out of 89.722 TCF estimated reserve of offshore and onshore gas.
52. "Energy focus as Prime Minister heads for Myanmar", *The Times of India*, 28 May 2012.
53. Sachin Parashar, "India Co. Allotted Myanmar oil Block", *The Times of India*, 29 May 2012.
54. Nirupma Subramanian, "In Myanmar, Manmohan to Focus on Trade", *The Hindu*, 28 May 2012.
55. "Hope in Myanmar", *The Times of India*, 3 April 2012.

9

Rising Indonesia's Global Diplomacy: Principled Pragmatism and Multilateral Activism

Vibhanshu Shekhar

Introduction

A consensus is gradually emerging among the IR aficionados that the nature and character of the emerging global order is going to be fundamentally different from that of the existing US-led global order. Scholars have characterised these system-level changes differently, such as 'the Post American World,' 'the end of American World Order,' 'the end of American Century,' the rise of 'Eastphalia' or 'the Great Convergence' of the East and West.[1] The emerging global order is being shaped by (a) a shifting gravity of political and economic transactions from trans-Atlantic to the Indo-Pacific, (b) resurgence of Asian civilisational powers—China, India and Indonesia, (c) relative decline in the power of the US and West, and (d) enormous increase in the material capacities of the global South. The rise of new powers has relocated the gravity of power towards the Indo-Pacific region and pushed the US-led unipolar global world towards multipolar power structure. Moreover, China is gradually taking over the US as the number one economic power, and the US share in the global economy has seen sustained decline. The rise of the Global South has exerted considerable demand for democratisation of existing global institutions, such as the United Nations, World Bank and International Monetary Fund. Moreover, new institutions of global significance, such as the BRICS Development Bank and Asian

Infrastructure Investment Bank (AIIB), which are, in reality, warning signals to the existing institutions to choose between improvisation and irrelevance. These system-altering developments have raised some pertinent questions as encapsulated by a noted IR scholar, John Ikanberry:

> "If the United States is losing its position of preeminence, will the order that it created weaken and break apart, giving way to a new type of global order? Or will non-Western rising states ultimately become stakeholders in the existing order? Do rising states want great authority and privileges in the existing international order or do they want to use their growing power to reorganise the basic principles and norms of the system?"[2]

These questions lie at the heart of rising Indonesia's global diplomacy as it grapples with the issues of what Indonesia's appropriate responses should be, what position and status befits the country and how Indonesia should contribute to the new debates of the 21st century. As Indonesia grapples with these questions, one can identify two distinct trends evident in Indonesia's global diplomacy—principled pragmatism and multilateral activism. While delivering lecture at Harvard University in 2009, the Indonesian President laid out nine imperatives to transform the world into a better living place.[3] Reinforcing the President's principled approach towards the global politics, Marty Natalegawa declared, "Our foreign policy was always carried out on the basis of a principled approach, one that is visionary and yet pragmatic and anticipatory in responding to global and regional developments."[4]

The idea of principled pragmatism has been applied in various contexts of international relations, such as international law, global multilateralism, international businesses, political movements, and global popular resistance.[5] The concept of principled pragmatism has roots both in the conceptual debates of political realism as well as in the explanations of the functioning of the global multilateral bodies, such as the United Nations (UN). The UN Secretary General, Ban Ki Moon, has suggested that the UN works and approaches should be seen in terms of the spirit of principled pragmatism and made three key recommendations.[6] First, the international community must work towards real solutions to building peace in the world. Second, 'development cannot take back seat to the issues of peace and security.' Finally, 'we cannot wait for a perfect time and perfect leadership to address global challenges.' Surprisingly, Ban Ki Moon's spirit of principled pragmatism remains confined to a proactive UN working towards greater global good but does not include a reformed and represented UN critical for its sustenance and relevance as a global voice in the 21st century. In a similar context, John Gerrard Ruggie, a well-known IR scholar, explained the concept of principled pragmatism in the field of business and human rights as 'the world's fundamental human rights expectations in a balanced way that takes account of the varied, complex global business landscape.'[7] While situating the idea of principled pragmatism in the context of feminist anti-globalisation global movement, Bice Maiguascha has identified its three elements—its normative orientation, its complex understanding of and response to power relations, and its specific temporality.[8]

The idea of principled pragmatism is used here in a context of Indonesia's emphasis on a global order that is just, representative and democratic; that is feasible, practical and rooted in the appreciation of the existing global system; that best serves Indonesia's global projection; and that is essential for the survival of the global order itself. In other words, the principled approach is also a pragmatic approach. This approach involves (a) Indonesia's projection of its democratic identity and its role as a responsible global citizen, and (b) demand for democratisation of global institutions and greater representation of the Global South in the global distributive practices. Indonesia follows a pragmatic approach rooted in normative contexts. For example, the discussion on climate change can be both pragmatic as well as principled. Similarly, Indonesia's demands for reforms in the international institutions, such as the United Nations, World Bank, International Monetary Fund today appear not only normative but also pragmatic. These representation and character of these institutions are reflective of the Cold War and therefore need to be changed if they have to deliver and stay relevant. The Indonesian leadership has reiterated its democratic normative global worldview at regular intervals. Amitav Acharya argues, "the goal of the global diplomacy of new Indonesia is to be 'accepted' by the international community 'as a country that highly regards its human rights and pays attention to environmental issues and (promotes) an international regime that upholds and respects Indonesia's cultural heritage'."[9]

The second element of multilateral activism reflects emerging Indonesia's desire for greater role in shaping the emerging global order. While speaking at the Wilton Park Annual Conference, London in November 2012, the Indonesian President, Susilo Bambang Yudhoyono identified five important aspects of Indonesia's global role as: (a) norm setter, (b) consensus-builder, (c) peacekeeper, (d) bridge-builder, and (d) voice of the developing world.[10] The State Guideline on foreign policy (1999-2004) and the Act No. 37, 1999 on Foreign Relations once again laid emphasis on two critical components of Indonesia's global positioning – 'restore Indonesia's international image and promote international cooperation that helps build and maintain world peace.'[11]

The democratic Indonesia has shown a great deal of alacrity in presenting its image and role as a responsible stakeholder in the global deliberations over critical challenges.[12] Indonesia's new activism aims at advocating reforms in the existing international order, calling upon the urgent necessity of a greater exchange of wisdom from diverse civilisational worldviews and value systems, and building a democratic and representative global order.

Projection of Indonesia's Democratic Identity

Jakarta's pro-democracy campaign reflects its aspirations to project its democratic image to the world. Democratic Indonesia has earned considerable normative capital that it has been trying to project for the country's overall principled global positioning in the 21st century. Its democratic experience has been examined as a standard case for observation, examination and emulation for the developing world, and Muslim and multi-ethnic societies, including countries of the West Asia and North Africa. Various writings have appeared equating the Arab Spring with the Indonesian Reformasi and suggesting lessons for the former to learn from the latter.[13] The Economist ran a special debate on equating the Middle East issue with the Indonesian transition to democracy.[14] Indonesia's former Foreign Minister, Hasan Wirajuda, while taking part in the Bali Democracy Forum in 2011, indicated his country's desire to 'share its experience with the Arab countries and learn from each other's mistakes.'[15]

The drivers for the projection of its democratic credentials seem to have come from its desire to regain its normative capital by eradicating its authoritarian and undemocratic past and projecting its new identity based on democratic credentials. Its policy makers have relied principally on the global and regional multilateral institutions to propagate its democratic character—global multilateral forums such as the United Nations and regional forums such as ASEAN Cooperative Processes. Indonesia, during the last five years, has hosted various multilateral meetings and has been represented at the highest levels in different multilateral global and regional meetings taking place abroad.[16] In this context, Indonesia's efforts at the Bali Democracy Forum (BDF) warrant a closer scrutiny. The BDF was set up by the democratic

Indonesia in 2008 as 'an annual, inclusive and open intergovernmental forum on the development of democracy in the Asia-Pacific region.'[17] The BDF website lists its basic objectives as to establish and maintain a forum among Asian countries that promotes political development through dialogue and cooperation in strengthening adherence to democratic values and development of democratic institutions.' Moreover, the forum also allows Indonesia to project its democratic outlook at the regional level.

While discussing the achievement of the half-a-decade old Bali Democracy Forum, the Indonesian President highlighted its three important contributions —involvement of increasing number of countries in the BDF deliberations, increasing shared commitment to democratic policies and values, and giving a greater push to the democratic momentum building in the countries of the Asia-Pacific.[18] The number of stakeholders in the BDF has gone up from 43 in 2008 at its first annual meeting to 91 after half a decade of life and the growing participation is, according to Susilo Bambang Yudhoyono, indicative of the fulfillment of the basic objective of the BDF of sharing experiences and best practices in democracy.[19]

However, the promotion of democracy has not been a smooth ride for the democratic Indonesia. It has faced constant challenges at two levels – national as well as at the ASEAN level. Indonesia has faced strong contestation while pushing for the adoption of democratic values at the ASEAN level. Many of the non-democratic ASEAN member-states have opposed such moves and threatened their withdrawal from the membership if pushed further. Myanmar's case was a good example. Myanmar threatened to withdraw from ASEAN if pushed on the issue of democratic reforms and Yangon's fierce contestation prompted a writer to call it 'a case of one versus nine.'[20] Indonesia's democratic progress has faced two important national challenges in the form of growing Sunni majoritarianism in the country and irregular functions of the legislatures emanating from the nature of coalition politics.

Democratic Indonesia has also sought to play the role of a bridge-builder between the West and Muslim world. While the 9/11 awakened Indonesia as a Muslim country to a new set of discourse regarding the growing radicalisation of Islam, the Bali Bomb Blast made Indonesia an active participant of the global discourse on radical Islam. Three trends can be identified in Indonesia's facilitating role between the Muslim world and West —its moderate Muslim democratic society, its role as a bridge-builder and its expression of solidarity with the Muslim world. Jakarta responded to these trends by projecting itself as the largest Muslim democracy in order to win over the global Muslim constituencies and offer a powerful and alternative discourse confronting the relations between the world and the second largest religion. Notwithstanding being the largest Muslim country of the world, 'Indonesia is neither an Islamic state nor is Islam the official religion of the state.[21] The Post-Suharto Indonesia has projected its successful counterterrorist campaigns against the home-grown terror network with regional and global tentacles.[22] So far, the democratic Indonesia is known to have launched the most effective measures against the terrorist networks.

Highlighting Indonesia's bridge-building role between Islam and the West, the then Indonesian Ambassador to the United States, Dino Patti Djalal, characterised Indonesia-US partnership as a 'constructive 21st-century partnership between the West and the Islamic world.'[23] Barrack Obama, the President of the United States of America, while giving his speech at Istiqlal mosque in Jakarta in November 2010 called upon Indonesia to play a greater role in facilitating dialogue between the West and Muslim world and build trust. On the other hand, the International Conference on Cultural Diplomacy in the European Union held in Brussels on December 2011, identified Indonesia as a bridge between Islam and the West and a model of compatibility between Islam and democracy.

At the same time, democratic Indonesia has also tried to express unequivocally its leadership role for the cause of Islam. Expressing its solidarity with the Muslim world, Indonesia has shown its continued support for the cause of Palestine. Indonesia continues to have no diplomatic relations with Israel. In this regard, Indonesia has participated actively in the Organisation of Islamic Conference and campaigned for peace and stability in the Middle East. The Megawati government of Indonesia had openly criticized the US interventions in Afghanistan and Iraq.[24] On 26 September 2012, the Indonesian President, Susilo Bambang Yudhoyono, while addressing the UN General Assembly, called for greater global sensitisation about the Islamic values and an international codification to prevent insult to the global religions. He suggested greater UN role in facilitating inter-civilisation engagement and greater global sensitisation about the religious issues. Proposing the case for a global anti-blasphemy law under the aegis of the UN, Susilo Bambang Yudhoyono declared,

> "I seized the opportunity to stress this point at the UN General Assembly. I called for the promotion of a universal culture of mutual tolerance and

mutual appreciation. We are deeply disturbed by the fact that defamation of religions persists. We have seen yet another one in the film "Innocence of Muslims", that has caused an international uproar....Hence, I also called for the establishment of an international instrument that stipulates norms, rules, and responsibilities with regard to this very issue."[25]

These pronouncements and prescriptions highlight Indonesia's growing international image as a bridge between the Muslim world and West, and its willingness to facilitate 'sanitised and sensitised' dialogue between the two worlds. The potential of Indonesia's mediation again came onto the main stage when the world witnessed violent protests against an obscenely mediocre film, called Innocence of Muslims, produced in the US in 2012. The Indonesian President during his speech at the UN called for the 'adoption of a legally binding instrument to ban blasphemy against religious symbols and to promote dialogue between different faiths, civilisations and cultures.'

Building an Equitable and Representative UN Order in the 21st Century

Jakarta has linked the growth and efficacy of global multilateralism with the efficient functioning of the UN system and its global and representative character. Indonesia has advocated the UN leadership in addressing global challenges, impartial and effective participation of the UN Security Council in building global peace and security, greater engagement and cooperation among the UN members, greater global representation in the UN institutions, and active support for the UN deliberations and negotiations.

In addition to greater role of the global multilateral institutions, the rising Indonesia has also been advocating fundamental reforms in the international institutions—UN, World Bank, International Monetary Fund and WTO. These institutions in their current shapes do not reflect the changing reality of the 21st century and growing aspirations and roles of the developing world. Jakarta considers the existing international order as outdated, moribund, ineffective, triumphalist, reflective of World-War II reality and skewed in favour of the advanced West and the developed world. These institutions no longer represent the vast majority of countries and growing power of the emerging Global South. It believes that 'its (United Nations) democratic intentions are diluted by the workings of an embedded oligarchy.'[26] In other words, the rules of engagement need to be changed to make these institutions representative, efficient, harmonised and coordinated, and in tune with the changing times.[27] Jakarta's energy and advocacy for the restructuring of the international institutions has revolved around the idea of greater global visibility, finding its rightful place in these institutions amidst its new-emerging profile and the country's growing advocacy for equitable global order and greater cooperation among the developing world.

Indonesian leaders have brought to the table tangible suggestions for discussions regarding the restructuring of the UN system. The then Indonesian Foreign Minister, Ali Alatas was chosen as one of the Commissioners of the Commission of Global Governance that was constituted in 1992 under the Secretary Generalship of Boutros Boutros-Ghali. The Commission laid out various suggestions, such as, a standing UN army, end of Veto, and a system of global taxation.[28] Since then, Indonesia has actively participated in various working groups and deliberations both within and outside the UN mandate for reforms within the UN. The Indonesian Foreign Minister, Marty Natalegawa, while speaking at the 66th UN General Assembly, declared that the only way through which the United Nations can remain relevant and multilateralism can flourish is for them to be able to 'address new and emerging challenges, and not least, and identify new opportunities, full support for, and reform of the United Nations.'[29] Indonesia has also used other international organisations and forums to advocate the UN reforms and project its normative credentials, such as its membership of G-77 and China. Indonesia has shown its intent towards entering into the African market and joining other Emerging Powers' Club such as BRICS and IBSA. The G-77 grouping under the chairmanship of Indonesia in 1998 stressed on the UN reforms and set up 'an expert group that would help articulate the vision of the South on the future role of the UN.'[30]

The reform of the UN Security Council has drawn the maximum attention. Indonesia came up with a concept paper in September 1995 titled 'Criteria for Permanent Membership in the Security Council.'[31]

While highlighting the failure of the UN Security Council in ending violent conflicts in different parts of the world, Susilo Bambang Yudhoyono declared, "world peace should not be determined by only one country among the five veto holders within the Security Council. I suggest that the council be reviewed because it is no longer relevant to the current world situation."[32] Indonesia wants a Security Council that is 'transparent, democratic, representative, and effective in fulfilling its immense responsibility to maintain international peace and security, in an even handed and just manner.'[33]

Moreover, it has projected its own candidature as a potential permanent member of an expanded and reformed UN Security Council. The former Australian Prime Minister, John Howard, supported the Indonesian candidature as a permanent member on the UN Security Council without veto along with India, Japan, Brazil and Germany for two reasons of its contribution to the global peace and security and as the world's largest Muslim nation.[34]

The democratisation of the international financial institutions and greater representation of the global South in these institutions have been another important area of campaign. This campaign has its genesis in the manner in which these institutions have interacted with the non-developed world in time of economic crisis. Three critical issues of the quota system, the process of decision-making, and the nature of participation of the developing and under-developed economies in the IMF and World Bank have come under attack from the emerging economies of the Global South including Indonesia. Moreover, the global economic crisis of 2008 and its genesis in the developed economies of the West have exposed the prevailing bias in the global financial architecture towards the developed world, ruthlessly exploitative and unsparing approach towards the developing world, an urgent necessity of greater role of the developing world in the decision-making process, and re-allocation of the quota-system. While receiving a contribution of the US$ 1 billion from Indonesia as a part of the European bailout package, the IMF chief, Christine Lagarde, declared, "to enhance the global effectiveness of the Fund, dynamic emerging market countries like Indonesia need to have a greater say. In this context, I welcomed Indonesia's support for the IMF's quota and representation reforms."[35] The Indonesian contribution is part of a commitment made in the G-20 meeting in June 2012 to support the IMF, which needs US$ 430 billion to help countries facing financial difficulties.[36]

Indonesia considers itself a victim of discriminatory mandate and the policies of the international institutions. The image of humbled and weak Suharto, the then Indonesian President, signing the US$40 billion bail-out package with the then IMF chief, Michael Camdasus, overseeing the signing ceremony continues to reverberate in the minds and hearts of common Indonesians.[37] The arrangement, symobilisng the victory of the Washington Consensus, had led to the fall of the Indonesian Rupiah, large-scale retrenchment of Indonesian workers, and pushed the country towards a comprehensive political, economic and social crisis.

Indonesian Multilateral Activism at the United Nations

The democratic Indonesia has come a long way during the last 13 years from the point of being an object of the UN mission in 1999 to an active contributor to the UN processes in 2012. Indonesian leadership has suggested greater UN role in ending the conflicts in different parts of the world, such as in Libya, Syria and Palestine.[38]

The post-colonial Indonesia laid stress on its active participation in the UN peacekeeping operations as an attempt towards projection of its normative capital. The Indonesian peacekeepers, known as Garuda Contingent, has been deployed during the Cold War in the Republic of Congo (ONUC) in 1961-1963, the Middle East (UNEF II) in 1973–1979, Iraq (UNIMOG) in 1988–1990, Namibia (UNTAG) in June–December 1989, and during the Post Cold War era in Kuwait (UNIKOM) in 1991–2003, Cambodia (UNTAC) in 1992–1993, Somalia (UNOSOM) in 1992–1995, Bosnia and Herzegovina (UNPROFOR and UNMIBH) in 1993–2002, Sierra Leone (UNAMSIL) in 1999–2005, and in the Democratic Republic of the Congo (MONUC—now MONUSCO) from March 2001 until today.[39]

Indonesia's active role in the 65th UN General Assembly for the period of September 2010-September 2011 can be gauged from its different roles in different capacities as Vice President of the UN's 65th General Assembly Meeting, Chairman of Commission on Population and Development, member of Governing Council UNEP and Governing Council UN Human Settlements Program (UN-HABITAT).[40] In addition to taking part in the 67th UN General Assembly in September 2012, the Indonesian President co-chaired 'the first and historic meeting of the High-level Panel (HLP) of Eminent Persons to discuss the global development agenda after 2015."[41]

Indonesian contribution today to the UN operations is considered as entering into a new chapter for two reasons: (a) both quantitative as well as qualitative jump in the country's contribution to the UN peacekeeping operations, and (b) widening geographical horizon.[42] Indonesia is planning to increase the total strength of its peacekeepers to 4000. The contribution of naval unit to the Indonesian operations in Lebanon attests to the first trend and the presence of the Garuda contingent in Haiti, for the first time in the Americas, confirms the second trend.[43] Besides, there is growing desire among the political leadership to project Indonesia as 'a regional hub of the UN peacekeeping operations in Asia.' According to the Indonesian Foreign Minister, Marty R.M. Natalegawa, "...Indonesia has actively contributed to the development of strategic concept for global peacekeeping missions. In 2011, Indonesia will attempt to be a hub for the peacekeeping network in the region."[44] Indonesia ranked among the top 20 contributors of the UN peacekeeping operations in 2010 and its goal is to become one of the top ten contributors of the UN peacekeeping missions.[45]

The UN Secretary General, Ban Ki Moon, during his visit to Indonesia in March 2012, appreciated the country's significant role in the UN peacekeeping operations.[46] Approximately 2000 Indonesian troops are currently engaged in six of the most difficult UN missions—Lebanon, Haiti, Darfur (Sudan), Liberia, South Sudan and the Democratic Republic of Congo.[47] The Indonesian President, on the request of the visiting UN Secretary General, also agreed to contribute three Russian-made Mi-17 transport helicopters to the UN operations in the Democratic Republic of Congo (DRC), where Indonesia had sent its first ever peacekeeping mission in 1957. Moreover, the country's announcement to commit 4000 troops to various UN peacekeeping missions has made it one of the largest contributors to the UN peacekeeping operations.[48] In order to lend greater credence to its peacekeeping role, the Indonesian government has decided to set up a peacekeeping facility as part of the Indonesian Peace and Security Center in Sentul, Bogor that is the largest international facility in Southeast Asia for the UN peacekeeping purposes.[49] The Indonesian government decided in June 2012 to send one battalion of troops to the UN peacekeeping operations in Darfur, South Sudan.

Indonesian Activism at the UN Climate Change Negotiations

The issue of Climate Change has seen Indonesia's active participation as a responsible stakeholder at the multilateral level. Indonesia, being one of the richest bio-diverse countries of the world and the third largest GHG-emitting country, remains extremely vulnerable to the climate change and therefore is an important stakeholder in the multilateral negotiations over the climate change under the UN auspices.[50] The country hosted the 13th Conference of the Parties to the United Nations Framework Convention on Climate Change (UNFCCC), also known as the Third Meeting of the Parties to the Kyoto Protocol in Bali in December 2007. The conference adopted a Bali Road Map that also includes a Bali Action Plan (BAP), which launched a 'new, comprehensive process to enable the full, effective and sustained implementation of the Convention through long-term cooperative action, now, up to and beyond 2012.'[51]

The BAP set the target of COP 15 at Copenhagen in 2010 for an agreed outcome on various issues of commitments for their operationalisation. The UNFCCC meet in Bali is believed to have not only successfully projected Indonesia's role as an active and powerful contributor to the Climate Change negotiations but also created greater awareness among the common Indonesians by introducing Climate Change as an important agenda at the domestic level.[52]

Since then Indonesia has played a pro-active role in supporting the Climate Change negotiations taking place under the auspices of the UN. The former Vice-President of the US, Al Gore, in his testimony before the Senate Foreign Relations Committee in January 2009 identified Indonesia as a constructive force in the climate negotiations.[53] Indonesia has played an active and supportive role in the negotiations over Reducing Emissions from Deforestation and Degradation (REDD) and the establishment of the adaptation committee.[54] It finally, after much dilly-dallying, approved in December 2012 the Rimba Raya rainforest conservation project 'that sets aside an area roughly the size of Singapore and rewards investors with tradeable carbon credits in the first of its kind to win formal backing in the country.'[55] The Rimba Raya conservation project is an important component of the UN-led REDD scheme.[56]

Indonesia and the G-20: Deliberating over the Global Economic Order

The membership of G-20[57] has not only elevated Indonesia to an important position in the global hierarchy of nations but also provided a powerful avenue for the projection of its international image. Indonesia is aware of this mutually reinforcing relationship and has tried to utilise it effectively as evident from expressions coming from the country on the significance of the G-20 membership. Moreover, the rising Indonesia also represents an underlying paradox that characterises a developing society—rapid economic growth amidst all-pervasive poverty. According to the report of the World Economic Forum, released in June 2011, Indonesia has emerged as the third fastest growing G-20 economy.[58] Moreover, developing economies including Indonesia have proved to be the main driver of global economic recovery and a critical support-base for the world in time of need. Notwithstanding its rapid economic growth during the last five years, Indonesia continues to remain the second poorest member-state (after India) of the G-20 in terms of per capita income.[59] Therefore, the Indonesian representation in the G-20 deliberations highlights both confidence as well as insecurity, and an assertion of demand for greater democratisation of the global economic order along with the projection of its own national interests.

The initial years of Indonesia's participation did not draw much attention due to, as identified by one writer, (a) poor capability of the negotiators, (b) lack of home work in terms of agenda-building, (c) limited national budget, and (d) somewhat stand-alone approach.[60] Since then, Indonesia's role in the G-20 forum has revolved around 'promoting the interests of developing countries, maintaining an inclusive and sustainable global economic system, and encouraging the achievement of a consensus while acting as a bridge builder.'[61] In addition to maintaining the grouping's democratic and problem-solving character, Jakarta seeks to utilise its membership to promote and project the country's growing prosperity as it transitions from 'being a low income country to a middle income country and a beneficiary country to a beneficiary and concurrently a donor country.[62]

Indonesia co-chaired along with France the Working Group – 4 in 2008 to discuss reforms in the Multilateral Development Banks and called for the cleaning up of the infected assets of financial system and greater market access for developing countries.[63] The Pittsburgh summit of G-20 in 2010 saw increasing appreciation from among the member-states for Indonesia's success-story of transforming direct fuel subsidy into direct subsidy (BLT program).[64] Indonesia's performance in the June 2012 G-20 summit, held in Los Cabos, has been viewed by some as (a) focused due to its concentration on three issues—its 'middle-way' approach to balancing austerity and job creation, financial inclusion and infrastructure investment; (b) strategic since it refrained from discussing controversial issues such as green growth; and (c) effective given general appreciation given by the grouping to its two critical proposals—a global financing initiative on infrastructure facilities, and a framework to help develop the pipeline of bankable projects to boost infrastructure development in developing and emerging economies.[65] Moreover, these proposals found space in the final communiqué in the form of G20 Finance Ministers' and Central Bank Governors' Agenda, and was 'well received by other developing countries.'[66] As an ASEAN Chair in 2011, Indonesia mobilised ASEAN resources towards greater ASEAN representation in the G-20 meetings.[67] It becomes amply clear that rising Indonesia is more confident, innovative and forthcoming in its participation in the G-20 deliberations, while putting forth the interests and concerns of the developing world.

Reviving Non-Alignment and Solidarity of the Global South: towards Bandung II

The Bandung summit of April 1955 of Afro-Asian Conference occupies an important position in the conceptualisation of the foreign policy of the post-Colonial Indonesia. It symbolises Indonesia's assertion of (a) a strong and collective voice of countries of Asia and Africa, (b) non-partisan view of the global bodypolitik, (c) free and independent (*bebasdan Aktif*) foreign policy, (d) shared worldview and cooperation among the developing countries, (e) steering of the post-colonial developing world towards peace and prosperity by walking the path of non-alignment, and (f) relevance and necessity of a non-aligned foreign policy. The principle of Non-Alignment has come to shape the basic tenets of Indonesian foreign policy, ever since its encapsulation by Mohammad Hatta in 1948 and in his two subsequent writings.[68]

Democratic Indonesia has made a renewed effort to project the country's long-standing solidarity with the Non-Aligned Movement. In a bid to express its solidarity with the global South and emphasise its independent foreign policy in the 21st century, Indonesia hosted an Asia-Africa Summit in May 2005 to commemorate fifty years of Non-Aligned Movement.[69] The summit adopted a Joint Declaration on the New Asian-African Strategic Partnership (NAASP) that was aimed to be an expression of Indonesia's intent to be an important part of the Afro-Asian solidarity. Moreover, the NAASP Declaration called for close cooperation among the member-states and laid down important objectives of the partnership in the 21st century. It highlighted the need to (a) 'continuously strengthen the process of nation and state-building, as well as social integration; (b) actively pursue a common view and collective action to ensure the equitable sharing of the benefits of globalisation; (c) support and strengthen multilateralism in order to address global issues, including reforming multilateral institutions; (d) support the creation of a viable and sovereign Palestinian state, in accordance with relevant United Nations resolutions; and (e) facilitate dialogue among civilisations to promote a culture of peace, tolerance and respect for religious, cultural, language and racial diversities as well as gender equality.'[70] Moreover, the NAASP laid out a 'framework to build a bridge between Asia and Africa covering three broad areas of partnership, namely political solidarity, economic cooperation, and socio-cultural relations' based on nine principles.[71] As a result of Indonesian advocacy, the G-77 and China agreed during the Second South Summit at Doha in 2005 to adopt a clause regarding the NAASP as recognition of the importance of regional and inter-regional cooperation in improving South-South Cooperation.[72]

In an expression of its continued pursuit of the Non-Aligned Movement and its solidarity with the developing world, the Indonesian leadership also convened a commemorative meeting of the Non-Aligned Movement in Bali in May 2011. While hosting the XVI Ministerial Conference and Commemorative Meeting to celebrate the fifty years of the NAM, the Indonesian President, Susilo Bambang Yudhoyono, called upon the member-states to develop the movement into 'a greater force for peace, justice and prosperity in the 21st century.'[73] He also declared that even though the NAM today has the power of numbers (118 member-states), the platform needs to convert its power into influence and called upon the member states to work in that direction.[74] Indonesia also hosted in April 2015 the 60th Anniversary of Asian-African Conference and the 10th Anniversary of the New Asian-African Strategic Partnership, under the theme of 'Strengthening South-South Cooperation to Promote World Peace and Prosperity,' in which representatives of nearly 100 countries including more than 30 heads of the state from Asian Africa, Europe, Latin America participated.

Conclusion

As rising Indonesia's confidence expands, it is positioning itself as a leader and active stakeholder in the development of a democratic, representative, benign, and stable global order. As such, Indonesia does not seek to radically transform the existing international order, but rather incrementally reform and correct deficiencies in the existing order.

Indonesia's global diplomacy of activism and image-building has faced domestic challenges in the form of an unwillingness to pursue this path seriously and the continuing problem of radicalism. Though Indonesia took an important initiative in reviving the Bandung Spirit, it has remained somewhat lukewarm in taking the step further towards promoting Indonesian profile within NAM. On the other hand, radicalism on the domestic front has challenged Indonesia's global diplomacy and tainted Indonesia's moderate democratic image Notwithstanding global acceptability of its moderate Islamic outlook, attacks on minorities have continued to limit its global projection. It is imperative that a multi-religious, moderately Muslim, democratic, fast-growing, and institutionalising Indonesia addresses challenges, which can, otherwise, undercut a somewhat perfectly crafted success story of a civilisational power from the East.

END NOTES

1. David S. Mason, The End of the American Century, (Lanham: Rowman & Littlefield Publishers, 2008); Fareed Zakaria, The Post American World, (New York: W W Norton & Company, 2009); Sung Won Kim, David P. Fidler, and Sumit Ganguly, "Eastphalia Rising?: Asian Influence and the Fate of Human Security," World Policy Journal, (Summer 2009), pp. 53-64; Kishore Mahbubani, "The Great Convergence: Asia, the West and the Logic of One World, (New York: Public Affairs, 2013); Amitav Acharya, "The End of American World Order, (Cambridge: Polity Press, 2014), Joseph S. Nye Jr., Is the American Century Over? (Cambridge: Polity Press, 2015)
2. G. John Ikanberry (ed.), *Power, Order, and Change in World Politics*, (Cambridge: Cambridge University Press, 2014) (Kindle Edition, Locations 128-131)
3. These nine imperatives are make the 21st century the century of soft power, intensify global dialogue and outreach, find a solution to political conflicts that drive a wedge between the Western and Muslim worlds, strengthen voices of moderation in our communities, multiculturalism and tolerance, make globalisation work for all, reform global governance, educational opportunities in both our homes and our classrooms, and global conscience Susilo Bambang Yudhoyono, "The Confluence of Civilisations," *Common Ground News Service*, 13 October 2009, http://www.commongroundnews.org/article.php?id=26530&lan=en&sp=0
4. "RI's Foreign Policy Consistently Promoting Positive Change," *Antara*, January 4, 2012
5. Ban Ki Moon, "The spirit of Principled Pragmatism," The Economist, November 15, 2007, http://www.economist.com/node/10120161; John Gerrard Ruggie, "UN Guiding Principles for Business & Human Rights," Harvard Law School Forum on Corporate Governance and Financial Regulation, April 09, 2011, http://corpgov.law.harvard.edu/2011/04/09/un-guiding-principles-for-business-human-rights/; Bice Maiguascha, "Looking Beyond the Spectacle: Social Movement Theory, Feminist Anti-Globalisation Activism and the Praxis of Principled Pragmatism," in Laura Montesinos and Karen Tucker (eds.) Situating Global Resistance: Between Discipline and Dissent (New York: Routledge, 2012), pp. 141-156;
6. Ban Ki Moon, "The spirit of Principled Pragmatism,"
7. John Gerrard Ruggie, "UN Guiding Principles for Business & Human Rights," op.cit.
8. Bice Maiguascha, "Looking Beyond the Spectacle: Social Movement Theory, Feminist Anti-Globalisation Activism and the Praxis of Principled Pragmatism," op.cit. p. 150
9. Amitav Acharya, Indonesia Matters: Asia's Emerging Democratic Power, (Singapore: World Scientific, 2014), pp. 99-100
10. Susilo Bambang Yudhoyono, "Indonesia's Role as Regional and Global Actor," *The Wilton Park Annual Address*, London, 2 November 2012, http://www.presidenri.go.id/index.php/eng/pidato/2012/11/02/2001.html
11. Dewi Fortuna Anwar, "Key Aspects of Indonesia's Foreign Policy" in *Trends in Southeast Asia Series*, no. 9, (Singapore, ISEAS, 2003), p. 2; "Indonesia's Foreign Policy," *Embassy of the Republic of Indonesia in Ottawa, Canada*, http://www.indonesia-ottawa.org/discover-indonesia/foreign-policy/
12. Anthony L. Smith, "Indonesia's Foreign Policy under Abdurrahman Wahid: Radical or Status Quo State?," *Contemporary Southeast Asia*, vol. 22, no. 3, (December 2000), pp. 499-504

13. Ehito Kimura, "Indonesia in 2011: A Glass Half-Empty," *Asian Survey*, vol. 52, no. 1, p. 186; Thomas Carothers, "The New Republic: A Lesson for Egypt In Indonesia," *National Public Radio*, 03 February 2011, http://www.npr.org/2011/02/03/133461179/the-new-republic-a-lesson-for-egypt-in-indonesia; Joshua Kurlantzik, "Is Egypt the Next Indonesia?," *Council on Foreign Relations*, 07 February 2011, http://blogs.cfr.org/asia/2011/02/07/is-egypt-the-next-indonesia/; Robin Bush, "Indonesia: An Example for Egypt, or a Democracy in Retreat?," *The Asia Foundation*, 16 February 2011, http://asiafoundation.org/in-asia/2011/02/16/indonesia-an-example-for-egypt-or-a-democracy-in-retreat/
14. "The Indonesian example: Remember 1998," *The Economist*, 07 February 2011, http://www.economist.com/blogs/asiaview/2011/02/indonesian_example
15. Shada Islam, "Indonesian example," *The Dawn*, 10 December 2012, http://dawn.com/2011/12/10/indonesian-example/
16. Bantarto Bandoro, "Democracy and Indonesian Diplomacy Beyond 2009," *Jurnal Diplomasi*, vol. 1, no. 1, (June 2009), p. 37
17. "What is the Bali Democracy Forum," *Bali Democracy Forum*, Department of Foreign Affairs,
18. "Opening Statement by the President of Republic of Indonesia at the Bali Democracy Forum V," *Presidential Secretariat*, 8 November 2012, http://www.presidenri.go.id/index.php/eng/pidato/2012/11/08/1999.html
19. Ibid.
20. Rizal Sukma, "Indonesia Finds a New Voice," *Journal of Democracy*, vol. 22, no. 4, October 2011, p. 119; Meidyatama Suryodiningrat, "ASEAN 9, Human Rights 1," *The Jakarta Post*, 24 July 2009
21. Azymardi Azra, "Islam, Indonesia and Democracy," *Strategic Review*, vol. 1, no. 1, August 2011, p. 74.
22. "Indonesia-U.S. Relations: A Comprehensive Partnership," *Metropolitan Corporate Counsel*, vol. 19, no. 3, 28 February 2011, p. 45, 48, http://www.metrocorpcounsel.com/pdf/2011/March/45.pdf
23. Ibid.
24. Kai He, "Indonesia's foreign policy after Soeharto: international pressure, democratisation, and policy change," *International Relations of the Asia-Pacific*, vol. 8, no. 1, 2008, p. 66.
25. Susilo Bambang Yudhoyono, "Indonesia's Role as Regional and Global Actor," op.cit.
26. "Indonesia and the United Nations: Working Together for Peace and Development," *Permanent Mission of the Republic of Indonesia to the United Nations*, (New York, 2005), p. 356.
27. Ibid, pp. 353-356
28. Ibid;
29. "Indonesia Calls for UN Reform," *Antara*, 27 September 2011
30. "Indonesia and the United Nations: Working Together for Peace and Development," op.cit. p. 356
31. Quoted in Bardo Fassbender, *UN Security Council Reform and the Right of Veto: A Constitutional Perspective*, (Netherlands, Martinus Nijhoff Publishers, 1998), p. 251
32. Bagus BT Saragih and Yohanna Ririhena, "Composition in UNSC no longer Relevant," *The Jakarta Post*, 01 October 2012.
33. Statement by H.E. Mrs. Adiyatiwidi A. Adiwoso, Deputy Permanent Representative of the Republic of Indonesia to the United Nations at the Meeting of the Open-ended Working Group on the Question of Equitable Representation on and Increase in the Membership of

the Security Council and Other Matters related to the Security Council, New York, 2 September 2008, http://www.indonesiamission-ny.org/NewStatements/ps090208.htm

34. "Indonesia and the United Nations: Working Together for Peace and Development," op. cit. p. 382.
35. "IMF Managing Director Visits Indonesia, Meets President Susilo Bambang Yudhoyono," *IMF Press Release*, no. 12/254, 10 July 2012, http://www.imf.org/external/np/sec/pr/2012/pr12254.htm
36. Arientha Primanita, Francezka Nangoy and Tito Summa Siahaan, "Indonesia's Pledge of $1 Billion to IMF Marks an Era Of Financial Independence: SBY," *Jakarta Globe*, 11 July 2012.
37. Peter Alford, "Fifteen years after Humiliation, Indonesia turns the tables on IMF," *The Australian*, 11 July 2012
38. "Indonesia, Countries urge UN to Implement cease fire in Libya," *People's Daily Online*, 28 March 2011, http://english.peopledaily.com.cn/90001/90777/90855/7333132.html
39. Yayan G.H. Mulyana, "Peacekeeping operations and Indonesian Foreign Policy," *The Jakarta Post*, 03 January 2012
40. "RI Elected to UN Human Rights Council for Third Time," *Antara*, 21 May 2011
41. Andre Omer Siregar, "SBY's strong message, sense of optimism at the UN," *The Jakarta Post*, 05 October 2012
42. Yayan G.H. Mulyana, "Peacekeeping operations and Indonesian Foreign Policy," op.cit.
43. Ibid.
44. "Indonesia wants to advance peacekeeping role in 2011," *The Jakarta Post*, 08 January 2011.
45. Ibid.
46. "On regional tour, Ban salutes Indonesia's commitment to UN peacekeeping," *UN News Centre*, 20 March 2012, http://www.un.org/apps/news/story.asp?NewsID=41589&Cr=Indonesia&Cr1#.UMwig6V33dk; "Indonesia to Send 4,000 Troops, Helicopters to UN Peacekeeping Missions," *The Jakarta Globe*, 20 March 2012
47. Ibid.
48. Ibid.
49. Nani Afrida, "Indonesia to send peacekeeping battalion to Darfur," *The Jakarta Post*, 08 June 2012
50. Agus P. Sari (ed.), *Indonesia and Climate Change: Current Status and Policies*, (Jakarta, Peace, 2007), p. 9
51. "Bali Climate Change Conference, December 2007," *United Nations Framework Convention on Climate Change*, http://unfccc.int/meetings/bali_dec_2007/meeting/6319.php
52. Frank Jotzo, "Indonesia a key player in climate deal?," *East Asia Forum*, 08 February 2009, http://www.eastasiaforum.org/2009/02/08/indonesia-a-key-player-in-climate-deal/
53. Ibid.
54. Fitrian Ardiyansyah, "Durban climate talks bring mixed results for Indonesia," *East Asia Forum*, 20 December 2011, http://www.eastasiaforum.org/2011/12/20/durban-climate-talks-bring-mixed-results-for-indonesia/
55. David Fogarty, "Indonesia Approves Landmark Forest Protection Project, *Jakarta Globe*, 05 December 2012
56. Ibid.
57. Established in 1999 as an informal grouping of nations, the G-20 has gained significance in the aftermath of 2008 economic crisis that swept the advanced West but spared the emerging economies of the developing world. The G-20, since then, has focused on (a) developing ways and means for global economic recovery, (b) reforms in the international

financial institutions, including greater representation of the developing world in the IMF and World Bank, (c) international monetary reform including greater integration of finances and curbing of excessive volatility, and (d) pursuing an agreed development agenda. The members of G-20 are Argentina, Australia, Brazil, Canada, China, European Union, France, Germany, India, Indonesia, Italy, Japan, Mexico, Russia, Saudi Arab, South Africa, South Korea, Turkey, UK, and USA.

58. "Indonesia's Economic Competitiveness Improving: WER Report," *Asia Pulse*, 08 June 2011,
59. Zamroni Salim, "Indonesia in the G20: Benefits And Challenges Amidst National Interests and Priorities," in Wilhelm Hofmeister (ed.), *G20: Perceptions and Perspectives for Global Governance* (Singapore, Konrad Adenauer Stiftung, 2011), p. 97
60. Ibid; p. 98
61. "Ministry of Foreign Affairs – Multilateral Cooperation," *Government of Indonesia*,http://www.kemlu.go.id/Pages/IFPDisplay.aspx?Name=MultilateralCooperation &IDP=11&P=Multilateral&l=en
62. Ibid.
63. Zamroni Salim, "Indonesia in the G20: Benefits And Challenges Amidst National Interests and Priorities," op.cit. p. 103
64. "Ministry of Foreign Affairs – Multilateral Cooperation," op.cit.
65. Maria Monica Wiharja, "Indonesia and the G20: a door left half open," *East Asia Forum*, 29 June 2012, http://www.eastasiaforum.org/2012/06/29/indonesia-and-the-g20-a-door-left-half-open/
66. Ibid.
67. Winfried Weck, "ASEAN and G20 – Indonesia 's Foreign Policy Perspectives," *Konrad Adenauer Stiftung International Reports*, no. 2, 2011, http://www.kas.de/wf/doc/kas_21871-1522-2-30.pdf?110209123433
68. Mohammad Hatta, "Indonesia's Foreign Policy," *Foreign Affairs; an American Quarterly Review*, vol. 31, no. 1, (1952-53), pp. 441-452; Ide Anak Agung Gde Agung, *Twenty Years of Indonesian Foreign Policy 1945-65*, (The Hague, Mouton, 1973)
69. "Background Notes: Indonesia," *State Department Press Release*, Government of the United States of America, 03 November 2010, http://www.state.gov/r/pa/ei/bgn/2748.htm#foreign
70. "Declaration on the New Asian-African Strategic Partnership," http://www.kbri-canberra.org.au/lains/Hasil%20KTT%20AA%202005.pdf
71. Ibid.
72. The South Summit is the highest level of meeting involving the member states of G-77 and China. So far only two summits have taken place – Havana in April 2000 and Doha in June 2005. "Ministry of Foreign Affairs – Multilateral Cooperation," op.cit.
73. Abdul Khalik and Desy Nurhayati, "RI Wants NAM to play Greater Role on World Stage," *The Jakarta Post*, 26 May 2011, http://www.thejakartapost.com/print/325293
74. Ibid.

10

Post-Coup Fiji and Political Reform: Westminster under the 2013 Constitution

Richard A. Herr

Introduction

India has variety of reasons based in history, demographics, culture, and the new geo-politics of the Asia-Pacific region for maintaining its close ties with the Republic of Fiji. One of the less appreciated factors, perhaps, has been the shared experience of the Westminster model of parliamentary democracy. This has been an important direct political linkage both broadly through the Commonwealth of Nations and more specifically through such parliamentary ties as the Commonwealth Parliamentary Association (CPA). Although often under-rated by foreign affairs commentators, these parliamentary connections have been significant contributor to international networking through common political expectations and experience. Indeed, the cultural adaptability of the Westminster model has provided a political lingua franca that helps to explain why the Commonwealth of Nations has been such a robust political association for so long. Thus, from the most rarefied philosophical debates to the most practical personal interactions, parliamentary arrangements based on the Westminster model, such as the CPA, have provided a useful platform for cross-national understanding and cooperation within the Commonwealth.

At the time this chapter is being written, it is not clear that the Commonwealth will continue to link India and Fiji. Recent decisions to remove the Queen from its currency, the crown from police insignia and the Union Jack from Fiji's flag have heightened speculation that a complete disengagement from the Commonwealth is likely.[1] Nevertheless, the parliamentary connection will remain a relevant influence in bilateral relations as evidenced by the training of parliamentary staff in India in the lead-up to the restoration of the Fijian Parliament in 2014. Just how important the lingua franca of parliament may prove to be for India will depend, in part, on parliament's role in the new post-coup domestic political environment of Fiji. Prime Minister Voreqe Bainimarama, the architect of the both the 2006 military coup and the return to parliamentary democracy in 2014, has wrought significant changes to the role and operation of the newly restored parliament. Many of the culturally and racially based non-liberal aspects of Fiji's pre-2006 parliamentary system have been removed. Indeed, his roadmap for the return to democracy was grounded in reversing the communalism and ethnic divisions that he believed had been strengthened since independence. This chapter reviews Bainimarama's cure for the perceived malignancy of communalism with a special emphasis on the changes to the Westminster model of parliament in Fiji. Arguably, his cure has created a more liberal, non-racial order for Fiji albeit with a strong corporatist (party political) side effects and a noticeable undertone of personal leadership. These pose some new, perhaps, unintended consequences for the Parliament and its emerging role in the politics of Fiji.

Some Pre-2006 Historical Context

Mutual political adaptation with the intrusion colonial regime in Fiji began very early. The British Government applied significant aspects of indirect rule to Fiji after Ratu Seru Cakobau ceded the country to Queen Victoria in 1874. Traditional elites served in administrative posts using largely traditional mechanisms to maintain British authority in the colony.[2] The process was a two-way street as the traditional political authorities used the indirect rule system to strengthen and entrench their political power and their control of land within indigenous society. Thus the colonial experience for Fiji found both foreign administrators and indigenous chiefs benefiting from the process of cultural adaptation.

The colonial system fossilised perceived political status through both the recognition of titles and lands in a way that prevented further changes. The rising indigenous elites especially those close to the colonial administration were happier than those that lost out in historic challenges to the claims of the winners. Even less happy were latecomers from South Asia brought to Fiji to work as indentured labour in the colony's plantations. Unlike the indigenous Fijians (now known officially as *iTaukei*) or the European plantation owners, the indentured labourers had almost no access to land or to positions of influence with the system of indirect rule. Not only did this provide fuel for social disharmony as the ethnic balance within Fiji shifted, when the "winds of change" began to stir, it imposed political constraints on just how to end colonial rule in Fiji.

The issue of traditional political authority emerged as a significant independence issue from the late 1940s when the former indentured labourers; their children and grandchildren became the majority ethnic community in Fiji. Inter-communal strife in the wake of decolonisation in such former colonies as Cyprus, Kenya and Singapore were very much in the minds of the British authorities contemplating the timing of Fiji's independence. The expectation of communal tensions made the search for some acceptable form of parliamentary democracy fraught at every turning and delayed Fiji's independence longer than would have been expected. The Indo-Fijian leadership favoured a liberal one vote-one value approach while the Fijian leadership wanted traditional political values and power structures recognised and retained in some measure. A set of compromises was reached in the late 1960s. These provided for the inclusion of some traditional Fijian political elements as well a voting system that guaranteed communal representation. The blend of communal and liberal accommodations went far enough at the time politically to temper ethnic fears regarding the demographic imbalance and independence was achieved October 10, 1970.[3]

Fiji's independence Constitution gave constitutional status to customary political processes when it recognised the Great Council of Chiefs (*GCC* or *Bose Levu Vakaturaga*). This body had served an advisory role to the Governor shortly after Cession. In the decade or so before independence, the GCC had added indigenous institutional leaders to its number who did not hold chiefly titles. The GCC became virtually a third chamber to the formally bicameral parliament through its power to appoint more than a third of the Senate and its influence on *iTaukei* policy including the sensitive area of communally owned land. The 1970 Constitution also entrenched an ethnically based electoral system that reinforced the communal compromise in the 52 member House of Representatives. Three communities divided reserved seats that were not entirely proportional in terms of ethnic numbers. The majority

Indo-Fijian community shared an equal number of seats with the indigenous Fijians (22 seats each) with the remaining 8 preserved for "General Electors" (Europeans, Chinese, Pacific Islanders etc.). The Senate also showed the ethnic compromise. The Prime Minister nominated 7 Senators, the Leader of the Opposition nominated 6, the GCC 8 and the island of Rotuma one.

The two military coups of 1987 brought about a number of changes to further enhance *iTaukei* influence in Government through the incorporation of traditional mechanisms and processes. An attempt was made to constitutionally preserve the prime ministership for an *iTaukei* leader and a permanent majority for *iTaukei* in the House of Representatives in a failed 1990 Constitution. This was replaced in 1997 by one that promoted the powers of the GCC while removing the *iTaukei*-preserved majority in parliament and *iTaukei* ownership of the office of the Prime Minister. Nonetheless, under the 1997 Constitution the GCC retained the authority to appoint the President and 14 of the 32 Senators. The 1997 Constitution also further entrenched *iTaukei* ownership of the majority of land held through communal titles.

The 2006 Military Coup

Unlike the military coups elsewhere in the world or, indeed, the coup d'états of May 1987 and September 1987 or the civilian-led coup in May 2000, Fiji's December 2006 military coup came as no surprise. The Commander of the Republic of Fiji Military Forces (RFMF), Commodore Voreqe Bainimarama, signalled his intention to stage a coup months in advance. However, the intention was always followed by an "unless"—that is, unless certain demands of the Government of Prime Minister Laisenia Qarase were met. His conditions revolved around undoing the mistakes that Bainimarama believed that the Qarase Government was making in governing Fiji. The reason he felt entitled to impose conditions on the continuance of the Qarase Government stemmed from the personal responsibility Bainimarama for having put Qarase into power after the 2000 coup.[4]

The Commander of the RFMF was particularly sensitive to his responsibility for Fiji's circumstances following the 2000 coup for a number of reasons. The RFMF did not engineer the coup. George Speight, a civilian businessman, and a handful of i*Taukei* nationalist supporters did when they seized the Prime Minister Mahendra Chaudhry, much of his cabinet and other MPs holding them as hostages in the parliamentary precincts in order to bring the Government down. A week later, a small number of RFMF officers and soldiers mutinied in support of Speight. The mutineers made an attempt to assassinate Bainimarama and succeeded in killing three other loyal soldiers. As head of the RFMF, Bainimarama was profoundly affected by the awareness that a civilian could undermine so lethally the military's chain of command. In deciding to take charge of the situation, Bainimarama turned a faltering civilian insurrection into a full military coup. Rather than restoring Chaudhry to the prime ministership, Bainimarama installed Laisenia Qarase, a banker, who he regarded as a political "cleanskin" unsullied by political ties.

For such reasons as these, Bainimarama felt a strong sense of continuing responsibility for, bordering on ownership of, the aftermath of the 2000 coup. He saw Qarase's actions in power as less those of a cleanskin and more those of an old-style politician. Bainimarama became increasingly vocal in attacking the Qarase Government's agenda, which he perceived to be implementing a racial agenda in favour of *iTaukei* interests. Bainimarama opposed the election of the Qarase Government in May 2006. He believed its narrow win rested on some corrupt practices and challenged its validity. In the months prior to December, Bainimarama encapsulated his challenge to the Qarase in three (sets of demands of Qarase that would) obviate the need for military intervention. Bainimarama demanded the Qarase drop proposed legislation entrenching *iTaukei* control of land and water resources, legislation that seemed to support the Speight coup, and the use of some convicted coup-plotters in political offices.

There were a variety of other reasons that have been advanced for the 2006 coup and the complexity of events from 2000 suggests that any simplifying explanation would certainly be simplistic. However, the influences identified above had a bearing on Bainimarama's personalised approach to democracy and politics subsequently. Of course, it is highly improbable that these influences explain all that have shaped the constitutional and political developments in Fiji's return to parliamentary democracy. Nonetheless, they do appear relevant to some of the compromises made with Fiji's earlier constitutional and Westminster experience.

The New Parliament—Mostly Westminster?

After nearly eight years without a parliament following the 2006 military coup, Fiji returned to parliamentary democracy through a national election in September 2014. Fiji returned to a basically Westminster model parliament but one with some important qualifying changes. These changes were embedded in a new order portrayed by the post-2006 coup Government of Fiji as a watershed between the old communal politics and a new, non-racial, more liberally based politics. Indeed, in a post-election speech to the United Nations General Assembly, the Prime Minister characterised all of Fiji's previous systems as "undemocratic, unjust and unfair" and asserted that now Fiji had "true democracy".[5] The basis for the coup Government's broad reform agenda was a five-year roadmap announced in July 2009. Its underpinnings were grounded in principles articulated in the 2008 *Peoples Charter for Peace Progress and Change*[6] (herein after *Peoples Charter*) and expressed in 2013 through a new Constitution.[7]

The 2013 Constitution along with some crucial implementing decrees sought to remove both ethnic and customary influences from the new Parliament and, indeed, from the politics of Fiji. The communal influences in the pre-2006 parliamentary institutions were eradicated. Ethnic influences in the Senate were eliminated by eliminating the Senate altogether. The Great Council of Chiefs had been formally abolished a year earlier in 2012. The 2014 Parliament was a unicameral composed of 50 elected Members and a non-elected Speaker who served four-year terms. The Constitution established a strong liberal base for the Parliament through the electoral system. Core liberal values were expressed directly through Sec 53(1), which provided that "each voter has one vote, with each vote being of equal value..." Ethnic and racial discrimination is proscribed by its Bill of Rights and underscored by provisions in both party and electoral decrees. Perhaps, the most historically significant change was the elimination of racially based voting by the creation of a single national common roll for all voters and a single national constituency without any communally reserved seats. The Political Party (Registration, Conduct, Funding and Disclosures) Decree of 2013 provides an example of a decree reinforcing the Constitution protections. It required any association attempting to register as a political party to demonstrate its bona fides as non-discriminatory and not to "advocate hatred that constitutes ethnic or religious incitement or vilification of others or any other "communal antagonism".[8]

The one area where the Constitution could not avoid recognising traditional custom and practice was in the area of land ownership. Although a continuing source of political contention amongst some *iTaukei* as to its value, Sec 29(1) of the Constitution provides: "The ownership of all *iTaukei* land shall remain with the customary owners of that land and *iTaukei* land shall not be permanently alienated, whether by sale, grant, transfer or exchange, except to the State…". Nevertheless, even this, demonstrated in its own way the extent to which Bainimarama and his Government had reduced the effects of ethnicity in at the national level. This issue had defeated the concerted efforts of the NCBBF despite profound sensitivity to the divisiveness of not having a common name. Bainimarama cut through the Gordian knot of symbolic communalism by finding a single name for all citizens. He simply declared a common name through a 2010 decree to call all citizens "Fijian".[9] The word "*iTaukei*" (owner of the land) is now officially used to describe both the indigenous people and the language of Fiji.

The Constitution preserved core elements of the Westminster form of responsible Government by providing that only a Member of Parliament can be appointed a Minister with the possible exception of the Attorney General. The Attorney General may be appointed from outside the Parliament if the Prime Minister deems there is no suitable person available from amongst the elected Members [Sec 96(3)]. A non-elected Attorney General would sit in the Parliament but not be eligible to vote. Once the Parliament elects the Prime Minister, the PM elects the ministry as a Cabinet that serves the dual purpose as an executive council as well as the Government in Parliament. The Speaker is appointed from outside the membership of the Parliament but the individual must be qualified to stand as a candidate for the Parliament. Significantly, the Constitution elevates the Leader of the Opposition to an office of the Parliament (Sec 78) rather than leaving this to Standing Orders or conventional practice.

The electoral system rests in the cusp between the Constitution's liberal intentions and a corporatist implementation. Section 53 provides for the open list system of proportional representation (PR). The open list PR system was deliberately recommended by the *Peoples Charter* process precisely to limit the influence of political parties in determining electoral outcomes.[10] Yet, significant constraints on these liberal aspirations were imposed subsequently through the decrees regulating the registration of political parties and the election. Importantly from the parliamentary perspective, a strong party corporatist approach was taken in the Constitution that serves to undermine some of the liberal aspects of the electoral system. Political party discipline overrides constituency influence in Parliament even to the point of breaching the privileges standard for most Westminster Parliaments by giving constitutional validity to external bodies controlling the actions of an MP on the floor of the parliament. A Member may be expelled from the Parliament if the MP:

> votes or abstains from voting in Parliament contrary to any direction issued by the political party...without obtaining the prior permission of the political party [Sec 63(1)(h)].

Other provisions of this section take the party's control of a Member even further as the seat can be lost if the MP resigns from the party or is expelled from the party. Thus the membership of the Parliament can be determined outside the electoral process by unelected party machine officials if these officials impose party discipline over MPs unrelated to parliamentary duties. However, it is uncertain how to interpret the qualification that expulsion from the party should "not relate to any action taken by the member in his or her capacity as a member of a committee of Parliament" [Sec 63]. It is not clear why parliamentary committee activities are privileged from disciple by the party machinery more than actions on the floor of the Parliament.

Individual ministerial responsibility is another area where the Constitution supports a party corporatist approach over individual obligation and accountability. The Constitution provides that "Cabinet members are accountable individually and collectively to Parliament, for the exercise of their powers and the performance of their functions" [Sec 91(1)]. However, while accountability might be individual, Sec 95(3) suggests that responsibility may not be. Ministers continue in office unless removed by the Prime Minister, ceasing to be a Member of Parliament, or by resigning. There is no provision for removing an individual Minister by a parliamentary want of confidence motion. While in the event, perhaps, not much different in practice from other Westminster parliaments, the absence of a specific reference to the role of the parliament seems an unusual oversight. On the other hand, a successful motion of no confidence in the Prime Minister deems every other Minister to have resigned. As is the case in Papua New Guinea, for example, any motion against a PM must be constructive; e.g. propose the name of the alternative PM [Sec 94(1)].

Chapter 8 of the Constitution requires the enactment by statute of a "code of conduct" for all public officers established under the Constitution. Members of Parliament are so listed. The Constitution also established an independent authority, the Accountability and Transparency Commission, which is to oversee compliance with this code of conduct once enacted. The Commission will have the power to investigate breaches of the code. Even more, however, the Commission will have the power to enforce this code "through criminal and disciplinary proceedings, and provide for the removal from office of those officers who are found to be in breach of the code of conduct". Again, it appears that an outside body unelected agency will have control over MPs that, at least in this case, would be more normally the responsibility of the Parliament through its privileges committee.

Aspects of personal power have been expressed somewhat curiously through the 2013 Constitution in ways that appear at odds with standard Westminster practice. Not only are Ministers not directly responsible to Parliament, Sec 92(3) states that the Prime Minister "appoints" and "dismisses" Ministers. This may not seem surprising at first blush since generally it is accepted that PMs make these determinations around the Westminster world. However, its significance becomes clearer when contrasted with the more conventional wording regarding this relationship. For example, Sec 99(1) of the 1997 Constitution states, "The President appoints and dismisses other Ministers on the advice of the Prime Minister." Under the 2013 Constitution, the President's role is limited to administering the oath of office. He plays no formal role in the appointment or dismissal of Ministers.

Technically, the usual Westminster description of the Prime Minister as "primus inter pares"—the first amongst equals – does not apply in Fiji today. Arguably, under the 2013 Constitution, the Ministers are subordinates of the Prime Minister. Thus, the 2013 Constitution underscores the personal authority of the PM. This locates the current Fijian parliamentary system in a hybrid grey area somewhere between the Westminster model and the American model of executive autonomy. It is closer to the Westminster model but clearly altered significant relationship between the parliamentary and executive arms of government in Fiji and between these at the state of Fiji.

Some Concluding Thoughts

Deep ethnic divisions have been a tragically central feature of Fiji's adoption and adaptation of the Westminster model. The implicit preference of the Westminster model for stable Government based on controlling a majority in Parliament contributed to the ethnic tensions that have bedevilled Fiji since before independence. Customary *iTaukei* political forms had been a central part of the administration of colonial Fiji but confecting majority role for *iTaukei* while in the minority at independence left a legacy of political tension and strife. Indeed, it is impossible to treat the past half-century of parliamentary development in Fiji without acknowledging that the struggle to control its institutional norms has played a critical role in this fractured and fractious political narrative. Whether a liberal electoral system to elect a parliament with no inbuilt accommodations to customary *iTaukei* political processes might have worked is only conjecture now. Whether it can work today, given a contemporary *iTaukei* majority now exists, is in the process of being tested.

The newly re-instituted Fijian Parliament is a principal crucible in which this experiment will be carried out. Trying to surmount old ethnic tensions, claims of an entrenched coup culture and the persistence of non-liberal customary political influences, are not the only challenges the Parliament is facing. It will have to confront some factors that appear to undermine the supremacy of the Westminster parliament. The 2013 Constitution has created a high level of dependence on political parties as mechanisms for accountability as well as undermining some of the traditional privileges of parliament. The entrenchment of the authority of political parties in Parliament and, at times, over it in the Constitution is a source of concern for the doctrine of the supremacy of parliament. The institutional fragility of political parties adds significantly to such apprehensions. The personal power of the Prime Minister may also be factor in the operation of such important Westminster principles as ministerial responsibility.

The elimination of racial tensions and finding representational compromises that will allow Fiji to put its troubled parliamentary history behind it may prove these risks appropriate and effective. The future stretches forward as a blank page yet to be written. However, there is a further constitutional uncertainty overhanging Fiji's new parliamentary system to adjust to teething problems, new challenges or altered priorities. So much of the operation of the Fijian Parliament is set in constitutional "concrete" that much of the traditional flexibility of the Westminster parliament may be lost. Chapter 11 of the 2013 Constitution requires three quarters of the Parliament to support a proposed amendment and three quarters of the registered voters in a subsequent referendum vote in favour for the amendment to be passed. This is such a high bar that few believe the Constitution can ever be amended. If this proves to be the case, it seems likely that adaptation and reform will become sources of political contention. If this debate comes, perhaps, it will proceed without the racial rancour of the past.

The understanding and support of other democratic parliaments will be important regardless of how challenging the way forward is for Fiji's restored Parliament. India has a role in this today just as it has had since 1948 when independent India established a representational post in Suva more than two decades before Fijian independence. India's role in co-chairing (with Australia and Indonesia) the Multinational Observation Group (MOG) played an important role in insuring international acceptance of the election result. Material support from India for the conduct of the election also contributed to this success. Whether, bilaterally or multilaterally through such mechanisms as the CPA, parliamentary relations will be a significant arena in the years ahead for India to assist in maintaining and deepening Fiji's return to democracy.

END NOTES

1. Fiji has been a republic since 1987 but all these elements were retained out of affection for the British monarch and a continuing role in the Commonwealth of Nations.
2. For a very useful introduction to these cultural interactions, see: Peter France, *The Charter of the Land: Custom and Colonisation in Fiji* (Melbourne: Oxford University Press, 1969).
3. For an historical survey of the events leading to independence, see Brij V. Lal, *A time bomb lies buried : Fiji's road to independence, 1960-1970* (Acton, A.C.T.: ANU E Press, 2008).
4. This interpretation of the initial causes of the 2006 coup were covered in the author's "External Influences and the 2006 Fiji Military Coup" *Harvard Asia Pacific Review*, Winter 2007, Vol 9, no 1 (2007), pp. 10-13. Other elements in this passage of the chapter have been based on the author's personal experience as an advisor to the National Council for Building a Better Fiji and involvement with the development of the *Peoples Charter*.
5. Rear Admiral J. V. Bainimarama, Speech at the 69th Session of the United Nations General Assembly, 27 September 2014. Accessed at: http://www.un.org/en/ga/69/meetings/gadebate/pdf/FJ_en.pdf.
6. Government of Fiji, National Council for Building a Better Fiji, *Peoples Charter for Peace Progress and Change*, 15 December 2008. Accessed at: http://www.itaukeiaffairs.gov.fj/docs/finalcharter.pdf.
7. The 2013 Constitution of the Republic of Fiji can be accessed at: http://www.fiji.gov.fj/getattachment/8e981ca2-1757-4e27-88e0-f87e3b3b844e/Click-here-to-download-the-Fiji-Constitution.aspx.
8. Government of Fiji, *Government of Fiji Gazette*, Political Parties (Registration, Conduct, Funding And Disclosures) Decree 2013 (Decree No. 4 of 2013), 15th January 2013. Accessed at: http://www.electionsfiji.gov.fj/wp-content/uploads/2013/04/PoliticalPartiesDecree20131.pdf.
9. Government of Fiji, *Government of Fiji Gazette*, Fijian Affairs [Amendment] Decree 2010 (Decree No. 31 of 2010), 2nd July 2010. Accessed at: http://www.fiji.gov.fj/getattachment/edb60dd9-82c3-4064-9e2a-478c0f34d261/Decree-No-31—Fijian-Affairs-(Amendment)-Decree-2.aspx.
10. As an advisor to the National Council for Building a Better Fiji (NCBBF) that developed the Peoples Charter, the author was intimately aware of the debate on the merits of the open list system and its alternatives.

11

Coups, Constitutions and Struggle for Power:
Contours of Racial Politics in Fiji

Amba Pande

Fiji, the Pacific Island country, with 37 percent ethnic Indian population, went to polls on 17 September 2014, ending the eight year wait after the coup in 2006. This is a notable step forward for a fragile democracy fraught with racial politics and prone to coups and changing constitutions.[1] The elections were held on the basis of 2013 constitution which introduced radical changes in the political system of Fiji by bringing the ethnic Indians almost at par with the ethnic Fijians. However, the bigger challenge is how well the transition is managed and the democracy progresses and above all, to what extent Bainimarama, the ex-coup leader who swapped his position to become democratically elected prime minister is able to act as the bulwark between Indo-Fijians and a Fijian nationalist (already irked by the changes introduced by his government) backlash. The chapter seeks to situate the ethnic Indians in the deep rooted racial politics of Fiji inherited from its colonial past and analyse how Indians were made a convenient scapegoat in the power struggle of the Fijian society. The chapter would also try to assess the Constitutional changes introduced in Fiji over the years and its impact on the ethnic Indians who have been emigrating in large numbers from Fiji.

Race Relations in Fiji: A Historical Sketch

The race problem in Fiji has its roots in its colonial past when the first British Governor Gordon (1875-80) of the colony established a regime under the policy of 'Paramountcy of Fijian Interests', to protect the Fijian people, society and culture from encroachments by Europeans. Strict restrictions were imposed on the recruitment of ethnic Fijians in the plantations and the ownership of almost 83 per cent of the country's land was confirmed to ethnic Fijians. Gordon also, 'standardised the Fijian social structure by the innovation of 'Council of Chiefs' which became the basis of Fijian administration and an instrument of chiefly domination.[2] The rights to control the bureaucratic management of the traditional land further strengthened the position of the Chiefs 'condemning the Fijians to the tutelage of their own Chiefs'.[3]

Fiji's colonial economy was based primarily on the sugar industry for which a constant supply of labour was needed. As a result, indentured recruitment for Fiji was started in 1879 and by the time it ended in 1916, there were around 61,000 Indian indentured labour on the Fijian soil. The British followed a policy of complete segregation between Indo-Fijians and ethnic Fijians. Most of the Indo-Fijians were employed in sugarcane plantations concentrated in western Fiji while most of the indigenous Fijians were confined to their traditional occupations in their villages. The British also evolved separate local administrations for the two ethnic communities. In the words of Stephanie Hegan "Gordon introduced a form of indirect rule by way of a separate native administration which was to keep Fijians in an economic backwater and in a relative isolation from the mainstream of colonial politics. Indeed, it can be argued that these effects are largely responsible for many of the economic problems that the Fijians continue to experience but which are frequently blamed on the Fiji Indian community which has become a convenient scapegoat."[4]

As the Indians completed their indentured terms (5+5 years) majority of them decided to stay back, took land on lease, made it cultivable, and started sugarcane cultivation for big sugar producing Australian multinationals which were running Fiji's sugar industry. Over the years, Indians succeeded, prospered and as John Davis says, "largely managed to transcend them, creating through their sweat, blood and enterprise the modern economy of Fiji while continuously improving themselves through education, application and discipline."[5] With economic prosperity came entrepreneurship which brought them into direct competition with European traders. Other than indentured labourers there were also 'free migrants' from India, mainly Gujarati business people and traders who too were making their impact on Fijian economy. It was the fight for economic survival and progress that brought the political awareness and pushed the Indians in the political mainstream of Fiji.[6] Their century old presence in the island country has largely been a success story, which has remained the major source of resentment against them. The Indians also had multiplied and outnumbered Fijians by 1946 in the population, which made it easier for the British to inspire the belief that if they were given equal political rights, they would take over the country which legitimately belonged to the Fijians.

Democracy versus Race versus Traditionalism

Thus from the very beginning, the general debate over democracy and equality in Fiji got entangled with the issues of race and traditionalism. The ethnic Indians who had a long history of labour and peasant movement behind them pitched for equal political rights, franchise rights, one man, one vote system, common electorate and a common identification for all the citizens of Fiji. On the other hand, this idea was unacceptable to the British; as well as most of the Fijians on the ground that it might dilute their political identity. Hence, the democratic ideas professed by the ethnic Indians came to be regarded as being against Fijian interests. Democracy was seen a 'Foreign flower'[7] which by putting ethnic Indians on equal footing was directly confronting with ethnic Fijian traditional order represented by systems of chieftaincy. The idea of 'Paramountcy of Fijian interests' conveniently shifted its focus from Europeans to Indians as the main threat to the Fijian society. So much so that independence was opposed by the Fijians not willing to come out of the protective cover of the Europeans.

Land was another contentious issue which remained at the helm of the racial politics in Fiji. The land rights were entrusted to ethnic Fijians but as the main commercial cultivators of sugarcane, Indians held most of it as tenant farmers on lease. All native land leases are managed by the Native Land Trust Board (NLTB) controlled by Council of Chiefs with no representation of Indians. Despite the fact that the land was legally made inalienable by the constitution of 1970, and all the later constitutions, the fear of losing it had always been there among the Fijians. It is important to note here that the Indians actually never challenged the customary rights of the Fijian people over land but their major concern was about adequate agricultural leases and ensured security of tenure for Indo-Fijian farmers, something that was also in the interest of the Fijian economy. However, the ever present "bogey of Indian land grab" became a political gizmo to maintain Fijian support base by the ruling feudal elite. In the 1990s, when large number of leases expired due to racial tensions, thousands of Indo-Fijians lost their occupation and moved to cities crowding in squatter settlements.

Constitutional Development and Race Relations

Against this backdrop when constitutional reforms started in Fiji, the above concerns/fears/interests had to be accommodated under the outward façade of democracy. The process of constitutional development and the establishment of democracy got completely entangled with the race politics and the political aspirations of the feudal elements in the Fijian society. The phrase 'Paramountcy of Fijian interests' was invoked over and over again to stake special claims and to influence the direction of constitutional change.

When Fiji got its first constitution, after independence in 1970, it adopted communal representation and one of the most complex legislative systems in the world with each voter having a total of four votes, one in the communal electorate and three in the national electorate.[8] In the lower house, a symmetrical parity of ethnic representation was maintained but in the upper house special representation given to the Council of Chiefs with a veto power over any legislative attempt to interfere with core Fijian interests and way of life. The constitution also guaranteed to the indigenous Fijians, the traditional rights over 80 per cent of the country's land. In other words, "The outwardly symmetrical parity of ethnic representation was more than outweighed by defence of Fijian interests, through the composition and powers of the nominated Senate".[9]

For the first 17 years Alliance party dominated the Parliament and Ratu Sir Kamisese Mara—a powerful feudal chief—remained the Prime Minister. Although, during the second general elections in 1977 National Federation Party (NFP, the Indian dominated party) managed to secure majority -which clearly indicates voting crosscutting racial lines—but it failed to form government. However, in 1985 Fiji Labour Party was formed under Dr. Timoci Bavadra and Mahendra Chaudhary. The new party had its base in the cross section of the society i.e. urban Fijians (who had moved away from the villages due to industrialisation and urbanisation weakening the traditional hold of the feudal system), western Fijians (who despite having the bulk of the sugar industry were deprived of adequate development and political power) and the Indo-Fijians. As a result, FLP and NFP in coalition won the 1987 elections and Dr Timocy Bavadra, who belonged to the middle class and was from western part of the country, became the Prime Minister. However, only after few months a coup was staged by Lt.-Col. Sitiveni Rabuka in the month of May, followed by another coup in September.

The coup reinstalled the Fijian elite led regime which espoused the traditional order and the 'Fijian way.' Thus, interpreting the two coups by Rabuka in 1987 merely from the race perspective would be naïve. It was a counter reaction by the traditionalists, aimed to preserve their own privileged position and dominance over Fijian society and economy which they enjoyed during the long rule of the Alliance Party. As Anthony J. Payne explains it, "The problem was that these old men had come to believe that the government of Fiji was their natural fiefdom. Led for many years by Ratu Mara the Fijian ruling elite was simply unable to tolerate the existence of FLP and the coalition as a government".[10] According to Prof. Brij V. Lal stated that "both Bavadra's class and regional origin posed the danger for traditional scheme of things in Fijian society.[11] In the words of J. Sandy "The coup of 1987 overthrew a newly elected multiracial government and reinstalled the former Fijian elite led regime which espoused the traditional order and the 'Fijian way' yet also aimed to preserve its own privileged position in both Fijian society and modern economy".[12]

Despite protests by Indo-Fijians a highly discriminatory constitution was promulgated in 1990 by the Rabuka Government in which parity in the lower house was done away with by reducing the Indian seats.[13] In the Upper House, the powers of the 'Great Council of Chiefs' were further increased. In effect, the new constitution further relegated the Indians to a position from where they could not attempt to ever become politically powerful.[14] The post-coup period was one of trauma and turmoil for the ethnic Indians. The professionals, the businessmen and those who could obtain emigrant visas left Fiji for other countries thereby bringing in demographic change, which ended their predominant position.

However, the new regime as well as the 1990 constitution badly affected Fiji's position in the international and regional order and had serious consequences on its economy. As a result, Rabuka, introduced a new constitution in 1997 amongst great deal of opposition from ultra-nationalists. The new Constitution continued with communal representation in the Lower

House its giving more seats to ethnic Fijians but made 25 seats were open to all. In the Upper House the dominant position of 'Council of Chiefs' and the land ownership rights of the ethnic Fijians were retained as before.[15] Yet several other privileges denied to Indians were restored. The 1997 constitution was called a 'unique experiment', an amalgam of ideas which attempted to establish an interesting balance to bring diverse people together.[16]

Following the adoption of the new Constitution, Fiji was back on the path of reconciliation and co-existence. Fiji conducted general election on the basis of the new constitution in May 1999 in which the FLP led People's Coalition came to power and Mahendra Chaudhary became the Prime Minister. Chaudhary treaded cautiously attempting to build "a secure multiracial foundation."[17] Not only did he include his alliance partners but also Ratu Sir Kamisese Mara's daughter and her Christian Democratic Alliance into his government. He allocated portfolios central to Fijian interests—Agriculture, Fisheries & Forests, and Tourism etc—to ethnic Fijians. However, the land remained the most contentious issue throughout Chaudhary's rule. The issues involved this time were not only about denying political rights to the Indo-Fijians but also to strike at their economic backbone by taking away the land they farmed on for generations. Every move of the government to find a solution and get the expiring land leases renewed was blocked by the opposition groups and ultranationalist under the Taukei banner.[18]

Exactly a year after the assumption of power, Chaudhary government was overthrown in a civilian coup led by George Speight. What is notable here is that twelve out of 18 members of the sacked cabinet and 14 of the 31 members among Speight's hostages were ethnic Fijians.[19] In the aftermath of the coup an interim government was formed under Laisenia Qarase who later floated a political party and formed government after elections in 2001 and 2006. However, frictions with the military continued which resulted in a coup in 2006 by Commodore Frank Bainimarama. The coup of 2006 is a clear representation of the internal power play of the Fijian society as the Fijian dominated military toppled the Fijian dominated regime.

Bainimarama blamed Fiji's 'communal voting' system for ethnic tensions and a 'lack of a strong feeling of shared national identity and citizenship' for the state of affairs in Fiji. He argued that the 'intervention was needed to end widespread corruption and root out entrenched discrimination against ethnic Indians' and that 'the army was the only institution disciplined enough to usher in real reform'. The new Constitution which he brought in September

2013 is a landmark and a bold departure from the past in several ways. It replaced the racially weighted formula by 'one person, one vote, one value principle' and opened the use of the term 'Fijians' to identify all its citizens as against the previous race based identification. It dismantled the unelected upper chamber, the Great Council of Chiefs, and brought the youth into political fold by reducing the voting age.[20]

These changes were welcomed by many including ethnic Indians who got equal rights with indigenous Fijians. There were signs of improvement with cheap education for all and better infrastructure especially in villages. Life got better, for nearly half of Fiji's population living below the poverty line in growing squatter settlements (dominated by ethnic Indians) and helped lift Bainimarama's support base. Fiji's economy grew at 3.8 percent in 2014, exceeding its historical average. After much delay elections were held on 18 October 2014 in which seven parties took part: with 248 candidates. A multinational observer group comprising about 90 officials from more than a dozen countries including India, was set up to monitor the election and ensure it is free and fair. The results show big support for Bainimarama among ethnic Indians reducing Fiji Labour Party and National Federation Party—traditionally Indian dominated parties—into minor players.

Nevertheless, the constitution also came under sharp criticism for curb on freedoms. Amnesty International accused Bainimarama regime for creating 'climate of fear'. There have been concerns about media gagging and the role of the government media watchdog. The independence of the judiciary was constantly under question, with little transparency in the conduct of government. Most of the changes introduced by the government were all decreed with no consultation whatsoever with principal stakeholders. Fairness of Fiji elections also was a big concern. Ban on trade unionists and public servants being candidates or having disqualified several respected candidates at the eleventh hour for trivial issue (like 12 year old traffic offence) has all remained questionable.

Conclusion

Racial segregation/discrimination has existed in Fijian politics in an institutionalised manner since the colonial times. However, interpreting Fijian politics merely from the race point of view would give only an incomplete picture. The winning of Indian dominated party (NFP, FLP) in the general elections, thrice (i.e. 1977, 1987 and 1999) in the history of Fiji is clear enough evidence to show that people have voted across racial lines and that there are more important issues than race for the people of Fiji. As a matter of fact, modernisation, education and migrations among the ethnic Fijians, has led to a constant change in the character of Fijian society and brought both Indian and Fijians on a common ground. Race has been a crucial factor in the analysis of the politics of Fiji, but the problem is aggravated as the race card was used as a tool by the vested interests in the power struggle at various levels in the Fijian politics.

Bainimarama has taken bold strides, such as trying to break the racial divide at the institutional level. However, only time will tell, how well the democratic transition in Fiji is preserved and how well Bainimarama government is able to build bridges between the two communities and control the power struggle within the Fijian society. Although things appear to be moving in the right direction (in terms of economic conditions) as of now there is a long way to go towards giving fair representation to ethnic Indians in civil services, judiciary, police, army and educational institutions which are heavily tilted towards ethnic Fijians and above all rehabilitate the ethnic Indians who had emigrated following the regressive policies of the previous regimes.

END NOTES

1. Constitutions of the Republic of Fiji 1970-1013, Government Documents, Suva Fiji.
2. S.K Bhutani, "Fiji: Self Inflicted Wounds", *World Affairs*, vol. 3 (1991), 54.
3. Shanti Sadiq Ali, "Institutionalised Racial Discrimination," *Mainstream*, 30 (10) Dec. 2, (1991), 19.
4. Stephanie Hegan, "Race, Politics and the Coup in Fiji", *Bulletin of Concerned Asian Scholars*, 19 (4) (1987), 3.
5. John E. Davis, "Ethnic Competition and the Forging of the nation State of Fiji," *Round Table*, 94 (1), (2005) 59.
6. See for example Ahmed Ali, Political awareness among Fiji Indians, 1879-1919 Asian profile, *Asian Affairs*, 6 (5) (1978) 477-491
7. P. Larmour, "A Foreign Flower?' Democracy in the South Pacific" *Pacific Studies*, 17 (1), (1994) 45–77.
8. Colonial Papers, Fiji Government Documents, Suva, Fiji.
9. Rod Alley, "Fiji at the Cross Roads?" *Round Table*, 342, (1997), 247.
10. Anthony J. Payne, "The Fiji Effect: A Review of Trends in the South Pacific," *Round Table*, 312, (1989) 442.
11. Brij V. Lal, "Fiji Indians and the Politics of Exclusion", *Foreign Affairs Report*, 38 (7-8), (1989) 105-106.
12. J. Sandy, "The Coups of 1987: A Personal Analysis," *Pacific Viewpoint*, 30 (2) (1989) 116-31.

13. Constitution of the Republic of Fiji 1990, Government Documents, Suva, Fiji.
14. M.M Kaul, *Pearls in the Ocean* (New Delhi: UBSPD, 1993), p 40.
15. Constitution of the Republic of Fiji 1997, Government Documents, Suva, Fiji.
16. Rajeev Dhawan, "The Fiji Crisis", *the Hindu*, 2000.
17. As quoted in "Crossing Fiji's Racial Divide," *Pacific Islands*, 69 (6), ", 1999.
18. *News Time*, Hyderabad, May 20, 2000.
19. *The Fiji Times*, July 4, 2000.
20. Constitution of the Republic of Fiji 2013, Government Documents, Suva, Fiji.

12

A Perspective on the Socio-Political Analysis of Indian Migration to Australia

Jasvinder Sidhu

Introduction

This chapter provides a socio-political analysis of Indian migration to Australia, primarily examining the most recent wave of migration within the context of Australian multiculturalism. The chapter also comments on the Indian community's recent journey towards gaining its identity and space within the social context in Australia and analyses the possible challenges faced by Indian community. This chapter employs a critical approach to both historical and contemporary evidence providing a narrative based on the personal and professional experiences of author.

Early Links between India and Australia

The relationship between Australia and India is as old as the British settlement in Australia. As settlement took place in Australia, the East India Company contributed to the commodities and livestock trade from India to Australia.[1] In 1790, the colonial governor of New South Wales was given permission to gain supplies from India which considerably increased the volume of imports from India. Trade from Australia to India included coal and timber as early as 1799.[2] The Sydney Cove is a classic example of frequency of trade[3] between

India and Australia. The ship sailed from Calcutta, Bengal on November 10th, 1796 carrying 44 Indian seamen.[4]

Over the next three decades 129 vessels from India carrying in total 30,000 tonnes of supplies arrived in New South Wales. This comprised 35 per cent of the total number of overseas ships arriving in all Australian ports until 1820.[5]

The first wave of migration from India was from the 1790s to the early decades of 1800s when Anglo-Indians began to settle in New South Wales.[6] From the 1860s, Indians were recruited to work in the regional and rural Australia. The early Chinese, Afghani, Indian and Pacific Islander migrants were largely replaced by Southern Europeans when Australia became a Federation due to the enactment of the White Australia Policy in 1901.[7]

These fragments of historical evidence indicate that India has had a significant direct and indirect influence on early settlement in Australia through its commodities trade and supply of manpower. However, the present day identify of Indian community in Australia warrants more attention. The general awareness among Australians about India is not very great. After the 1970s, the White Australia Policy was progressively dismantled by the Whitlam and Fraser Governments leading to a new wave of Indian migration. Modern Indian migrants are largely unaware of the earlier contributions of Indians in Australia. Outside the Indian community there is significant ignorance around Indian society and India's broader political and economic position.

There are a number of reasons for the ignorance and a significant reason is the starkly difference in cultural heritage between India and Australia. There are profound cultural and religious differences between the Australia, Judeo-Christian system and the hierarchical, Hindu/Vedic practice. These cultural differences have acted as a barrier to superior integration and knowledge of Australia and India as well as contributing to the difficulties faced by Indian migrants when integrating into Australian society.

Australian Society: Its Core Values, Egalitarianism

The Australian and Indian societies have a dearth of differences regarding how these societies are structured, operate and perform social functions. Indian culture is vibrant, rich and dominates social context in all aspects. When Indians migrate to Australia they confront a society which is significantly different from their own society and its social practices back in India. The foundations of Australian society are based on the principles of egalitarianism where ideally no social class differences exist and social value is based primarily on hard work and ability. Australia has its own challenges with race and gender related bias. Although progressive laws in both Australia and India make such discriminations a punishable crime.

Indians initially are perplexed by a society where occupational status doesn't affect status in the public domain whether a janitor or a judge. In restaurants or hotels it is considered a serious social faux-pas to click or point at staff. Indian migrants are also surprised that, regardless of the high household wealth, domestic servants are extremely rare in Australian society. Subject to income levels people do utilise the services of cleaners, laundries and cooks etc.

In the Australian society the idolisation of personalities is discouraged and uncommon. Whether it is politicians, cricket or film stars, the general public may respect and honour their contribution but will not personally idealise and endow that person with god-like attributes. In India, Sachin Tendulkar and Amitabh Bachchan have achieved a status beyond mere mortals for their fans. Such achievements in Australian culture would engender respect but there would not be such a desperate desire for personal contact or photographs. The VIP culture is not part of Australian society. Politicians do not attract the level of public attention as they would in India. It is very common for Ministers and even Premiers of States to walk on the street or have a meal in a restaurant without creating any disturbance to public. People are usually unfazed by VIPs and allow them their private space.

However, in the Indian social system status is conferred by group identity and the desire to be well known in your social circles is quite prevalent. Politicians and personalities have significant influence in the various operations and structures of society and thus a desire to be associated with such public figures is particularly strong.

Conspicuous displays of wealth and income are considered as poor taste in Australia. Significant spending on social indicators of wealth such as jewellery, weddings or gifts is not considered socially necessary or is generally scorned. In Indian culture, families are forced to spend beyond their financial capacity by the demands of society.

Australia is an individualistic society where considerations are driven primarily by individual utility. The perceptions of other members of society, whilst still important, are not accorded as great a value. For example, the purchase of a luxury car as a means to impressing your social circle would be generally considered as unwise and socially ignorant.

However, social class differences are still part of Australian society as they would be of any other society however these differences aren't generally acknowledged. In Australia, friends and family are not generally considered to be entitled to private information such as income levels or relationship details.

The Indian community typically finds it difficult to become accustomed to these vastly differing social practices and customs. In many respects the Indian and Australia social practices are directly in conflict. This clearly poses a challenge to multiculturalism. In this respect, however the Indian diaspora is not the first cultural group to experience these issues.

Multiculturalism in Australia

Australia actively encourages and celebrates a multicultural society. This policy is reflected in the economic, political and legal structures of Australia society. From the early waves of migration to nearly 70 years (from 1901 to mid-1970s) of a discriminatory White Australia Policy, Australia has come a long way from exercising a deliberately discriminatory migration policy. The White Australia Policy or Immigration Restrictions Act 1901 actively restricted entry of non-Europeans into Australia and it continued until Labor Prime Minister Gough Whitlam and successive Federal Governments dismantled the policy and eradicated systemic discrimination from Australia law. Since then various laws have been passed which prohibit racism and protect the ethnic communities. The state of Victoria, has always been a progressive state in this right and introduced multiple changes to the legal framework including the *Racial and Religious Tolerance Act of 2001*. The Victorian government also has a government department, the Victorian Multicultural Commission, led by Minister for Multicultural Affairs.

In a similar period to the dismantling of the White Australia Policy, Australia also recognised and extended equal rights to Aboriginals who are the inhabitants of this land and are one of the oldest continuous civilisations in the world with continuing cultural practices and land rights dating back thousands of years.

A shift in Australian politics was seen in 1967 when a referendum was supported by more than 90 per cent Australians which gave powers to the Federal government to implement policies that benefited indigenous Australians. In the State of Victoria the referendum received the highest votes with 95 per cent people supporting such change. This clearly shows that the core beliefs of Australian society are non-discriminatory, welcoming and accepting of major changes, once provided with a rational argument.

Former Prime Ministers Gough Whitlam, Malcolm Frazer, Bob Hawke, Paul Keating and Victorian Premier Steve Bracks implemented socially progressive and inclusive polices in last four decades which has shaped modern day Australia. Paul Keating led the nation and made laws that gave land titles to aboriginal Australians by bringing the Native Title Act 1993.

In modern Australia 28 per cent of Australians are born outside Australia and India has the fourth largest share of migrants only behind UK, New Zealand and China. However, 60 per cent of Australian population is of European decent. If we disregard the British and New Zealand population then Indians are only behind Italians, Germans and Chinese in terms of total population share in Australia. A big chunk of this population has migrated in last 10-15 years.

Thus the extent of Indian migration in the recent past has been unprecedented both in Australia and for the Indian diaspora. As was noted there are some fundamental differences between Indian and Australian cultures. Such a big wave of migration naturally poses many cultural challenges. The issues linked with acceptability, adaptability, professional mobility etc. are not automatically resolved.

The strength of Australian society is that it is tolerant and accepting of alternative cultures. Australia is home to people of many backgrounds and cultures and encourages a similar inclusiveness and tolerance in the various migrant communities within Australia.

Contemporary Indians in Australia and Challenges

The current population of the Indian community in Australia is close to 500,000 with Melbourne being home to the largest Indian diaspora in Australia. The sources of migration to Australia have primarily been from Punjab, Gujarat and the South Indian states. The US, UK and Canada have stronger Indian diaspora which are now well integrated in to the broader community. That is primarily due to the Indian community being largely third or fourth generation residents. Canada is unique, out of the million Indians in Canada approximately 60 per cent are Sikh. Due to the White Australia Policy most Indians could migrate only recently. So there are many challenges linked with settlement, social inclusion and social adaptability.

The major factor responsible for the large number of Indians migrating to Australia has been the Skilled Migration system. In this scheme people from other countries of the world could migrate either by applying direct Permanent Residency (PR) or first coming to Australia as students and then gaining PR. During 2008-2009, upto 80,000 Indian students were granted a visa in various study programs.

While studying students were employed in jobs which typically don't attract the interest of Australians. These jobs are usually low paid, involve late night or over-night work and also expose students to predatory employers who may not pay entitlements, tax or workers compensation insurance. Students were frequently employed in hospitality, taxi driving, retail and working as a security guard. Students typically sought late night shift work to accommodate their university study and due to the higher pay rate. This exposed them to general risks of late night work which included drunk and abusive customers, drug affected people, assaults and other associated risks.

In April 2008 an Indian taxi driver, Jalvinder Singh aged 23, was stabled to death in Melbourne leading to a major protest by taxi drivers on 29 April 2008 in which more than five hundred Indian taxi drivers blocked Melbourne's major intersection at the historic Flinders Street Station. The following year a number of attacks took place on Indian students and leading to over 4,000 students blocking the Flinders Street Station intersection on May 31, 2009. These incidents were widely reported in Indian and international media. The Indian media formed many conclusions based on secondary sources of information and repeatedly ran stories labelling Australia as a racist country. This happened before any enquiry had been commenced. After the attacks and the wide spread negative publicity, the relationship between two nations at a political, cultural and social level suffered a major blow.

The murder of 25-year old fruit picker Ranjodh Singh in Griffith, New South Wales, three year old child Gursharan Singh and the murder of 21 year old Indian student Nitin Garg on 3 January 2010 in Melbourne and associated reporting by Indian media further damaged the relationship of the two countries. However, in these three cases the first two murders involved fellow Indians and the murder of Nitin Garg was an act of robbery at the hands of another migrant. After initially reporting such incidents in a racially inflammatory manner the Indian media never corrected itself or followed the story further.

Subsequent to these events the Indian government ordered a probe by the Overseas Indian Ministry which submitted its report in early 2010. The report concluded that of the 152 attacks that the Indian consulate was aware of, 23 had "racial overtones". These attacks included racial abuse, or "anti-Indian remarks". This means that as per a report tabled in Indian Parliament and based on first hand evidence provided by Indian consulate 130 out of 152 reported cases did not involve racism. This also means that only 14 per cent of attacks were racially motivated. However, this report did not attract same level of media attention because reporting this did not suit media and would not create same level of sensation as an attack and a claim that Australia is a racist nation.

Indian Diaspora in Transition Phase

The Indian diaspora in Australia is quite large, diverse and integrating well into Australian society. However, the community is in transition phase. Such transition is the result of recent migration. Most people from India migrated under the skilled migration scheme and hence most Australian Indians are in their youth. They are gaining their citizenships, getting married, buying houses and are going through a phase of complete transition.

Issues linked with settlement are exposing young couples to family violence issues. Although family violence is a universal problem there are in the Australian-Indian community some particular problems including lack of a social circle and friends, having no relatives locally and a lack of support at home (e.g. typically domestic servant or mother-in-law as in India) to look after the child and assist in home duties, thus exposing young women to more risks than if they were in India. This has led to a significant number of murders and suicides in Melbourne potentially linked with family violence. Police and support services are generally not clear how to offer culturally sensitive assistance in the context of family violence.

Another major issue has been growing problems linked with migration of older Indians through parental visas. The migration of parents to Australia is difficult because one must meet the family balance test stipulating that at least half of the siblings must be in Australia before one can seek their parents' migration. Additional, non-refundable, payments in excess of $100,000 are made to gain PR for parents within 12-18 months. Otherwise the general queue could take 15-20 years due to quota based PR and the length of the applications queue. There are now thousands of parents who have migrated to Australia mainly in the last 5 to 10 years. They have language barriers, mobility issues and are not capable or confident in navigating Australian society. Most parents are generally confined to the home, to looking after the grandchildren and are totally dependent on children for taking them out. They have lost their years' long friendship and social circle. The only place where they can meet fellow seniors are temples and mainly Gurdwaras. Due to mobility issues they generally they can only visit these places on Sundays. This is another big social issue confronting the Indian community. However, other issues linked with migration and settlement are so profound that the Indian community is still not looking at solving the problems of senior migrants in an organised manner.

Another cultural issue is professional acceptance and the general inability to find employment in relevant fields to one's education. A lot of university graduates drive taxis or do less skilled jobs that are unrelated to their field and are usually for lower pay. An issue which often filters out Indian candidates from professional jobs is a lack of, 'soft skills'. Each society has certain social and professional attributes which are minimum requirements. For example in Indian society it is important to show respect to elders by not addressing them with names but in Australian society everyone is referred to by their first name. Social and professional skills that are expected from professionals in an Australian context are not necessarily evident to migrants. A lack of such skills has been a major reason for the inability of Indian students to find jobs immediately after finishing their qualifications.

A last issue that I would like to address is political representation. Due to the vast differences based on regions and languages the Indian diaspora is diverse. This diversity also brings divisions in the community. Internal division within the community hampers effective political communication, resulting in a confused political message. Diversity and division pose challenges to lobbying regulators and government effectively. At present there are no Indian-born Members of Parliament at either a State or Federal level. Representation of the Indian community at even a local government level is almost negligible. The lack of representation makes it difficult to highlight issues within the community before they become severe.

Conclusion

The Indian community is tightknit and involved leading people to avoid significant exposure to non-Indian culture. This means that the broader Australian culture and community is sometimes poorly understood and disregarded by many Indian migrants. It also contributes to an ignorance of Indian culture beyond the obvious touchstones of curry, cricket and the Taj Mahal.

The Indian community in Australia is rich, diverse and vibrant. Australia is the only country in the world in recent years where such a large number of Indians have settled in a short period of time. Such migration has brought with it other social issues as they have been briefly touched on in this paper. Social mobility at those levels is really important and governments from both countries can assist in creating projects and programs to increase social inclusion, social cohesion and the empowerment of the Indian community in Australia. An empowered Indian diaspora is very important for improving relationship between two nations. Indian migrants offer a gateway to the massive opportunities for trade and business for India. Australia has a huge knowledge base in professional services, food technology, bio-technology, medical research, waste management and also has abundant supplies of natural resources such as coal and uranium. Trade between two countries is surprisingly low and there are many avenues for future growth. In such a situation the role of Indian diaspora to establish cultural ties and people to people contacts becomes crucial. First, however, the Indian diaspora must address its internal issues linked with settlement and migration. Only an empowered and confident diaspora can make a significant impact.

END NOTES

1. L. Kena, "Are Indians an ethnic minority—Discovering Victoria", 1, (2005) Jika Publishing, Bundoora, Victoria.
2. M. Nash, *Cargo for the Colony: The 1797 wreck of the merchant ship Sydney Cove*, (Navarine Publishing, Canberra, 2001).
3. The Sydney Cove carried rice, sugar, tobacco, salted meat, Chinese tea, tar, vinegar, soap, candles, leatherwear, Indian textiles, livestock and luxury items.
4. Ibid., n 2.
5. Rickard J. Broadbent, S. and M. Steve, *India, China, Australia: Trade and Society 1788-1850*, (Historical Houses Trust of New South Wales, Sydney, 2003).
6. Historical Records of Australia, Vol 2 cited in Kena, 2005.
7. See website, http://www.australia.gov.au/about-australia/australian-story/changing-face-of-early-australia.

PART III

Maritime Security: Challenges and Cooperation

13

The South China Sea:
Conflict in a Complex Maritime Security Environment

Aileen S.P. Baviera[1]

Overview of the Maritime Security Situation

Describing the overall security situation in the South China Sea (SCS), one can say that it is at the very least a complex maritime security environment. Maritime security in the SCS and in the seas that connect Southeast Asia involves at least four interconnected layers of challenges, having different sets of stakeholders and interests. These include: first, territorial sovereignty disputes over islands and other features; second, disputes over maritime rights and jurisdictions (e.g. access to fish, energy and mineral resources, regulation of other activities at sea) arising from undefined or overlapping boundaries and in part from the territorial disputes themselves; third, transnational challenges common to many littoral states (e.g. threats to safety of life at sea, piracy, effects of natural and man-made disasters and of climate change); and fourth, increasing geopolitical competition among major powers, amid expectations of an impending power shift-based on long-term changes in the relative capabilities of states that comprise the international system.

The sovereignty disputes and competition over maritime jurisdictions are distinct but interrelated questions. They continue to be the most sensitive issues that have triggered the sharpest tensions among the various states concerned over a longer period of time. China, Taiwan, Vietnam, the Philippines, Malaysia and Brunei have competing claims over part or the whole of the Spratly Islands. Clashes between China and Vietnam there in 1988 caught the attention of ASEAN member states and triggered efforts to address the issue through multilateral consultations. China and Vietnam have also long been at loggerheads over the Paracel Islands, fighting a short, limited war over the area in 1974. Since the late 1990s, but especially following a 2012 standoff between maritime authorities of China and the Philippines triggered by fishing disputes, Scarborough Shoal also became an arena for escalating tensions.

The territorial disputes, so long as they remain unresolved, have prevented states from obtaining recognition of the maritime rights that the UN Convention on the Law of the Sea (UNCLOS) accords them as coastal states, such as development of fishery resources on their Exclusive Economic Zones (EEZ) or of oil and gas on the continental shelf (CS), and regulation of passage by foreign ships or other activities at sea that may potentially affect their interests. China's so-called 9 dashed line claim, enclosing ninety percent of the SCS, is the most problematic in the manner it appears to deny other states' rights already assured by international law.

The overlap between disputed territories and the maritime zones that should otherwise be covered by UNCLOS and other legal regimes (e.g. International Maritime Organisation conventions) lead instead to a lack of clear rules of behavior, with certain countries trying to exercise domestic laws in contested areas. Further complicated by asymmetric power relations among the major players, such disputes have led to deep mistrust, nationalism turning violent in some cases, and countries resorting to arms buildup, as we have seen in recent years.

Transnational maritime security challenges, on the other hand, are often touted as desirable areas of cooperation and confidence building, possibly even leading to the mitigation of the sovereignty and jurisdictional disputes, as states would recognise the need to work together for shared goals despite their differences on other counts. In the SCS region, despite the clear necessity of cooperating to combat such challenges as piracy and marine environmental challenges, and despite some progress made in fostering new habits of consultation and coordination, serious political obstacles remain and mistrust among certain key actors seems to be growing rather than diminishing.

It is however the last layer of security challenge—geopolitical competition and the trend towards open confrontation among major powers—that many find the most worrisome. If unconstrained, it can have potential far-reaching effects, the extreme scenario (even if a still improbable one) being a more generalised conflict involving certain states in the SCS area.

Lessons from Dialogue and Cooperation Initiatives

Amidst this complexity of the different layers of security challenges in the SCS and Southeast/East Asia more broadly speaking, there have emerged many mechanisms, institutions and cooperation initiatives dedicated to addressing the wide range of maritime concerns. From the defense and security side alone, a non-exhaustive list may be drawn up.

The ASEAN Regional Forum Inter Sessional Meeting (ISM) on Maritime Security in 2012 identified three priority areas: information/intelligence exchange and sharing of best practices, including on naval operations; confidence building measures based on international and regional legal frameworks, arrangements and cooperation; and capacity building of maritime law enforcement agencies in the region.

The ASEAN Defense Ministers Meeting (ADMM) process, being Southeast Asia's highest ministerial defense and security consultative and cooperative mechanism, has since 2006 been leading efforts to move ASEAN forward from engaging in confidence-building initiatives to the implementation of concrete cooperative security efforts.

Also under the ASEAN umbrella are the ASEAN Maritime Forum, the ASEAN Chiefs of Defense Forces Informal Meetings; ASEAN Service Chiefs Meetings; ASEAN Military Intelligence Exchange Meetings, and ASEAN Senior Defense Officials' Meetings.

The ADMM Plus process, which since 2010 brings ADMM together with defense officials of ASEAN's eight dialogue partners, has also identified cooperation in maritime security as one of its main goals, aside from cooperation in counterterrorism, humanitarian assistance and disaster relief, peacekeeping operations and military medicine.

The biennial Western Pacific Naval Symposium is an initiative (since 1988) involving navies of some 25 countries focused on improving communications and information exchanges, and finding new ways of cooperation among countries that have strategic interests in the Western Pacific. In April 2014, WPNS members agreed to implement a multilaterally negotiated Code for Unplanned Encounters at Sea (CUES). There are currently some proposals to set up a similar network of national Coast Guards (or counterparts).

Not to be ignored are so-called "Track 1.5" efforts such as the Shangri-La Dialogue or the Asian Security Summit organised annually in Singapore by the UK-based International Institute for Strategic Studies. While "unofficial" in nature, this forum provides ample opportunity for defense chiefs to conduct bilateral or minilateral dialogues in an informal setting.

Meanwhile, ASEAN and China are engaged in continuing efforts to define how to effectively implement the Declaration of Conduct of Parties in the South China Sea (DOC) which is now going on its twelfth year since its signing, while holding incipient discussions on a legally-binding Code of Conduct.

Among the maritime authorities of Indonesia, Singapore and Malaysia there are joint arrangements for patrolling the Malacca Straits; among these three countries and Thailand there are as well joint air surveillance operations. Similarly there is a multilateral mechanism known as Regional Cooperation Agreement on Combating Piracy and Armed Robbery against Ships in Asia (ReCAAP) which has an Information Sharing Center in Singapore.

The proliferation of maritime security dialogues and incipient coordination efforts are probably reassuring to some but they also indicate that the region is very far removed from the regional order it aspires for. A closer assessment will demonstrate that most of these mechanisms are consultative and focused on information sharing and confidence-building rather than actual cooperation at sea.

Arguably, among the lessons learned from the dialogues and developments of the last two decades, particularly with respect to the South China Sea, are that: first, a clear demonstration of political will to resolve the sovereignty disputes—as opposed to 'managing' them for one's own advantage—has been sorely lacking at the highest level among the states concerned; second, that confidence building measures and picking the "low-hanging fruit", "low politics" or non-controversial functional areas to cooperate on (e.g. disaster response, search and rescue,...) may be important in themselves but they may not be adequate for conflict prevention; third, that all concerned states need to develop agreement on what rules to apply during operations at sea rather than risk misunderstanding by relying on unilateral rules of engagement;

fourth, that transparency of intent and capability alone without mutual security assurances can be counterproductive; and fifth, that self-restraint by great powers always plays an important role but cannot always be relied upon so that at some point, deterrence and hedging strategies have to be put on the table and so on.

Growing Power Competition and its Impact on Southeast Asia

In the last five years or so, great power competition has slowly moved to occupy center stage of the South China Sea situation, and this is manifested in a number of developments. On the one hand, we find China becoming much more assertive in the pursuit and defense of its territorial claims, particularly vis-à-vis Vietnam (e.g. oil rig incident) and the Philippines (e.g. Scarborough Shoal takeover)., with its latest move being the reclamation of seven reefs and construction of an airstrip on Fiery Cross Reef. On the other hand, is the US policy of "rebalancing" or pivot to Asia, evident in its growing security coordination with various regional states, increased military presence and scope of military exercises, more explicit criticisms against Chinese coercive approach and behavior, all while still trying to avoid direct provocation of China and simultaneously engaging in high level dialogues with Beijing counterparts.

Moreover, we are for the first time in many years seeing competitive defense buildups in the region (particularly among big powers but also involving smaller states), as countries seek to acquire new technologies, advance their capabilities, build new security partnerships, and conduct bigger and more complex military exercises, having in mind scenarios of conflicts over resources, island takeovers, or other explicit maritime threats.

One recent development has also been Japan's active pursuit of cooperation with Southeast Asian states to help strengthen their maritime security capabilities. This takes place against the backdrop of its so-called 'normalisation' efforts and the Abe government's reinterpretation of their constitution to provide for Japan's participation in collective security. Japan's conflicts with China over the Senkakus/Diaoyutai resonate with those in ASEAN who find themselves in similar straits in the South China Sea, particularly Vietnam and the Philippines.

India likewise has demonstrated its growing interest and engagement in security affairs of the South China Sea region, inasmuch as its "Look East

Policy" prioritises economic relations with East Asia. Moreover, border conflicts with China, China's longstanding close ties with archrival Pakistan, and China's growing influence on some of India's neighbouring countries underscore India's need for hedging options involving China's own strategic backyard in East Asia. US, Japanese, and to some extent Australian encouragement of an Indian counterbalance to China in East Asia is manifested in the new concept of an "Indo-Pacific" security region.

There is a need to focus discussion on US-China relations as this is the most critical issue for stability of the South China Sea right now, and has serious impact on Southeast Asia.

The reason the South China Sea has become quite central to the question of power shift and the future East Asian regional security order is because this ocean space is simultaneously China's critical area for maritime power projection in its drive to become a global maritime power, while being a locus of US naval primacy and at the same time, Southeast Asia's maritime heartland.

With this resurgence in power rivalry, the Southeast Asian states, particularly the major claimants in the South China Sea but also ASEAN as an institutional actor, may find themselves losing the initiative and relinquishing their driving role in pushing for order-creating codes of conduct and cooperative security arrangements as they have been doing since the 1990s. If they risk being sidelined, this is also in no small part due to lack of unity of perspective on how to deal with the South China Sea issues and with China. Southeast Asian countries are now hard-pressed to make adjustments in their bilateral relations with China and the United States, as the need for hedging between these two giants increases, given the unpredictable outcomes of great power competition.

During the Cold War era, ASEAN states preserved strategic autonomy by trying to keep all the great powers at bay, while after the end of the Cold War they succeeded in extending ASEAN's influence by their ability to engage all the great powers while keeping largely to a posture of equidistance among them and neutrality with respect to inter-great power disagreements.

Under the current situation, it has become impossible for ASEAN to exclude great powers, and yet including everyone within its ambit of regional community building has become fraught with challenges such as those arising from Sino-Japanese conflicts and the now growing Sino-US competition. This new situation makes it more difficult for ASEAN to maintain equidistance.

China has been exerting pressure on certain ASEAN states to make a choice, or more specifically to choose China rather than the United States, leading naturally to a counter-reaction by the US and its allies. One outcome is that we have an absurd situation where new multilateral arrangements intended as a matter of principle to be inclusivist and cooperative now appear to be becoming exclusivist and competitive. There have been, for instance, debates among regional states on whether to emphasise the ASEAN Plus Three which excludes the US, or the East Asia Summit which includes it; whether to support what is bound to be a China-dominated Regional Comprehensive Economic Partnership (RCEP) or the US-led Trans Pacific Partnership (TPP); whether or not to join China's new Asian Infrastructure Investment Bank which many believe will compete with and undermine Japan-dominated Asian Development Bank and the US-dominated International Monetary Fund-World Bank.

Southeast Asia's Response to China's Assertiveness and US Rebalance

There is no single uniform view in Southeast Asia on either China's new assertiveness or the US rebalance to Asia. As a top trading partner of Southeast Asian states, and a major source of investments and development assistance for a few, China is given much importance in the diplomacy of its neighbouring states. But net assessments, especially comparing the situation now with that which prevailed even five years ago, indicate that as far as the issues impinging on the uses of the South China Sea are concerned, there is generally greater concern among Southeast Asian states over the possibility of China seeking a dominant position as a great power in East Asia on the one hand, and more interest in keeping the US (and possibly its allies Japan, Australia) actively engaged in Southeast Asian security affairs, on the other hand. Incidents such as the Philippines-China Scarborough Shoal standoff in April-June 2012, the Vietnam-China oil rig crisis of 2014, China's forays into Malaysian-claimed James Shoal and North Luconia Shoal, and largely unpublicised displays of its coercive power against Indonesia over fishing, and many other acts of Chinese assertiveness over territorial and maritime rights account for this.

It is this assertiveness of China, the increase in its military power projection capabilities, but most especially its recent demonstrations of willingness to use coercive means to gain advantage in its maritime disputes with the various contending countries, that have provided strong reason for littoral states around the South China Sea to doubt China's pledges of peaceful rise and non-hegemonic intentions; and therefore reason to welcome the American rebalance. While other countries have indeed also contributed their share to the increase in tensions, China's moves have elicited the greatest concern by sheer size, scope of actions and potential impact. The global financial crisis since 2008 and perceived decline in overall US capability may also have provided added opportunity and temptation for China to step forward both with respect to territorial claims and challenging US pre-eminence in the Western Pacific.

How do Southeast Asian states look at US rebalance? Deducing from the foreign policy postures and national interests of the Southeast Asian states, one can observe that some welcome the US rebalance rather unconditionally (Singapore, Vietnam and the Philippines), some welcome it but with certain reservations (Malaysia, Indonesia and possibly Brunei), while the others have expressed no position at all. Naturally, how the US' regional role and its rebalance policy are perceived by each ASEAN country is shaped not only by perceptions of China but by their own historical experiences, domestic politics, the current status of bilateral relations with the US, differing threat perceptions, and how they view the dynamics of great power competition in East Asia itself.

The US moreover faces complex challenges in terms of sustaining and promoting its influence in the region through rebalancing. These include the fact that regional states are not certain that the US government will continue to have a sustained commitment to a strong presence in East Asia– due to fiscal issues, domestic politics, and other foreign policy priorities. The effect of the unpredictability of US policy is that regional states may tend to hedge against the possibility of a US pullback, including by cultivating closer ties with other powers, or engaging in their own internal arms buildup, or both.

Some countries in Southeast Asia for domestic political reasons (e.g. popular anti-Americanism and/or a historical preference for non-alignment or neutralism), cannot openly support a strong US military presence due to such sensitivities, even though some may quietly be working with the US to keep its active regional presence. There is also residual concern still expressed that the rebalance may result in revival of US interference in internal affairs of countries in the region, such as setting normative and other conditions for US support that may lead to unacceptable infringements on sovereignty.

Most importantly, there is fear that US military presence and activities, including the conduct of large-scale military exercises and material as well as political support for allies, may lead to heightened risk of confrontation between US and China, as both compete for influence over the regional states and over the shaping of future regional institutions and architecture. The current perception is that US alliances and new security partnerships are being invigorated or built to help certain countries strengthen their response to China's assertive actions and policies in relation to territorial and maritime jurisdiction claims, thus highlighting the security dilemmas.

To mitigate these challenges to the rebalance, US can help reassure governments that the rebalance is genuinely more than a mere consolidation of US military power—with social, cultural, economic and developmental dimensions. Over the long run, these will also help the US widen and deepen ties with the region. US renewed engagement will likely be more welcome in Asia if seen to be constant and institutionalised through the region's existing inclusivist multilateral arrangements and institutions. Finally, the rebalance should not only provide security assurances to small and middle powers but also opportunities for the big powers themselves to work together to address each other's legitimate security concerns.

The US seems to be moving step by step in this direction, but perhaps still rather tentatively as the imperative of a strong forward presence and reliance on its own hard power cannot be denied. More recent US diplomatic engagement with regional mechanisms such as East Asia Summit (EAS), APEC, the ARF, and ASEAN itself are therefore encouraging, whereas all concerned states should help ensure that new initiatives like the TPP, Regional Comprehensive Economic Partnership (RCEP), the Asian Infrastructure and Investment Bank (AIIB), and China's 21st Century Maritime Silk Road Initiative, need to evolve into arenas for cooperation and order-building rather than mere power competition.

This leaves ASEAN with the question: Will US participation in addressing the South China Sea questions help resolve or mitigate the territorial and sovereignty disputes?

Two schools of thought may be forwarded. The first will argue that US involvement will make matters more complex. It will heighten China's security concerns and lead to more tensions between the powers. It may divide ASEAN as some prefer non-involvement of third parties. It may also in fact divert attention from the resolution of maritime issues and the search for effective maritime cooperation and towards US-China maritime issues like freedom of navigation and military activities at sea. Finally, China's fears that US support will embolden allies to be more provocative towards China will need to be addressed.

The second school of thought will argue that US involvement can help. US diplomatic engagement may increase the chances of resolution by putting pressure on as well as offering incentives for both China and ASEAN claimants to territory to pursue a rules-based, multilateral approach. US support for political settlement combined with maritime security capability building may also help build the confidence or leverage of Southeast Asian states to collectively or individually pursue a negotiated political settlement with China, by reducing the effects of asymmetry. Also by becoming a supporter, participant, or possibly even a party to a future regional code of conduct, US can help provide assurances to China that constraints on behavior of powers will not only target China but bind other big powers as well.

Conclusion: Is the Situation Ripe for Compromise?

China's own efforts to contribute to a thawing of relations, even the halfhearted handshakes between Xi Jinping and Shinzo Abe, or Xi Jinping and Benigno Aquino at APEC Summit in Shanghai last November 2014, and its support for regional code of conduct talks, should be applauded and encouraged. It is especially important to follow through and reciprocate these with prudent behavior on all sides in the coming months. However, more recent developments such as China's massive reclamation and expansion of features in the South China Sea give pause to any optimism, and indeed, have provoked the US and its allies into discussions of appropriate coordinated responses of a military nature.

In the current conjuncture, there are certain motivations for China to want to return to a less coercive path and more importantly to try to restore the trust of its smaller neighbours. The increasing involvement of the United States and Japan in security cooperation with several Southeast Asian countries, the growing mistrust of China by its peripheral states, and statements of concern not only in the region but by institutions like the G7 also do not bode well for China's aspirations to become a respected leader.

There are also incentives for China's neighbours to reopen channels of dialogue. Regional instability is bound to hurt efforts to sustain economic growth. The persistence of territorial conflict prevents, among others, sustainable use of fisheries as well as offshore energy resources. The sharp escalation of disputes in 2014 alone brings to mind William Zartman's concept of ripeness of a conflict situation for negotiation. A situation becomes ripe for conflict resolution by negotiations, he says, when the parties find themselves in a mutually hurting stalemate. We do not know if we are yet in a situation where the principal countries involved in the South China Sea disputes feel they are in a mutually hurting stalemate, but the trajectory of developments do seem to be heading in this direction.

END NOTE

1. This paper is based on a presentation delivered at the 6th International Conference on the South China Sea, organized by the Diplomatic Academy of Vietnam, on 17-18 November 2014 in Danang, Vietnam.

14

South China Sea Dispute:
An Indian Perspective

Amit Singh

The recent upsurge in tensions in the South China Sea (SCS) represents a security flashpoint with global consequences. The SCS is a strategic maritime link and a vital gateway for shipping in East Asia. It is thus economically and strategically important to the emerging economies of the Asia-Pacific region. The dispute has the potential to turn into a military conflict thereby affecting the adjoining maritime nations and consequently, the peace and security of entire region.

The tensions in the South China Sea are also affecting India's maritime, commercial, strategic, and most importantly, energy interest in that region. Recently, a top official of Chinese of Foreign Ministry underlined/warned New Delhi that it cannot explore oil and gas blocks in South China Sea without seeking Beijing's approval. The official also added that pending the final settlement of territorial disputes in South China Sea, China would encourage "joint development" in the region.[1] However, India again responded to the Chinese objections by reiterating that its cooperation with Vietnam is in accordance with international laws and commercial in nature.

Accordingly, this chapter aims to analyse the strategic and economic significance of the South China Sea vis-à-vis India, especially for its energy security. The chapter highlights the overlapping and conflicting claims in the

SCS and explores possibilities for New Delhi to improve its bilateral and multilateral relations with Southeast Asian countries to safeguard their interests for freedom of navigation in the SCS and maritime security in the region.

Strategic and Economic Importance of the South China Sea

The South China Sea is the world's second busiest international sea-lane. More than half of the world's super tanker traffic passes through these waters. The main reason behind the scramble for the two island chains (Spratly and Paracel) is their richness in natural resources, especially oil and gas. On April 19, 2011 China's *Global Times* published a special report that termed the region as the "Second Persian Gulf"— a repository of 50 billion tons of crude oil and more than 20 trillion cubic meters of natural gas (about twenty five times China's proven oil reserves and eight times its gas reserves). The US Energy Information Administration (EIA) estimates that the South China Sea contains approximately 11 billion barrels of oil and 190 trillion cubic feet (Tcf) of natural gas in proven and potential reserves.[2]

The SCS is not a mere strategic maritime link between the Pacific and the Indian Oceans; it is also a vital gateway for shipping in East Asia. Eighty per cent of China's energy imports and Japan's and South and North Korea's oil supplies pass through these waters. Almost, 55 per cent of India's trade with the Asia Pacific region transits through the SCS to China, Japan, Korea and the United States.[3] The economic potential and geopolitical importance of the SCS are the primary motivating factors for the surrounding countries to claim the islands and their resources. The bountiful fishing opportunities within the region are yet another factor for the overlapping territorial claims in the SCS.[4] This pattern of claims, counter claims and military skirmishes continues in the SCS and if these issues are not resolved to the satisfaction of all maritime stakeholders including the littoral nations, heightened global tension will be inevitable.

The South China Sea Dispute

The overlapping and conflicting claims over islands and maritime zones in the SCS are one of the most longstanding security issues between China, Taiwan and half of the ASEAN (Association of Southeast Asian Nations) countries. The recent upsurge in tensions in the SCS has turned the issue into a major regional security flashpoint with global consequences.

China, Taiwan, Vietnam, Philippines, Malaysia and Brunei are the claimants of island chain within the SCS. The South China Sea stretches roughly from Singapore and the Strait of Malacca in the southwest to the Taiwan Strait in the northeast. There are more than 200 tiny islands and several uninhabited rocky outcrops, atolls, sandbanks and reefs; majority of them located in the Paracel and Spratly Island chains. The Spratly and Paracel islands are the major flashpoints of overlapping territorial disputes within the South China Sea.[5]

Beijing claims almost the entire SCS, citing "historical" records, which purportedly show Chinese control in the region over the past two millennia. Taiwan's claims are similar to those of China, as the island considers itself the Republic of China. Indonesia is also a party to the dispute; however, Jakarta is seeking only maritime rights without claiming any island of the region. In fact, Indonesia's EEZ and continental shelf overlap China's claims, which include Indonesia's largest natural gas reserves called Natuna. Vietnam rejects

Map 1: South China Sea

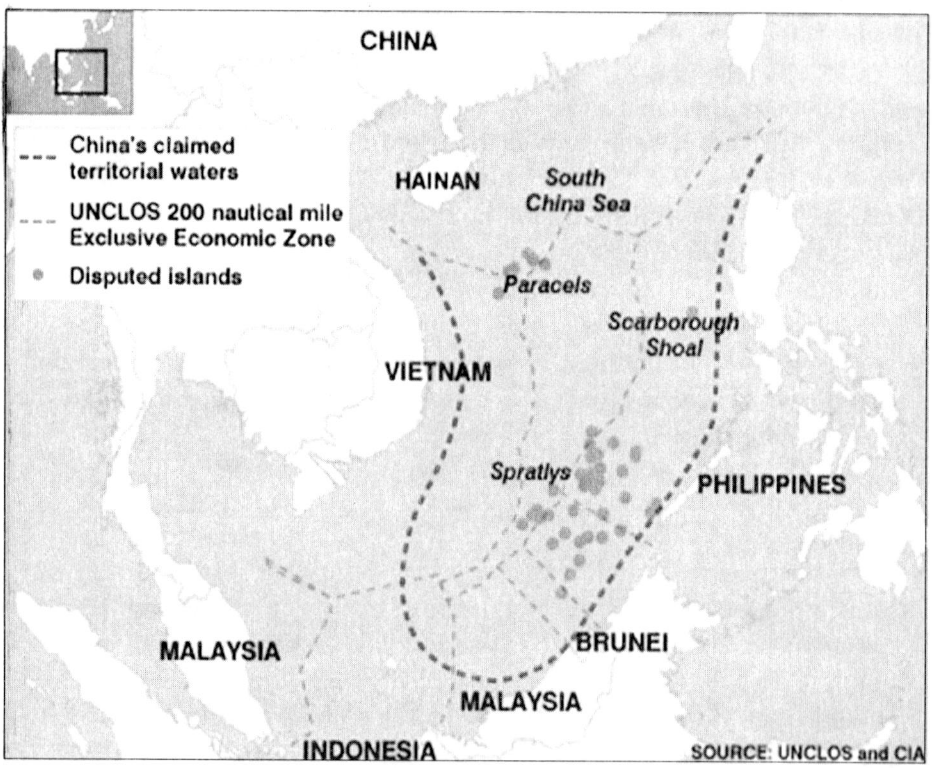

China's historical explanation and asserts that Beijing had never claimed sovereignty over the islands until the 1940s. Hanoi is convinced that both Spratly and Paracels are entirely within its own territory and has the documents to prove that the islands have been ruled by Vietnam since the 17th century.[6]

The SCS disputes between the involved nations have been going on for decades, but with the United Nations Commission on the Limits of the Continental Shelf (UNCLCS) setting a deadline of May 13, 2009 for submitting claims for extended continental shelves beyond 200 nautical miles, the issue has exacerbated.[7] After Vietnam and Malaysia submitted their respective claims, China made a submission to the UN in May 2009 and claimed that it had "indisputable sovereignty over the islands in the South China Sea and the adjacent waters, and enjoys sovereign rights and jurisdiction over the relevant waters as well as the seabed and subsoil thereof."[8] Beijing is also making an effort to include the SCS as its *"core national interest"* and in the non-negotiable territorial claims category—the same phrase it uses for Taiwan, Tibet and Xinxiang province.[9]

In the recent years, China has been growing increasingly assertive in pressing its claims over SCS matters. However, the other nations in the region do not acquiesce to China's claims. In fact, during the 2010 ARF meeting, it was reported that 12 of the 27 participating countries, including India, had backed the United States' multilateral approach instead of China's bilateral approach for resolution of the SCS disputes.[10]

The ASEAN as a regional organisation of the Southeast Asian countries maintains a deep interest in the peace and stability of the SCS. Since all ASEAN countries are not equally involved in the dispute and consequently have no equal stakes, there is not one ASEAN approach to the SCS dispute. Each member country pursues its own policy vis-à-vis China. Therefore, one can say that the ASEAN countries are in reality divided over their approach towards China, as well as on the exact mechanism to diffuse tension in the region. As a result, ASEAN's position on political and strategic issue towards China is rather weak. To compensate for this weakness, ASEAN had often used diplomacy and tried involving external powers by internationalising the regional issue. Such a strategy may have helped it avert regional tension in the short term but it failed to hide its inherent weakness in dealing with the regional hegemon, i.e. China.[11]

After the end of the Cold War, US policy on the South China Sea dispute has been consistent. At the height of the Mischief Reef Crisis in 1995, a statement issued by the US State Department articulated that Washington had a "fundamental interest in freedom of navigation" and the claimants should intensify diplomatic efforts to resolve the problem in accordance with international law and not by force.[12] As tensions have been rising, the fundamentals of this policy have remained unchanged but there has been a change in tone and emphasis.[13]

The US national interests in the South China Sea are readily apparent. The free flow of maritime trade through the Sea Lines of Communications (SLOCs) is crucial to the American economy.[14] At the strategic level, the SLOCs allow the US Navy to transit between the Indian and Pacific Oceans, greatly facilitating America's global military posture. Therefore, the US cannot be seen to be conceding the SCS, thus appearing to be falling under the Chinese sphere of influence. Consequently, Washington has taken a series of measures to bolster its military presence in Asia, including forward deployment of a modern nuclear powered aircraft carrier i.e. USS George Washington.[15] Recently, the US has also sent its most advanced surveillance and submarine hunting aircraft, the P8-A Poseidon to swoop over an artificial island built by Beijing to extend its zone of influence in the SCS. The Chinese Navy issued almost eight warnings to the US surveillance aircraft and asked it to leave what it described as Chinese territory. The US Defence Secretary Ashton Carter urged Beijing to put "immediate and lasting halt" to such construction.[16] The series of fabricated islands and the massive Chinese military build-up on them have alarmed the Pentagon, which is carrying out the surveillance flights in order to make clear that the US does not recognise China's territorial claims.[17]

Subsequently, the US tightened its military-to-military relations with a number of Southeast Asian countries, including capacity-building support for Malaysia, Vietnam, the Philippines and Indonesia. The deployment of American troops to Northern and Western Australia, along with a heightened naval and air force presence may put the US in a better position to dominate the critical sea-lanes between the Indian and the Pacific Oceans, through which a large proportion of world trade passes.[18]

The ongoing skirmishes between China and disputant countries run counter to the spirit of the Declaration on the Conduct of Parties (2002) in the SCS, drawn up between the ASEAN countries and the People's Republic of China. Under the terms of the agreement, the countries had agreed to "resolve their territorial and jurisdictional disputes by peaceful means, without resorting to the threat or use of force, through friendly consultations and negotiations". However, recent developments have negated the 'friendly tenor' that underpinned the agreed mechanism for conflict resolution.[19]

Most scholars believe that the SCS dispute is regional in nature with global consequences. Robert D. Kaplan emphasized that "most of the contested areas of the globe in the last century lay on dry land, but over the span of the decades, the demographic and economic axis of the earth shifted measurably towards the opposite end i.e. maritime, and the SCS will be the major focal point of the future conflict."[20] Hence, this is an opportune time for India to engage with the Indo-Pacific region substantially rather than symbolically.

India's Interest in the South China Sea

India cannot isolate itself from the dispute, especially after Beijing denounced plans by an Indian company to develop oil fields in the SCS. However, China insists on building strategic projects in Pakistan Occupied Kashmir, including deploying troops there. In April 2013, the Chinese forces intruded 19 kilometres deep into Indian Territory in the Depsang region of Ladakh (later withdrawn), but protests Indian oil exploration in SCS. There are also unconfirmed reports of confrontation between the Chinese warship and INS Airavat in the South China Sea.

The Indian Navy document *"Freedom to use the Seas: India's Maritime Military Strategy"*, highlighted that India's area of interest "extends from the north of the Arabian Sea to the South China Sea".[21] During the 17th ASEAN Regional Forum (ARF), meeting India joined other countries to declare that the SCS should remain open for international navigation but unfortunately, it went unnoticed.[22] In an address at National Maritime Foundation, New Delhi on July 28, 2011, Indian Foreign Secretary Nirupama Rao reiterated India's stand on the SCS dispute and emphasised that it is an important shipping route and India supports the freedom of navigation in the SCS.[23]

On August 31, 2011, the UK media reported that an "unidentified Chinese warship confronted an Indian Navy vessel". However, India downplayed the reported confrontation between the Indian Naval ships and PLA Navy in the international waters of the disputed SCS on July 19-28, 2011 when INS Airavat was on a "friendly visit" to Vietnam. The MEA said in a statement, "There was no confrontation involving the INS Airavat." The Indian Navy, too, issued a statement stating: "There was no confrontation with any vessel." Beijing too maintained silence over the incident. However, the fact of the matter is that China is closely observing Indian activities in the SCS and its growing relations with the ASEAN countries.[24]

On September 14, 2011, Beijing objected to ONGC Videsh's (OVL) venture in Vietnam to scout for hydrocarbons in the SCS, and asked India to refrain from entering into deals with Vietnamese firms exploring oil and gas in the disputed SCS over which China claims sovereignty.[25] India responded to the Chinese objections by saying that its cooperation with Vietnam is in accordance with international laws.[26] In response, China announced its plan to expand its exploration of 10,000 sq km of seabed in Southwest Indian Ocean.[27] During the then External Affairs Minister, SM Krishna's visit to Hanoi in September 2011, India underlined that OVL will go ahead with oil and gas exploration in the disputed region or the two offshore blocks (127 and 128) which Vietnam claims as its own. In 2011, India and Vietnam also signed a three-year deal covering investment and cooperation in energy exploration, production and refining.[28]

India is the fourth largest consumer of energy in the world after the US, China and Russia. India's economy is growing rapidly and to sustain this growth uninterrupted energy supply is essential. The NITI Aayog (erstwhile Planning Commission of India) in the 12th Five Year plan (2012-17) has underlined that coal dominates the country's energy mix with a robust 52 per cent share in primary energy consumption, followed by oil at 30 per cent and gas at 10 per cent. Other sources include two per cent hydroelectricity and less than one per cent nuclear energy. Import dependence of oil is currently about 75 per cent, which is projected to increase to 80 per cent by 2016-17. Import of gas is currently ruling at 19 per cent, slated to increase to 28 per cent by 2016-17. Similarly, coal import is expected to rise from about 90 million tons at present, to over 200 million tons in 2016-17.[29]

As per the US Energy Information Administration (EIA), India imported approximately, 62 per cent of its oil from the Middle Eastern countries in 2012 (see diagram-1). However, due to political instability in the region and some 'political compulsions' (US urged India to delink/reduce its energy requirement from Iran), New Delhi has found it prudent to diversify its energy resources and take a look eastwards. Even though the availability of oil and gas in the South China Sea (SCS) has, somewhat limited potential to satisfy India's energy quest in comparison to West Asia, it is still an attractive option for India's energy security and related diplomacy. Significantly, on November 23, 2011 during an address on *Security dimensions of India's Foreign Policy* at the National Defence College (NDC), Ranjan Mathai, then Foreign Secretary of India, underscored that "the South China Sea remains crucial to our foreign trade, energy and national security interests".[30]

Diagram 1: India Pertoleum and other Liquids Imports by Source, 2013

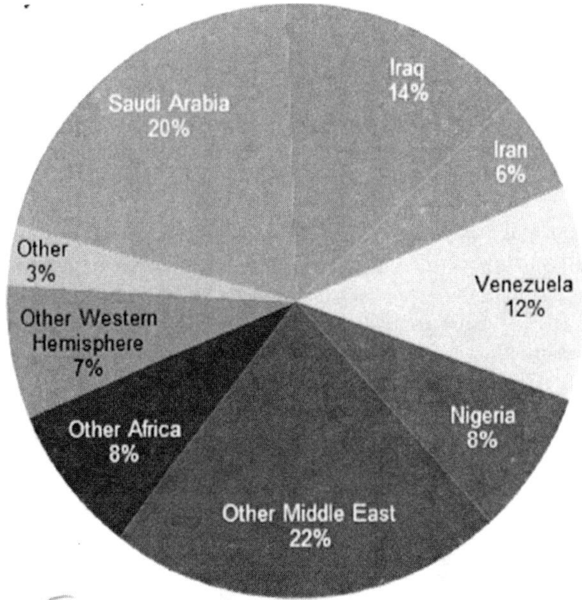

eia Source: U.S. Energy Information Administration, Global Trade Atlas.

Therefore, one must take note of India's exploration activities in the SCS region, especially the blocks given by Vietnam. The ONGC Videsh Ltd. (OVL) provides the following information:

Block 06.1	Block 06.1 is an offshore Block located 370 km southeast of Vung Tau on the southern Vietnamese coast with an area of 955 sq km. The exploration License for Block 06.1 was acquired by OVL in 1988. After subsequent assignments and transfers of Participating Interest (PI) between the parties to Block 06.1 and Petro Vietnam, the present holdings of PIs with effect from October 17, 2011 are ONGC Videsh 45 per cent, TNK Vietnam BV 35 per cent (Operator) and Petro-Vietnam 20 per cent. Lan Tay field in the Block has been developed and the field started commercial production in January 2003. OVL share of production from the project was 2.023 BCM (Billion Cubic Metres) of gas and 0.036 MMT of condensate during 2011-12 as compared to 2.249 BCM of gas and 0.038 MMT of condensate during 2010-11. Lan Do field in the Block is under development with first gas expected in October 2012. Wells Lan Do-2P and Lan Do-1P have been drilled and completed between January 14, 2012-April 18, 2012. Presently, subsea construction works are in progress and first gas from Lan Do field is expected in October 2012. OVL's share of the development expenditure in the block was about $342.78 million till March 31, 2012.
Block 127	Block 127 is offshore deep water Block, located at water depth of more than 400 meters with 9,246 sq km area in Vietnam. The PSC for the Block was signed on May 24, 2006. OVL holds 100 per cent PI in the Block with Operatorship. OVL has

	acquired 1,150 sq km 3D seismic data in the Block and the interpretation of the seismic data has been completed. Location for drilling of exploration well was identified and the well was drilled in July 2009 to a depth of 1265 mts. As there was no hydrocarbon presence, the Company decided to relinquish the block to Petro-Vietnam. OVL has invested approx $68 million till March 31, 2010.
Block 128	Block 128 is offshore deep water Block, located at water depth of more than 400 metres with 7,058 sq km area in Vietnam. The PSC for the Block was signed on May 24, 2006 and the extension to the exploration Phase-I for the Block 128 was valid till June 15, 2012. OVL holds 100 per cent PI in the Block with Operatorship.1650 sq km of 3D seismic data was acquired and interpreted in the Block by OVL and location for drilling of exploration well was identified. Drilling was attempted on the location during September 2009; however, the well could not be drilled as the rig had difficulty in anchoring at the location due to hard carbonate sea bottom.Meanwhile, OVL has found solution to the anchoring problem and asked for extension to the exploration phase to undertake review of additional G&G data to find out a viable location for drilling to fulfill the PSC commitment. Petro-Vietnam (PVN) has suggested OVL to continue the exploration programme in the block for additional two years with effect from 16th June 2012 by revisiting the geological model with the integration of data likely to be available with the assistance from PVN. Till March 31, 2012, OVL has invested about $49.14 million in the Block.

Source: ONGC Videsh Ltd., http://www.ongcvidesh.com/Assets.aspx?tab=0, (accessed July 08, 2013). See also ONGC Videsh Ltd., http://www.ongcvidesh.com/assets/cis-far-east/, (accessed June 10, 2015).

Map 2: Block 06.1

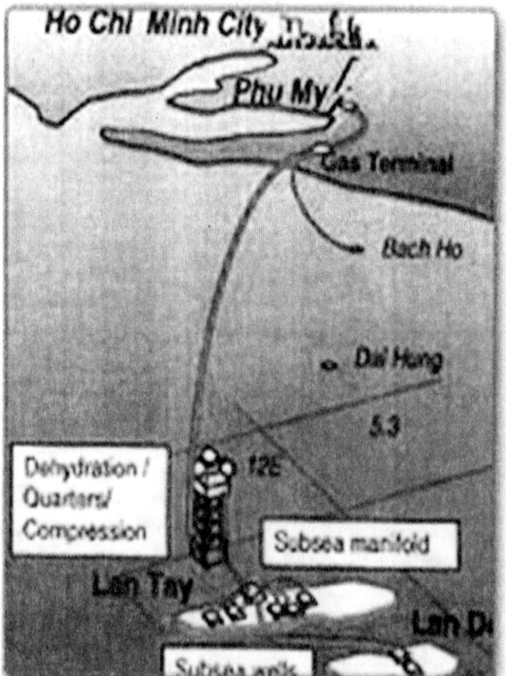

Source: http://www.ongcvidesh.com/assets/cis-far-east/, (accessed June 10, 2015).

Map 3: Blocks 127 and 128

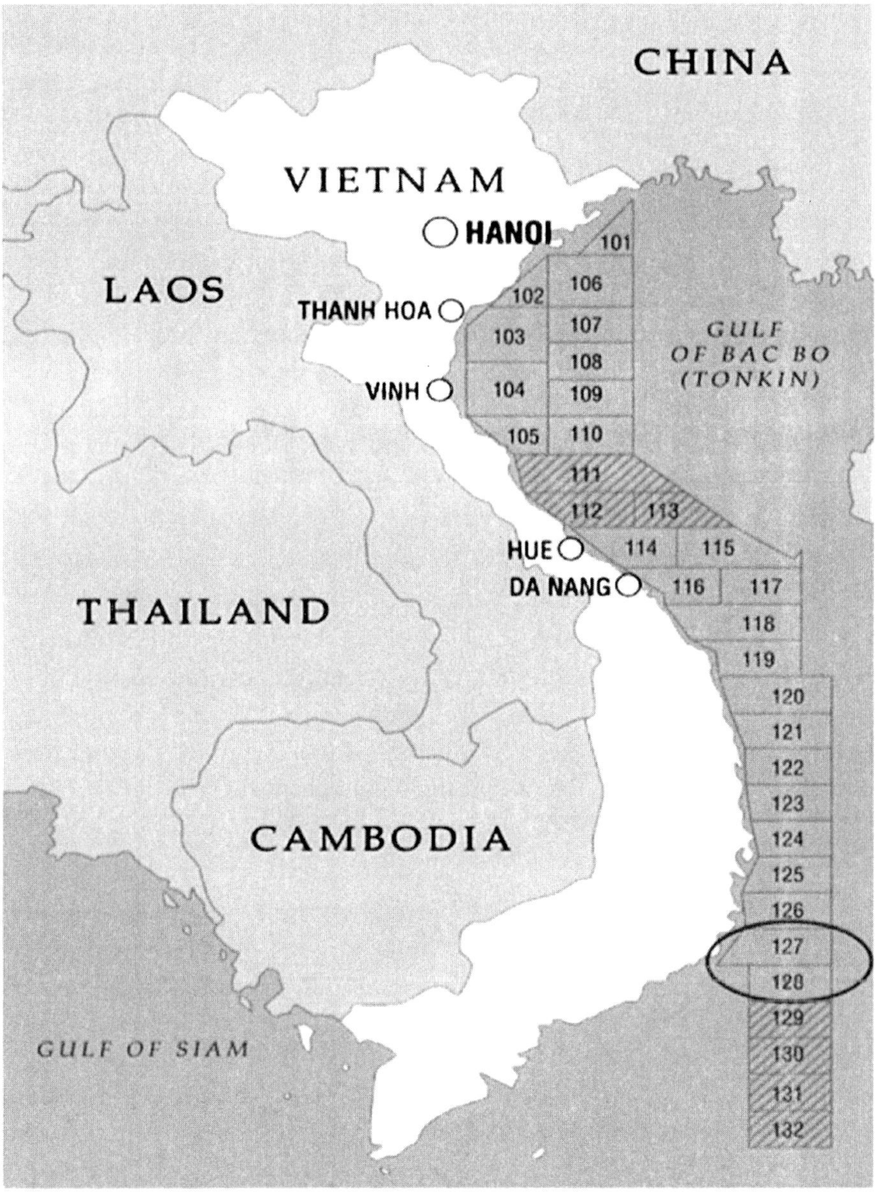

Source: http://www.gazprom.com/f/posts/63/322243/vietnam_1_eng.jpg, (accessed June 10, 2015).

Interestingly, the OVL is working in the region since 1988, especially on block 06.1 but only recently, China has started opposing India's oil exploration in the SCS. However, Russia's Gazprom is also exploring oil and gas in the Vietnamese block 112 and 129-132 in the South China Sea since September 11, 2000 but Beijing has never uttered a single word against the Russian exploration.[31]

On December 3, 2012, while responding to media questions on the South China Sea, the then Chief of Naval Staff, India, Admiral DK Joshi underlined that "not that we expect to be in those waters very frequently, but when the requirement is there for situations where the country's interests are involved, for example ONGC Videsh, we will be required to go there and we are prepared for that."[32] Admiral Joshi's remark came at the same time when the then National Security Advisor (NSA) of India, Shivshankar Menon was in China on his two-day visit, but the latter downplayed the remarks, saying that the issue did not figure during his talks with the Chinese leadership. Mr. Menon told that the media had "manufactured" a story by getting the Navy Chief to comment on the matter, adding that the Chinese side recognised that "the media plays a role."

However, India's diplomacy has failed at that time on this issue as Beijing advised caution to New Delhi for its exploring activities in the SCS. In response to Admiral Joshi's comments, the Chinese Foreign Ministry spokesperson Hong Lei said, "We hope relevant countries respect China's sovereignty and national interests", and emphasized that China opposes any unilateral energy exploration and development activities in the disputed areas in the South China Sea.[33] Recently, China highlighted that the Beijing would encourage "joint development" in the SCS, especially on the issues related to oil and gas explorations.

The issue at stake here is that if India truly supports freedom of navigation in the SCS, then it will be necessary for India to assert, back up and safeguard its own interests in the region. The SCS is not only a strategic maritime link between the Pacific and the Indian Oceans; it is also a vital gateway for shipping in East Asia. Almost 55 per cent of India's trade with the Asia-Pacific transits through the SCS. Therefore, it is quite evident that India derives considerable economic benefits from the SCS being an area where all actors enjoy a level playing field. The recent upsurge in tensions in the SCS represents a security flashpoint with global consequences. The dispute has the potential to turn into a military conflict that could end up affecting the peace and security of the entire region and any disruption or conflict relating to SLOCs will hurt India's energy and economic outlook severely. As it may compel

New Delhi to adopt some alternative route to channelize their economic activities in the region, which could force time constraints, increase overheads and consume more energy.

Therefore, keeping in mind the volatile situation of the South China Sea and India's energy interests, New Delhi is deliberately increasing its maritime profile in the region. Indian Naval warships are frequently visiting this region and engaging the SCS littorals in maritime exercises. India has stepped up its strategic partnership with ASEAN in the recent months as the newly elected Prime Minister of India Shri Narendra Modi visited some of the Southeast/ East Asian countries and emphasised upon maritime security and safety.

The arrival of the Modi Government in 2014 with a nationalist fervour, has given new impetus to the ties with the Southeast Asian countries since the latter is repeatedly urging New Delhi to play a crucial role in balancing Beijing in the Indo-Pacific region. Prime Minister Modi has impressed the entire world with his various initiatives on India's foreign policy and related diplomacy. Since the forming of the new government, several bilateral and multilateral interactions between India and the East Asia nations have been taken place. It is due to Prime Minister Modi's dynamism and enthusiasm that New Delhi has rejuvenated its more than two-decade-old 'Look-East' policy to the 'Act-East' policy.[34]

Prime Minister Shri Narendra Modi and his ministers, NSA and President of India have visited few of the Southeast and East Asian countries, especially Japan, China, South Korea, Myanmar, Vietnam, etc. and signed various agreements of mutual interest, keeping an eye on the future developments of the entire region. Significantly, Modi also visited United States and Obama visited New Delhi as a Chief Guest to India's Republic Day celebration. During the visit, both India and the US brought out a strategic vision document for the "Asia-Pacific and Indian Ocean Region" in which they highlighted that 'a closer partnership between the United States and India is indispensable to promoting peace, prosperity and stability in those regions'. The Joint Strategic Vision, also underscored that the 'regional prosperity depends on security; we affirm the importance of safeguarding maritime security and ensuring freedom of navigation and over flight throughout the region, especially in the South China Sea'. The vision document urges 'all parties to avoid the threat or use of force and pursue resolution of territorial and maritime disputes through all peaceful means, in accordance with universally recognised principles of international law, including the United

Nations Convention on the Law of the Sea'.[35] This joint strategic vision signifies that the Modi Government is more proactive and vigilant with regard to Asia-Pacific and Indian Ocean Region, including the SCS, as compared to the Manmohan Singh Government. Prime Minister Modi is also expected to visit Malaysia and Vietnam during the 27th ASEAN Summit, November 18-22, 2015. Vietnam is looking to increase defence cooperation between New Delhi and Hanoi including aiming to buy BrahMos supersonic cruise missiles from India. Hanoi is also materializing few more oil and gas blocks to New Delhi in the South China Sea for joint exploration and production.[36]

The growing influence of China in the Indian Ocean Region (IOR) and in Southeast Asia is a decisive reason for both India and ASEAN to engage strategically in the region. China has strengthened its naval presence in the SCS and is endeavouring to do the same in the Indian Ocean. It has reportedly installed a listening post in the Burmese territory of Coco Islands and thus, is aiming to establish its strategic presence in the IOR purportedly through the "String of Pearls" strategy.

After the Chinese claims over the entire SCS, Southeast Asian countries are preparing themselves against the possibility of further Chinese aggressive stances. From the ASEAN perspective, India is seen as a possible counterweight against China in the region. Therefore, India and some members of the ASEAN countries began holding joint maritime exercises. The seventh edition of Exercise Milan in 2010 was held in the backdrop of India's "Look East" policy wherein naval ships of Singapore, Sri Lanka, Thailand, Australia, Bangladesh, Indonesia, Malaysia and Myanmar, with representatives from navies of Brunei, Philippines, and Vietnam, participated.[37] Significantly, most of the navies of the region, especially ASEAN countries, also participated in the Milan 2012[38] and the recent Milan 2014 exercises hosted by the Indian Navy in the Andaman and Nicobar Islands.[39]

At the same time, China does not welcome the ASEAN moves to interact with major powers. However, the Indian Navy has conducted joint exercises with the Singaporean, Vietnamese, Japanese and South Korean navies in the South and East China Seas. The Indian Navy has also conducted exercises with the PLA Navy whenever Indian ships have visited the region.[40]

Witnessing overarching Chinese claims over the SCS, there is significant scope for the Indian and Southeast Asian Navy to engage constructively. India has helped Malaysia in building up its Coast Guard in the past and it has the expertise to help other ASEAN countries. However, maritime cooperation between India and ASEAN is still in the nascent stages. Cooperation with regard to capacity building and patrolling piracy-infested areas or jointly facing non-traditional threats at sea like drug-trafficking, human-trafficking and possible maritime terrorism remain inadequate. India has a strong Navy with technological credibility that can be leveraged by ASEAN. Frequent joint naval exercises similar to India-Singapore exercises and deeper cooperation in training and exchange of defence personnel could form additional and viable confidence-building measures. Collaboration on missile technology, radar systems, defence component systems and supporting hardware are again areas where ASEAN countries can work in partnership with India.[41]

India has provided training to Malaysia's Air Force pilots on MiG-29s in the past and has offered training on the Sukhoi. It has also shown keenness to sell BrahMos missiles to friendly countries, including the neighbouring Southeast Asian countries.[42] At present, most of the ASEAN countries are engaged in a defence modernisation programme and would like to obtain assistance in weapons up-gradation and systems integration. Like India, most of the Southeast Asian countries also rely on Russia for their defence procurements. India with its long experience in using Russian products has developed the technological capabilities for low cost servicing and hence could be a potential ally for ASEAN in this field. Assisting ASEAN will also improve India's relations with the Southeast Asian countries bilaterally and multilaterally and it will boost India's image/standing in the region as having the potential to balance China in the IOR.

Conclusion

China's recent acts in the SCS indicate that it is working on a 'revisionist agenda' in the region and trying to unilaterally change the status quo in the SCS. China's rising economic and military might could compel the ASEAN countries to rally together as well as to seek assistance from the United States and other nations to balance China. The US posture has raised tensions in the region as China warned its neighbours not to "play with fire". Further, Beijing believes that Washington is eyeing to control the Spratlys through Vietnam and the Philippines. If the territorial disputes relating to the SCS are not resolved soon to the satisfaction of all maritime stakeholders including the littoral nations, heightened regional and global anxiety will spiral out of control causing a bitter diplomatic fracas over this issue.

It is a fact that India is a growing military power and a growing economy and to sustain eight to nine per cent of economic growth annually, New Delhi has to diversify and looks for new avenues for its energy resources. It is interesting to note that after getting an observer status in the Arctic Council, New Delhi is in the process of acquiring an icebreaker for a whopping $144 million for conducting scientific and business exploration in the polar region as the Arctic is also reasonably rich in hydrocarbons.

As far as hydrocarbon resources in the South China Sea are concerned, India has not invested enough in the region. Till March 31, 2012, the OVL had invested around $460 million in the Vietnamese Blocks and this can be increased. However, the repository of oil and gas elsewhere in the SCS also attracts New Delhi and in some way or the other, India is dependent on this region too for its energy security as she is shipping oil from Sakhalin (Russia) to Mangalore through this sea route. New Delhi is also importing a significant amount of coal from SCS littorals, namely Indonesia and the Philippines, through this maritime channel itself. India's OVL is also eyeing stakes in one of the three joint ventures announced in the Arctic region by the Russian state oil company Rosneft. If India gets this project, then New Delhi will have to ship oil through the South China Sea, as this is the shortest sea route for India to transport oil from the Arctic region. OVL has produced 2.104 BCM (Billion Cubic Metres) of gas in 2012-13 as compared to 2.023 BCM in 2011-12 and 2.249 BCM during 2010-11 from Block 06.1 of Vietnam. This is more than what the OVL is producing from Sakhalin-I, AFPC-Syria and BC-10 of Brazil collectively.[43] In addition, if China controls these waters, it will be difficult for India to continue its unencumbered economic and energy ventures through this region.

India's national interest lies in the freedom of navigation and any disruption or conflict relating to SLOCs will hurt New Delhi severely as the South China Sea channel is significant for its energy security. It is therefore an opportune time for India to channelize its foreign policy with the littorals of the SCS substantively, rather than symbolically. It has also been noted that the second phase of the India's Look East policy is over and now the time has come for India to lay the groundwork during the third phase, in which, New Delhi has already rechristened its Look East policy to 'Act East' policy. Therefore, New Delhi now must concentrate on the strategic aspects of the bilateral relations with all the Southeast/East Asian countries. Moreover, it is an opportune time for India to interact strategically with its allies in the region. In this context, maritime cooperation and capacity building between India and the Southeast Asian countries will be of utmost importance. This recalibration can pay rich dividends to New Delhi's ongoing 'Act-East Policy'.

END NOTES

1. Sachin Parashar, *"No oil hunt in South China Sea without nod: Beijing to Delhi"*, Times of India, May 31, 2015, New Delhi, available at http://timesofindia.indiatimes.com/india/No-oil-hunt-in-South-China-Sea-without-nod-Beijing-to-Delhi/articleshow/47486463.cms, (accessed June 10, 2015).
2. US Energy Information Administration (EIA), *South China Sea*, February 7, 2013, available at http://www.eia.gov/countries/analysisbriefs/South_China_Sea/south_china_sea.pdf, (accessed July 08, 2013).
3. Amit Singh, "South China Sea Dispute and India", SAEA Group Research, Singapore, September 25, 2011, available at http://saeagroup.com/articles/2011/sept/south-china-seadispute- and-india.html, (accessed June 10, 2015).
4. Amit Singh, "South China Sea Dispute: A New Area of Global Tensions", July 23, 2011, available at http://www.maritimeindia.org/CommentryView.aspx?NMFCID=1291, (accessed June 10, 2015).
5. Amit Singh, 'South China Sea Disputes: Regional Issue, Global Concerns', *Maritime Affairs*, 8:1, 2012, London: Routledge, p.116-135.
6. US Energy Information Administration (EIA), *South China Sea Tables and Maps*, September 2003, available at http://community.middlebury.edu/~scs/maps/US%20EIA,%20South%20China%20Sea%20Tables%20and%20Maps.htm, (accessed July 08, 2013).
7. Tran Truong Thuy (ed.), *The South China Sea: Cooperation for Regional Security and Development,* (Hanoi: Diplomatic Academy of Vietnam, 2010), p. 137-138.
8. K.K. Agnihotri & Sunil Agarwal, "Legal Aspects of Marine Scientific Research in Exclusive Economic Zones: Implications of the Impeccable Incident", *Maritime Affairs*, 5 (2), (London: Routledge, 2009)), pp. 142-43.
9. "The South China Sea: A Sea of Disputes", *The Economist*, February 21, 2011, available at http://www.economist.com/node/21016161, (accessed June 10, 2015).
10. Amit Singh, "India's Energy Security and South China Sea: A Maritime Perspective", in *'Strategising Energy: An Asian Perspective'*, ed. by Dr. Sreemati Ganguli, (New Delhi: Knowledge World, 2014), pp. 61-79.
11. Baladas Ghoshal, "ASEAN and South China Sea Dispute", *World Focus*, April 2011, pp. 207- 210.
12. "US warn against restriction in South China Sea, *Straits Times*, May 12, 1995.
13. "China's 'aggressive' build-up called worry", *The Washington Times*, 14 January 2010, See also "China 'more aggressive' at sea", *Straits Times*, 24 July 2010.
14. US Department of Defence, Naval Operations Concept 2010: Implementing the Maritime Strategy (Washington D.C., US Department of Defence, 2010), p. 35.
15. James Kraska, "How the United States Lost the Naval War of 2015", *Orbis*, Winter 2010.
16. Nayan Chanda, "A Chinese Lake", Times of India, June 6, 2015, p. 22, New Delhi.
17. Jim Sciutto, "China warns US Surveillance Plane", CNN, available at http://edition.cnn.com/2015/05/20/politics/south-china-sea-navy-flight/, (accessed June 10, 2015).
18. James Cogan, "Obama increases US military presence in Australia and Asia", November 17, 2011, available at http://www.wsws.org/articles/2011/nov2011/asia-n17.shtml, (accessed June 10, 2015).

19. Leszek Buszynski, "Rising Tensions in the South China Sea: Prospects for a Resolution of the Issue", *Security Challenges*, 6 (2), 2010, pp. 85-104.
20. Robert D. Kaplan, *The South China Sea is the Future of Conflict* (2011), available at http://www.foreignpolicy.com/articles/2011/08/15/the_south_china_sea_is_the_future_of_conflict, (accessed June 10, 2015).
21. "Freedom to use the Seas: India's Maritime Military Strategy", (New Delhi: Ministry of Defence, GOI, 2007), pp. 59-60.
22. Indrani Bagchi, "India to discuss China with US later this month", The Economic Times, September 4, 2010.
23. Nirupama Rao, "Maritime Dimensions of India's Foreign Policy", Ministry of External Affairs, India, July 28, 2011, http://www.mea.gov.in/Speeches-Statements.htm?dtl/53/Address+by+FS+on+Maritime+Dimensions+of+Indias+Foreign+Policy, (accessed June 10, 2015).
24. India, Vietnam ties irk China? *Asian Age*, September 2, 2011, p. 5.
25. Li Hongmei, "Wise to Refrain from Churning up South China Sea", available at http://news.xinhuanet.com/english2010/indepth/2011-09/16/c_131142806.htm, (accessed June 10, 2015).
26. This information was given by the Minister of State for External Affairs, Shri E. Ahamed in written reply to a question in Rajya Sabha on December 15, 2011, available at http://www.mea.gov.in/rajya-sabha.htm?dtl/15481/Q2516+Agreement+signed+with+Vietnam, (accessed June 10, 2015).
27. Indrani Bagchi, "India, China square off for sea fight", *Times of India*, September 19, 2011, p. 10.
28. Sachin Parashar, "Undeterred India to hunt for oil in South China Sea", *Times of India*, New Delhi, September 17, 2011, p. 18.
29. Twelfth Five Year Plan (2012–17) Economic Sectors, Vol. 2, Planning Commission, India, (New Delhi: SAGE Publications, 2013), available at http://planningcommission.nic.in/plans/planrel/12thplan/pdf/vol_2.pdf, pp.130-194, (accessed July 08, 2013).
30. Address by Foreign Secretary at NDC on "Security dimensions of India's Foreign Policy", November 23, 2011, Ministry of External Affairs, India, available at http://www.mea.gov.in/SpeechesStatements.htm?dtl/6946/Address+by+Foreign+Secretary+at+NDC+on+Security+dimensions+of+Indias+Foreign+Policy, (accessed June 10, 2015).
31. Gazprom, Vietnam, Blocks 112 and 129–132, available at http://www.gazprom.com/about/production/projects/deposits/vietnam/, (accessed June 10, 2015).
32. Manu Pubby, "Ready to protect Indian interests in South China Sea: Navy Chief", *Indian Express*, December 4, 2012, available at http://www.indianexpress.com/news/ready-toprotect-indian-interests-in-south-china-sea-navy-chief/1040119/, (accessed June 10, 2015).
33. Ananth Krishnan, "China opposes 'unilateral energy exploration' in South China Sea", *The Hindu*, December 5, 2012, available at http://www.thehindu.com/news/international/chinaopposes-unilateral-energy-exploration-in-south-china-sea/article4167002.ece, (accessed June 10, 2015).
34. C. Raja Mohan, *Modi's World: Expanding India's Sphere of Influence*, (New Delhi, Harper Collins, 2015) p. 133.
35. US-India Joint Strategic Vision for the Asia-Pacific and Indian Ocean Region, Ministry of External Affairs, Government of India, January 25, 2015, available at http://www.mea.gov.in/bilateral-documents.htm?dtl/24728/USIndia_Joint_Strategic_Vision_for_the_AsiaPacific_and_Indian_Ocean_Region, (accessed June 10, 2015).

36. Satya Prakash, 'Vietnam eager to host PM Narendra Modi', Hindustan Times, April 26, 2015, available at http://www.hindustantimes.com/world-news/vietnam-eager-to-host-pmnarendra-modi/article1-1341322.aspx, (accessed June 10, 2015).
37. "Indian Navy Hosts Milan 2010", available at http://indiannavy.nic.in/Milan12/sub-pages/history.php, (accessed July 08, 2013).
38. "Indian Navy Milan-12", available at http://indiannavy.nic.in/Milan12/index.php, (accessed July 08, 2013).
39. Press Information Bureau, "17 Nations 15 Ships Demonstrate a Momentous 'Milap': Milan 2014 an Unequivocal Success", Ministry of Defence, Government of India, February 9, 2014, available at http://pib.nic.in/newsite/PrintRelease.aspx?relid=103278, (accessed June 10, 2015).
40. Faizal Yahya, "Challenges of Globalisation: Malaysia and India Engagement," *Contemporary Southeast Asia*, 27 (3) (2005), pp. 472-98.
41. Amit Singh, India-Malaysia Strategic Relations, *Maritime Affairs*, 7 (1), (London: Routledge, 2011), pp. 85-105.
42. "Export Market of BrahMos Missile", *Press Information Bureau*, Government of India, August 9, 2010, available at http://pib.nic.in/newsite/erelease.aspx?relid_64459, (accessed July 08, 2013).
43. *"Indian Petroleum and Natural Gas Statistics 2013-14"*, Ministry of Petroleum & Natural Gas Economics and Statistics Division, Government of India New Delhi, October 2014, available at http://petroleum.nic.in/docs/pngstat.pdf, (accessed June 10, 2015).

15

Maritime Security Cooperation with Southeast Asian Littorals: Role of the Indian Navy

Shishir Upadhyaya

Background

The ancient historical linkages and deep bonds of trust and friendship between the people of India and Southeast Asian states, established through trade and cultural exchanges were underpinned by maritime links spanning several millennia. These links were temporarily disrupted with the arrival of the colonial powers in the region in the 15th century. However, presently these very ancient bonds form a key element of India's 'Look East' foreign policy for engagement with Southeast Asia.

The strategic environment of the region in the post-Cold War era is dominated by the Indian Ocean, shared by India and Southeast Asian littorals as a global common. Thus, both India and the Southeast Asian littorals are destined to jointly face the emerging threats and challenges of the 21st century, ranging from transnational maritime crimes such as piracy, illegal immigration, smuggling etc at one end of the spectrum to the more serious challenges of natural disasters, climate change and even interstate maritime disputes erupting into full-fledged conflicts at the other end. These challenges have now taken centre stage and demand the undivided attention of the regional navies and security forces.

It has been seen, that given the common nature of maritime threats and the evolving political consensus amongst states—an outcome of the post-Cold War era—regional navies are willing, more than ever before, to cooperate with each other. Consequently, in recent years several cooperative security mechanisms have emerged in the IOR in order to address the common maritime security challenges. These include organisations such as the IORA (Formerly IOR-ARC or Indian Ocean Region–Association for Regional Cooperation), the ADMM (ASEAN Defence Ministers Meeting) and the IONS (Indian Ocean Naval Symposium) at the regional level and the Malacca Strait Patrols, the *Milan* series of exercise hosted by India, etc at the sub regional levels.

The aim of this chapter is to define a maritime security cooperation strategy for India, based on the framework of the regional security complex propounded by Buzan and Weaver.[1] A regional security complex represents;[2] 'a group of states whose primary security concerns are linked together sufficiently closely that their national securities cannot realistically be considered apart from one another.' This chapter highlights the key maritime security challenges before India and defines the broad strategy that could be adopted to foster maritime security cooperation in the IOR. The chapter concludes with specific recommendations for forging close maritime security cooperation with Southeast Asian littorals, led by the Indian Navy.

Challenges for India

In its 66 years of existence, India has seen five major conflicts with China and Pakistan. All three countries are now nuclear weapon states. Historically, China has followed a strategy of 'creeping invasion' to usurp island territories in the region including the Paracel Islands in 1974, the Johnson Reef in 1988, the Mischief Reef in 1995 and recently the Scarborough Shoal in 2012 and the Second Thomas Shoal in 2013. Evidently, China has now turned its focus on the disputed Senkaku Islands with Japan. Further, recent events of border incursions reported from the northeast Indian state of Arunachal Pradesh are a clear indication of China's persistent attempts at 'territorial nibbling'[3] on land. Meanwhile, Pakistan, an all-weather ally of China has systematically exploited the nuclear 'umbrella' to inflict cross border terrorism against India. It is thus amply clear that India's relations with China and Pakistan will continue to remain adversarial with little hope for improvement in the foreseeable future.

In the IOR, the emerging nontraditional challenges of the 21st century, not only threaten India's maritime security – as demonstrated during the 26/11 attacks in Mumbai—but also impose a moral and legitimate duty upon it to ensure the safety and security of the sea lanes in the region. According to Admiral Sureesh Mehta (Retd),[4] the smaller maritime powers of the IOR look up to India to ensure a measure of stability and tranquility in the region. Thus, for India, in order to preserve a favourable balance of power in the Indian Ocean in the face of a rising China and an adversarial Pakistan and to maintain good order and peace in the Indian Ocean, it is imperative to maintain an all-round balanced naval capability. It is therefore, imperative for India to adopt a maritime cooperation strategy that would enable it to leverage its inherent advantages of geographical position, historical ties and diaspora in the region over China and Pakistan. Clearly, such a strategy for maritime cooperation would need to be dovetailed with India's foreign policy and crafted in close collaboration with various stake holders including its domestic defence and maritime industry.

Maritime Doctrine

The framework for employment of India's maritime power in the 21st century is laid down in the maritime doctrine (2009) promulgated by the Indian Navy. It outlines the diplomatic role of the Indian Navy as follows:

> Naval Diplomacy entails the use of naval forces in support of foreign policy objectives to build 'bridges of friendship' and strengthen international cooperation on the one hand, and to signal capability and intent to deter potential adversaries on the other. The larger purpose of the navy's diplomatic role is to favourably shape the maritime environment in the furtherance of national interests, in consonance with the foreign policy and national security objectives.

The Indian maritime doctrine and strategy promulgated by the Indian Navy's have served well to provide the basic guiding principles and framework for the employment of the Indian Navy. However, the lack of a formal national maritime strategy, curtails the efforts of the navy to favourably shape the maritime environment as envisaged above.

Maritime Security Cooperation

India's maritime security (or defence) cooperation with the Southeast Asian littorals states is conducted at two levels. Firstly, at a multilateral level India interacts with the region through regional fora such as the Indian Ocean Rim Association for Regional Cooperation or the IOR-ARC (now renamed as IORA), the ASEAN Defence Ministers Meet Plus (ADMM), the IONS and the multinational annual exercise *Milan* series. Secondly, India has various bilateral/trilateral agreements with most littoral states. During the preceding decade the Indian Navy has evolved its own cooperative engagement programmes with various littorals and extra regional powers and signed Defence Cooperation Agreements (DCA) with virtually every littoral.

Multilateral Fora

A brief discussion on the various fora for multinational maritime security cooperation is as follows:

IONS

This organisation was established in 2008 as the outcome of an Indian Navy initiative to build a regional 'Track–I' forum of navies and coast guards of the IOR. The IONS was inspired by the Western Pacific Naval Symposium (WPNS)—of which India has been an observer for several years. It was formed two decades earlier in 1988 to promote maritime cooperation and interoperability amongst the Pacific navies. However, over the years, it has been seen that while the IONS has conducted several 'talkshops',[5] it has failed to conduct a single naval operation under its aegis. In comparison, the WPNS has been able to leverage the close cooperative ties or *spirit de corps* established between member states to conduct combined operations at sea. It could be argued that the WPNS has been in existence longer than IONS, but it is noteworthy that it initially drafted a more ambitious charter which seeks to promote cooperation and interoperability.[6] In 2008, even as the IONS was being inaugurated, critics had warned that it encompasses a region that is too disparate to be treated as a coherent entity and because it was not built around a common trade or economic interest—as the ARF has been an offshoot of the ASEAN grouping—it would fail to deliver.[7] It was perhaps felt that common security concerns could be a binding factor for member states only if it impinged on a common economic interest.

IORA

An economic forum in the form of the Indian Ocean Rim Association for Regional Cooperation or the IOR-ARC, established in Mauritius in 1997, is the only summit level forum encompassing the IOR. While the original charter made no reference to maritime cooperation, this has now been included under the Chairmanship of Australia. It is opined that the time has now come for a 'handshake' (as suggested by Vice Admiral Pradeep Kaushiva[8]) between the only two pan Indian Ocean organisations. This could perhaps provide the much needed impetus to the IONS.

ADMM Plus

In 2007 the ASEAN Defence Ministers' Meeting (ADMM) was expanded beyond ASEAN to include China, India, Japan, South Korea, Australia, New Zealand, Russia, and the United States. The ADMM Plus has identified five areas for cooperation viz., maritime security, counter-terrorism, disaster management, peacekeeping operations and military medicine. Each issue is addressed through five Experts' Working Groups (EWGs) who work towards practical cooperation. In June 2013, a multinational HADR exercise was conducted under the aegis of ADMM. The success of ADMM in facilitating military participation of all stakeholders of the region in an effort to prepare for natural disasters highlights the role for navies in promoting a friendly environment in the region. India thus should continue to offer full-fledged participation of the Indian Navy in the ADMM.

Strategy for Multilateral Cooperation

Broadly, India's strategy for cooperation at the multilateral level should seek to combat the common threats of piracy, maritime terrorism, transnational crimes, etc and also contribute to HADR. India should also seek to promote its maritime and defence interests in the region and prevent China from dominating the agenda. This implies that India should not only be present in every multinational fora but also be an active participant. It is clearly a difficult task for India to match China in terms of capacity and scale for maritime cooperation. Therefore, India would need to reach out to other stakeholders with common security concerns. In Southeast Asia, it is thus imperative for India to leverage its ties with Australia, Japan and USA to sustain and promote its national interests in the region.

Recommendations

A few specific projects that could be initiated by the Indian Navy and undertaken jointly with other navies of the region for the benefit of all are enumerated in the succeeding paragraphs.

Pan IOR Intelligence Grid

Given the recent experience of combating Somali piracy in the Indian Ocean and the extant security environment in the Indian Ocean, it is opined that constant surveillance especially over the sea lanes and intelligence or in other words complete Maritime Domain Awareness will continue to remain the key factor to maintaining good order in the region. To this end several sub regional organisations have evolved. These are as follows:

- The Piracy Reporting Centre (PRC) of the International Maritime Bureau (IMB) in Malaysia.
- The ReCAAP Information Sharing Centre (ISC) at Singapore.
- The Information Fusion Centre (IFC) of the Republic of Singapore Navy (RSN).
- The newly established Indian Coastal Radar cum AIS Network under the Director General Lighthouses and Lightships (DGLL).
- The Maritime Security Centre, Horn of Africa or MSC HoA.
- NATO Shipping Centre (NSC). Both the NSC and the MSC HoA are based in London but maintain a watch on the shipping off the African Coast.

It is opined that a Pan Indian Ocean Intelligence Grid, connecting all the above organisations into one common platform (accessed via the internet) could provide all the IOR littorals a complete MDA picture. This could be achieved under the aegis of the IONS and led by the Indian Navy.

IONS Series of Naval Exercises

The Indian Navy conducts several joint naval exercises. The *Milan* series is the largest multilateral exercise conducted by the Indian Navy; the exercise in 2013 was attended by 13 countries. In order to promote multinational naval cooperation and provide an operation focus to IONS, the *Milan* series could be brought under the aegis of IONS. The format of the exercises could also be tailored to prepare navies to combat common nontraditional challenges. Further, in order to encourage participation from all navies, member states could be allowed to invite sea riders/ observers from smaller navies.

HADR and Climate Change

It is a well-known fact that a majority of the world's population resides within

300 km of the coast. Asian coastal areas have the most significant concentrations of populations close to the coast with the attendant increased vulnerability to maritime disasters. This vulnerability was witnessed during the Tsunami of 2004 which killed over 226,408 people in the IOR. According to the IFRC world disasters report of 2012, in 2011, Asia alone accounted for 77 per cent of all lives lost to disasters globally.

Natural disasters can strike anywhere at any time and early warning and quick response is the key to reducing damage. It is universally accepted that the armed forces are best suited to respond to disasters. In the IOR the navies thus have a key role to play and the IONS is thus an ideal platform to discuss and prepare for such contingencies in the future. In fact, a regional early warning system linked with the Pan Indian Ocean Intelligence Grid (as discussed above) and IONS series of naval exercises to foster interoperability amongst navies could significantly improve the disaster preparedness in the IOR.

Maritime Security Cooperation at the Bilateral/Trilateral Level

During the preceding decade the Indian navy has evolved its own cooperative engagement programmes with various littorals and extra regional powers and signed Defence Cooperation Agreements (DCA) with virtually every littoral. A list of such engagements is appended below (Table 1). The key challenge for the Indian Navy, in the future, would be to sustain and/or extend its current level of naval engagement with various littoral states in the face of growing competition from PLAN.

Strategy for Bilateral/Trilateral Cooperation

Since the 1990s when China turned towards South Asia and thence towards the rest of the Indian Ocean, it has sought to develop maritime cooperation with various littorals. According to C. Raja Mohan (2012),

> China, has steadily raised its profile in the Indian Ocean. Initially, China's strategic focus was aimed at Burma (Myanmar), where Beijing sought a range of security cooperation. Since then, its interests in South Asian waters came to light, as it moved into the development of maritime infrastructure in Gwadar (Pakistan) and Hambantota (Sri Lanka), China as begun to look beyond South Asia in recent years towards the key island states in Western Indian Ocean-Seychelles and Mauritius.

Pakistan has sought to develop defence/maritime ties with several littoral states principally on the Islam card. It has thus sought to counter Indian naval influence in Indonesia, Malaysia, Bangladesh and Maldives in Southeast Asia and other Islamic states in West Asia. Pakistan Naval (PN) ships occasionally visit ports in these countries and the PN also offers training assistance to naval officers from the region. However, the PN is severely constrained by capacity to match the scale of Indian Navy's foreign cooperation programmes. It is thus opined that the principal challenge to Indian maritime influence in the region would be from China and not Pakistan, though the possibility of Pakistan actively facilitating Chinese influence in certain states can't be ruled out.

The Chinese dependency on maritime trade to transport strategic resources to fuel its burgeoning economy is its greatest vulnerability in the Indian Ocean, sometimes expressed as the 'Malacca Dilemma'. China has sought to counter this weakness by promoting close maritime cooperation with Pakistan (Gwadar), Sri Lanka (Hambantota), Mauritius and Seychelles. While it is difficult to prognosticate on the type of support that China could potentially receive from these states, the Indian strategy for bilateral cooperation should seek to balance if not neutralise the Chinese efforts. As discussed, above, India would need to reach out to extra-regional partners such as Australia, Japan and the US to complement its efforts in the region.

Table 1: Ongoing Maritime Security Cooperation Initiatives of the Indian Navy with Southeast Asian States

Sl.	*Country*	*Programme*
1.	Indonesia	• Navy to Navy Staff talks. • Ind-Indo coordinated Patrols or CORPAT. • *Milan* participant. • Training assistance and training exchanges. • Visits by defense/civilian officers. • OTR. • HADR assistance.
2.	Brunei	• Ship visits. • *Milan* participant.
3.	Malaysia	• Training assistance. • *Milan* participant. • Navy to navy staff talks.
4.	Myanmar	• Training assistance. • Gifting of naval platforms.

Sl.	*Country*	*Programme*
		• OTR. • *Milan* participant. • Navy to navy staff talks. • Joint exercises and Coordinated Patrols along EEZ Boundary Line.
5.	Singapore	• Navy to Navy Staff talks. • Joint Exercises codenamed SIMBEX. • *Milan* participant. • Training assistance. • Visits by defense/civilian officers. • Information sharing for MDA. • OTR.
6.	Thailand	• Training assistance. • *Milan* participant. • Indo Thai Coordinated Patrols (CORPAT). • Navy to navy staff talks.
7.	Timor Leste	—
8.	Vietnam	• Ship visits. • Training assistance. • Navy to navy staff talks. • Material and technical assistance in maintenance of vintage platforms.
9.	Cambodia	• Ship visits.
10.	Laos	—

Souce: Compiled from various MoD Annual Reports. Please see www.mod.giv.in.

Analysis

It can be seen from the above table that the Indian Navy has wide ranging foreign cooperation programmes with most the Southeast Asian littorals, however, a lack of depth and trust in the ties is evident. For instance, since 2004 the Southeast Asian littoral viz., Indonesia and Malaysia, have consistently prevented the participation of the Indian Navy in security patrols in the Strait of Malacca, despite the fact that the Andaman and Nicobar Islands lie in close proximity of the region and that the Indian Navy could have significantly augmented the naval capacity in the region. Clearly, a lot remains to be done by India to bridge this trust deficit and establish a close maritime cooperation with the littorals.

The navies of the Southeast Asian region, with the exception of Singapore, are in various stages of modernisation. This offers huge potential for India to develop close maritime security cooperation with the region. As the largest navy in the Indian Ocean the Indian Navy has considerable expertise and capacity to offer in terms of naval training, technical support and defence collaboration. These are discussed in the following paragraphs.

Naval Training

Indian Navy's sophisticated training infrastructure which includes world class basic training facilities (the medium of instruction being English) as well as highly specialised training schools and defence colleges which are a great asset to foster close naval cooperation. Training helps to build everlasting bridges of friendship. Australia has used defence training as an effective tool to promote defence ties with all its neighbouring Island states. The Australia Defence International Training Centre at Melbourne, conducts orientation programmes for all foreign personnel deputed for training. The Indian Navy has training programmes for almost every littoral navy and imparts training to sailors and officers at various levels of seniority. The newly launched Cadet Training Academy at Ezhimala has been designed to accommodate an additional load of foreign trainees. The fact that naval training in India, even at the level of sailors is mostly in the English medium is a significant advantage over the PLAN and the Indian Navy should capitalise on this advantage. Yet a formal institution like the DITC in Australia does not exist in India. Thus, the Indian Navy should develop a focused strategy to promote training as an effective means to foster close maritime security cooperation in the region.

Defence Exports

India overtook China as the largest importer of arms globally in 2011 and has since maintained the lead. However, in terms of defence exports, the situation is quite the reverse. India's defence exports from 2010-2012 totaled a mere $ 183 Million.[9] In comparison, China's defence exports which include high end aircraft, missiles, ships and artillery, amounted to $ 2.2 Billion in 2012 (*New York Times*, Nov. 2013) alone! The top 10 largest recipients of Chinese arms include Pakistan, Bangladesh, Saudi Arabia, Iran, Thailand and Vietnam in descending order.[10]

The key reason for India's poor record of defence sales is widely attributed to a perceived lack of quality and sophistication of equipment produced by Indian manufacturers. However, it would be grossly inaccurate to attribute the lack of defence exports to quality alone. After all, the Indian industry has produced some world class military hardware that includes modern naval platforms such as the Delhi Class destroyers, the *Shivalik* Class stealth frigates and one of the world's fastest and most accurate cruise missiles, the *Brahmos*. Even the private sector has had a few success stories. The high speed interceptor boats made by L&T for the Indian Coast Guard are one of the fastest boats in the world in the sub 28 mtr, 100 T category! Similarly, in what is touted as India's largest defence order, the Pipavav Defence and Offshore Engineering Company has bagged a US$ 450 Million order for four OPVs for an African state, Nigeria (Grevatt, Jon. 2013).

It is assessed that one of the key reasons for low defence exports is the lack of a national strategy involving all the stakeholders viz., the armed forces, Defence Research and Development Organisation (DRDO), Defence Public Sector Units and various private sector players to promote defence exports. The Indian Navy could play a vital role in stimulating the defence exports within Southeast Asia as it is currently engaged with almost every littoral state in the region through its various ongoing foreign cooperation programmes/initiatives. In the recent past, the Indian Navy transferred some of its own ships, *gratis*, to Mauritius, Seychelles, Maldives and Sri Lanka to help them augment their surveillance/policing efforts. In a similar initiative by Australia, known as the Pacific Patrol Boat programme (PPB), the RAN donated 22 vessels to various Pacific island states to assist them in protecting their respective EEZs. Perhaps the Indian Navy could emulate or remodel the PPB programme with a 'buy one get one free scheme' to help promote sales of the high speed interceptor craft by L&T, which could find many takers in the region, particularly in Cambodia, Myanmar, Thailand and Vietnam.

Repair and Refit Facilities

A large number of littoral states operate platforms, weapon and sensors common to the Indian Armed Forces. For example, both the Indian Navy and the RMN are the only two navies in the region inducting *Scorpene* submarines. While the Indian Navy is yet to acquire a *Scorpene* Class Submarine the RMN is already operating them. Similarly, Indian and Indonesia are two navies operating the Type 209 HDW submarines and the Kilo Class submarines in service with the Indian Navy for several years are now also been inducted by Vietnam. The Airforce Su 30 is another platform operated by India and others including Indonesia and Malaysia. In addition to these platforms there are many common weapon systems and sensors that are operated by India and others in the region. The development of dedicated support facilities in India could potentially help India to emerge as the regional hub for all defence requirements including repair and refit of various platforms, weapons and sensors operated by various littorals in the region. This could be an important factor to promote long term defence relations.

Maritime Domain Awareness

India should also explore the feasibility of linking up the recent Trilateral Cooperation on Maritime Security or TCMS for with Sri Lanka and Maldives with the ongoing Malacca Strait Security initiative. The TCMS is an initiative sharing information on merchant vessel traffic to build regional Maritime Domain Awareness (MDA) and could be a useful source of intelligence for the Southeast littorals. Sharing of information in the maritime domain with the Southeast Asian littoral could also be confidence and trust building measure.

Conclusion

The formation of an international coalition of naval forces from almost every G20 state to combat piracy in the Gulf of Aden, would have been unimaginable during the Cold War era. However, presently, 20-23 ships from the US led multinational Task Force 151, the European Union Naval Force, the NATO, China, Russia, India, Iran, Japan, South Korea, etc are on patrol in the Gulf of Aden operating as a loose international Task Force. This is clearly the shape of future maritime security cooperation.

India's relations with its immediate neighbours on land viz., China and Pakistan, remain adversarial with little scope for improvement in the foreseeable future. The emerging nontraditional threats of the 21st century in the IOR and the apprehensions of a rising China are common concerns shared by many littorals states, thus creating a "regional security complex" as defined by Buzan. The key challenge for India is to ensure a stable and secure environment in the IOR. Clearly, this will be a task spearheaded by the Indian Navy in the role of a catalyst for fostering maritime security cooperation. However, India faces challenges, both internal as well as external. Internally, there is a need to evolve a national maritime security cooperation strategy leveraging the inherent strengths of the Indian Navy and the capabilities of various stakeholders in the country including the domestic defence and maritime industry. Externally, it is appreciated that Indian influence in the IOR will be increasingly challenged by China and Pakistan.

India's maritime engagements with the IOR at the multilateral level should seek to address the larger common nontraditional threats and maintain a stable and secure environment. At the bilateral level the Indian should prioritise its engagements with the littorals and focus on building robust partnerships and a high degree of interoperability with a few select states and their navies. In the post-Cold War period, as the world moves towards a multipolar world, defence diplomacy will be a key factor in preserving a balance of powers. Thus for India, an effective national maritime security cooperation strategy that creates a synergy between its foreign policy, the employment of the Indian Navy and the domestic defence and maritime industry is the key to maintaining peace and stability in the Indian Ocean Region.

END NOTES

1. B. Buzan, and O. Wæver, *Regions and Powers: The Structure of International Security*, (Cambridge: Cambridge University Press, 2003).
2. Dennis Rumley (ed), "The Indian Ocean Region: Security, Stability and Sustainability in the 21st Century."AII, Task Force on Indian Ocean Security, Mar 2003. P11.
3. Brahma Chellaney, "The Chinese Art of Creeping Warfare", The Mint, New Delhi, 25 December 2013.
4. Note 3 ibid. p. iv.
5. See Seng Tan, *Future of ADMM-Plus: Asia's Growing Defence Engagements.* RSIS Singapore Commentary No. 158/2013 dated 26 August 2013.
6. See http://www.navy.mi.th/wpns2013/, Accessed on 01 September 2013.
7. Kanwal Sibal, *Contemporary Transnational Challenges: International Maritime Connectivities*, ed. Ravi Vohra, et al. (KW Publishers, NMF, New Delhi, 2008), p. 4.
8. See http://maritimeindia.org/article/regional-maritime-co-operation, Accessed on 01 September 2013.
9. Jon Grevatt. Jane's Defence Industry report dated 01 January 2013.
10. http://www.nytimes.com/2013/10/21/world/asia/chinas-arms-industry-makes-global-inroads.html?pagewanted=2&_r=3&. Accessed on 22 October 2013.

16

India-Malaysia Relations in the Regional Geo-Politics: A Maritime Perspective

Ashok Rai

India and Malaysia, two maritime neighbours have had a common historical past as both these nations were colonies of the British Empire. Post-independence, their relations have undergone phases of highs and lows. This article examines the prevailing maritime security dynamics of the Asia-Pacific Region, the existing India-Malaysia maritime engagements and recommends areas where India and Malaysia could cooperate to further enhance their maritime security.

Historical Background

India and Malaysia are maritime neighbours. The politico-economic and socio-cultural ties between the two countries go back to the pre-Christian era. India gained her independence on 15th Aug 1947. Diplomatic ties were established soon after Malaya's independence in 1957, an event that was celebrated by all citizens of India including the Indian Prime Minister Jawaharlal Nehru. The Malaysian Prime Minister Tunku Abdul Rahman had made efforts to advance links between the two countries and during a period of grave crisis like the Sino-Indian war of 1962, Malaysia proved to be a good friend of India by openly condemning the Chinese aggressors. Later, India supported the Malaysian candidature for the non-permanent membership of UN Security Council. This allowed the two countries to embark on a new phase of understanding in political and economic fields. In the 1965 Indo-Pakistan War, Indonesia supported Pakistan, while Malaysia backed India. On the issue of Kashmir, Malaysia also supported India's stand. India reciprocated the support to Malaysia during the Konfrontasi despite the fact that India's move caused resentment in Indonesia. This showed the commitment of both the nations towards each other and thereafter the relationship between the two grew considerably. During Indira Gandhi's premiership, relations between the two countries concentrated on cultural and technological exchanges. India's opposition to any military presence in the region was unanimously welcomed. Consequently, Malaysia came out openly to extend help and cooperation to India during the 1971 Bangladesh crisis and was amongst the first few countries to recognize Bangladesh in 1972.

In May 1974, India conducted a peaceful nuclear test to become self-reliant in the field of nuclear power which forced Malaysia to criticize India. Subsequently, the goodwill between India and Malaysia during Mrs. Gandhi's tenure was short-lived. However, there was a thaw in the relationship during the Morarji Desai led Janata Party Government in 1977 and subsequent Govts resulting in signing of some important agreements.

During the Cold War period, India and ASEAN drifted apart. In 1991 with the launching of India's Look East policy an economic reconnect was established between India and its eastern ASEAN neighbours which included Malaysia. As India's economic reforms unfolded, there was no let-up in the pace of diplomacy towards the region, which saw steady gains. Neither the controversial Indian nuclear tests of 1998, nor the economic crisis in East Asia in the late 1990s, came in the way of rapid expansion of India's relations with the region. Trade between India and ASEAN most of which is sea-borne multiplied fourfold - from $3.1 billion in 1991 to about $12 billion in 2002. Today the trade between India and ASEAN and India and Malaysia stands at about US$ 80bn and US$ 13bn respectively. This indicates that India – Malaysia relations have gone through some high and low phases in the last five decades or so.

Once again the two countries have realised the need for greater engagement, and in 2007, which marked the 50th anniversary of the establishment of diplomatic ties between India and Malaysia, many an agreements for further enhancing bilateral ties were signed, notable among these agreements included Trade & Industry, Railways, Road Transport &

Highways, tourism, Energy (especially renewable), Higher Education and Knowledge etc. The two countries also agreed to explore the possibilities of joint collaboration on projects of mutual interest in the defence sector including enhancing cooperation in counter-terrorism strategy through information sharing and the establishment of a bilateral Joint Working Group. The leaders acknowledged that the partnership has moved beyond the bilateral framework and that the two countries share a mutual interest in cooperating for peace, prosperity and security of the Asia-Pacific region and beyond.

Asia-Pacific Region

The Asia-Pacific region encompasses almost half the world's population, three of the four largest economies, more than fifth of world's GDP, one-third of world exports and half of world's maritime tonnage. It is home to an enormously populous and diverse mix of ethnicities, cultures, political systems, religions and economies, which further enhances its growing geo-strategic importance. Over the next five years, nearly 50 percentage of all growth outside the US is expected to come from Asia. The region is the maritime trade highway of the world and joins Southeast Asian states with the Western Pacific. The South China Sea, apart from being rich in fisheries also provides passage to roughly two–thirds of South Korea's energy supplies, 60% of Japan's and Taiwan's, and about 70% of China's. The seabed of South China Sea and East China is reputed to hold valuable reserves of energy deposits.

Of late, the Asia-Pacific region has witnessed the aggravation of territorial disputes in the East China and South China Seas as well as the Sea of Japan. Add to that recently there have been strained relations between China and some of the Southeast Asian countries involving maritime disputes. These factors have resulted in the region seeing a competitive modernisation of military capabilities in almost every nation of the region[1]. Many analyst have remarked that what is going on in the region is not really an arms race, but rather a military build-up with a wary eye on one's neighbours, fuelled by nationalist sentiments[2]. Spending on the modernisation of the naval forces in Asia-Pacific countries now accounts for 24 per cent of all defence spending globally[3]. According to the International Institute for Science Studies (IISS), Asian countries have begun to spend more than European countries.

The "Pivot to Asia" or "rebalancing to Asia" policy adopted in 2011 by the administration of US President Obama, reflects, the US desire to retain preponderance in this strategically high–priority region. Of the 26 ships equipped with Aegis systems with SM Block 1A interceptor missiles, 16 ships are currently located in this region. In 2013, whilst the USA's defence budget was US$ 640 billion, for the first time in the last ten years, Japan's Defence budget saw an increase to US$ 48.13 billion (SIPRI), South Korea's at US$ 33.97 billion (SIPRI) with a significant naval component for its modernisation and Australia at US$ 23.96 billion (SIPRI).

Another important player in the region has been an assertive China, which has along with its economic rise also enhanced its military budget. According to SIPRI, China's defence spending increased by 750 per cent, from US$ 18 billion to US$157 billion, from 1989 to 2012. In 2013, according to SIPRI, China's military budget was $188 billion.

According to many experts, an important development of China's policy along with its growing assertiveness since late 2000's is that not only are Tibet, Xinjiang and Taiwan now regarded as 'core interests', but also disputed islands in the East Asia Sea (Senkaku/Diaoyu/Tiaoyutai islands) and the South China Sea (the Spratly and the Paracel islands) including other maritime claims, have been characterised as issues of utmost importance where no concessions or compromises are possible and where a state can resort to coercive measures. Malaysia has a maritime dispute with China on some of the Spratly Islands[4]. Additionally, Malaysia has a dispute with Indonesia on the Ambalant Island. Ambalant is known to be rich in oil and gas reserves. Though the media reports suggest that there was tension around the area which escalated with the "brushing" of naval vessels of the two countries, the diplomatic relations between the two ASEAN members have reduced tensions between the two ASEAN neighbours.

Malaysia and Singapore had a dispute with regard to three maritime features namely Pedra Branca/Pulau Batu Puteh, Middle Rocks and South Ledge[5]. This dispute was referred to the International Court of Justice. On 23 May 2008, the Court pronounced its Judgment on the case. It ruled that sovereignty over Batu Puteh belongs to Singapore, and that of Middle Rocks to Malaysia. The Court further ruled that sovereignty over South Ledge belongs to the state in the territorial waters. Both Singapore and Malaysia have accepted the judgement by the ICJ and later establish a Joint Technical Committee to enforce the ICJ's decision.

In addition to the traditional threats, the Asia-Pacific region also has non-traditional threats of piracy, maritime terrorism, drug trafficking, gun running and climate change being prominent among them.

India-Malaysia Maritime Security Engagements

In the early 1990's, the collapse of the Soviet Union, and the launching of India's Look East policy, led to a major reassessment of India's relationships with the littorals of South East and East Asia. Among of the plethora of activities undertaken, friendly port visits by the Indian naval ships to Malaysia and vice versa commenced. Over the years, the operational interaction between the Malaysian navy and the Indian navy has increased, be it, in terms of training interactions, visits by high-level delegations or regular reciprocal port calls by respective warships. The Chief of the Royal Malaysian Navy (RMN) visited India in September 2004. Between 2003 and 2004, six Malaysian officers underwent training in India and three Indian navy personnel received training in Malaysia. Both navies also interact regularly under the aegis of the Western Pacific Naval Symposium (WPNS)[6]. Both the Navies have been carrying out PASSEX[7]. The Indian High Commissioner in Malaysia stated that there was a substantial enhancement in the defence exchanges between Malaysia and India since Mr Najib's visit as deputy prime minister to India in 2006. Another important platform for India's and Malaysia's navy-to- navy cooperation is in the biennial LIMA exhibition and Milan exercises. The LIMA exhibition is seen as one of the major aerospace and maritime industry showcases in the world. LIMA provides a platform for the global aerospace and maritime industry to exhibit and promote cutting-edge defence technology in the Asia-Pacific region.

Milan is a Multinational Exercise conducted at Port Blair, A & N Islands. The number of participants in Milan has been increasing since it was initiated in 1995. From four navies in 1995, it has grown to 16 in 2014. The RMN has been sending naval ships to the Milan exercises since 1997. Malaysia believes that Milan serves as a good platform for the RMN to build friendship and mutual understanding between participating navies and is an effective forum to discuss common concerns in the Indian Ocean region. It also helps to forge cooperation initiatives. Furthermore, the Malaysian navy has purchased two French-made Scorpene-class diesel-electric submarines. India has also placed an order for six similar class submarines. Both countries are keen to collaborate on training, logistics and certain operation procedures in terms of maritime security to protect their maritime interests and sensitive sea-lanes[8]. According to a Malaysian maritime analyst, one such area of security cooperation that India may offer is through securing the northern sphere of the Malacca Straits from the threats of transnational crimes. These include the trafficking of weapons, humans and drugs, which have been a concern to the littorals.

In order to undertake joint anti-piracy patrols in the Malacca and Singapore Straits several rounds of consultation between the United States, Indonesia, Malaysia, Australia, India and other littoral states were held. Warships were required to escort ships carrying high-value goods in the Straits of Malacca. The operation commenced after intelligence agencies warned of a major terrorist threat in the region[9]. The operation was undertaken by Indian navy vessels INS Sukanya and INS Sharda under code named **Operation Sagittarius**[10]. However, when INS Sukanya began patrolling the Straits of Malacca in coordination with the US Navy, as part of India's commitment to assist the international coalition against terrorism, Malaysia showed its discomfort. Malaysia argued that as per UNCLOS (1982), the repetitive passage of warships through Malaysian territorial water was considered a breach. Therefore, INS ships were not cleared for rest and recreation in Malaysian ports. Again, in June 2004, Malaysia, Indonesia and Singapore enunciated their policy by issuing a joint declaration to initiate stepped-up 'Coordinated Patrols' as the main strategy for securing the Malacca Straits, especially for curbing piracy attacks, without the participation of US forces. These patrols were termed MALSINDO. MALSINDO is an acronym for Malaysia, Singapore and Indonesia. MALSINDO involved the navies of these three countries patrolling in a coordinated fashion in their respective territorial waters[11]. However, the lack of a provision for cross-border pursuit into each of the participating states' territorial waters has been cited as the main flaw in this measure. India showed interest in being part of the MALSINDO exercise, India has been offered the role of 'Eye in the Sky' that is Joint military air patrols over the Straits of Malacca[12].

Way Ahead

India does not have any dispute what so ever with any of the nations of Asia-Pacific Region in general and ASEAN littorals in particular. With a resurgent Indian economy growing at about 7.5 per cent[13], and about 90 per cent of Indian trade by volume flowing through the Sea Lanes of Communication (SLOCs), India is genuinely concerned about the safety and security of the SLOCs. India is a votary of freedom of navigation. The Indian and Malaysian Navies are two of advanced navies in the region and have displayed professionalism whilst meeting their mandated charter of duties.

Indian Navy's role during the disaster relief operations undertaken post Tsunami 2004 was well commended globally. India has also been actively engaged in anti-piracy patrols off Somalia. In the recent past Indian Navy's assistance in locating the Malaysian Airline MH 370 was also well appreciated. Post 26/11 Mumbai terrorist attack, India has put in place a well-integrated Coastal Security architecture called IMAC (Information Management and Analysis Centre). IMAC links 51 Naval and Coast Guard stations located along the 7500 km coast as well as island territories. The network provides these stations coastal surveillance information obtained from various sensors such as the coastal radar chains, the automatic tracking system as well as electro-optical cameras. Apart from sharing expertise on Humanitarian Assistance And Disaster Relief (HADR) operations and IMAC, India and Malaysia could share expertise on type-specific training on Scorpene and pollution control procedures from the Indian Naval and Coast Guard formations respectively.

Conclusion

On the naval front, although Malaysia does not see China as a threat, and does not have any major issues with any nations, given the present security architecture in the region, such as maritime interests in the South China Sea and the Malacca Straits, Malaysia could look to India as a viable option for defence cooperation. There have been many developments between the two nations in terms of training, PASSEX, visits at the level of service chiefs, reciprocal visits of ships, sports and adventure activities and strategic security dialogues. The burgeoning defence ties with Malaysia are an indicator of India's willingness to enhance its interaction with Malaysia. India also possesses one of the largest military forces in the world, its navy is the largest in the Indian Ocean littoral and is one of the very few that operate aircraft carriers. India and Malaysia could set actively engage each other, to oversee different aspects of maritime security cooperation in the Asia-Pacific region.

END NOTES

1. Kireeva Anna, Regional Strategies and Military Build-up in East Asia and Indo-Pacific: A Russian Perspective, *Maritime Affairs*, Vol 10, No 2, Winter 2014, pp. 42.
2. Ibid
3. Ibid
4. Malaysia is a claimant in the Spratly Island in the South China Sea. In 1979 Malaysia published a map defining the limits of its continental shelf claim that enclosed several Spratlys

features. Malaysia has occupied five islands that it considers to be within its continental shelf. Malaysia has built up one atoll by bringing soil from the mainland and has built a hotel and dive facility centre on Swallow Reef (Pulau Layang Layang). Malaysia's navy currently occupies Ardaseir Reef (Terumbu Ubi), Mari Veles Reef (Terumbu Mantanani), Erica Reef (Terumbu Siput), and Investigator Reef (Terumbu Peninjau). Recently Malaysia and Vietnam jointly submitted the extension of is Continental Shelf to the Commission on the Limits of the Continental Shelf. This extension of territory beyond 200 nautical mile limit is allowed under Article 75 of the UNCLOS. In its immediate reaction, China objected to the joint submission by Malaysia and Vietnam, claiming that the expansion would encroach into its sovereign territory. The Chinese government also urged the Commission not to consider the joint submission.

5. Pedra Branca/Pulau Batu Puteh (hereafter Pedra Branca) is a granite island, measuring 137 m long, with an average width of 60 m. It is situated at the eastern entrance of the Straits of Singapore – one of the busiest maritime passages in the world. It lies approximately 24 nautical miles to the east of Singapore, 7.7 nautical miles to the south of the Malaysian state of Johor and 7.6 nautical miles to the north of the Indonesian island of Bintan. Middle Rocks consists of two clusters of small rocks that are permanently above water, and is located 0.6 nautical miles to the south of Pedra Branca. South Ledge is a low-tide elevation and lies at 2.2 nautical miles to the south-south-west of Pedra Branca.
6. CNS: Press Release, Press Information Bureau, Government of India, Ministry of Defence, on the occasion of commissioning of new Naval Air Station 'INS Baaz' on July 14, 2005.
7. 'India, Malaysia Hold Joint Naval Exercise', The Times of India, May 3, 2008. PASSEX is conducted as per an approved pre-planned schedule when one nation's naval ship(s) meets up with the naval ship of another country whilst enroute to another final destination.
8. Vijian, P, 'Delhi, KL Examine Scorpene Submarine Cooperation', National News Agency of Malaysia (BERNAMA), February 15, 2008, at http://www.bernama.com/bernama/v3/news_lite.php?id=314129 (accessed 20 Mar 15)
9. Josy Joseph, 'Navy Replaces Vessel on Patrol in Malacca Straits', athttp://www.in.rediff.com/news/2002/jul/16josy2.htm (accessed 20 Mar 15)
10. Commodore (Retd.) Ranjit B. Rai, International Correspondent for 'India Strategic', April 17, 2013
11. Official Releases, 'Launch of Trilateral Coordinated Patrols—MALSINDO Malacca Straits Coordinated Patrol', Ministry of Defence, Singapore, July 20, 2004, at http://www.mindef.gov. sg/imindef/press_room/official_releases/nr/2004/jul/20jul04_nr.html#.UVv_Tzdv7Gg (accessed 20 Mar 15)
12. Given that India has developed capabilities in various aspects of maritime security, India was willing to share its expertise with other countries in the region. However, Malaysia's objection was that if external powers were allowed, it would set a precedent for other powers to come into the region. Because of this concern, Malaysia preferred the littoral states to coordinate the patrols. However, later, Malaysia and other ASEAN countries offered India a role in the 'Eye in the Sky' project relating to joint military air patrols over the Straits of Malacca.
13. IMF Chief Christine Lagarde speaking at LSR College, New Delhi on 16 Mar 15.

PART IV

Conflicts and Conflict Resolution

17

Islands of Discontent:
The Arduous and Convoluted Path to Peace in the Southern Philippines

Mohor Chakraborty

The year 2014 will be commemorated in the 'peace' history of Southeast Asia in general and the Philippines in particular, since it marked the successful finale of a protracted religio-ethnic separatist insurgent movement in its southern island of Mindanao. Conceived as a nationalist struggle which had as its goal the establishment of a separate independent homeland for the thirteen ethno-linguistic groups[1] comprising the Philippine Muslims (Moros), the movement was systematically and successfully organised under the leadership of Nur Misuari—the co-founder of the Moro National Liberation Front (MNLF) in the late 1960s. However, in 1978, the MNLF disintegrated and the other co-founder of this separatist group, Hashim Salamat, formed the Moro Islamic Liberation Front (MILF) as its splinter.

Since then, the two branches of the once indivisible identity have continued their fight for an autonomous, independent Muslim homeland (Bangsamoro) on separate pedestals. The quest for the fundamental bases of a modern Philippine nation motivated the development of 'Morohood' (Muslim consciousness), with its roots impregnated in the search for a concerted, ebullient and persistent Muslim resistance to colonial Spain's aggression in the 16th Century. This anti-colonial sentiment was fortified by the feelings of deprivation and exploitation of the Muslims fuelled by the migration of Christians and non-Filipinos in the south in the post-1898 scenario, when the Spanish colonisers were vanquished by the Americans from the Philippine archipelago. It is exactly at this juncture that the roots of the conflict in the southern Philippines can be traced.

The spell of colonial occupation of the Philippines (Spanish colonisation: 1565-1898, followed by American occupation: 1898-1946) not only altered the political and social structures of the indigenous peoples, but also had an impact on their cultural and psychological frame. It deserves mention in this context that, the rise of Islamic political institutions in Southeast Asia is a 15th century phenomenon, marking the culmination of over two centuries of Islamisation following the introduction of Islam by the Arabs directly to the masses. This stimulated the genesis of Muslim nationalism and society in different parts of Southeast Asia and the Philippines was no exception to this rule.

The first Muslim community in the southern Philippines to establish a central government was the Sulu Sultanate in 1450, under which, indigenous institutions were Islamised, thus imposing a superstructure without eradicating the rudimentary foundations. At the height of its power in the 18th century, the stronghold of this Sultanate encompassed Zamboanga, Basilan, Sulu, Tawi-tawi, Palawan and Sabah. With their national identity shaped by Islam, it was further developed in course of their heroic struggle against Western colonialism. Subsequent to their first encounter with foreign aggression (Spanish colonisers) in 1570, the Muslims won a distinct honour as "Moro" —an identity accorded by the Spanish colonisers, based on the Moors of Spain. Interestingly enough, the Muslim inhabitants of the southern Philippines were christened 'Moros' by the Spaniards on account of their Islamic ideology and cultural similarities with the 'Moors' who ruled over Spain for more than seven hundred years.

Even after the departure of the Spanish colonisers from the Philippines, the term 'Moro' lived on, though pejoratively, and was widely used by the Christian Filipinos, primarily through the cultural institution of the "Moro-Moro"—a form of folk theatre in which Christian heroes fought against cruel and barbarous 'Moro villains'.[2] Evidently, the history of the Muslims (Moros) in the Philippines constitutes the backbone of the politico-historical development of the country. As a dominant religious group, entailing a civilisational heritage of over five centuries, the Muslims represent the longest political experience, when compared to the other ethno-religious groups in the country. While the Muslims account for about 20 per cent of the entire population, the other dominant religious group—'Lumad'—a generic term for "native", applied in reference to non-Muslim indigenous people, constitutes about 5 per cent of the populace. Apart from the Muslims and the Lumads, the other demographically dominant group is constituted of the 'Dumagat' (literally meaning "people from over the sea") indicating Christian settlers. Mostly originating from Luzon and Visayas (in the north), the Dumagat migrated to the southern Philippines at the dawn of the 20th century, encouraged by the American colonial government. Demographically speaking, the Muslims were originally concentrated in the southern provinces of Mindanao, Palawan and Sulu, and later spread to Basilan, Cotabato, Davao, Kudarat, Lanao, Tawi-Tawi and Zamboanga. The Christian settlers dominated Mindanao, Sulu and Palawan constituting 75 per cent of the total population of the region. Thus, a combination of religion and colonial policies brought the principal religious groups in the Philippines, namely the Muslims (Moro), Lumad and Christian settlers together in the southern Philippines, creating the matrix of mutual suspicion and animosity.

Such a psychology of misgiving, deprivation and apprehension sowed the seeds of animosity and violence, reflected in frequent and intermittent wars and feuds, which blemished the complexion of the political landscape of the southern Philippines. This plunged the southern islands into a vicious cycle of poverty and underdevelopment, which formed the bedrock of subsequent rebellions, insurgent movements, snowballing into vociferous demands for secession. This chequered situation acted as the incubator of the struggle for self-determination of the Moros, with parallel assertive overtures of the Lumad to a rightful ancestral domain and regional identity.[3] Given this backdrop, this chapter will analyse the trends of the separatist movement led by the Moros and the manner in which it has been dealt with by the Government of the Philippines, starting primarily with the tenure of President Ferdinand Marcos. The chapter will conclude with the present status of this conflict under President Benigno Aquino III, thereby flagging this case study as the culmination of a long and arduous process of conflict resolution, which could well be a panacea for countries both within the region and beyond for forging peace with secessionist groups.

The Marcos Era (1965-1986): The Sprouting and Entrenchment of the 'Moro' Problem

With the United States granting Independence to the Philippines on 4 July 1946, the demand for statehood by the Moros was blatantly overlooked. In this scheme of things, the incorporation of the Sultanates in the region into the overall Philippine Republic, without the provision of democratic consultation on whether the majority of the Moro population intended to be a part of the new Republic as individual citizens or as Sultanates was the principal bone of contention. Thus, the Republic was arbitrarily imposed, notwithstanding the relentless demands for autonomy of the Moro leaders, in denial of the forced inclusion of their homeland within the Philippine Republic.[4]

In this context, historical re-tracing of the *Dansalan Declaration* (18 March 1935) becomes significant, since it expressed the Moros' desired exclusion from the proposed independent Republic to the US colonial government. This Declaration asserted in no uncertain terms the desire of the Moros not to be "included in the Philippines for once an independent Philippines is launched, there would be trouble between us and the Filipinos because from time immemorial these two peoples have not lived harmoniously together. Our public land must not be given to people other than the Moros."[5] Unfortunately, the call for Moro autonomy was rejected and following the incorporation of the region into the Republic, certain administrative changes ensued: first, the Moro Sultanates lost their independence, paving way for the establishment of provincial and municipal governments; secondly, the political control was handed over to Catholic Filipinos from the north; thirdly, several Muslim inhabitants were deprived of their ancestral lands; and finally, the Moros were marginalised in their homeland.[6] The restoration of independence to the Philippines did not improve the socio-economic conditions of the Moros, since the Philippine government retained the colonial socio-economic policies. For instance, the control and monopoly of the economy by multinational corporations, particularly in the export of pineapple, banana, rubber, sugarcane (agribusiness) was extended.[7]

Furthermore, during the decade of the 1950s and 1960s, Manila induced migration to the southern Philippines because of its fertile land and tremendous abundance of other natural resources, specifically as a means to tide over the agrarian problem in the northern regions of Luzon and Visayas. In fact, under the administration of President Ramon Magsaysay (1953-1957), several resettlement programmes like the National Authority for Reforestation and Rehabilitation Administration (NARRA) and Land Settlement and Development Corporation (LASEDECO) prompted huge influx from the northern Philippines to the south. Resultantly, the Filipino Christian migrant settlers outnumbered the Moros consequently not only dominating the socio-economic and political life in Mindanao, but also fuelling increased marginalisation and underdevelopment of the Muslim populace.[8]

This stream of perceived exploitation of the 'Moros' aggravated their discontent, which found its organised and systematic expression in the Muslim Independence Movement (MIM) in May 1968. The MIM was founded by the retired Governor of Cotabato, Udtug Matalam, with the explicit goal of the secession of Muslims from the Republic of the Philippines in order to establish an Islamic State. The Movement put forth the following reasons behind their agitation and demand for secession: first, the establishment of the provincial and municipal governments was believed to not only undermine the status of the traditional leaders, but also dislocate the authority and communication infrastructure, thus negating the then existing coalition formation patterns, imperative for cooperative and community-oriented ventures that the Muslims were accustomed to; secondly, the imposition of a new legal system negated the traditional judicial functions of the village elders, consequently disintegrating social order and fuelling socio-economic problems; thirdly, the educational sphere was not immune to dislocations since the public school organisation systematically alienated the school students, who were forced to learn new sets of values alien to their socio-cultural milieu; and fourthly, the influx of settlers from the north to the southern provinces, in conjunction with the creation of agricultural colonies out of their lands, which effectively reduced the economic base of the Moroland caused severe resentment among the Moros.

The MIM vehemently called for the outright secession of Mindanao, Sulu and Palawan regions from the Philippine government's control, besides proclaiming a 'Jihad' (holy war) to defend the Moro homeland. Subsequently, the protesters also supplanted the word "Muslim" with "Mindanao" in order to accommodate the non-Muslim inhabitants of southern Philippines as well. Later, the name "Muslim Independence Movement" was changed to "Mindanao Independence Movement" to have room for the Christian majority in the Island. However, the MIM was never a popular secessionist movement and its public political actions were pronouncements in the form of manifestos and declarations of policy in the national and international press, disseminated to politicians and Muslim leaders in the Philippines and abroad. The manifestos of the MIM also drew the prompt attention of the then President of the Philippines, Ferdinand Marcos, who met Udtug in October 1968, acknowledged Udtug's self-proclaimed role as "the leader of the more than four million Muslims in the Philippines", and appointed him presidential adviser on Muslim affairs. Thereafter, Udtug retreated publicly from his initial positions.[9]

Birth of the MNLF: The Sword-Bearers of the Secessionist Movement

However unsuccessful it might have been operationally, the MIM successfully created the groundwork for the formation of the Moro National Liberation Front (MNLF) in 1969 under the leadership of Hashim Salamat and Nur Misuari. Founded as a vanguard organisation, the MNLF demanded the creation of a Bangsa Moro Republik (Moro National Republic) encompassing Mindanao, the Sulu Archipelago and Palawan Island (MinSuPala). The young blood behind this organisation was drawn mostly from the University of Manila. The demands of the MNLF were charted out in their Manifesto (of April 1974), which read, "That henceforth the Bangsa Moro people and Revolution, having established their Bangsa Moro Republik, are throwing off all their political, economic and other bonds with the oppressive government of the Philippines under the dictatorial regime of President Ferdinand E. Marcos to secure a free and independent state for the Bangsa Moro people".[10]

The trajectory of the MNLF's demands underwent transformation in the context of the imposition of martial law by Marcos on 21 September 1972, the rationale of which was cited as the existence of armed conflict between Muslims and Christians and a Muslim "secessionist movement" in the Philippine South. The armed Muslim insurgency led by MNLF, which had prompted an unprecedented level of violence and political disruption, was cited as the raison-de-etre of the imposition of Martial Law.

MNLF activities turned 1973 and the first quarter of 1974 into a critical and harsh period. The violence frequently consisted of attacks on Christian civilians, and the rebels were determined to demonstrate their power and sinews to the rest of the Filipino population. Therefore, Marcos' imposition of Martial Law was the tip of the proverbial iceberg. This transformed philosophy of the movement was apparent in the *MNLF Manifesto*, Clause 2, which read: "That we believe armed struggle is the only means by which we can achieve the complete freedom and independence of our people, since Marcos and his government will never dismantle the edifice of Philippine colonial rule in our national homeland of their own accord". Furthermore, while spelling out the ultimate objective of the movement, Clause 3 of the Manifesto spelt out in no uncertain terms: "That the Moro National Liberation Front and its military arm, the Bangsa Moro Army, shall not agree to any form of settlement or accord short of achieving total freedom and independence for our oppressed Bangsa Moro people."[11]

Under such circumstances, given the burgeoning intensity of the violent MNLF activities, President Marcos emerged as the most redoubtable challenge to the Front, who, armed with the twin strategies of collaborating with some Muslim leaders (Datus) and the stringent provisions of Martial Law, could ensure the dismantling of this rebellion from the exclusive preserve of the MNLF outfit. President Marcos de-legitimised the MNLF, branded it as a militant group of communists and "Maoist Muslims", besides attempting to associate Misuari with the Communist Party of the Philippines in order to convince Muslims at home and abroad that he was a Marxist-Leninist ideologue. In a closely coordinated strategy, Marcos promoted returned rebel commanders as legitimate spokesmen not only for Philippine Muslims, but also for the MNLF. Moreover, Marcos convened a couple of meetings, read "peace talks" in Zamboanga in April and July 1975, in which he invited more than two hundred rebels to the negotiating table, who rejected Misuari as their leader and pledged loyalty to the Philippine Government. Evidently then, Marcos' deft diplomatic handling of the collaborators successfully, though temporarily, served to considerably fracture the backbone of the MNLF.[12]

One of the major achievements of Marcos' Presidential tenure towards resolving the Mindanao problem was the signing of the Tripoli Agreement with the MNLF in December 1976. Essentially an agreement on a cease-fire and tentative terms for pacific settlement supported by the Organisation of Islamic Conference (presently Organisation of Islamic Cooperation/OIC), it laid out the general principles for Muslim autonomy in the Philippine South. The principal clauses of this agreement were: the establishment of Autonomy in the Southern Philippines within the realm of the sovereignty and territorial integrity of the Republic of the Philippines (Clause 1); the areas of the autonomy for the Muslims in the Southern Philippines shall comprise the following: Basilan, Sulu, Tawi-Tawi, Zamboanga del Sur, Zamboanga del

Norte, North Cotabato, South Cotabato, Maguindanao, Sultan Kudarat, Lanao del Norte, Lanao del Sur, Davao del Sur, Palawan and all cities and villages situated in the above-mentioned areas (Clause 2); Foreign Policy shall be of the competence of the Central Government of the Philippines (Clause 3, Section 1); In the areas of the autonomy, the Muslims shall have the right to set up their own Courts which implement the Islamic Shari'ah laws (Clause 3, Section 3); The authorities of the autonomy in the South of the Philippines shall enjoy the right of representation and participation in the Central Government and in all other organs of the State (Clause 7) and Cease-fire shall be declared immediately after the signature of this agreement, provided that its coming into effect should not exceed the 20th January 1977 (Clause 12).[13] The Tripoli Agreement were considered favourable to the MNLF demands. However, since the Agreement allowed autonomy for only thirteen provinces and nine cities, instead of all twenty-three provinces in the Southern Philippines, this was considered unfair to the vast Christian majority and many considered it absurd that the entire MinSuPala region would become autonomous.[14]

Subsequently, negotiations were renewed from 5 February to 3 March 1977 in Tripoli towards the implementation of the peace settlement. However, the talks collapsed over widely divergent interpretations of the key terms of the Agreement, which were considered vague and unrealistic. On his part, Marcos endeavoured to "implement" the Tripoli Agreement on his own terms, principally by creating two special "autonomous regions"—one for Central Mindanao and the other for Sulu. But, his unilateral actions provoked unfavourable responses from both the MNLF. The failure to implement the Tripoli Agreement was largely due to the terms of the final clause of the Agreement, which stated: "The Government of the Philippines shall take all necessary steps for the implementation of this Agreement".[15] This gave little room for the MNLF to make decisions regarding its own autonomy, and left all respective action in the hands of the Philippine Government, which it felt repressed Islamic religious and cultural freedom. Besides, the failure of the Tripoli Agreement not only unmasked the ineptitude of the MNLF leadership to script successful negotiations with Manila, but also facilitated the emergence of more radical insurgent groups like the Moro Islamic Liberation Front (MILF).

A splinter of the MNLF, the MILF was formed in 1978 by the MNLF co-founder, Hashim Salamat, as a manifestation of his disillusionment with Nur Misuari. The two groups differed on the very principle of governance:

While the MNLF was more secular, the MILF wanted a State fully governed by the Koran and Islamic Shari'ah law. Thus, while on the one hand, the former recognised the Philippine Constitution, the latter did not recognise the Constitution and fought the Government.[16] Although the 1976 Agreement had included a ceasefire of hostilities under its main principles, the late 1970s and early 1980s witnessed violence as Muslim insurgents retaliated against the Government. In this backdrop, President Ferdinand Marcos attempted to reinstitute the goals of the Agreement, calling for the creation of an Autonomous Region in the Southern Philippines. However, his proclamation was struck down by a plebiscite and it was under the administration of Marcos' successor, President Corazon Aquino that the demand for full autonomy for the Southern Philippines surfaced. Summarily then, though the issue was not resolved under Marcos' tenure, the signing of the Tripoli Agreement was a significant stride in the pursuit of peace in the sense that the Agreement was the first official acknowledgement of the problem in the Southern Philippines.

Picking up the Threads from the Marcos Era: the Legacy of Corazon Aquino and Fidel Ramos

When Corazon Aquino took over as President of the Philippines (25 February 1986-30 June 1992) from Marcos after a peoples' revolt in February 1986, one of the very first moves she made was to restore democratic institutions in government and pursue a national reconciliation programme. As a result, negotiations between the MNLF and the Government of the Philippines were resumed, with the Tripoli Agreement as its reference point. Eventually in January 1987, after several meetings, the MNLF and the Government reached a cease-fire. In this context, the MNLF relinquished its goal of complete independence for Muslim regions and accepted Manila's offer for autonomy. The new Philippine Constitution of 1987 ultimately honoured the Tripoli Agreement, and provided for autonomous regions in Muslim areas of Mindanao. By late 1987, Aquino established the Regional Consultative Commission (RCC) in an attempt to maintain dialogue between the Government of the Philippines and rebel groups in preparation for the constitutionally mandated autonomy legislation for Mindanao. Finally, in August 1989, the Aquino administration approved Republic Act 6734 that created the Autonomous Region in Muslim Mindanao (ARMM) as a response to the rebels' clamour for autonomy. The affected regions of Mindanao and Sulu were given the right to avoid membership in the ARMM if they so voted in a plebiscite.[17] Since most provinces had majority Christian populations, only four (two in Mindanao and two in Sulu) of thirteen provinces voted for autonomy in the November 1989 plebiscite. It was at this juncture that another point of departure emerged between the MNLF and MILF, since the latter rejected the ARMM and demanded a delineation of what it claimed a Bangsamoro juridical entity or a 'sub-state'.

When Fidel Ramos succeeded Corazon Aquino as the President of the Philippines (30 June 1992 to 30 June 1998), he was faced with the issue of implementing the provisional government for the ARMM. Initially, he called for a consultation meeting with MNLF leaders, who in turn, proposed the establishment of an administrative structure instead of a provisional government, through a realignment of local government units. In this perspective, Ramos assured the MNLF leadership that their sentiments would be taken into consideration, and he resumed fresh talks in 1993, within the scaffold of which, the Government representative, Simeon Datumanong submitted a "compromise proposal" intended to set up a Southern Philippines Consultative Development Council (SPCDC) to govern the MNLF areas of autonomy to be headed by its Chairman, Nur Misuari. This proposal was initially rejected by MNLF as its legal representative, Randolph Parcasio alleged: "It is not pursuant to what is in the Tripoli Agreement."[18]

Subsequently, in June 1996, President Ramos brought the MNLF to the negotiating table in Davao. At the Davao meeting, both sides reconsidered their respective postures and arrived at a much-needed compromise. Besides, the MNLF agreed to establish the SPCDC as the transitional mechanism to implementing the Tripoli Agreement.[19] Eventually, the final round of peace talks were held in Jakarta on 30 August 1996 confirming the acceptance of the Peace Agreement drafted during the Davao meeting. This initiative culminated in the signing of the Final Agreement on the Implementation of the Tripoli Agreement, in Manila on 2 September 1996 between the Government of the Republic of the Philippines (GRP) and the MNLF, aided by the OIC Ministerial Committee of the Six and the Secretary General of the OIC, Dr. Hamid, thereby marking the most remarkable achievement of the tenure of President Ramos.

The basic provisions of this Agreement were: implementing the structure and mechanism of the Tripoli Agreement; the establishment of a Special Zone of Peace and Development in Southern Philippines (SZOPD); the establishment of SPCPD; and the local government units in the area including the ARMM shall continue to exist and exercise their functions in accordance with existing laws.[20] This Agreement constituted the endorsement of the full implementation of the Tripoli Agreement (1976) and was a path-breaking measure towards conflict resolution in the Southern Philippines. The cornerstone of the 1996 Agreement—the creation of an autonomous region in Mindanao—was confirmed by a plebiscite in 1999. However, by the end of 1998, the peace process had been weakened owing to the following factors: the transitional autonomous structures had failed to provide a good test for future autonomous institutions due to mismanagement and corruption; the inability to address the issue of land rights which was crucial to any long-term peace in Mindanao; and the inability to produce many of the expected benefits, the responsibility for which could be accorded partly to the lack of commitment of MNLF leadership.

In the second phase, a new autonomous government would replace the ARMM and the SPCPD after the approval through a plebiscite in 14 provinces and 9 cities. Nur Misuari was made the SPCDP Chairman and was also elected the Governor of ARMM. Thus, by appointing Misuari in charge of both institutions, it was believed that the peace settlement would gain recognition among the Muslim community and demonstrate to the non-Muslims that autonomy could potentially benefit all communities. The Agreement also provided for the region's representation in the institutions of the national Government, the creation of special regional security forces and the inclusion of Islamic curriculum in the education system as well as the integration of Madrasas with the educational system of the ARMM. The regional government was given the right to establish Shari'ah courts as well. Therefore, the Final Peace Agreement marked an important beginning to resolving the long-standing conflict to Mindanao and its accomplishments were unprecedented since, under its aegis, it was for the first time that, the Philippine Government and the MNLF not only converged on the principle of autonomy, based on a shared understanding of the territorial claims of the Muslims, but also on a process of implementation. Furthermore, the MNLF leaders immediately gained access to the control of resources and power in Mindanao with the opportunity to govern during the transition to a fuller institutional autonomy.

Subsequently, the MNLF leaders were accused of contributing to its characteristic waste and corruption. Summarily then, while the 1996 Agreement was a grand step towards peace in the Southern Philippines, it was not enough to ensure the sustenance of the Agreement. It also depended on a broader and holistic agreement to guarantee that the peace process would culminate in conflict resolution, towards which, the fulfilment of the following factors became imperative: first, new institutions had to be provided with access to resources, or at the most, with the power to raise resources immediately. Alternatively, a limited autonomy had to be effectively combined with more adequate representation by Muslims in the central institutions of the Philippines; secondly, the issue of land in future settlements had to be addressed; thirdly, the non-Muslim communities had to be included more systematically in negotiations for future autonomous institutions if they were expected to support the process; and finally, the MNLF leadership had to prove its commitment to peace by eliminating their corrupt practices and using resources more effectively.

Amidst such allegations of corruption and administrative mismanagement, Misuari tried to lobby for an extension of his term after the 2001 ARMM elections, and when the Philippine Government denied his request, he ordered his troops to break into violent revolt. However, the rebellion in Sulu and Zamboanga was easily crushed, and Misuari fled to Sabah. Later, he was extradited to the Philippines and imprisoned. Consequently, the MNLF regenerated into a spent force, paving the way for the MILF to step into the void left by the MNLF.[21] Since then, the MILF emerged as the largest, the most potent and influential militant group in the Philippines fighting for the cause of a Bangsamoro Republik. Among the demands of the MILF, the most important was the call for self governance and a constitutional amendment that would create a Moro 'sub-state', whereby a Bangsamoro basic law could be crafted, thus manifesting the highest expression of the Moros of their right to exercise self-determination without jeopardising national sovereignty and territorial integrity of the Philippines.[22] The MILF also called for expediting the peace negotiations with the Philippine Government. Although formal negotiations between Manila and the MILF had taken off in January 1997 after the conclusion of the peace talks between the Philippines and the MNLF, it took another seventeen years to finally seal the Comprehensive Agreement on the Bangsamoro (March 2014) with the Government, under the able leadership of President Benigno Aquino.

The New Wave in the Trajectory of Conflict Resolution under President Gloria Macapagal Arroyo and President Benigno Aquino III

When Gloria Macapagal-Arroyo assumed power in January 2001 (20 January 2001 to 30 June 2010), the peace process was revived with a unilateral declaration of ceasefire on the part of the Government. Interestingly enough, Arroyo's peace initiatives almost coincided with the 11 September 2001 terrorist attacks on the World Trade Centre (New York), which not only unleashed the macabre face of terrorism and its global inter-connectedness, but also branded the region of Southeast Asia as the "Second front" in the scheme of America's Global War on Terror. Given this international milieu, President Arroyo was swept with a new-found urgency to strike a peace deal with the MILF expeditiously. Arroyo's peace efforts reversed the "all-out-war" policy undertaken by her immediate predecessor, Joseph Estrada (30 June 1998 to 20 January 2001), whose strategy of launching a military campaign against the Moro secessionists had resulted in enhanced pursuit of violence by the MILF.

A couple of important events took place during the initial days of Arroyo's tenure in the pre-September 11, 2001 phase, which may be briefly recounted: first, on 31 March 2001, the Republic Act, 9054 ("An Act to Strengthen and Expand the Autonomous Region in Muslim Mindanao (ARMM)") lapsed into law, amending the Organic Act of the ARMM to provide for the region's expansion from the original four provinces under its jurisdiction.[23] Secondly, the Presidential Advisor on the Peace Process, Eduardo Ermita and MILF Vice-Chair, Al Haj Murad Ebrahim concluded the Tripoli Agreement on Peace with the GRP on 22 June 2001, which constituted the roadmap for the initiation of successive agreements for ushering in peace in the Philippines. Another important step taken by President Arroyo was to bring the MNLF and MILF together at the negotiating table for signing a Reunification Agreement on 29 October 2001. Although hailed by both Misuari and Hashim Salamat as a "major turning point in our common quest for total peace, development and freedom of the Bangsamoro people",[24] the Agreement fell apart barely a month later when Nur Misuari allegedly led a rebellion in Sulu and Zamboanga City to stall the scheduled ARMM elections, following which, he escaped to Sabah. In any case, President Arroyo was successful in resuming the Fourth Round of Formal Peace Talks between Manila and the MILF on 6 May 2002, which resulted in the signing of two agreements: One was in the form of a Joint Communiqué that provided an "ad hoc joint action group" of the Philippine Government and MILF forces to isolate and interdict "criminal syndicates and kidnap-for-ransom groups."

The second was an Agreement on "Implementing Guidelines on the Humanitarian, Rehabilitation and Development Aspects of the Tripoli Agreement on Peace of 2001" (signed respectively on 6 and 7 May 2002 in Cyberjaya and Putrajaya, Malaysia).[25] Eventually, the First Exploratory Talks on the Final Draft of the Peace Accord was initiated between the two sides in Kuala Lumpur (Malaysia) in March 2003, with a further commitment from both sides for a "mutual secession of hostilities". Besides, the provision for a Muslim Ancestral Domain, divided into four strands—concept, territory, resources and governance—was laid down as the prominent agenda of the next round of future Exploratory Talks.[26]

As a follow-up on the pursuit of peace under the Arroyo Presidency, a Memorandum of Agreement on the Muslim Ancestral Domain (MoA-AD) was signed on 5 August 2008 in Kuala Lumpur, within the scaffold of which, the Contracting Parties agreed that the "Bangsamoro Juridical Entity (BJE) shall have the authority and jurisdiction over the Ancestral Domain and Ancestral lands, including both alienable and non-alienable lands encompassed within their homeland and ancestral territory, as well as the delineation of ancestral domain/lands of the Bangsamoro people located therein."[27] About 700 villages in Mindanao were entitled to hold a referendum within a year to determine their intention to join the "Bangsamoro Juridical Entity." Although the signing of the MoA-AD paved the way for the conclusion of the Final Peace Agreement by October 2008, its trajectory was not devoid of its fair share of obstacles.

Subsequently, President Arroyo took a significant step by signing the "Mindanao Development Authority Act (MinDa)" or Republic Act, 9996 on 17 February 2010, in a declared policy of the State "to accelerate the socio-economic growth of Mindanao, increasing its trade, tourism and investments, encouraging private enterprise and advancing efforts towards peace and development.[28] Mindful of the fact that the neglect of Mindanao's economic development was the principal contributing factor to violence, separatism and widespread poverty, the MinDA ended five decades of waiting for the creation of a Mindanao-wide body dedicated to the integration of peace and development efforts of the Island. It was also an acknowledgement that the ubiquitous and compelling problems of Mindanao would be addressed by a permanent and institutionalised agency, which would help ensure unity among diverse cultures, religious denominations and synchronise the programmes and projects for alleviating poverty and underdevelopment in the region. It was also projected to "promote, *coordinate and facilitate the active and extensive participation of all sectors to effect the socio-economic development of Mindanao.*"[29]

The baton of the final lap of this "marathon" peace process was passed on by President Arroyo to her successor, Benigno Aquino III (30 June 2010 onwards), who, soon after assuming power, resumed peace parleys with the MILF in February 2011, in the wake of the latter's announcement that it no longer sought secession from the Philippines. This paved the way for President Benigno Aquino's unprecedented meeting with the MILF Chairman, Ibrahim Al Haj Murad in Japan on 5 August 2011, in a bid to fast-track the peace negotiations and ensure that any agreement(s) undertaken be implemented within the remaining five years of his administration (which lapses in 2016).[30] Unfortunately, this meeting could not guide the peace process to its destination since Manila's offer of a 3-for-1 proposal that limited its commitment to "massive economic development; political settlement with the MILF; and cultural-historical acknowledgment" was rejected outright by the MILF, which accused the Government of failing to address its ancestral domain claim.

In any case, President Aquino, without being frustrated by the failure of the August 2011 negotiations, undertook a bid to salvage the stalled peace talks between the GRP and the MILF, within the frame of which, a Joint Statement, facilitated by Malaysia was signed in April 2012, scrapping the ARMM and acknowledging Bangsamoro as the New Autonomous Political Entity (NPE) in place of the ARMM. (Clause 1) The Declaration contained ten principles to guide both parties in addressing the prospects and challenges to final peace in Southern Philippines. In addition to being identified as "commitments that can be properly accommodated by our current legal and political realities" by the Philippine Peace Panel Chair, MarvicLeonen, these principles focused on power-sharing and wealth-sharing between the national Government and the New Political Entity, with the following matters reserved for the competence of the national Government: defence and external security, foreign policy, coinage and monetary policy, citizenship and naturalisation, postal service, common market and global trade, though it added a footnote that the power to enter into economic agreements already allowed under RA 9054 "shall be transferred to the new political entity." (Clause 6)[31] Eventually, the signing of the Joint Statement (of April 2012) paved the way for the sealing of the *Framework Agreement on the Bangsamoro* in October 2012. This Agreement, stated that "the Bangsamoro is the new autonomous political entity (NPE) referred to in the Decision Points of Principles as of April 2012" (Clause 1), thereby realising the long-cherished desire for the establishment of the Bangsamoro as an independent political entity.[32]

It may be recalled that, though the Final Peace Agreement was signed between Manila and the MNLF in 1996, the MILF faction, dissatisfied with the creation of the ARMM and touting the Agreement as a compromise, carried out acts of insurrection in the southern Philippines. Thus, during that time, while the MNLF was successfully incorporated into the political process, the MILF kept fighting. Almost sixteen years after the signing of the Final Peace Agreement between the Philippine Government and the MNLF, the inking of the Framework Agreement (2012) was supposed to have addressed the MILF's concerns and create a path forward to a lasting peace. Yet, as if showcasing a historical retrospect, the Agreement irked the MNLF, which, under Misuari's leadership, in 2013, declared independence from the Philippines in Sulu province and attacked the southern port city of Zamboanga, taking hostages, and sparking a siege that lasted more than three weeks, ending with the execution or capture of at least 400 MNLF rebels, loyal to Misuari. Misuari's declaration of Independence and the attack on Zamboanga could have been prompted by the Philippine Government's pace and position in peace talks with the MILF and the MNLF's feeling of alienation under the Aquino administration. Furthermore, the termination of the Tripartite Review of the 1996 Peace Agreement, with Indonesia acting as a mediator in all such past tripartite reviews since 1996, could have disenchanted the MNLF.[33]

Under such volatile circumstances, the iron determination of President Benigno Aquino to culminate the peace process with the MILF led to the signing of the *Comprehensive Agreement on the Bangsamoro* in Manila on 27 March 2014. This Agreement signalled the termination of seventeen years of negotiations with the MILF (which had taken off in July 1997, with the signing of the Agreement on General Cessation of Hostilities, and continued thereafter). Under the terms of the Comprehensive Agreement on the Bangsamoro, the MILF agreed to bring an end to violence and its demand for a separate state in lieu of greater degree of autonomy. This momentous Agreement would pave the way for the creation of the political framework for the "more powerful, better-funded and potentially larger" autonomous region, to be christened "Bangsamoro", which Manila aims to set up the region by 2016, under a "basic law" to be approved by the Philippine Congress. The Agreement also calls for Muslim self-rule in parts of the southern Philippines in exchange for a deactivation of rebel forces by the MILF. Besides, the MILF forces have agreed to surrender their firearms to a third party to be selected unanimously by the MILF and Manila.[34]

Conclusion

The Comprehensive Agreement on the Bangsamoro has swept this archipelagic Southeast Asian nation with a sense of long-awaited optimism and developmental aspirations. Nevertheless, it is now contingent on the President of the Philippines, Benigno Aquino III and the MILF leadership to sustain this new-found spirit of optimism and consummate the protracted peace process through scrupulous implementation of its provisions, especially before President Aquino's tenure expires in 2016. Unfortunately, a major incident which has emerged as a stumbling block to the peace process within a period of nine months of signing of the Comprehensive Agreement was the ambush which broke out between the Philippine police force and the MILF on 25 January 2015. The origin of the contention can be traced to a secret police operation to capture two terrorists thought to be sheltered by the Bangsamoro Islamic Freedom Fighters (BIFF)—another rebel group outside the purview of the peace agreement with the MILF. However, in this case, the police failed to coordinate their operation with either the Army or the MILF, thereby going against the terms of the truce.[35]

The immediate fallout of this incident was a public demonstration urging Senators to withdraw support for the "basic law" bill, thereby bringing into question the Congressional passage of the Bangsamoro Basic Law, which is part of the implementation of the Comprehensive Agreement on the Bangsamoro.[36] Naturally, a delay in the legislative procedure would only shrink the timeframe for implementing the peace agreement signed in March 2014. In the face of possible delays in implementation of the peace agreement, there is increasing speculation of extending the transition through 2019, though such an extension would mean greater uncertainty and procrastination.

Under such circumstances, the next two years will be extremely crucial for the Government and the MILF to fulfil the hopes, objectives and promises for ensuring the return and survival of ultimate peace in the Southern Philippines. Unfortunately, as demonstrated by the January 2015 massacre, the implementation of the Agreement runs the risk of being eclipsed by violent activities of some separatist strands like the MNLF, Abu Sayyaf Group, BIFF and the New People's Army (the armed unit of the Communist Party of the Philippines) which suffer from a feeling of alienation and disillusionment vis-a-vis the policies of the Government of the Philippines. Given this milieu, one can only hope that even in the face of grave provocations, the peace process, in its implementation phase, reaches its prized destination with success.[37] It is only through the facilitation and safeguard of the avenues of peace in the southern Philippine islands, which have languished in their hunger for peace, prosperity, inclusion and development for decades together, that its people would ultimately find the keys to unlock their elusive 'El Dorado', thereby unleashing a virtuous cycle of security, development and equitable progress.

END NOTES

1. Composed principally of thirteen indigenous groups, namely Badjao, Molbog (or Melebugnon), Iranun, (also known as Ilanun), Palawani, Jamamapun, Sama, Kalagan, Sangil, Kalibugan, Tausug, Maguindanao, Yakan, and Maranao.
2. Hannbal Bara, "The History of the Muslim in the Philippines", *Publications of National Commission for Culture and the Arts*, the Philippines, http://www.ncca.gov.ph/about-culture-and-arts/articles-on-c-n-a/article.php?i=232&igm=4 (accessed on 23 June 2014)
3. Ronald E. Dolin, Philippines: A Country Study, the Library of Congress, Washington, 1991, http://countrystudies.us/philippines/ (accessed on 23 June 2014)
4. Jamail A. Kamlian, "Ethnic and Religious Conflict in Southern Philippines: A Discourse on Self-Determination, Political Autonomy and Conflict Resolution", (Lecture), Islam and Human Rights Project, School of Law, Emory University, Atlanta, 4 November 2003, http://www.law.emory.edu/ihr/worddocs/jamail1.doc, (accessed on 23 June 2014)
5. *Dansalan Declaration Overviews*, http://www.acmaly88.page.fl/DANSALAN-DECLARATION.htm (accessed on 23 June 2014)
6. Leodivico Cruz, *Philippine History and Government*, (Phoenix Publishing House, Quezon City, 2009), p. 156
7. For details, see Eduardo C. Tadem, "Technological Changes and the Filipino Peasantry", *Akademika: Journal of South East Asia Social Sciences and Humanities*, National University of Malaysia, Vol. 30, No. 1, January 1987, http://ejournal.ukm.my/akademika/article/view/3693
8. Patricio N. Abinales and Donna J. Amoroso, *State and Society in the Philippines*, (Rowman and Littlefield Publishers, Inc., United States of America, 2005), p. 182.
9. Alunan Glang, *Muslim Secession or Integration?*, (Garcia Publishing Company, Quezon City, 1969), pp. 91-92.
10. The Manifesto of the Moro National Liberation Front (MNLF), 28 April 1974, Clause 1, cited in Patricio N. Abinales and Donna J. Amoroso, *State and Society in the Philippines*, n. 8, p. 218
11. Ibid., Clauses 2 and 3.

12. Jamail A. Kamlian, "Ethnic and Religious Conflict in Southern Philippines: A Discourse on Self-Determination, Political Autonomy and Conflict Resolution", (Lecture), n. 4
13. *Text of the Tripoli Agreement,* Government of the Republic of the Philippines and the Moro National Liberation Front, Tripoli, Libya, 23 December 1976, *Official Gazette,* Government of the Philippines, www.gov.ph/1976/12/23/the-tripoli-agreement-december-23-1976; Full Pdf available at pcdspo.gov.ph/downloads/2012/10/Tripoli-Agreement-December-23-1976.pdf (accessed on 23 June 2014)
14. William Overhalt, "The Rise and Fall of Ferdinand Marcos", *Asian Survey,* 26 (11), (November 19860, p. 247.
15. *Text of the Tripoli Agreement,* Government of the Republic of the Philippines and the Moro National Liberation Front, n. 13.
16. Maria A. Resse, *Seeds of Terror: An Eyewitness Account of Al-Qaida's Newest Center of Operations in Southeast Asia,* (Free Press, New York, 2003), p. 126.
17. For details, see *Republic Act No. 6734: An Act Providing for an Organic Act for the Autonomous Region in Muslim Mindanao,* Eighth Congress of the Philippines, Republic of the Philippines, Manila, 1 August 1989, National Economic and Development Authority, Cordillera Administrative Region, Republic of the Philippines, http://www.car.neda.gov.ph/organic-act-for-the-autonomous-region-in-muslim-mindanao/ (accessed on 25 June 2014)
18. Jacques Bertrand, "Peace and Conflict in the Southern Philippines", *Pacific Affairs,* 73 (1), (Spring 2000), p. 45.
19. Eliseo R. Mercado Jr., "Mindanao Peace Process", http://www.philippineupdate.com/frjun.htm (accessed on 25 June 2014).
20. *Final Agreement on the Implementation of the Tripoli Agreement signed between the Government of the Republic of the Philippines and Moro National Liberation Front,* Presidential Communications Development and Strategic Planning Office, Manila, the Philippines, 2 September 1996, http://www.pcdspo.gov.ph/dpwnloads/2012/10/Final-Peace-Agreement-MNLF-September-2-1996.pdf (accesses on 25 June 2014).
21. Patricio N. Abinales and Donna J. Amoroso, *State and Society in the Philippines,* n. 8, p. 293.
22. *Excerpted from the Interview of* Mohager Iqbal, *Chairman of the Moro Islamic Liberation Front (MILF) Peace Panel, by Dr. Aland Mizell, Mindanao, the Philippines, 2011,*http://kurdistantribune.com/2012/peace-process-philippines-lessons-for-turkish-government-part-ii/ (accessed on 25 June 2014).
23. *Republic Act No. 9054: To Strengthen and Expand the Organic Act for the Autonomous Region in Muslim Mindanao, Amending for the Purpose Republic Act No. 6374,* 31 March 2001, Office of the Presidential Adviser on the Peace Process, Office of the President of the Philippines, Republic of the Philippines, Manila, http://www.opapp.gov.ph (accessed on 25 June 2014).
24. The three-point agenda tackled during the joint meeting were: To strengthen the unity and cooperation of the MNLF and the MILF so as to hasten the resolution of the Bangsamoro problem in the South of the Philippines; Assessment of issues confronting the Bangsamoro people and their struggle; and Holding of continuing dialogue and meeting to further discuss all remaining issues of the Bangsamoro people; "MNLF Unites with MILF", 29 October 2001, http://www.mnlfnet.com/The_Jeddah.htm (Official Website of the Moro National Liberation Front) (accessed on 25 June 2014).
25. Rizal G. Buendia, "The GRP-MILF Peace Talks: Quo Vadis?", p.4, https://eprints.soas.ac.uk/4430/1/GRP-MILF_Rizal_Buendia.pdf, (accessed on 26 June 2014).
26. Abhoud Syed Lingga, "Reasons Behind the Non-Signing of the MOA-AD", *The Mindanao*

Think Tank: Perspectives, Issues and Concerns on the Mindanao Peace Process, Monograph 4 (Supported by the Centre for Humanitarian Dialogue, Geneva, Switzerland), 2010, p. 12, http://www.hdcentre.org/uploads/tx_news/70Monograph4.pdf (accessed on 26 June 2014).

27. *Memorandum of Agreement on the Ancestral Domain Aspect of the GRP-MILF Tripoli Agreement on Peace of 2001*, Clause 6, 5 August 2008, Kuala Lumpur, Malaysia, Official Website of Presidential Communications Development and Strategic Planning Office, Republic of the Philippines, http://pcdspo.gov.ph/downloads/2012/10/MOA-%E2%80%93-Ancestral-Domain-August-5-2008.pdf), (accessed on 26 June 2014)
28. *Republic Act No. 9996, Mindanao Development Authority (MinDA) Act of 2010: An Act Creating the Mindanao Development Authority, Defining its Powers and Functions, Providing Funds Therefore and for Other Purposes*, Section 2, *Official Gazette*, 17 February 2010, Congress of the Philippines, Republic of the Philippines, Manila, http://www.gov.ph/2010/02/17/republic-act-no-9996 (accessed on 26 June 2014).
29. Ibid., Section 3.
30. "PNoy Does a Cory: Historic Meet with MILF Chair Praised", 5 August 2011, Office of the Presidential Adviser on Peace Process, Office of the President of the Philippines, http://www.opapp.gov.ph/features/pnoy-does-cory-hstoric-meet-milf-chair-praised (accessed on 26 June 2014).
31. *Joint Statement and Decision Points of the Government of the Philippines and MILF on the 27th Round of Exploratory Talks*, Kuala Lumpur, Malaysia, 24 April 2012, *Official Gazette*, Government of the Philippines, Manila, http://www.gov.ph/2012/04/24/joint-statement-and-decision-points-of-the-gph-and-milf-on-the-27th-round-of-exploratory-talks/, (accessed on 26 June 2014).
32. *2012 Framework Agreement on the Bangsamoro*, *Official Gazette*, Government of the Philippines, Manila, 15 October 2012, http://www.gov.ph/the-2012-framework-agreement-on-the-bangsamoro/ (accessed on 26 June 2014).
33. Nikko Dizon, "Misuari, MNLF Felt Betrayed when Philippine Government Withdrew from 1996 Peace Pact Review", *Philippine Daily Inquirer*, 9 September 2013, http://newsinfo.inquirer.net/484267/misuari-mnlf-felt-betrayed-when-ph-govt-withdrew-from-1996-peace-pact-review (accessed on 27 June 2014).
34. *Comprehensive Agreement on the Bangsamoro*, *Official Gazette*, Government of the Philippines, Manila, 27 March 2014, http://www.gov.ph/2014/03/27/document-cab/, (accessed on 28 June 2014).
35. Shirley Escalante, "More than 40 Philippine Police Officers Killed in Clash with Muslim Rebels", 26 January 2015, http://www.abc.net.au (accessed on 12 May 2015).
36. Excerpted from an Interview by Steven Rood, Country Representative (for the Philippines and Pacific Island Nations), Asia Foundation, with Gabriel Domínguez, 29 January 2015, http://dw.de/is-the-Philippine-peace-process-in-jeopardy/a-18223688 (accessed on 12 May 2015).
37. *Speech of President Benigno Aquino III during the Signing Ceremony of the Comprehensive Agreement on the Bangsamoro*, 27 March 2014, n. 37.

18

The Genesis of the Scarborough Shoal Dispute between the Philippines and China

Premesha Saha

Introduction

Maritime issues are emerging as a matter of grave concern in the international security environment. After the scramble for occupation over the land resources, now the attention has turned towards the oceanic resources. According to Barry Buzan, oceans have "become areas of intense competition for scarce goods."[1] He further goes on to say, after the end of the Cold War, disputes between states take place for competition over access to vital resources like oil and natural gas, and not for differences along ideological lines. The international legal framework, namely the United Nations Convention on the Law of the Seas will not be successful in creating order as it will be difficult to get the countries to abide by its legal obligations. This can be clearly seen in the case of the South China Sea and the Scarborough shoal disputes, where the main concern is the demarcation of maritime boundaries between the states. If the boundary delimitation or demarcation problem is taken care of then the sovereignty dispute will automatically be resolved. Though there might be both cooperation and conflict in future, conflicting interests would somehow be counter balanced by the considerations of trade, development and cost of disputes.[2]

Buzan's observation provides the basis for critically examining the situation in the Indo-Pacific region, where maritime issues are becoming a key concern. China's economic and military rise has made her involved in territorial disputes with nearly all the countries of Southeast Asia over maritime delimitations and sovereignty of offshore islands, namely the Spratly and the Paracel Islands. Control over these islands would guarantee the rights of resource exploitation, control of the Sea Lines of Communication and regional naval power projection. Confrontation rather than cooperation marks the history of the South China Sea dispute and hence acts as a major irritant in the bilateral and multilateral relations in the Southeast and East Asian region. In addition to the dispute over the Spratly islands, the scramble for occupation between China and the Philippines over the Scarborough Shoal, which is considered the largest atoll in the South China Sea and lies further to the north of the South China Sea, has also emerged as a potential trouble spot in Southeast Asia. Though the Scarborough Shoal is not a part of the Spratlys, yet it has become of special significance to the whole South China Sea issue.

The dispute may not appear to be as complex as the Spratly issue since it concerns less number of claimants and the weakest military powerof the region, the Philippines is the only other claimant, besides China. Nonetheless, the Philippines have taken a very strong stand on its claims, given the memory of the 1995 Mischief Reef clash. Though the possibility for a big armed confrontation is unlikely, nevertheless there is a high chance of the dispute escalating into a more serious one in the future. Moreover the U.S. intervention in the dispute in the future cannot be ruled out, since it is the erstwhile ally of the Philippines and committed to the Mutual Defence Treaty signed with the Philippines in 1951.

This chapter seeks to examine the overall importance of the Scarborough Shoal, the origin of the Scarborough Shoal dispute and the present status of the dispute between the Philippines and China. While enumerating the course of the dispute, it also examines the impact the dispute might have on the "politico-strategic" landscape of Asia.

What is the Scarborough Shoal?

The Scarborough Shoal, or what China calls the Huangyan Island, comprises a barely submerged reef enclosing a lagoon. The feature is located about 600 nautical miles east of China's Hainan Island and about 1000 nautical miles from China's mainland. It is about 128 nautical miles west of Luzon.[3] The nearest landmass is the Palauig, Zambles, on the Luzon Island in the Philippines, 137 miles away. It is about 123 miles west of Subic Bay.[4] The Scarborough reef is actually a large atoll including the North and the South rock. According to a Chinese authority on the South China Sea, the reef is the biggest atoll in the South China Sea submerged at high tide with a few rocks above sea level. It lies approximately 170 nautical miles east of the Macclesfield Bank, and approximately 115 nautical miles off the Zambles province on the western side of Luzon Island.[5]

The Shoal is claimed by three countries, namely, China, the Philippines and Taiwan. But it is mainly the Philippines and China who are asserting their claims steadfastly. The area is under the permanent occupation of the Philippines. Though the Scarborough Shoal is outside the Philippine Treaty Limits, it is still within the 200 nautical miles EEZ of the Philippines.

The Scarborough Shoal had been used as a target range by the U.S. military with the permission from the Philippine military authorities. Like the Spratlys, the Scarborough Shoal is also believed to possess huge potential of oil and gas as well as minerals such as manganese, cobalt, nickel and chromate. It is an important fishing ground and an international navigational route.[6]

Approximately three hundred ships pass in the vicinity of the shoal daily and Japan uses this route to transport 80 percent of its petroleum from the Middle East. Majority of energy shipments to China and Japan pass through the waters of the shoal on their way to and from the Philippines port of Subic Bay. Washington also considers this route as the world's second busiest trade route and therefore safeguarding the freedom of navigation through this waterway is crucial for the U.S. interest as well.[7] Therefore,it will not be surprising if, like the Spratly dispute, the Scarborough shoal dispute also attracts a lot of global attention, if not resolved timely.

From the end of the Second World War up to the 1990s, the shoal was not taken notice of by the governments of China, Taiwan and the Philippines. At that time the status of the shoal in the high seas was still not clear. The Shoal was located very closeto the American Naval Base, the Subic Bay and neither Taiwan, nor mainland China would risk taking control over it at that time. Even in the Philippines, the name Scarborough shoal appeared in newspapers mostly due to smuggling operations conducted by syndicates based in the province of Cavite and abroad using the Scarborough shoal as a transshipment point. Hence the Shoal was seen as a potential trouble spot by the officers of the Armed Forces of the Philippines (AFP). In October 1963, for instance, the Philippine Navy had discovered that the shoal was used for smuggled goods coming from Macao by Taiwanese fishermen. The point to be noted is even before the Chinese authorities had realised the potential of the shoal, the Filipino authorities patrolled the shoal, made arrests and the area was monitored by the Philippine Air Force when it was necessary. A Filipino flag was also raised on an 8.3 meter high iron pole. The government also built and operated a small light house near the mouth of the lagoon of the shoal. Meanwhile the Chinese authorities were inactive on the shoal except in 1978 when the Chinese had send their first official mission on the shoal and in 1983 the shoal was renamed Huangyan Qundao.[8]

The Importance of the Scarborough Shoal to China

China regards the South China Sea as the "lost territories to be recovered like other lost territories on China's periphery".[9] Hence Chinese claims in the South China Sea has been said to represent China's "core interest" by their officials in 2010. For China, the Scarborough Shoal is of paramount significance for its claim over the "ZhongshaQundao" and consequently the features located inside the controversial "U-shaped line". The Zhongsha Qundao is composed of the Macclesfield Bank, Truro Shoal, Saint Espirit Shoal, Dreyer Shoal and the Scarborough Shoal. The Chinese officials are aware that without the Scarborough Shoal, their chances of having ownership over the Zhongsha Qundao is very remote, which will lead the Zhongsha Qundao to be divided by the EEZs of the neighbouring countries or be placed under the regime of the high seas. Therefore, this will automatically make China's claim to the South China Sea supported by the "U-shaped line" "moot and academic".[10]

Another reason for China's assertiveness in the Scarborough Shoal is domestic pressure. The coverage of the recent events at the Shoal by China's state-run media has raised a strong nationalist fervour in the populace and there have been calls for a strong assertive action on the shoal.[11] Furthermore, with the U.S. trying to make its return in the region through its "Asia Pivot" policy, it is pertinent for Beijing to show her naval projection and rising military assertiveness to ensure the Chinese influence in the region.

To support their claim over the Zhongsha Qundao, the Chinese describe the Scarborough Shoal as an island (Huangyan Island). Article 121 of the UNCLOS defines an island as a "naturally formed area of land, surrounded by water which is above water at high tide."[12] In theory, island status would permit the drawing of, from Scarborough Shoal's baselines, not only a territorial sea (12 nm) and a contiguous zone (24nm), but also an EEZ (200 nm) and a continental shelf. This means, that the Scarborough Shoal would provide China a "huge and disproportionate maritime territory". Nonetheless, it is doubtful that the UNCLOS would designate the Scarborough Shoal as an island. Rocks are defined in UNCLOS Article 121(3) as, "elements that cannot sustain human habitation or economic life of their own."[13] The Scarborough Shoal satisfies both the criteria as neither the Filipino nor the Chinese fishermen can live on these rocks and have to live in their boats during the fishing season. In this case, the rocks of the shoal could give to China at most, only a territorial sea and a contiguous zone, but not an EEZ or a continental shelf. This controversial reading of the shoal as an island prevents the Chinese officials from getting the competing claim adjudicated by any international tribunal. Instead they insist on a bilateral settlement of the dispute with the Philippines.[14]

The Importance of the Scarborough Shoal to the Philippines

For the Philippines, the stake is primarily economic. The rich fishing grounds of the Scarborough Shoal serve as a means of livelihood for the Filipinos residing in the coastal provinces of Zambales, Pangasnian, and Bataan. Though till date no gas and oil exploration has taken place around the shoal, but still some deposits of polymetallic nodules have been found around the shoal, at a depth of more than 3,000 meters. Besides these economic benefits, virtually the whole EEZ of the western side of Luzon could also be claimed by the Chinese.[15] The shoal is also of strategic importance to the Philippines, as with the control of this shoal, the Filipinos can, in a small way, block or limit China's claim over the whole South China Sea. Finally, the memory of the 1995 Mischief Reef clash with China still lies fresh in the minds of the Filipino officials. China has now built a strong naval base equipped with a sophisticated system of communications on the Mischief Reef. The occupation of the shoalcould mean another communication and intelligence hub being set up and this time may be near to Luzon to undertake surveillance activities in the northern part of the main Singapore-Hong Kong and Manila-Hong Kong sea lanes or could also become a shelter for Chinese fishermen.[16]

The Philippines President, Benigno Aquino III is also dedicated to show that his government will not be browbeaten by China. In lieu of this, the

Aquino government is concentrating on strengthening Manila's ties with the U.S. to get its backing for its claims in the Scarborough Shoal. The Philippines is also willing to let the dispute be resolved through the International Tribunal for the Law of the Sea, despite China's firm rejections.[17]

After a lot of speculation in the aftermath of submission of limits of the extended continental shelf to the UNCLOS in 2009, the Filipino policymakers seem to have reached a consensus that the shoal is a "low tide elevation with some rocks (not islands) above sea level at high tide."[18] According to Article 13 of the UNCLOS, a low tide elevation is a "naturally formed area of land which is surrounded by and above water at low tide but submerged at high tide."[19] The main argument of the Philippines is that the shoal is located within its EEZ. The Philippines by all means is trying to let the issue be adjudicated by the International Tribunal of the Law of the Sea (ITLOS) by just focusing on its maritime rights and setting aside the issue of land titles on the rocks/islands. The ITLOS does not have the competency for dealing with matters on land territories, but can speculate on whether the shoal is a low tide elevation with rocks or an island. If the ITLOS decides that the feature is made of few rocks above sea level, the Scarborough shoal would totally be within the EEZ of the Philippines. China would not be in a position to claim the ZhongshaQundao, which would be seen "as a group of five rocks above the sea level at high tide, constantly submerged banks, some reefs above sea level at low tide."[20]

History of the Claims of the Philippines over the Scarborough Shoal

The Philippines' claim over the shoal can be traced back to the time of the Spanish colonisation of the country, when the fishermen took shelter at the reef during poor weather.[21] The reefs and shoals of the South China Sea had been known to mariners as dangers to be avoided at all times. The Paracel Islands, Macclesfield Bank, Scarborough Shoal and the Spratly Islands were surveyed and mapped by the colonial powers of the 19th Century. These mapping activities were mainly conducted to rid the sea lines bordering the South China Sea of all the hurdles in the way of navigation and trade mainly in tea and opium. On September 12, 1748 a British boat named "Scarborough", carrying tea, broke down near a feature named the 'Maroona Shoal' by Spanish cartographers. Later the Maroona Shoal became internationally known as the Scarborough Shoal. The first survey on the

Maroona Shoal was conducted in April 1800 by a Spanish frigate, *Santa Lucia*, sent by Admiral Malaspina in Manila. The outcome of the survey was published ina chart in 1808, and henceforth the Maroona Shoal came to be known as "Bajo de Masingloc", the name which is still used by the Philippine government.[22] Another survey of this feature was conducted in May 1866 by the British vessel, *H.M.S. Swallow* under the command of E. Wilde. Besides these two surveys, the shoal had not attracted the attention of the colonial authorities. During this period up to the 20th century, claiming a sandbank, a reef, rocks, or an atoll in the high seas was unimaginable. Hence, a territorial claim on the shoal by the Spanish authorities could not have materialised at that time.[23]

It was in 1957, in conjunction with the U.S. Navy, that the Philippines government carried out an oceanic survey of the area and used the shoal as a testing range for defence purposes. Manila also constructed a small lighthouse there in 1965, although it is no more operational. Legally, the Philippines' claim is based on theUnited Nations Convention on the Law of the Sea (UNCLOS) principle that an EEZ is measuredup to 200 nautical miles (370 kilometres) from a country'scoastline from which its territorial sea is measured. Recently, in February 2009, the Philippine Congress passed the Baselines Law for identifying the country's archipelagic baselines. The act did not include the Kalayaan and the Scarborough shoal as a part of the Philippine territory, but placed them in an ambiguous category as a "regime of islands under the Republic of the Philippines."[24]

History of the Claims of China over the Scarborough Shoal

According to the Chinese embassy in the Republic of the Philippines, the Huangyan Island was first discovered and drawn into China's map under China's Yuan dynasty (1271-1368 AD). In 1279, Chinese astronomer GuoShoujing conducted surveys in the seas around China for Kublai Khan, and the Huangyan Island was chosen as the point in the South China Sea.[25] In 1935, the Chinese Ministry of Interior published a list of names of the islands in the South China Sea, in which the Scarborough shoal was listed as per its English name under the group definition of the Nansha Islands. In 1947, it was named Minzhu Jiao (Democracy Reef) and was designated as a part of the Zhongsha Islands. A map published by the government in 1947 claimed that the shoal lies within the Hainan Province.[26] China's sovereignty over the Huangyan Island has been made clear in all the government announcements and statements on the South China Sea. These claims were made much before the UNCLOS came into force in 1994. Since ancient times the Huangyan Island and its surrounding waters has been used as a traditional fishing ground by the Chinese fishermen. Many scientific expeditions were also organised on the island by China's State Bureau of Surveying, National Earthquake Bureau and National Bureau of Oceanography in various periods.[27]

In 1983 the People's Republic of China renamed the shoal as the Huangyan Island which became the official name of the reef. Minzhu Jiao was reserved as the second name. In 1958 China promulgated its "Declaration on the Territorial Sea", in which it states that: "...the breadth of the territorial sea of the People's Republic of China shall be 12 nm. This provision applies to all the territories of the PRC, including the Chinese mainland and its coastal islands, as well as Taiwan and its surrounding islands, the Peghu Islands, Dongsha Islands, Xisha Islands, Zhongsha Islands, Nansha Islands and all other islands belonging to China which are separated from the mainland and its coastal islands by the high seas".[28]

The Chinese government reiterated its claim shortly after the U.S. Navy withdrew from the Subic Bay in the 1990s.[29] The 1992 Law on the Territorial Sea and Contiguous Zone reaffirmed China's claim to sovereignty over the Zhongsha Islands. The Scarborough Reef also falls within China's 1947 unilaterally drawn U-shaped map, which also includes the South China Sea as its territory. For administrative purposes, China places the South ChinaSea islands, including the Scarborough Shoal under the administration of the Hainan province.[30]

It is said it was not before 1909 that China developed its interest on some group of islands in the South China Sea. It was after China discovered that the Japanese traders had been exploiting the natural fertiliser found on the Pratas Island (Dongsha) since 1907 without its knowledge, did China develop an interest over the South China Sea and its surrounding islands. In the past neither the British nor the Spanish naval authorities while surveying or organising rescue operations in the Scarborough Shoal took permission from the Chinese authorities. The Chinese were aloof tosuch operations.[31]

There have been ongoing debates sans conclusion as to who claimed the Scarborough Shoal first. The main point is both the parties are steadfastly backing their claims. However, till the legality of both the claims is established as per the conventions of the UNCLOS, no party can be said to have an upper hand in the disputing claims. Given that there is still no conclusion on the claims over the South China Sea, we can hardly assume that the future of the Scarborough Shoal claims will be any different.

The Scarborough Shoal Dispute between the Philippines and China

The Philippines and China have been embroiled in a sovereignty dispute over the Scarborough shoal since April 2012. This bilateral dispute first came to surface in 1997 when vessels owned by the Chinese State Oceanic State Administration were discovered by the Philippine Navy near the shoal. The captains of the Chinese vessels informed their Filipino counterparts that the PRC considered the Scarborough shoal as part of its territory, a claim that was rejected by the then Ramos administration. The Chinese vessels withdrew from the area then not wishing to escalate the dispute any further. In mid-May a group of Filipino Congressman sailed to the Scarborough shoal and planted the Philippine flag there.[32] Again in the year 2000 tensions arose on the shoal when in January a Philippine Navy patrol vessel fired three warning shots at two Chinese fishing boats near the shoal. China then accused the Philippine Navy of "firing at, harassing and forcibly boarding its fishing boats and even robbing its fisheries in the waters near the shoal."[33] The Philippines rejected these accusations and later accused the Chinese fisheries of harvesting endangered coral and illegal dynamite fishing. When China warned the Philippines of "provocative acts", the then Philippine Senate President, Blas Ople referred to the U.S.-Philippines Mutual Defence Treaty and declared that the U.S. would support it in case of an armed clash with China. Subsequently, in May 2000 one Chinese fisherman was shot dead by the Philippine marine patrol forces in the disputed shoal.[34]

The dispute again flared up on 8 April, 2012, when the Philippines sent the officers of the Navalship, BRP Gregorio Del Pilar, a Hamilton class cutter obtained from the U.S. to search Chinese fishing vessels operating in the disputed area. Large amounts of illegally collected corals, giant palms and live sharks were discovered. The Filipino officials tried to arrest eight Chinese fishermen for illegal entry and poaching in Philippine waters. China then dispatched surveillance ships to put pressure on the Philippines so that it freed the detained Chinese fishing boats.[35] The standoff lasted nearly two weeks and both sides agreed to just station their patrol boats near the shoal.

The Philippines was unable to contend with China which used threats like banning Philippine exports to China, as well as stationing numerous large maritime and fishing security vessels to make sure that the Chinese fishermen had access to the shoal and the Philippine fishermen were excluded.[36] The then Chinese Vice Foreign Minister, Fu Ying warned in early May 2012 that Beijing was prepared for "any escalation" in the standoff.[37] Philippines diplomatic manoeuvres to involve the ASEAN and the United Nations in the dispute and to imply that the U.S. was supportive of Manila, did not prove effective in the dispute. Though the China-Philippines consultations led to the retreat of the Chinese vessels from the shoal, they still continued their patrolling in the surrounding waters. Later in the month, Manila was forced to withdraw its security vessels due toa coming typhoon. Following the typhoon, the Philippines reported that five Chinese security vessels along with various fishing boats were still stationed in the vicinity of the shoal. In July 2012, it was reported that China had placed barriers that prevented the Philippines fishing vessels from entering the shoal.[38] The dispute intensified and led to diplomatic protests and exchange of strongly worded statements between Manila and Beijing. The China-Philippines standoff also coincided with the U.S.-Philippines military exercises on April 16, 2012, involving 'mock beach invasions' along Philippine coastlines facing China. President Aquino and other officials defended this by stating that the exercises had been planned "way, way ahead" of the current standoff.[39]

The possibility of small skirmishes cannot be ruled out, but the chance of a major confrontation is not on the horizon soon. Nonetheless, it cannot be discarded completely seeing thatthere have been instances of China's aggressive attitude in the past, for instance, in its occupation of the Paracel Island and Mischief Reef despite Vietnam's and Philippines' claims on it respectively. With neither of the parties showing any inclination to soften their stance, the prospect of resolution remains low. Even though China has not deployed the People's Liberation Army Navy (PLAN) assets and is using the paramilitary vessels from China's Marine Surveillance Force, Philippines is still aware of the superiority of the Chinese naval strength. Additionally, China is Philippines' important economic partner. On the other hand, China is concerned about the involvement of "outside powers" like the U.S. in this dispute. Therefore, it can be presumed that both the claimants will take their steps carefully and not coax one another.

The 2012 China-Philippines Standoff: A Matter of Concern

The China-Philippines confrontation over the Shoal has long history. The dispute came to fore in 1997, and erupted in 2000, andthe standoff in April 2012 ledto a severe crisis. In this crisis, there was escalation beyond the exchange of strong diplomatic protest notes. China employed coercive measures against the Philippines; for instance, at one point China deployed nearly one hundred surveillance ships, fishing boats and utility craft in the lagoon, targeted economic sanctions, repeated diplomatic warnings to intimidate and coerce Philippine officials, security forces and fishermen to respect China's claim to the disputed Scarborough Shoal. In addition, China extended its annual unilateral fishing ban to cover the waters around the shoal and quarantined tropical fruit imports from Philippines. China also failed to obey a verbal agreement reached with Manila to withdraw vessels from the lagoon in early June 2012. It roped off the mouth of the lagoon so that the fishermen of no other country could enter the shoal during April-August, 2012.[40]

Meanwhile, there has been wide scale exploitation of fishing resources by China in the South China Sea. It deployed one of the world's largest (32,000 ton) fish processing ships in the area. It also proclaimed that it dispatched a fleet of thirty fishing boats supported by a supply ship to fish in disputed South China Sea areas. Beijing created a new, comprehensive administrative structure backed by a new military garrison that covered wide stretches of disputed areas in the South China Sea. Finally, Beijing used its diplomatic skills with Cambodia, the then chair of the ASEAN. Beijing promised Cambodia huge economic assistance in its development projects to prevent reference to the Scarborough Shoal and the EEZ issues in the text of the joint communiqué at the annual meeting of ASEAN foreign ministers. This led to a failure of ASEAN to issue a final communiqué at the 45th Foreign Ministers Meeting in Phnom Penh on 13 July, 2012 for the first time in the organisation's history.[41]

Beijing is not in favour of indulgingin multilateral discussions. It does not support the interference of any outside or third party like the U.S., Japan and does not even recognise the role of the ITLOS and the ICJ in the resolution of the dispute. Beijing feels that through bilateral discussions, it can use its 'leverage' over any small power. On the other hand, China has agreed, in due course, to engage in negotiations with the ASEAN to reach a Code of Conduct on the South China Sea. Within the ASEAN, Beijing has its supporters like Cambodia and it is very much aware that the ASEAN stands divided on the South China Sea issue. Additionally, the 2002 Declaration on the Conduct of the Parties in the South China Sea has no dispute resolution mechanism and is also not legally binding. This unwillingness of China to undertake serious diplomacy is also a matter of concern. China's emphasison the 2002 Code of Conduct is also an indication that the use of force in the assertion of the claims is also not ruled out.[42]

China's tendency to defy international law and norms is an upsetting trend. The result of Beijing's constant refusal to obey the verbal agreement that was reached with Manila in early June 2012 to pull out all its ships from the lagoon and the area around the Scarborough shoal is that a new "status quo has been established that favours Chinese interests."[43] China is conducting regular patrols to prevent Filipino fishermen from fishing in the disputed waters. No country has publicly protested against this action and this has set a dangerous example.

China's attempt to make use of "economic leverage" to get its way with weaker countries which are economically dependent on it is also a disturbing phenomenon. Its move to quarantine imported tropical fruit from the Philippines to force it to relinquish its control over the Scarborough shoal was a violation of international norms. Chinese customs officials cited unjustified reasons that the fruit was infested. Philippines' economy underwent immense loss as the country exports nearly one third of its banana crop to China, as well as papayas, pineapples, mangoes, and coconuts. Additionally, Chinese travel agencies cancelled tourist charter flights to the Philippines on the premise that the safety of Chinese tourists was in question.[44] In November 2012, China released its new passports with the inclusion of the controversial nine-dash line rejected by the other claimant countries. Manila protested against this move and ordered the Bureau of Immigration to require Chinese travellers carrying the new passport to get their visa stamped on a separate application document to make it clear that Manila does not recognise the map. In late June 2012, China put all its territories in the area under the jurisdiction of Sansha, a new city belonging to the Hainan province in charge of enforcing Beijing's policy over the region. Chinese authorities are planning to take up development projects on the island – establish a military garrison, an airport and other infrastructure to put across a clear message to the other countries that "China is here to stay".[45] To Beijing, these are "means of satisfying domestic pressure for a tougher foreign policy to match its economic might, all while trying to cling to the mantra of peaceful development."[46] As

Fu Ying, then Vice Minister for Foreign Affairs, had said, "when facing provocations, the Chinese public hopes that China will be even more assertive."[47]

The Hidden Weapons of Philippines

Philippines is undoubtedly at a position of disadvantage when judged from the point of military or naval strength in comparison to China. The Philippine government fully realisesthat even with new military assistance and inflows coming from the U.S., including a sister ship to the Gregorio Del Pilarshortly, still it will still not be in a position to challenge the overwhelming Chinese superiority.[48] According to the Philippines Foreign Secretary, Albert Del Rosario, Philippines wanted to return to the 'status quo', "where both sides keep the dispute to one side, to improve economic, social and political relations."[49]

The standoff may have come to an end, but the dispute still continues. China has constantly rejected the plea of the Philippines to take the dispute over the shoal to the International Court of Justice. The court also requires the consent of both the parties before a dispute related to "disputed sovereignty" can be brought before it. Many may think the hands of the Philippines are tied in this regard. But officials in Manila, with the help of international legal consultants, are quietly examining other legal means under which they can possibly compel China to arbitration or an international tribunal for the resolution of the dispute, even if China is reluctant.[50]

The Philippines can take unilateral action, according to a range of international lawyers. Though the UNCLOS cannot be used to solve disputes on sovereignty, itcan be used to deal with a wide range of related disputes. It is a unique feature among UN conventions which allows a State to contest another's actions or positions without the consent of that state, and this is known as "compulsory binding dispute statement".[51] China which signed and ratified the convention when it came in force in 1994, has long been wary of such "unilateral action". In 2006, it took the formal step of exercising its right to be exempted from such action in certain cases, like cases on military activities, maritime boundaries and historic waters. But unilateral action can still be possible over disputes centered on fishing rights within another country's claimed economic zone; or, whether a rock or reef could be considered an island under the law, and therefore entitled to possible economic zone status. The disputed Scarborough shoal can fall under this category.

Some lawyers believe that the "disputes concerning China's objections to activities within the exclusive economic zone of Southeast Asian claimants may be subject to the compulsory dispute system".This has been pointed out by Robert Beckman, a scholar of International Law at the National University of Singapore.[52] Another veteran Southeast Asian envoy stated,"International law is one way of solving the dispute. We know it could be a better solution than having to negotiate with a power like China one by one. We are all watching to see if the Philippines is brave enough to take the first step down that road and face a potential backlash from Beijing."[53]

Besides legal arbitration, Manila has proposed that ASEAN take the lead in transforming the South China Sea into "a Zone of Peace, Freedom and Cooperation" (ZoPFC). This concept calls for determining which maritime areas are disputed and which are not as a starting point to initiate a negotiation on joint cooperation zone. In launching this new initiative, President Aquino explained, "what is ours is ours, and what is disputed, we can work towards joint cooperation."[54] According to the Department of Foreign Affairs, the ZoPFC provides a framework for separating the disputed waters that may be considered for joint cooperation activities from the non-disputed territorial features in the West Philippine Sea (South China Sea) in accordance with international law in general and UNCLOS in particular.[55]

Manila appears convinced that it is time to 'move beyond confidence building to a resolution of the conflict'. The Aquino government is no longer convinced that the slow "ASEAN Way" of decision making will bring any constructive solution to the dispute. He also has to make other ASEAN countries believe that the "Aquino Way" is not meant to further Philippines' interest and gang up against China. The larger aim is to "institute cooperative solutions in addressing the roots of the conflict based on international law."[56] The need is for all member countries to bring about a rules-based cooperative solution like the ASEAN-China regional code of conduct on the South China Sea, else the potential for instituting military power for the resolution of the dispute will become a reality.

The Impact of the Current Standoff on the Sino-Philippines Relations

Tensions have beenon the rise since April 2012, but both sides claim they seek a peaceful solution, even if the means of achieving it may be different. The standoff has drawn to a close, but there is no indication of the dispute drawing to a close. Both sides are determined to not back down from their claims, so there is reason to be concerned about the dispute escalating into an armed conflict; however, there is also reason to be hopeful that both countries have a threshold they will choose not to cross. China's then Defence Minister, Liang Guanglie said the Ministry of Foreign Affairs is handling the confrontation for now, and any military action would be "according to the needs of diplomacy".[57] At the same time, on March 20, 2012, the two countries celebrated the launch of the Sino-Philippines Friendship and Exchange Year. Despite the mounting tension, given the current standoff, the launch of thefriendship year is a positive sign. China is currently the Philippines' third largest trading partner, and in 2011 bilateral trade reached an all time high, exceeding $30 billion. Last year the two countries announced plans to double their bilateral trade by 2016. Such contradictions demonstrate the complexity of the Sino-Philippines relations.[58]

The standoff may have been predictable, but the 2012 standoff has been the most serious escalation of the territorial dispute thus far. Economic ties have improved, but the impact of this on the standoff and overall relations seems negligible. Philippine President Benigno Aquino III made his first visit to China from August 30 to September 3, 2011. During the visit, both sides emphasised cooperation by concentrating on economic relationsand not bringing up the territorial dispute. In January 2012, China represented the highest percentage of the Philippines' imports, which increased by 13.9 percent year-by-year to $535.63 million.[59]

Whetherincreasing economic ties prevent the dispute from further escalating and taking a worse shape is yetto be seen. Philippines' distrust in China is very clearly seen in its increasing security ties with the U.S. and Japan. The U.S. "Rebalancing towards Asia" has played a role in escalating the Sino-Philippines tensions. In January 2012, the Pentagon announced it was holding a bilateral strategic dialogue with Manila. A U.S. spokesman said Washington would discuss "how our enhanced posture in Asia can be useful to them as we expand our cooperation."[60] Indeed the U.S.-Philippines ties are broadening and the U.S. is taking active interest in the South China Sea disputes. From April 16-27, 2012, the United States and the Philippines conducted an annual joint military exercise off the Palawan coast near the contested Spratly Islands.[61] This growing cooperation with the U.S. has probably given Philippines the confidence to assert its claims more unfalteringly.

Concluding Remarks

The Scarborough Shoal dispute is no longer confined tothe two claimants, Philippines and China.The United States is also using this dispute as a platform to stage its comeback in the Asia-Pacific region. This dispute has emerged as mutually convenient for the Philippines and the United States to strengthen their bilateral security relationship. The resolution of the dispute is desired by all. The lingering of it is the result of clashing opinions on the means of resolution of the dispute. The future of the Sino-Philippines relations with this ongoing dispute and whether it will take the same shape as the South China Seadispute is still to be seen. The situation seems calm at the moment.

The rising number of maritime sovereignty issuesin Southeast and East Asia, such as the South China Sea, the Senkaku Island dispute between China and Japan, and presently the resurfacing of the Scarborough Shoal dispute has compromised the peace and security of the region. Furthermore, these disputes are also having a negative impact on the working of very successful regional association, the ASEAN. Timely resolution of the Scarborough Shoal dispute is imperative, be it through bilateral discussions or multilateral diplomacy, before it also gets the tag of being the "potential hot spot" of the region and further hinder peace and tranquility of the region.

END NOTES

1. Quoted in Andy Yee, "Maritime Territorial Disputes in East Asia: A Comparative Analysis of the South China Sea and the East China Sea", *Journal of Current Chinese Affairs,* 40 (2), (2011), p. 166.
2. Ibid.
3. Lowell B. Bautista, "The Legal Status of the Philippine Treaty Limits and Territorial Waters claim in International Law: National and International Legal Perspectives" (PhD diss., University of Wollongong, 2010).
4. Ibid.
5. Zou Keyuan, "Scarborough Reef: a new flashpoint in the Sino-Philippines Relations", *IBRU Boundary and Security Bulletin,* no. 71 (1999), p. 71.
6. Bautista, *The Legal Status of the Philippine Treaty Limits and Territorial Waters claim in International Law: National and International Legal Perspectives,* p. 249-250.
7. Keuyan, *Scarborough Reef: a new flashpoint in the Sino-Philippines Relations,* p. 72.
8. Francois-Xavier Bonnet, "Geopolitics of Scarborough Shoal", *Irasec's Discussion Papers,* no. 7 (2012), p. 19-20.
9. Quoted in Beukel, *China and the South China Sea: Two Faces of Power in the Rising China's Neighbourhood Policy,* 7.
10. Bonnet, *Geopolitics of Scarborough Shoal,* 5
11. Sarah McDowall, "Scarborough Affair: Philippines and China in Sovereignty Deadlock", *Jane's Intelligence Review* 24, no. 7 (2012), p. 54-55.

12. Bonnet, *Geopolitics of Scarborough Shoal,* 6.
13. Ibid.
14. Ibid.
15. Ibid., 7-8.
16. Ibid.
17. McDowall, *Scarborough Affair: Philippines and China in Sovereignty Deadlock,* 55.
18. Bonnet, *Geopolitics of Scarborough Shoal,* 7-8.
19. Ibid.
20. Ibid.
21. McDowall, *Scarborough Affair: Philippines and China in Sovereignty Deadlock,* 54.
22. Bonnet, *Geopolitics of Scarborough Shoal,* 20-21.
23. Ibid., 21.
24. LeszekBuszynski, "Rising Tensions in the South China Sea: Prospects for resolution of the issue", *Security Challenges* 6 (2) (2010), p. 90.
25. Embassy of the People's Republic of China in the Republic of the Philippines (2012), *Some Basic Facts on China's Sovereignty over the Huangyan Island,* Embassy of the People's Republic of the Philippines. Accessed March 28 2013. http://ph.china-embassy.org/eng/xwfb/t922578.htm
26. Keuyan, *Scarborough Reef: a new flashpoint in the Sino-Philippines Relations,* p. 73-74.
27. Embassy of the People's Republic of China in the Republic of the Philippines (2012), n.30
28. Quoted in Keuyan, *Scarborough Reef: a new flashpoint in the Sino-Philippines Relations,* p. 73-74.
29. McDowall, *Scarborough Affair: Philippines and China in Sovereignty Deadlock,* p. 54.
30. Keuyan, *Scarborough Reef: a new flashpoint in the Sino-Philippines Relations,* p. 74.
31. Bonnet, *Geopolitics of Scarborough Shoal,* p. 14.
32. Ian James Storey, "Creeping Assertiveness: China, the Philippines and the South China Sea Dispute", *Contemporary Southeast Asia* 21, no. 1 (1999), p. 98.
33. DaojiongZha and Mark J. Valencia, "Mischief Reef: Geopolitics and Implications", *Journal of Contemporary Asia,* 31 (1), (2001), p. 90-91.
34. Ibid.
35. RodelRodis, "Scarborough will not be Mischief Reef Redux". Accessed October 21, 2012, available at http://globalnation.inquirer.net/35543/scarborugh-will-not-be-mischief-reefredux
36. Robert Sutter, "China-Southeast Asia Relations: China Muscles Opponents in South China Sea", *Comparative Connections,* 14(2), (2012), Accessed May 21, 2013, available at http://csis.org/files/publication/1202qchina_seasia.pdf
37. Ibid.
38. Ibid.
39. Robert Sutter, "China-Southeast Asia Relations: Hu Visits Cambodia as South China Sea Simmers", *Comparative Connections,* 14 (1) (2012), p. 73.
40. Bonnie S. Glaser. "Beijing as an Emerging Power in the South China Sea", Statement delivered at House Foreign Affairs Committee, United States, September 12, 2012.
41. Sutter, *China-Southeast Asia Relations: China Muscles Opponents in South China Sea*
42. Bonnie S. Glaser, n. 40
43. Ibid.
44. Bonnie S. Glaser, "China's Coercive Economic Diplomacy: A New and Worrying Trend",

*PacNet*14 (2012), Accessed May 28 2013, available at http://csis.org/publication/pacnet-46-chinas-coercive-economic -diplomacy-new-and-worrying-trend

45. Carlos Santamaria, "2012 Year ender: PH, China and Scarborough Shoal", Accessed March 29 2013, available at http://www.rappler.com/nation/18709-2012-yearender-ph-china-andscarborough-shoal
46. Stephanie KleineAhlbrandt, "China: New Leaders, same assertive Foreign policy". Accessed March 29, 2013, available at http://edition.cnn.com/2013/03/08/opinion/china-foreignpolicy-kleine-ahlbrandt
47. Ibid.
48. Donald E. Weatherbee, "China, the Philippines and the U.S. Security Guarantee", *PacNet* 28 (2012), Accessed May 28 2013, available at http://csis.org/pubication/pacnet-28-chinaphilippines-and-us-security-guarantee
49. Ibid.
50. Greg Torode, "Preparing for the main event: Manila is considering special legal action to pursue its territorial claims against Beijing over Scarborough shoal, but the risky, complex strategy may backfire", Accessed November 10 2012, available at http://cil.nus.edu.sg/wp/wp-content/uploads/2010/01/21Jun2012-SCMP-Manila-territorial-claims-against-Beijingove-Scarborough-Shoal1.pdf
51. Ibid.
52. Ibid.
53. Ibid.
54. Aileen San Pablo Baviera, "The South China Sea Disputes: Is the Aquino Way the 'AEAN Way'?",*RSIS Commentaries*, No. 004/2012 (2012), p. 1-2.
55. Thayer A. Carlyle, "China's New Wave of Aggressive Assertiveness in the South China Sea", Paper Presented at the Centre for International and Strategic Studies, Washington D.C., June 20-21 2011.
56. Baviera, *The South China Sea Disputes: Is the Aquino Way the 'AEAN Way'?*, p. 2.
57. Samantha Hoffman, "Sino-Philippine Tension and Trade Rising Amid Scarborough Standoff," *China Brief*, 12 (9) (2012), p. 133-14.
58. Ibid.
59. Ibid.
60. Ibid.
61. Ibid.

19

The Dispute over Preah Vihear Temple and Thailand's Domestic Unrest

Sushma Negi

This chapter analyses the trajectory of the border dispute between Thailand and Cambodia, on conflicting claims over Preah Vihear temple, and the land adjoining to it, in the backdrop of the dynamics of domestic politics in Thailand. Although, the issue has a long history, it was in 2008 that the dispute became a major irritant in the bilateral relationship, leading to violent border clashes. The chapter examines how domestic factors contributed to the inflaming of the dispute, thereby upholding the interest of a section of the political group. The connection between the domestic politics with Preah Vihear issue became particularly obvious during and after the administration of Prime Minister Thaksin Shinawatra. Thaksin came to power in 2001, after his party, Thai Rak Thai Party (TRT), won a landslide electoral victory. During his term, PM Thaksin introduced many popular initiatives for the population from the rural belt. According to Paul Chambers, who is a specialist on Thailand, during this period there was a "growth of political culture of populist entitlement among Thailand's lower and middle classes (with the exception of the South)".[1]

After completing his first term as Prime Minister, Thaksin was re-elected in 2005; however the election was invalidated by the Constitutional Court of Thailand. His Government was accused of corrupt shady business deals, authoritarian approach, and abuse of power. Thus, his second electoral win, where the opposition parties had not participated, resulted in a massive protest movement by his opponents, led by the PAD (People's Alliance for Democracy), popularly known as the "yellow shirts". Finally, he was overthrown in a military coup on September 19, 2006. But Thaksin managed to escape abroad and has since lived in exile. Nonetheless, he continues to influence the political narrative of Thailand, as was seen in the electoral victory of People's Power Party in 2008, an offshoot of the Thai Rak Thai Party, which had been banned in the aftermath of the coup of 2006. The leader of the party Samak Sundaravej became the Prime Minister and was known to be a Thaksin supporter.

Prime Minister Samak followed Thaksin's policy of engaging the immediate neighbours, including Cambodia. The policy was based on attaching importance to bilateral economic ties, rather than harping on emotive contentious issues, such as the Preah Vihear dispute. After coming to power in 2008, his first official trip was made to Cambodia. During this visit, Samak agreed with the Prime Minister Hun Sen's proposal of nominating Preah Vihear temple as a UNESCO World Heritage Site. In May 2008, the Thai Foreign Minister signed a joint communiqué with Cambodia's Deputy Prime Minister in Paris to confirm the Thai support for Cambodia's request to UNESCO.[2] However, it had been clarified in the communiqué that the disputed land would not be included in the "application" to UNESCO.[3] The nomination was expected to be a win-win situation for both Cambodia and Thailand, as it would help generate revenue through tourism. This did not appeal to a section of Thai population, since it would call for the government to amend the constitution. It was feared that the constitutional amendments would enable exiled Prime Minister Thaksin to return to Thailand. The domestic political unrest gave the opponents of Thaksin an opportunity to create a nationalist frenzy over the Preah Vihear dispute. They held that the nomination of the temple had jeopardised Thailand's claim over the surrounding area and criticised the government for failing to protect the country's "sovereign interests".[4]

Sondhi Limthongkul, the anti-Thaksin leader, was in need of an emotive issue to successfully carry out his protest against the current government. When Samak's government supported Cambodia's nomination of Preah Vihear temple, this gave an opportunity to royalist PAD to politicise the Preah Vihear issue.[5] PAD alleged that Samak's government agreed to the Preah Vihear nomination as a World Heritage site in exchange for Thaksin getting lucrative business deals in Cambodia.[6] In addition, PAD alleged that the nomination of the temple would undermine Thailand's claim over the disputed territory of 4.6 km surrounding the temple. This misrepresentation of facts enabled the opposition party to mobilise a large section of Thai people on the border, leading to a tense standoff. The immediate cause can be traced to three Thai people who intentionally entered the Preah Vihear temple, and were caught in the act by the Cambodian troops. In order to divert public attention, Samak sent 100 troops into the Cambodian territory to discuss the release of these three nationals. At the same time, Thai military occupied the Cambodian pagoda, Keo Sikha Kiri Svarak, which they considered to be within their territory.[7] In retaliation, Cambodia too deployed its troops, resulting in both countries increasing the number of soldiers on the border. When Cambodia saw that bilateral negotiations were not working, in order to diffuse the situation, it asked for an urgent meeting of the United Nations Security Council. On July 18, 2008, the permanent representative of Cambodia at the United Nations wrote to the Secretary General of the United Nations, lodging a complaint about Thai incursion into Cambodian territory.

The letter stated: "On 15 July 2008 about 50 Thai soldiers crossed into Keo Sokha Kiri Svara pagoda located in Cambodia territory about 300 meters from the Preah Vihear Temple. By 16-17th July 2008 the number of Thai soldiers, in the pagoda grounds had increased to 480."[8]

However, the response from the Security Council at this point of the conflict was lukewarm, as the request for UN's intervention in the conflict had only come from Cambodia, while Thailand had maintained its desire to solve the dispute through bilateral talks. According to some analysts, Thailand was conscious of its weak legal position vis-à-vis the Preah Vihear issue, and therefore was not keen to internationalise the problem. Thailand's stand that the resolution of the dispute must be through bilateral negotiations, received support from its main ally, the US, and from ASEAN as well. However, although Samak had succeeded in saving his government on the Preah Vihear issue, his government could not last long and was forced to resign.

Background

The boundary between Cambodia (France as a protectorate of Cambodia) and Siam (Thailand) was drawn in 1907. However, due to technical error in the boundary map, it showed Preah Vihear in the Cambodian territory.[9] Until the beginning of the Second World War, the Thai authorities had not objected to this map. With the beginning of the impact of the Second World War, the Thai Prime Minister Phibun Sonkgram (1938-44; 1948-57), pursued a foreign policy that took its clues from the transformation in international environment, especially from Japan's unchecked rise in Asia.[10] During his regime, nationalism became most implicit,[11] and he revived the issue of lost territories and embarked on a campaign to recover the lost provinces of Thailand from the French. He took the support of Luang Wichit Wathakan, a prolific nationalist writer to reconstruct the Thai history based on its past glories. In 1939, Phibun changed the country's name from Siam to Thailand —"land of the free." Through his extremely nationalistic economic and political approach, he wanted to create a "sang chat" (new nation).[12] He printed a map which showed Cambodia as being historically a Thai territory. In 1940, Phibun took advantage of the French defeat during the World War, by reclaiming Thailand's lost provinces in Indochina.[13] He was astute enough to assess that once France was defeated by Japan, the latter would take over the French colonies. In order to forestall such a move, the Thai army invaded North-western Cambodia in 1941, and after a fierce combat took control of the Preah Vihear temple. This was legitimised by Japan in a peace treaty signed in Tokyo in March 1941. Through this agreement, France agreed to return most of the Thai territory, including Preah Vihear.

After the end of the Second World War, Preah Vihear temple reverted to France.[14] However, soon after in 1949, it was re-occupied by Thailand as the French were busy trying to hold on to their other colonies in Indochina, and did not pay heed to Preah Vihear incident. After Cambodia's independence in 1953, its Prime Minister Norodam Sihanouk pursued the Preah Vihear issue.[15]

In the aftermath of the Second World War, both Thai and Cambodian governments responded to the changing world order in diverse manners based on their perceptions of what was best for their respective countries. After Phibun's return as Prime Minister in late 1940s, Thailand entered into the US led military alignment and became a founding member of the Southeast Asia Treaty Organisation (SEATO) in 1954. On the other hand, Cambodia followed a neutral foreign policy while maintaining close relations with China. The bilateral relationship between Thailand and Cambodia deteriorated during the Cold War period. As for the temple issue, it remained unresolved until International Court of Justice in 1962 placed Preah Vihear in the Cambodian territory.[16] This incident led to a protest march in Thailand.

Meanwhile, Thailand was going through a domestic political upheaval —a non-popular military coup overthrew the absolute monarchy in 1932, and since then the relationship between the military government and the King kept on deteriorating until 1957, when Sarit Thanarat led a military coup against Phibun. Although the coup that he staged was popular, he faced the problem of legitimacy and there was no constitutional mechanism by which this could be achieved. Therefore, he turned to the King for gaining support and instead of competing over power with the King he used his support in legitimising his role as Prime Minister.[17] Monarchy-military alliance took control over Thai politics at the cost of democracy. Anti-communist rhetoric also helped the military to dominate foreign policy while dealing with the neighbouring countries. The credit for making monarchy a respected institution goes to Thai historians, who represented the King as a quasi-divine figure that embodies virtues generally not found in the corrupt politicians. Laws of lèse majesté further kept the Thai King out of criticism.[18] Even after Sarit's demise, his military protégés continued to dominate Thailand, but the King ascended over them in political authority.[19]

The military succeeded in maintaining its dominant position in the government till 1973. It was only after the student-led protest against the authoritarian regime of Thanom Kittikachron that the middle class started to take part in politics. Henceforth, a compromise was achieved between the military and the civilian government in which power was shared between the elected politicians and the military.[20]

As the Cold War started to weaken by late 1980s, the military lost its role in determining bilateral relations with neighbouring countries. This gave opportunity to the elected government under Prime Minister Chartichai Choonhavan to adopt the policy of "turning the battlefields into a market place." Eventually, the discontentment between military and civilian government arose again, with the military leading a coup d'etat against Chartichai in 1991. This coup did not go down well with the masses and the subsequent "Black May" incident of 1992 played a crucial role in bringing political reforms and constitutional democracy to Thailand.[21] The new pro-democracy Constitution was promulgated in 1997, when Thailand was reeling from the impact of the Asian Financial crisis. Under the new Constitution, many independent institutions like the Election Commission (EC), the National Counter-Corruption Commission (NCCC) were created.

Thaksin Shinwatra and the Temple Issue

The financial crisis of 1997, with its negative impact on Thai economy helped Thaksin come into political prominence, backed as he was with his successful business empire.[22] In 2001, Thaksin Shinawatra, having formed his political party Thai Rak Tai over the years, was able to win the elections with a resounding victory. Once in power, he turned to building strong bilateral relations with Cambodia, by concentrating on mutually beneficial economic and trade links. He was aware that many politicians in Cambodia had business interests, and was hence convinced of a positive response from Cambodia.[23] This policy was in keeping with his focus to make Thailand a regional economic hub, and according to him, benefited from maintaining close relations with the heads of neighbouring countries. As per allegations his personal business interests stood to benefit too.[24] His personal equation with Prime Minister Hun Sen continued even after his ouster in 2006, and Thaksin became economic adviser to the Cambodian government in November 2009. However, within nine months, on August 23, 2010, he had to quit his post as it created a diplomatic row between the two governments, with both countries recalling their ambassadors.[25]

By emphasising economic interests rather than security issues with neighbouring countries during his rule, Thaksin was able to undermine the role of the military in foreign policy. Thaksin's domestic policies like cheap housing, providing free medical visits and introducing a scheme to purchase all bank debts, made him a popular leader among the masses. He assumed a position just below the monarchy, but above the military.

Thaksin however, soon alienated the Army and pro-royalists, when he began to undermine the 1997 Constitution, by delaying the selection process of important institutions like State Audit Commission, NCCC and National Broadcasting Commission.[26] A major conflict of interests arose between the monarchy and Thaksin over the promotion of military officers.[27] By the middle of 2005, anti–Thaksin forces came together including the military, Democrat Party, and the urban middle class under the leadership of Sondhi Limthangkul, who himself was a media tycoon.[28]

From 2001 to 2005, Thaksin, with his autocratic manner and his methods of doing things, such as killing of many innocent people extra-judicially in the name of controlling drug addiction, alienated many. A large number of non-government organisations and intellectuals came forward against him and charges were levied against him for showing disrespect to monarchy, a serious charge in Thailand. The time was right for a military coup, which took place under the leadership of General Sonthi Boonyaratglin on September 19, 2006, after a year-long unrest in Thailand.[29] The surprising support by a large section of the society to the coup was, as already stated, due to Thaksin's method of governance and his underhand dealings. The coup in which Thaksin was ousted was quickly endorsed by the King. In spite of the military takeover, there was no end to the political turmoil in Thailand as the people were divided into two opposite factions representing anti-Thaksin and pro-Thaksin groups.

After the coup, the military leadership pushed a new internal security law and tried to place a check on the electoral weight of the North and Northeast where Thaksin was popular. This strategy of exclusion led to social division and political tension. The divide was no longer between different political ideologies, it was a struggle between the poor northern and eastern states verses the powerful well to do classes from Bangkok and the influential South.[30] PAD proposed partial election of members of the Senate under the military initiated 2007 Constitution, in which seventy per cent of the members of the parliament were to be appointed from a list of nominees, by a high-level committee of judges and heads of independent agencies.[31] The conjectured objective of preventing Thaksin or his surrogates from winning the elections led to an uproar among the pro-Thaksin faction, who called for an amendment to the Constitution.[32]

PAD led protests had succeeded in destabilising two Thaksin backed governments of Samak Sundaravej and Somchai Wongsawat. Later, in the December 2008 elections, military and PAD helped Abhisit Vejjajiva [Democrat Party] to form the government. After coming to power, he revived the issue of Preah Vihear, and announced to reverse the unilateral declaration of Preah Vihear temple as a World Heritage Site. Relations worsened during his term, in December 2010, some Thai nationals (presumably with the support of the government), tried to cross the Cambodian border, and were subsequently arrested by Cambodia for illegally entering, and trespassing on a military area.[33]

On February 4, 2011, war between Cambodia and Thailand broke out, due to Cambodia's construction of an access road to the temple through the contested 4.6 sq km area, as part of Cambodia's plan to link the site with Angkor Wat in Siem Reap.[34] In late January 2011, the Thai military had also begun to build a connecting road towards the Kao Sikha Kiri Svara pagoda from Highway 221, which runs from the provincial capital Si Sa Ket to a border checkpoint west of the temple.[35]

The political climate in Thailand also became volatile by 2011, as PAD and the military combined, gave vent to nationalist rhetoric regarding the Thai-Cambodian border issue, in order to maintain their dominance in Thai politics. The military used this issue to have a say in the foreign policy with Cambodia. The Thai Army Chief, General Prayuth Chan-ocha, made more public appearances on television and assumed a full-time political role.[36] Meanwhile PAD also engaged itself in street demonstration on Jan 25, 2011, to put pressure on Abhisit Vejjajiva's government by demanding the ejection of Cambodia from the contested border areas which they held belonged to Thailand; and to cancel the Memorandum of Understanding signed in 2000, with Cambodia on border demarcation negotiations.[37] According to Amnat Barlee, director of the Thai Red Cross's Relief and Community Health Bureau, there was displacement of 15,000 people from the Thai side of the border and NGOs who were keeping eye on the dispute claimed that almost 30,000 people had fled to makeshift shelters.

Following the outbreak of fighting Cambodia requested the United Nations (UN), to intervene.[38] However, the UN informed that its role would be limited to supporting bilateral and regional efforts in negotiating an end to the conflict. Subsequently, an ASEAN meeting was held in Jakarta on February 22, 2011, in which parties agreed to peacefully resolve the dispute by following the norms laid out in the ASEAN Charter and the Treaty of Amity and Cooperation (TAC). It was agreed that Indonesia would send observers and play a facilitating role.[39] However, the talks came to a deadlock when Thailand demanded Cambodia withdraw its troops unilaterally before the observers could be deployed. Thai military also showed its dislike over Indonesian presence in their border region.

Cambodia and Preah Vihear

Interestingly enough, even the Cambodian political elite exploited the issue of Preah Vihear for their internal political gains. Since the Cambodian Prime Minister Hun Sen's government became extremely unpopular, the UNESCO nomination of Preah Vihear temple as World Heritage site came as a timely interlude. There was much jubilation among the people and Hun Sen used this occasion to divert the attention of his people from the ills of his government.[40] The nomination of the temple by UNESCO came in early

July 2008, during the election campaign period. In commemoration, the government sponsored programmes were broadcast across Cambodia on the State media, and people came out in large numbers to celebrate the nomination.[41] The occasion was very special as Cambodians generally felt that they had suffered humiliation for long at the hands of Thailand. Hun Sen emerged a strong leader and his People's Party won 58 per cent of the votes. The trajectory would have been different had Thailand not politicized the nomination of Preah Vihear temple; then perhaps the temple would not have aroused such nationalistic feeling among the people of Cambodia. After a brief fight over the temple in October 2008, Cambodia maintained a low profile till 2011.

The Cambodian government and its military force knew that if there is a full scale war, Cambodia was no match for Thailand. First, Cambodian military was well aware of the ground reality, that if war breaks out there would be supply problems, as all the supplies might have to be delivered through helicopters, which Cambodia lacked. Hence, the army avoided any major action that would blow into full scale war. At the same time, border skirmishes were used to further the interests of the government. Second, Hun Sen had harsh things to say against the Thai Prime Minister Abhisit Vejjajiva as he rightly perceived that Thaksin Shinawatra still commanded loyalty and support of the rural people. After 2006 military coup, two pro-Thaksin leaders Samak Sundaravej and Somchai Wongsawat managed to become Prime Ministers of Thailand. Nevertheless, the anti-Thaksin forces did not allow these pro Thaksin governments to last for long. Hun Sen, had found it advantageous to stand on the side of Thaksin, who during his tenure had opted for an engagement with Cambodia and personal friendship with himself.[42] He provided sanctuary to many UDD [United Front for Democracy against Dictatorship] leaders who fled to Cambodia to escape arrest by Thai authorities.

In the beginning of 2011, the Thai-Cambodian military were again involved in a conflict which was greater in severity than the earlier skirmishes. The Cambodian Prime Minister used the issue to gather international support by presenting Thailand as an aggressor. The most plausible reason behind internationalisation of Preah Vihear issue by Cambodia was its strong case over the temple and there were clear indications of its winning it.

Preah Vihear and the ICJ Ruling

Frustrated by the lack of progress, on April 28, 2011, Cambodia brought the case back to the ICJ (International Court of Justice), requesting a clarification of the 1962 decision. Hun Sen's government asked the ICJ for an interpretation of unclear passages of its 1962 verdict, especially the status of the 4.6 km² area surrounding the Preah Vihear complex. While the Court postponed the judgement on Cambodia's request for re-interpretation of 1962 judgement to a later date, it did give directions to both the countries to withdraw all military personnel from the demilitarised zone and refrain from armed activity. It also directed them to allow the observers appointed by ASEAN to have access to the provisional demilitarised zone."[43] ASEAN Regional Forum, the only forum within the framework of ASEAN that can discuss the security concerns of the region, also requested Cambodia and Thailand to follow ICJ orders. Abhisit Vejjajiva left the implementation of Court's order to the next government. After the July 3, 2011 elections Yingluck Shinawatra (younger sister of Thaksin Shinawatra), came to power. The Yingluck government, under domestic pressure, was unable to follow with the plan to allow Indonesian observers to be stationed at the conflict site.

The Current Situation

Finally, the ICJ on November 11, 2013, gave its ruling over Cambodia's reinterpretation of 1962 verdict. According to this verdict, Cambodia has sovereignty over the whole of the promontory of Preah Vihear, while the rest of the disputed territory was to be negotiated bilaterally by Thailand and Cambodia. As seen above, the Preah Vihear dispute did get intrinsically linked to the delegitimising of pro-Thaksin forces and Thaksin's policies both at the domestic and at the international level.

At this point of time, Yingluck Shinawatra's government was becoming unpopular with the "Yellow Shirts" and the military for wanting to amend the Constitution and introduce the Amnesty Bill. It was suspected that her attempt was to give amnesty to Thaksin, so that he could return to Thailand. The Amnesty Bill led to fierce protests from the opposition led by former Democrat MP Suthep Thaugusan. With her ouster by the army, Cambodian Prime minister Hun Sen adopted a pragmatic approach and ended all visible support to Thaksin and his "red shirt" supporters.[44] His realistic approach was to build army to army contacts and this became evident when Hun Sen, without delay congratulated Prayuth Chan-ocha, when he was appointed the

Prime Minister after he led a coup against the caretaker government of Yingluck, on May 22, 2014.[45] It is yet early to predict the depth of this new bilateral relationship, and the future shape of domestic politics in both the countries. These paradigms will have a definite impact on the border issue.

END NOTES

1. Paul Chambers, "Consolidation of Thaksinocracy and Crisis of Democracy: Thailand's 2005 General Election" in Auriel Croissant, Beate Martin (eds), *Between Consolidation and Crisis: Elections and Democracy in Five Nations in Southeast Asia*, (LIT Verlag, Berlin, 2006), p. 278
2. Ministry of Culture and ICOMOS Thailand (2008), Management Plan for Preah Vihear Mountain and Its Setting, Office of Archaeology, Fine Arts Department Ministry of Culture and ICOMOS Thailand 2551 B.E. (2008 AD.)
3. Available at http://www.swpberlin.org/fileadmin/contents/products/projekt_papiere/BCAS2013_Rosita_Dewi.pdf (Accessed on April 20, 2015)
4. James Ockey, "Thailand in 2008: Democracy and Street Politics," *Southeast Asian Affairs,* (2009), p. 315-333
5. Kitti Prasirtsuk, "Thailand in 2009: Colored by Turbulence" *Asian Survey,* 50 (1) (2010), p. 203-210
6. Prasirtsuk, Kitti, "Thailand in 2008: Crises Continued", *Asian Survey,* 49 (1), (2009), p. 174-184
7. Leng Thearith and Chheang Vannarith, "Cambodia-Thailand dispute and its impacts on Southeast Asian community construction", The *Cambodia Journal of International Affairs,* 1(1) (2008), p. 29-42.
8. Available at http://www.swpberlin.org/fileadmin/contents/products/projekt_papiere/BCAS2013_Rosita_Dewi.pdf.
9. Case concerning the Preah Vihear temple (Cambodia v. Thailand) Merits, (1962), 15 June 1962, *The International and Comparative Law Quarterly,* 11(4), p. 1183-1204, available at https://docs.google.com/viewer?a=v&q=cache:Htg9HjdGlKEJ:www.icj-cij.org/docket/files/45/4871.pdf+ICJ+report+of+1962+on+preah&hl=en&gl=in&pid=bl&s
10. Arne Kislenko, "Bending with the wind," *International Journal,* 57, (2001-2002), p. 537-60.
11. Lucus G. Barlow, *The Preah Vihear Temple: What's in a claim?, Ph.D Thesis,* Monterey, California, Naval Postgraduate School (2011).
12. Arne Kislenko, "Bending with the wind," *International Journal* 57, (2001-2002), p. 537-56.
13. Ibid.
14. Ibid.
15. Lucus G. Barlow, *The Preah Vihear Temple: What's in a claim ?, Ph.D Thesis,* Monterey, California, Naval Postgraduate School, 2011.
16. D.H.N. Johnson, The Case concerning the Temple of Preah Vihear, (1961-62), *The international and Comparative Law Quarterly,* 11 (4) (1961-62), p. 1183-1204.
17. Thak Chaloemtiarana, "Distinctions with a Difference: The despotic paternalism of Sarit Thanarat and the demagogic authoritarianism of Thaksin Shinawatra," *An Interdisciplinary Journal of Southeast Asian Studies,* 19 (1) (2007), p. 50-94.
18. Jack Fong,"Sacred Nationalism: The Thai Monarchy and Primordial Nation Construction," *Journal of Contemporary Asia,* 39 (4) (2009), p. 673-696.

19. Duncan Mc Cargo, "Network monarchy and legitimacy crises in Thailand", *Department of Psycho Pacific Review,* 18 (4) (2005), p. 499-519.
20. Prasirtsuk, From Political Reform and Economic Crisis to Coup d'état in Thailand, 876.
21. Ibid.
22. Micheal K. Connars,. "Thailand's four elections and a coup," *Australian Journal of International Affairs,* 62 (4) (2008), p. 476-498
23. Pavin Chachavalpongpun, *Reinventing Thailand Thaksin and his foreign policy,* (Silkworm Books Thailand, 2011)
24. Chookiat Panaspornprasit, "Thailand Politicized Thaksinization", *Southeast Asian Affairs,* (2004), pp. 257-266
25. "Thaksin Shinwatra quits role as adviser Cambodian government", The Guardian, 23 August 2010, available at http://www.theguardian.com/world/2010/aug/23/thaksin-shinawatraquits-cambodia-role
26. Mutebi, Alex M, "Thailand's Independent Agencies under Thaksin: Relentless Gridlock and Uncertainty," *Southeast Asian Affairs,* (2006), p. 303-321.
27. Paul Chambers, "Understanding civil-military relations: the case of Thailand with implications of emerging democracy in Asia," *Asia-Pacific Social Science Review,* 10(2) (2010), p. 1-24.
28. James Ockey, "Thailand In 2008: Democracy and Street Politics James", *Southeast Asian Affairs* (2009), p. 315-333.
29. Chairat Charoensin-o-larn, "Thailand in 2009 Unusual Politics Becomes Usual", *Southeast Asian Affairs,* (2010), p. 302-332.
30. Kitti Prasirtsuk, "Thailand in 2009: Colored by Turbulence," *Asian Survey,* 50 (1) (2010), p. 203-210.
31. McCargo, "Thailand: State of Anxiety", *Southeast Asian Affairs,* (2008), p. 333-356
32. James Ockey, "Thailand in 2008: Democracy and street politics," *Southeast Asian Affair,"* (2009), p. 315 -331
33. N. Ganesan, "Thaksin and the Politics of Domestic and Regional Consolidation in Thailand," *Contemporary Southeast Asia,* 26 (1) (2004), p. 26-44.
34. International Crisis Group Report, Waging Peace: ASEAN and the Thai-Cambodian Border Conflict, Crisis Group Asia Report N°215, 6 December 2011
35. Ibid.
36. Pavin Chachavalpongpun, "The Thai Military's Latest Sortie", *Asia Senitel,* Saturday, 23 April 2011, available at http://www.asiasentinel.com/opinion/the-thai-militarys-latest-sortie/
37. Martin Wagener, "Lessons from Preah Vihear: Thailand, Cambodia, and the Nature of Low-Intensity border Conflicts", *Southeast Asian Affairs,* 30 (3) (2011), p. 27-59
38. United Nations Security Council, S/PV.6480, Official communiqué of the 6480th (closed) meeting of the Security Council, February 14, 2011.
39. International Crisis Group, International Crisis Waging Peace: ASEAN and the Thai-Cambodian Border Conflict, Crisis Group Asia Report N°215, 6 December 2011.
40. Pavin Chachavalongpun, "The Reasons Behind the Thai-Cambodia Conflict", The Irrawaddy, Feb 10,2011. http://www2.irrawaddy.org/article.php?art_id=20722
41. Pavin Chachavalpngpun, "Hun Sen, Cambodia's agent provocateur?" KI-Media. (10 July 2009). Retrieved from http://ki-media.blogspot.com/2009/10/hun-sen-camboidasagentprovacateur.html
42. Martin Wagener, "Lessons from Preah Vihear: Thailand, Cambodia, and the Nature of Low-Intensity border Conflicts", *Southeast Asian Affairs,* 30 (3)(2011), p. 27-59.

43. Request for interpretation of the judgment of 15 June 1962 in the case concerning the temple of Preah Vihear (Cambodia *v.* Thailand) Request for the indication of provisional measures order of 18 July 2011.
44. Kevin Ponniah, "Prayuth to make first visit", *The Phnom Penh Post,* October 30, 2014. http://www.phnompenhpost.com/national/prayuth-make-first-visit
45. Nicole Jenne, "Uncertainty at home brings calm to the Thai–Cambodian border", East Pacific Forum, 20 November 2014.

Bibliography

Acharya, Amitav. 2014. *Indonesia Matters: Asia's Emerging Democratic Power*, Singapore: World Scientific.

Acharya, Amitav. 2014. *The End of American World Order.* Cambridge: Polity Press.

Anders, Leslie. 1965. *The Ledo Road: General Joseph W. Stilwell's Highway to China*, Oklahoma: University of Nebraska Press.

Ayoob, Mohammed. 1990, *India and Southeast Asia: Indian Perceptions and Policies*, London: Routledge.

Barlow, Lucus G. 2011. *The Preah Vihear Temple: What's in a claim?. Ph.D Thesis.* Monterey, California: Naval Postgraduate School.

Basu Das, Sanchita. 2013. *Enhancing ASEAN's Connectivity.* Singapore: ISEAS.

Bautista, Lowell B. 2010. *The Legal Status of the Philippine Treaty Limits and Territorial Waters claim in International Law: National and International Legal Perspectives.* PhD diss., University of Wollongong.

Beeson, Mark. ed. 2004. *Contemporary Southeast Asia: Regional Dynamics, National Differences*, Palgrave Macmillan, Hampshire.

Broadbent, J., Rickard, S. and Steve, M. 2003, *India, China, Australia: Trade and Society 1788-1850*, Sydney: Historical Houses Trust of New South Wales.

Butwell, Richard. 1963. *U Nu of Burma*, Stanford, CA: Stanford University Press.

Buzan, B. and Wæver, O. 2003. *Regions and Powers: The Structure of International Security*, Cambridge: Cambridge University Press.

Chachavalpongpun, Pavin. 2011. *Reinventing Thailand Thaksin and His Foreign Policy*, Books Thailand: Silkworm.

Chakraborty, Debashis and Amir Ullah Khan. 2008. The WTO Deadlocked: Understanding the Dynamics of International Trade, New Delhi: Sage.

Croissant, Auriel, Beate Martin. eds. 2006. *Between Consolidation and Crisis: Elections and Democracy in Five Nations in Southeast Asia.* LIT Verlag, Berlin.

Datta Ray, Sunanda K.. 2009. *Looking East to Look West: Lee Kuan Yew's Mission India*, New Delhi: Penguin Books.

Dennis Rumley. 2003. *The Indian Ocean Region: Security, Stability and Sustainability in the 21st Century*. AII, Task Force on Indian Ocean Security.

France, Peter. 1969. *The Charter of the Land: Custom and Colonization in Fiji*, Melbourne: Oxford University Press.

Funston, John. ed. 2001. *Government and politics of Southeast Asia*, Singapore: ISEAS.

Grare, Frederic and Amitabh Mattoo. eds. 2003. *Beyond the Rhetoric: The Economics of India's Look East Policy*. NewDelhi: Centre de Sciences Humanines and Manohar.

Gugler, P. and J. Chaisse. eds. 2010.*Competitiveness of the ASEAN Countries: Corporate and Regulatory Drivers*, Cheltenham: Edward Elgar.

Hlaing, Kyaw Yin and Talor Robert H. 2005. *Myanmar: Beyond Politics to Societal Imperatives*, Singapore: Institute of Southeast Asian Studies.

Htin, Aung 1965. *The Stricken Peacock: Anglo-Burmese Relations, 1752-1948*, Lieden: M. Nijhoff.

Ikenberry, G John. ed. 2014. *Power, Order, and Change in World Politics*, Cambridge: Cambridge University Press.

Jackson, Ashley. 2006. *The British Empire and the Second World War*, London: Hambledon Continuum.

Kaplan, Robert D. 2010. *Monsoon: The Indian Ocean and the Future of American Power*. New York: Random House.

Kaul, Man Mohini. 1993. *Pearls in the Ocean: Security Perspectives in the Southwest Pacific*. New Delhi: UBSPD, 27-50.

Kena, L. 2005, *Are Indians an ethnic minority- Discovering Victoria*. Bundoora, Victoria: Jika Publishing.

Lal, Brij V. 2008. *A time bomb lies buried: Fiji's road to independence, 1960-1970*, Acton, A.C.T.: ANU E Press.

Lampton, D.M. 2008. *The Three faces of Chinese Power: Might, Money, and Minds*. Berkeley: University of California Press.

Leckie, Jacqueline. 2007. *The story of a New Zealand South Asian Community Indian Settlers*. Dunedin: Otago University Press.

Mahbubani, Kishore. 2013. *The Great Convergence: Asia, the West and the Logic of One World*. New York: Public Affairs.

Mason, David S. 2008. *The End of the American Century*, Lanham: Rowman & Littlefield Publishers.

Mohan, Raja C. 2012. *Samudra Manthan: Sino-Indian Rivalry in the Indo-Pacific*. Washington: Carnegie Endowment for International Peace.

Nash, M. 2001, *Cargo for the Colony: The 1797 wreck of the merchant ship Sydney Cove*, Navarine Publishing, Canberra.

Nehru, Jawaharlal. 1974. *India's Foreign Policy: Selected Speeches*, September 1946-April 1961 New Delhi: Publications Division.

Nye Jr., Joseph S. 2015. *Is the American Century Over*. Cambridge: Polity Press.

Panikkar, K.M.1955. *In Two Chinas: Memoirs of a Diplomat*, London: George Allen & Unwin.

Panikkar, K.M. 1943. *The Future of South East Asia*, London: George Allen & Unwin.

Prasad, Bimla. 1960. *The Origins of Indian Foreign Policy*, Calcutta: Bookland.

Sari, Agus P. ed. 2007. *Indonesia and Climate Change: Current Status and Policies*, Jakarta: Peace.

Sarvepalli Gopal. 1979. *Jawaharlal Nehru, A Biography* Vol.1: 1947-1956, Delhi: Oxford University Press.

Sibal, Kanwal. 2008. *Contemporary Transnational Challenges: International Maritime Connectivities*, KW Publishers, NMF: New Delhi, 2008.

Singh, Uma Shankar. 1979. *Burma and India, 1948-1962*, New Delhi: Oxford and IBH.

Tan, See Seng. 2013. *Future of ADMM-Plus: Asia's Growing Defence Engagements*. Singapore: RSIS.

Thant Myint U. 2012. *Where China Meets India: Burma and the New Crossroads of Asia*, New York: Farrar, Straus and Giroux.

Tucker, Shelby. 2001. *Burma: The Curse of Independence*, Penguin Books.

Zakaria, Fareed. 2009. *The Post American World*, New York: WW Norton & Company.

Index